Sixth Edition

OBSERVING YOUNG CHILDREN

Transformative Inquiry, Pedagogical Documentation, and Reflection

Kristine Fenning

Humber Institute of Technology and Advanced Learning

Sally Wylie

NELSON

NELSON

Observing Young Children:
Transformative Inquiry, Pedagogical
Documentation, and Reflection,
Sixth Edition

by Kristine Fenning and Sally Wylie

VP, Product Solutions, K–20:
Claudine O'Donnell

Director, Qualitative Publishing:
Jackie Wood

Publisher
Carmen Yu

Executive Marketing Manager:
Amanda Henry

Content Manager:
Theresa Fitzgerald

Photo and Permissions Researcher:
Karen Hunter

Senior Production Project Manager:
Natalia Denesiuk Harris

Production Service:
MPS Limited

Copy Editor:
Christina Jelinek

Proofreader:
Nayyer Shamsi

Indexer:
Sonya Dintaman

Design Director:
Ken Phipps

Higher Education Design PM:
Pamela Johnston

Interior Design:
Sharon Lucas

Cover Design:
Sharon Lucas

Cover Image:
Severin Schweiger/Cultura/Getty

Compositor:
MPS Limited

**Library and Archives Canada
Cataloguing in Publication**

Wylie, Sally, author
    Observing young children :
transformative inquiry, pedagogical
documentation, and reflection /
Kristine Fenning, Humber College
Institute of Technology and
Advanced Learning, Sally Wylie. —
Sixth edition.

Revision of: Wylie, Sally. Observing
young children.
Includes bibliographical references
and index.
Issued in print and electronic
formats.

ISBN 978-0-17-680513-5
(softcover).—ISBN 978-0-17-682839-4
(PDF)

    1. Observation (Educational
method).   2. Early childhood
education.   3. Child development.
I. Fenning, Kristine, author II. Title.

LB1139.3.C3W94
2019 372.21 C2018-905990-7
C2018-905991-5

ISBN-13: 978-0-17-680513-5
ISBN-10: 0-17-680513-3

This sixth edition was made possible by the wonderful people and colleagues in my life who have supported me in so many ways.

I am forever indebted to Sally Wylie for her unwavering commitment to writing the foreword of this new edition. It is Sally's leadership, mentorship, and friendship that led me curiously and willingly down this exciting path of writing and contributing back to our profession. Sally's visions will be carried on, and her talents for writing will continue to be enjoyed through the writing of her amazing and creative short stories for young and imaginative minds.

My family continues to support me with their unconditional patience and support, which have been instrumental in my ability to develop leading-edge perspectives regarding observation and early childhood education. Observing my own children's growth reminds me of the magnitude of the role we have in engaging their voice, for they are indeed curious, competent, and capable.

I also offer thanks to my Humber College Institute of Technology and Advanced Learning family of 26 years. I am always inspired by their ingenuity, innovation, creativity, and passion for supporting the success and future of students, the profession, and the community. The leadership of Jason Powell and Lisa Salem-Wiseman enables and empowers the greatness of our team every day. For that, I am truly thankful.

Lastly, to the students and the early childhood community, it is an honour to be among you, to co-educate and co-learn with you; together we can ensure a positive and promising future for our community.

Kristine Fenning

Brief Contents

Contents

CHAPTER 5
OBSERVING AND DOCUMENTING TARGETED BEHAVIOURS ... 166

Foreword

Welcome to the world of observation! Even before I authored the first edition of *Observing Young Children* in 1999, I was passionate about it. Now, after Kristine and I have co-authored two editions, this edition is hers alone. When she asked if I would write a foreword, of course I agreed. What an opportunity!

Within the pages of this text is quite possibly all you need to know on the subject of observing young children, so I'll not spend my allotted pages saying what is more eloquently said throughout this text. Instead, I'd like to look at observation through a personal lens, one that covers at least three decades of talking and writing about observation and, more importantly, being an observer. Let's begin.

One of the first books I read from an ECE-recommended reading list was *The Politics of Parenthood* by Mark Gerzon (1973). At that time, the term *social activism* didn't exist, but the book's message of social responsibility resonated with my beliefs that to be an adult (parent, educator) is to be accountable for the healthy growth and development of young children. The book spoke to the need for understanding how a society functions and how it is governed, suggesting that the subject of child wellness goes far beyond the attention to children's daily care.

I have always believed in the right of children to be heard, their behaviour to be recognized, and their ideas and emotions to be acknowledged and respected. Consequently, I have been committed to the practice of observation and the documentation of children's lives.

I still remember my first college observation assignment. I wondered if I was "doing it right." I'd never written down observations of a child before, but once I did, I loved that class more than any other. One reason I loved the class was because it was one of the rare times in college where we had the opportunity to construct our own knowledge and contribute to our own self-awareness and education. The observation assignment wasn't an essay or a test. Through our observations, we created something that wasn't there before.

Your observations will have the same power and relevance to you, especially when you share your knowledge with parents, colleagues, or others within the learning circle. It's quite a unique social as well as educational experience.

In one of my last positions as an ECE consultant in northern Ontario, I loved the opportunities to not only observe but also help others see and understand what was meaningful and authentic to the children and the community in which they lived. Children asked, "Does your grandpa have a boat?" "Where do the leaves go in winter?" or "Do you have a fishing licence?" These questions were relevant to them. One day a group of kindergarten children came back from a field trip at a marina. I asked them what they saw and their ideas about that. As they told me, I wrote their comments down. I could hear the buzz among them: "She's writing down what we're saying!" They couldn't believe it. Their takeaway was that someone cared enough to listen and actually record their ideas. In that moment they knew they were appreciated.

This text has more than one section about appreciation. Spend time talking about that word and what it means so that when you enter the world of children, you are ready to observe and listen . . . not just for the obvious things but also for the subtle way children have of communicating their innermost thoughts. Find joy in the toddler's dizzy abandon, learn about the serious child sitting alone, and then reflect on the importance of your observations. Watch carefully how children play outside versus inside and the way they communicate with their peers. Keep asking yourself, What is meaningful to the children? What has significance for them? Listen to what children say, watch what they do, and think about what you've just observed. You will uncover the little things that matter to them as well as significant findings. For example, over time, I discovered a boy who needed glasses, a girl who was sexually abused, an autistic boy with amazing drawing talents, and a three-year-old whose mother didn't know he was deaf. How? Observation.

Generally, I've found that over the years, children haven't changed, but their childhood has. Think about that. Children have always had the same wants and needs: love, food, clean water, play . . . to name but a few. But whether in Ontario or elsewhere in the world, life keeps changing. Expectations of families and communities constantly evolve with the growing social, economic, and political influences plus technology and social media. But what has that got to do with observation? When you finish this course, you'll have the answers to that question plus a whole lot more.

I'm glad this edition speaks to the *Calls to Action* document prepared by the Truth and Reconciliation Commission of Canada, as it speaks to our own journey of learning. Being open to the richness of children's lives will transform your ideas of the pedagogy of observation and documentation.

Perhaps I'll see you one day amid a group of children examining bugs, playing a game, or telling stories. You can be sure I'll ask you, "What did you observe?"

Sally Wylie

Preface

The primary focus of this sixth edition of *Observing Young Children: Transformative Inquiry, Pedagogical Documentation, and Reflection* is to promote and encourage pedagogically sound observation and documentation practices in early childhood settings as a collaborative, meaningful, and reflective learning experience and process for all. Reflection and appreciative inquiry are key components of observation and pedagogical documentation; when we take the time to reflect and inquire through a variety of lenses, we can develop clarity in our image of the child as a competent, equal, and capable co-observer, co-documenter, and co-learning partner. Some of the many lenses used within this text to appreciate the whole child in context include the responsive inclusive approach, socio-cultural theory, Indigenous perspectives, and developmental theory.

Through observation and the creation of pedagogical documentation, we have the opportunity to learn about, appreciate, and make visible the daily experiences of children. Observing and co-documenting with children about their ability to create and hypothesize, their curiosities and theories about their world, and their capacity for wonder, open opportunity for significant learning to happen. It is through the lenses of appreciative inquiry and the cycle of observation that we invite you to create a new space in your mind where you can develop transformative ways of educating, inquiring, reflecting, and learning with children, families, the early childhood profession, your own community, and the global village.

This text provides a comprehensive investigation of the topic of observation and pedagogical documentation for students, educators, administrators, parents, and consulting professionals or clinicians (such as resource professionals, speech pathologists, occupational therapists, and physiotherapists) who are involved with young children. It is particularly relevant for educators of infants, toddlers, and preschoolers; children in junior or senior kindergarten around the globe; and children who are in home child care, after-school programs, elementary school, and other settings.

Throughout this text, the process of observation and pedagogical documentation of children is examined, along with the aspects of practice that support and influence the dimensions of an early learning environment. Through appreciative inquiry and reflection, children, educators, and families are brought together to form collaborative learning communities where mutual education and anti-oppressive observation and documentation practices are supported. Inquiry and reflection provoke questions such as, "How might we promote the voice and equitable participation of children and families in our observation and documentation practices?" "What elements compose quality, responsiveness, and inclusiveness in early learning communities or environments?" and "How will reflection be valued or promoted within the day?" This investigative and reflective process can be truly transformational as it takes us to new places of thought and practice. Seeing new possibilities that can transform any practice is exciting and rewarding, especially knowing that through a new lens, the observer is able to better appreciate how children think and learn, a newcomer family's experiences, or the ways that community resources can build capacity and provide for enriched experiences for children and their families.

As students and professionals of early childhood education, you will explore and discover the world of children with this text and learn about families and communities. You will be amazed, surprised, and rewarded, for this journey and career is a deeply meaningful experience and process. We hope that, by studying and applying the content of these chapters and the online NelsonStudy site, you will find a meaningful way to tell your own story, as well as the stories of children and families. We invite you to join in Chapter 1 and stay with us as the dialogue continues into the last chapter, where we explore the important role of observer as leader and mentor of future observers.

We are excited about your journey as you develop your observation skills and your sensitivities and abilities to co-document the world of children, portraying their experiences as meaningfully as you can. Once this process has begun, it leads to a lifelong pursuit of learning.

OBSERVING YOUNG CHILDREN: THE SIXTH EDITION

The sixth edition of *Observing Young Children: Transformative Inquiry, Pedagogical Documentation, and Reflection* has been updated to reflect the ongoing changes occurring in the early childhood profession and in the global community. One such important consideration is the *Calls to Action* document prepared by the Truth and Reconciliation Commission of Canada. This text empowers its readers to embark upon their own personal journey of learning about reconciliation through the engagement of observation and pedagogical documentation to record one's own journey of discovery. As author of this text, I am continuing my journey of learning about Indigenous perspectives, looking at ways in which we can apply Indigenous knowledge and teachings to reduce oppression, power, and injustices in our observational practices. The building discourse between pedagogical documentation and standardized environmental and individual assessments continues to also gain attention as educational settings learn and grow their understanding of the reciprocity and collaborative intentions of pedagogical documentation. This text draws attention to these discourses in various chapters as they relate to the cycle of observation.

Benefiting from the global reach of innovative educational practices and social media, the early childhood community in Canada has seen significant evolvement in both use and applications of observation and pedagogical documentation. During the research and writing phase of this new edition, I became reinspired about the possibilities for observation and pedagogical documentation. This inspiration led to increased care and concern for the participatory rights of children in this process, for I felt I had an important role to play in co-educating and co-learning with children, colleagues, families, and the community regarding how we might together make our learning visible (in online and hard copy forms) in a safe, positive, non-oppressive, and thoughtful way.

Observation has remained at the centre of our inclusive and responsive practice, reflecting who we are, what we believe, and how we reveal this to ourselves and others. How observation informs practice through appreciative inquiry is reflected in subjects such as but not limited to family-centred practice, team relationships, the environment, early intervention, and early identification.

Observing and documenting children's learning, growth, and experiences is a responsibility as well as a joyous practice. To support your learning, in this text you will find ideas, examples, guidance, strategies, and adaptations that are current and relevant, and that will be of benefit to you now and in the future. All chapters are abundant with photos, exhibits, and reflective textboxes that allow for the application of content to one's observational practices. Throughout the text, there have been intentional connections made to national and international examples, as well as to early childhood frameworks and standards of practice so as to connect readers to various observational practices around the world. This text is both practical and informative at the same time; observers will explore all facets of the cycle of observation to appreciate its significance in all aspects of professional practice.

For the seasoned educator, some of the content will be familiar, yet the appreciative inquiry approach and the updated cycle of observation may give you an inspiring framework for creating or continuing to build sound observation and pedagogical documentation practices that increase access, engagement, and collaboration of all educators, children, families, and communities together. Each chapter supports the child voice and participatory rights, as ethics in observation (hard copy and online forums) take a more prominent focus in the text. Appreciative inquiry and reflection remain at the heart of all chapters, prompting readers to reflect upon different examples and questions to self-assess their own observation and pedagogical documentation practices.

Part 1 focuses on observation in a broad sense, examining one of the most vital and complex educational practices in the field of early childhood. Observation is the primary means of acquiring the knowledge we have about how children learn and about all aspects of our professional practice. It is also the tool with which we are able to uncover the thinking and wonderings of children and families. It is in this portion of the text that we introduce the observer to the participatory rights of children and the important ethical considerations we must reflect upon as we prepare pedagogical documentation within the cycle of observation. Part 1 also introduces readers to the observation and documentation writing process. Understanding why the choices of words we use matter in our efforts to capture what is seen and heard is highlighted, in addition to exploring how settings might prepare for collaboration in all stages of the observation and pedagogical documentation process.

Our current professional practice requires educators to be innovative, creative, and co-constructive in their approach. Part 2 expands upon the foundation established in Part 1 by introducing a wide variety of pedagogical documentation methodologies. The documentation serves to demonstrate that with a wide variety of choices, observers can gather information that supports a holistic portrayal of any child. Premised on a pedagogical approach to documentation, these chapters highlight the importance of children, families, and educators co-observing, co-documenting, and making visible the voices of all in the learning environment. Each method in this text includes the practice and approach of appreciative inquiry and facilitates the use of inquiry, reflection, and interpretation within a team approach. Explored in depth are current and trending documentation methods, all of which can be technologically produced, prepared, accessed, and shared. Furthermore, these methods support choice and discussion; they can be adapted to support any philosophy or practice; and when these methods are combined or used alongside traditional observation or assessment methods, educators are better equipped to support transformation of their practices no matter where they are in the world.

Part 3 continues with the topic of pedagogical documentation, introducing curriculum and portfolio development (e-portfolios and hard copy portfolios), as well as examining early intervention and early identification. Administrators of early childhood programs who are working to develop responsive, inclusive programs will find expert advice and innovative ideas as they consider the best possibilities in collaboration with their learning community for their centre, school, or agency.

This sixth edition emphasizes the links between observation and appreciative inquiry; observation and pedagogical documentation; responsive, inclusive practice and the cycle of observation; ministry guidelines and professional frameworks; diversity within communities and capacity building; early identification / early intervention and professional relationships; and personal beliefs/values and the development of meaningful curriculum and environment. Using the cycle of observation, each link is examined to illustrate how observation may begin like a stone dropped into water—beginning with the observation of a child, which sends ripples out in all directions to reach the community and even global shores.

Structural Organization of the Sixth Edition

The structural organization of the text remains the same as in previous editions. Parts 1, 2, and 3 serve to organize content into three main parts.

Part 1 examines observation, how it reveals how children see their world, what they think about it, how they use the things that are in it, and whom they trust, play with, and want to be around. Observation is setting-independent, serving no one particular philosophy, and is used by educators the world over. Observation is still the most important investigative methodology we have to discover how young children grow and develop.

Part 1 is divided into three chapters. Chapter 1 begins with a discussion of observation and appreciative inquiry and illustrates why observation is important in all aspects of education, regardless of pedagogy and philosophy. The basic questions of observation—who, what, how, when, where, and why—are also explored. Diversity and culture are examined as a context for observation, along with a look at the role of the educator in responsive, inclusive practice. The chapter provides a foundation from which further learning can be pursued, linking current practice to all aspects of the observation process.

In Chapter 2, one of the most important concepts is introduced—one that you will see throughout the entire text—the cycle of observation. Topics related to the observation process, such as occupational standards and challenges to effective observation, are investigated. This chapter is also about getting ready to begin the actual process of observation and relevant concepts to reflect upon, such as the rights of children, codes of ethics, and confidentiality—concepts and ideas that will lay the foundation for ensuing chapters.

Chapter 3 is about pedagogical documentation. In this chapter, you will learn the influence that bias and judgment have upon the observation and documentation process. An expanded section on bias will assist you with exploring the very real world of perception, values, and bias and their impact on your development as a professional. Expanded significantly in this chapter is the interpretation process. Chapter 3 will explain how different documentation methodologies require us to approach interpretations in different ways.

Another area thoroughly examined in this chapter is the actual writing process, with concrete, practical examples, guidelines, and suggestions. Few texts in the field of early childhood provide relevant information on the unique writing process that is pedagogical documentation. Even fewer texts address the concerns of mature students who have been away from school or those of newcomer students from other countries. This chapter will support their development as observers and writers of observations.

Part 2 introduces two major categories of documentation methods and is composed of two chapters that illustrate a wide variety of ways in which to document and make visible the learning and thinking of children. Chapter 4 speaks to the narrative, open style of pedagogical documentation, such as the anecdotal record, photographs and text, learning stories, documentation panels, and video recordings. The closed types of records illustrated in Chapter 5 include those that target specific behaviours, such as ABC analysis or the participation chart.

Part 2 is the most pragmatic section in the text, as it provides numerous practical, current, and popular ways of gathering, documenting, and making visible the learning of children. We have tried to encompass a wide spectrum of documentation, including numerous examples of pedagogical documentation embraced and practised in schools and early childhood centres across Canada and around the globe. A wide variety of methodologies are discussed, as each holds value and specific purpose.

The text and the online site provide numerous methods for documenting the experiences of young children, the interactions and relationships of adults and children, and the environment. The examples found in these two chapters can be used with all ages and abilities. An advantages/disadvantages chart of the methods is included in NelsonStudy to allow for quick comparison.

The comprehensive exhibit examples in these chapters and online illustrate real student, educator, and family work that exemplifies the notion that, through observation and pedagogical documentation, together we can construct meaningful learning. We hope these examples will encourage you as you begin your journey as a student–observer.

The purpose of **Part 3** is to look through the lens of the cycle of observation to reflect and see new possibilities, creating a new space in your mind that can transform what you see and believe. Part 3 solidifies the importance of reflective practice—a key concept fundamental to observation, particularly when living in a society that is ever-changing, with research and practices that constantly evolve and reframe our thinking.

In Part 3, we explore how our beliefs and practices around observation are reflected in day-to-day interactions, families, communities, and the global village. With the immediacy of social media and the Internet, it is no wonder that we look not only to our own neighbourhoods but also outward to others for their philosophy and practices regarding children and families. Guided by responsive, inclusive practices, educators look to models and their principles, goals, and core values to reaffirm, discover, and reflect. Exploring alternative methods that assist us in creating the most useful, meaningful ways of sharing the learning and development of children is necessary.

Changes to the Sixth Edition

This text is the sixth edition of *Observing Young Children: Transformative Inquiry, Pedagogical Documentation, and Reflection*. The first edition was published in 1999, the second in 2004, the third in 2009, the fourth in 2012, and the fifth in 2016. Major changes in each edition reflect the changes in the field of early childhood, our knowledge base, legislation, and society, and an overall transformation of the pedagogy of observation and documentation.

The general structure and identified changes to each chapter are as follows:

- An Overview is presented at the start of each chapter.
- Focus Questions at the beginning of each chapter are included to prompt inquiry and discussion of key topics in the chapter. These questions are tied to the Chapter Reflections at the end.
- Reflective Exercises embedded in each chapter promote dialogue, collaboration, and the solidification of concepts.
- Key Terms are now defined in the margins for each chapter.
- Each chapter incorporates Exhibits designed to highlight a concept or provide a specific example of chapter material.
- Colourful designs with outstanding colour photos and print make this edition visually interesting and engaging. A significant number of photos and examples were added to this edition. Photos have also been made larger for use in discussions and class exercises.
- An Advantages/Disadvantages section for each of the observational methods in Chapters 4 and 5 has been included in NelsonStudy to allow readers to determine which best suits their purpose for observing.
- Connections between content in each chapter have been made to exercises within the NelsonStudy site.

It should be noted that care and attention has been given throughout the text to make as many associations as possible to important ministry documents and frameworks that may guide aspects of observational practices in several different provinces.

Chapter 1

Chapter 1 has been revised to include new research, photos, topics, terminology, reflective exercises, exhibits, and concepts that reflect current and leading-edge early learning observational practices. Chapter 1 begins with reflections and questions concerning the image of the responsive inclusive observer as a co-participant and partner in the pedagogical documentation process. The content in Chapter 1 speaks to the educator as part of a responsible early learning community and highlights the importance of understanding the complex nature of the observational process. Using a responsive and inclusive lens for observation, this chapter strengthens the reflective practices of today's educators and further emphasizes the role of the educator as a partner in a broader early learning community.

This chapter also introduces the image of the child in various contexts, as these views are not universal. Exploring the image of the child from an Indigenous perspective is also a focus. In this edition, the relationship between observation and appreciative inquiry is explored in depth once again to look for the "possibilities" where the voices of children can be heard. Inspired by socio-cultural theory, inquiry-based thinking forms the catalyst for learning and pedagogical documentation. Reasons to observe are covered as in previous editions, but references to new inquiries and new purposes for observation are explored.

Chapter 2

Foundations of the cycle of observation are introduced and explored in further detail than in previous editions, setting the stage for further connections of this content to all other chapters throughout the text. The observation cycle includes children, families, educators, the environment, the community, and much more. This concept is not new, but how it is used to support the main themes of this text is new and visionary; it is the primary vehicle for reflection and inquiry. With the infusion of new content, research, photos, exhibits, and reflective exercises, the changes to Chapter 2 are quite exciting. Readers can expect an in-depth orientation to the participatory rights of children in the observation and pedagogical documentation process. No other text pulls together the multitude of considerations that observers must reflect upon to ensure their observations are ethical and supported by integrity-based practices and one's respective code of ethics and standards of practice.

Social media and technology have augmented observation and pedagogical documentation in dynamic and exciting ways, increasing access and use for children, families, and educators. Chapter 2 prompts observers to consider and reflect upon possible power dynamics and bias that can exist when making children's learning visible through various means. Safety, privacy, and confidentiality are other important considerations in the use of technology-assisted observation and pedagogical documentations. Consulting with children about their consent is also discussed. The role of the ethical observer and documenter is then connected to the enhanced cycle of observation. Not only do readers become familiar with the interactive cycle of observation but they are also introduced to the foundations that support sustainable observation and pedagogical documentation practices. NelsonStudy and Instructor's Manual exercises provide additional opportunities for examination of content.

Chapter 3

Chapter 3 also continues to separate this text on observation from all others as it clearly addresses the unique yet complex style of observational writing and documenting what is seen or heard in a variety of ways. It also outlines the importance of creating a sustainable and accessible observational pedagogy that is inclusive of all. As a mature learner, a new student from high school, or a student who is an English-language learner, writing observations in the field of early childhood offers its own set of challenges. This chapter clearly addresses these challenges and opportunities through the consideration of the words and descriptive language we select and use in our documentation. This includes use of "people-first" and "person-centred" language. For example, showing respect for the language and traditions of Indigenous peoples in our observational practices is critical to our commitment to the 94 Calls to Action outlined by the Truth and Reconciliation Commission of Canada. As a result, to understand and appreciate the culture, traditions, and language of others in our observation and documentation, this chapter encourages the building of meaningful and reciprocal relationships that challenge our traditional views of children.

Student examples, photos, key terms, exhibits, connections to NelsonStudy, and new research in the text demonstrate what is possible while providing strategies and ideas. The Chapter 3 focus on skill development is supported by dozens of closed-captioned videos featuring a wide range of age groups from the online Instructor's Manual. Self-reflection is a continued focus in this chapter as it guides the reader to form and answer questions regarding new and existing areas of inquiry. The chapter supports the reader in examining perceptions of behaviour, internal conditions, and characteristics in addition to positioning developmental theory as but one lens with which to appreciate and make visible children's learning. This chapter also explores the topic of bias, cautioning students to document their observations in such a way that represents children fairly and equitably.

Chapter 4

Chapter 4 begins Part 2, introducing observational and pedagogical documentation methods that are open-ended, flexible, and focused on capturing the spontaneity of children's thinking and wondering. The infusion of new and current exhibits and photos are reflective of not only innovative educators in the profession who were interested in contributing to this text but also those who have co-constructed pedagogical documentation in various ways with children, educators, and families. Significant attention has been paid to presenting a variety of authentic methodologies, which include learning stories, documentation panels, and anecdotals. Other innovative approaches to observation and pedagogical documentation have been thoughtfully discussed in this chapter and include but are not limited to social media (Twitter, Instagram), blogs, and video/audio.

These observational tools form one of the major groupings that can be represented in a child's portfolio. This chapter helps answer the question, "What are the advantages of the visual and technology-assisted alternatives to print-dependent methods used to document the activity of children?" Using these observational methods offers ways to discover what is new about children, uncover what had been previously unknown, or begin to develop information about a story or project. Technology plays a role in the way we document the experiences of young children, and this chapter, along with the plethora of examples and photos from educators in the community, illustrates the changing nature of observation.

Pedagogical documentation allows students to see their own learning through their observations, which gives them another benchmark for their success besides tests and assignments. Students and instructors are again privy to resources and links for this chapter online.

Chapter 5

Chapter 5 offers many of the traditional methods that target behaviours or experiences seen by observers as a means to learn specific information about a child or situation. New and expanded exhibits complement this chapter, introducing connections to curriculum and other aspects of practice. ABC Analysis now rests here in this chapter with other methodologies such as rating scales, checklists, and behaviour tallying. Readers have the opportunity to examine the purpose of each method and draw conclusions as to how they might apply to practice or how they might fit within a pedagogical documentation approach. In this edition, Chapter 5 examines these methods more clearly and in more detail, explaining why they are useful and giving examples that are meaningful for all observers. These observational methods have been streamlined with new content and examples that more thoroughly explain their possible adaptations. They are presented to invoke discussion and reflection regarding how educators might use them to inform their practice. For Chapters 4 and 5, a chart listing each documentation method's advantages and disadvantages is provided in NelsonStudy.

Chapter 6

Chapter 6 is the first chapter of the last section—Part 3. Like many other chapters in this text, Chapter 6 has been completely revised since the last edition. This chapter asks and answers the question, "How do we determine a framework in which to organize our pedagogical documentation, and how do we share that information?" It also addresses the query, "How might observation, pedagogical documentation, and frameworks that support practice inform curriculum and other areas of professional practice?"

Chapter 6 is the application of previous chapters. This chapter takes a broad look at how the cycle of observation opens the door to mutual education between and among educators, families, and the community through reflection, inquiry, and appreciation. New research, exhibits, and content (within the text and online) highlight how reflection and observation build self-awareness in educators, how mutual education between children and adults facilitates "possibility" thinking, and the importance of building our own pedagogy of observation and documentation. Meaningful observation and documentation requires thought, time, and planning for sustainability. Chapter 6 prompts the reader to use a number of responsive and inclusive perspectives when observing young children, looking again beyond the traditional developmental lens to consider many other approaches, such as those of socio-cultural and psychological influences.

Approximately half of this chapter is devoted to the development of portfolios. The investigation of portfolios reveals a more intensive and comprehensive look into relevant subtopics such as e-portfolios, stages and content of portfolios, how to link documentation and curriculum to professional standards and frameworks across Canada, supporting metacognition and self-assessment, and the various types and forms of portfolios. In addition, resources online provide examples, research, and related topics.

Chapter 7

Chapter 7 connects the learning from previous chapters and describes how early identification and early intervention transform practice with the newly updated cycle of observation. This chapter explores the complex process of both topics, starting with family-centred practice, interprofessional education, teams, assessment tools, individual planning for a child with special needs and rights, child abuse and the duty to report, and the terminology associated with the individualized planning process.

Chapter 7 affirms the notion that observation is integral to everything we do as educators, especially when it involves children and families who need extra supports and services. In this edition, we realize that involvement in the cycle of observation takes us beyond the corridors of early childhood settings and schools out into the community, both local and global; it causes us to step out to look back in and be involved in appreciative inquiry that involves assessment (authentic and standardized), teams, collaboration, and mutual education. In this chapter, we also consider perspectives on authentic assessment and inquiry in various contexts such as the Ontario Ministry of Education's Kindergarten Program, the *Te Whāriki* approach from New Zealand, and Indigenous peoples' perspectives. The cycle of observation also leads to discussion of referrals, adjustments and adaptations, environmental design, and the ways that children and families can draw assistance from the knowledge and skills of educators and the community. Integral to this chapter are further resources and examples provided online.

Chapter 8

Chapter 8, like other chapters in this text, introduces new terms, exhibits, photos, reflective exercises, and content. College and university instructors will be pleased to see this content included in the sixth edition. This chapter begins with an exploration of the role of environment as co-educator and co-play partner with children. Understanding that a quality environment is much more than just the physical attributes of a space is important; educators must observe a number of environmental aspects, including relationships and the psychological tone of the space, Universal Design for Learning (UDL), and the temporal environment in order to understand its role and interactions with children. This chapter poses a number of responsive and reflective questions concerning observation and documentation practices in order to examine how UDL principles might be applied to an early childhood environment.

Chapter 8 carefully weaves together all previous chapters in this text; the role of the educator continues to transform so significantly that it is important to challenge our current professional paradigms of practice. Opportunities are vast for educators to take on the role of leader and mentor in evolving observational practices to reflect both pedagogical documentation methodologies and the necessary components within the cycle of observation that is discussed throughout this text. Sustainability of an observational pedagogy that is safe and non-oppressive requires observer leaders who can mentor and support children, educators, and families in their documentation practices. Examples are available online of educator leaders in the profession who are innovative in social media methodologies in order to function in a co-education role with children and families.

Legislation and frameworks supporting and planning for accessibility in our observation and documentation practices and early childhood environments are also examined in this chapter. To be a transformational observer, it is important to maintain currency in one's knowledge and skills regarding all relevant legislation. Participation in continuous professional learning and communities of practice, engaging in longitudinal and ethnographic research, and applying action research to improve aspects of our professional practices all support our capacity for innovativeness and meaning in our observation and documentation practices.

SPECIAL PEDAGOGY TO SUPPORT LEARNING

Instructor's Resources

These online instructor's resources provide password-protected content for use by any instructor, and are especially helpful to part-time instructors or instructors new to this course material. Included in the resources for each chapter are expected content such as a test bank of informal and formal assessment items, Microsoft® PowerPoint® presentation slides, and an instructor's guide that contains key concepts, engagement strategies, reflective questions, Internet and video exercises, and annotated lists of recommended resources, such as articles, texts, videos, and websites. The Instructor's Manual also includes sections on student motivation and challenges to learning, engagement strategies, and reflections on teaching.

The **Nelson Education Teaching Advantage (NETA)** program delivers research-based instructor resources that promote student engagement and higher-order thinking to enable the success of Canadian students and educators. Be sure to visit Nelson Education's **Inspired Instruction** website at nelson.com/inspired/ to find out more about NETA.

The following instructor resources have been created for *Observing Young Children*, Sixth Edition. Access these ultimate tools for customizing lectures and presentations at nelson.com/instructor.

NETA Test Bank

This resource was written by Kristine Fenning and Sally Wylie. It includes approximately 40 multiple-choice questions written according to NETA guidelines for effective question construction. Also included are more than 40 short answer and 80 essay questions that, together, cover the full scope of the text.

NETA PowerPoint

PowerPoint lecture slides for every chapter have been created by Kristine Fenning and Sally Wylie. There is an average of 18 slides per chapter, many featuring key figures, tables, and photographs from *Observing Young Children*. NETA principles of clear design and engaging content have been incorporated throughout, making it simple for instructors to customize the deck for their courses.

NETA Instructor's Manual

The Instructor's Manual to accompany *Observing Young Children*, Sixth Edition, has been prepared by Kristine Fenning and Sally Wylie. This manual is organized by chapter and contains sample lesson plans, learning objectives, suggested classroom activities, and a resource integration guide to give instructors the support they need to engage their students within the classroom.

As with the text, the Instructor's Manual represents a complete update of previous instructor manuals for this text. A key highlight or added value is that while students are using documents available online, instructors are able to access their own resources that connect to students' understanding of content explored within their text and online. This coordinated approach to learning and teaching offers a rich hybrid experience of research, examples, and content for all involved.

NelsonStudy

NelsonStudy for *Observing Young Children*, Sixth Edition, includes two sets of closed-captioned videos:

- Observation videos of children alone or in small groups are extremely valuable for instructors in the classroom and useful for students who do not otherwise have access to groups of children for observation. Question sets are provided with these videos.
- Video testimonials enhance the audiovisual experience for students by enlisting leading professionals in the early childhood profession and external community to examine and discuss key concepts from each chapter.

All the videos within NelsonStudy function well as visual resources to assist students with the application of their learning and understanding of text material as well as providing opportunities for direct application of observation and writing skills.

Student Ancillaries

NelsonStudy

NELSONstudy

The NelsonStudy website is available for purchase and brings course concepts to life with engaging and interactive learning tools, including chapter overviews, videos, self-study practice questions, readings, quizzes, and flashcards. Access NelsonStudy online from any device—no set up, just success!

Visit nelson.com/student to start using NelsonStudy. Enter the Online Access Code from the card included with your text. If a code card is not provided, you can purchase instant access at NELSONbrain.com.

About the Authors

Kristine Fenning is a program coordinator and early childhood professor with the Early Childhood Education program at the Humber College Institute of Technology and Advanced Learning. Kristine has an extensive background in adult education, community college, resource consultation, and early childhood education. Kristine's vitality and passion for early childhood has led her to fulfill a number of roles in her 26 years in the profession, including early childhood educator, resource teacher, resource consultant, and training coordinator. Kristine has presented various topics at conferences in both Canada, the United States, and internationally and has authored and published other articles and documents pertaining to cohort-based learning, academic integrity, inclusion, and supervisory leadership. In collaboration with Toronto Children's Services and Humber College Child Care Centres / Humber College Institute of Technology and Advanced Learning, Kristine was a co-developer and co-originator of the professional development system now in place for early childhood educators, resource consultants, supervisors, and directors in Toronto. Her passions are teamwork, educational advocacy, inclusion, observation and pedagogical documentation, assessment, the role of technology in observation, and resource consultation. Kristine continues to be a vital member of a number of projects involving community partnerships, collaborative learning, and inclusion. She is a proud wife and mother of two beautiful daughters, who continue to teach her and empower her to make a difference in the lives of others.

Sally Wylie has been in the field of early childhood for three decades as an early childhood educator, resource teacher and elementary school teacher, program advisor for the Ontario Ministry of Children and Youth Services, and college/university professor. She has this to say about the topic of observation: "After 30-plus years in the early childhood education profession, observation is still one of my greatest interests and passions. I believe strongly that there is no test that could ever take the place of an educator with keen observation skills and the ability to communicate to others what is discovered." Sally has partnered with the Humber College Institute of Technology and Advanced Learning for a videoconferencing project with the Regional Training and Resource Centre in Early Childhood Care and Education for Asia in Singapore and given workshops in Singapore on the topic of developing portfolios. Sally has co-presented at the National Association for the Education of Young Children in Canada and the United States, and collaborated with the Government of Ontario and TFO, Ontario's French-language educational authority, to produce a bilingual website for supervisors. She has published and co-published many articles. Sally finished her formal teaching career with Charles Sturt University–Ontario in the Bachelor of Early Childhood Studies Program, but has remained an active early childhood consultant with various early learning centres in northern Ontario. She is married and has three wonderful adult children and six grandchildren. Sally is currently writing fictional stories for young children.

Acknowledgments

We would like to thank the following people for their contributions to this text; we continue to appreciate that it takes a community to write a text. To these individuals, we offer our appreciation of their gift of time and expertise and their willingness to share their experiences with the readers of this book. Thanks also to the parents and children who shared their faces with us in photographs and videos.

We would like to thank our families, without whose support this text would never have been possible. It was with their support and encouragement that we were able to continue our writing journey forward once again with this sixth edition.

We also wish to thank our colleagues and friends, whose encouragement has meant so much. Without support, it is difficult to persevere and complete a project, and we take this space to acknowledge those whose support has been much appreciated.

We wish to also thank the individuals, agencies, and organizations who gave permission for their contributions to be used in this text. It is because of their expertise and commitment to children and families that we are able to bring such relevant and insightful examples, photos, and content to our readership.

To students embarking on their career as early childhood professionals: this book is not only about you but is written for you. To current early childhood professionals: we are excited about the many possibilities that this text can offer to your important roles and work with pedagogical documentation, appreciative inquiry, research, and mentoring. Thank you for all that you do.

Generous thanks to the peer reviewers of the sixth edition. It is with your support, knowledge, and feedback that this and future editions can continue to reflect the diversity of its readership as well as current needs and trends in the early childhood profession:

Rebecca J. Allsopp, Champlain College
Erin Cameron, Mohawk College
Farveh Ghafouri, Seneca College
Brenda Huff, St. Clair College, Thames Campus
Leslie Kopf-Johnson, Algonquin College
Dhanna Mistri, Sheridan College

Our appreciation is extended to the diligent staff of the editorial and production departments at Nelson Education, whose expertise and organization kept everything on track throughout the entire process. We wish to thank Carmen Yu, publisher, for her expertise, cooperation, and generous support of this edition; Theresa Fitzgerald, content manager, for her unwavering patience, insights, and support; Amanda Henry, executive marketing manager; Natalia Denesiuk Harris, senior production project manager; Joanne McNeil, manufacturing manager; Christina Jelinek, copy editor; and Daniela Glass, project manager, rights acquisition and policy; as well as all the members of the production team at Nelson for their many contributions to the success of this sixth edition.

Sincerely,
Kristine Fenning and Sally Wylie

OBSERVATION, PEDAGOGICAL DOCUMENTATION, AND THE RESPONSIVE INCLUSIVE OBSERVER

As you embark upon this transformative personal learning journey, we encourage you to ask questions, listen, reflect, inquire, research, collaborate, and so much more! This book is intended to inspire and guide all observers—whether they are preservice or seasoned educators, professors, supervisors, families, early interventionists or others—in their development of meaningful observation and documentation pedagogy. We invite everyone to share in our perspectives concerning observation and pedagogical documentation, and accept our invitation to join this examination of *Observing Young Children: Transformative Inquiry, Pedagogical Documentation, and Reflection.*

In this text, we are proud to be global in our approach, examining philosophies and practices reflective of early childhood and early learning settings in various countries. As we learn about observation and pedagogical documentation, we practise observing through a variety of lens including but not limited to socio-cultural theory, responsive inclusive education, emergent curriculum, perspectives of First Peoples and the wisdom of Aboriginal Elders, developmentally appropriate practice, Reggio Emilia, and other philosophies, theories, and practices so as to learn, understand, and appreciate.

It is intended throughout this text to demonstrate our respect for and acknowledgment of Indigenous teachings and wisdom, as we respond to the Truth and Reconciliation Commission of Canada: Calls to Action through our observations, our pedagogy, and our learning. We have much to learn from our Aboriginal peoples, as well as from children and families around the world. We recognize that everyone coming to the expansive topics of observation and pedagogical documentation will bring their own set of values, beliefs, and perspectives. We hope this text will fulfill all expectations, embrace all perspectives, and acculturate readers to a responsive, inclusive, and appreciative observational pedagogy that supports and enriches the lives of young children and their families.

Part 1 is divided into three chapters. Chapter 1 introduces us to the importance of observation and pedagogical documentation and how together they can assist observers (children, families, educators, and the community) in uncovering the learning and thinking of children within early childhood environments. Knowledge of different observational methodologies is not sufficient in itself as observation is also a value, a philosophy, an attitude, a skill, and, ultimately, an important responsibility. As part of the observational process, responsive inclusive observers have the privilege and opportunity to engage in appreciative

Truth and Reconciliation Commission of Canada: Calls to Action

A report by the Truth and Reconciliation Commission of Canada identifying 94 calls to action that promote reconciliatory action in order to right the unjust treatment of Indigenous peoples and the legacy of residential schools.

inquiry to dialogue, question, inquire, and wonder with children as they discover the world around them. While significant transformation in the profession continues to occur, the multitude of purposes for observing continue to be relevant and foundational for all observers within any program, school, or early childhood setting. As you continue to discover and uncover the possibilities that observation offers, we hope you will come to appreciate observation as we do.

Chapter 2 is a very meaningful chapter as it orients us to the participatory rights of children as equal partners in the observation and documentation process. Pedagogical documentation is more than simply inviting children to participate in the observational cycle; it expects that children and families will share the responsibilities for making learning visible. This chapter also posits the importance of educators building and maintaining ethics in all steps and aspects of their observational practices, it introduces the standards of practice concerning ethics as they relate to observation and pedagogical documentation for educators in different provinces, it explores what observers need to do in order to promote the participation of children in the observation and pedagogical documentation processes, and it prompts observers to increase their understanding of how bias can exist in their observations and what they can do about it. Technology-assisted documentation aided by social media is also a highlight of this chapter as technology introduces a whole realm of ethical dilemmas and considerations when making children's learning visible online. The discussion of ethics leads us into examination of the dynamic and interactive cycle of observation. Each component of the cycle is carefully explored and explained, outlining how it supports the creation of observation and pedagogical documentation.

Chapter 3 is about getting started with the actual process of observing, documenting, and interpreting and reflecting on the learning experiences of young children. In this chapter, we also explore preservice educator guidelines for observing as well as how to set the stage for equity, access, and opportunity for co-observing and the co-preparing of pedagogical documentation by everyone (children, families, educators). This chapter introduces how language usage, combined with observation and interpreting skills, produces an appreciative perspective and insightful knowledge about how children learn, and about how we might understand children's behaviour.

This chapter is also robust with discussion about how bias influences how and what we document and the important considerations we need to make when engaging in the observational process. As we interpret what we see and hear, we begin to understand our role in creating a culturally responsive environment and how our role is interwoven with those of the children and their families. We then begin as educators to appreciate the role of the family and its cultural influence on a child's development.

Chapter 3 is about writing and pedagogical documentation. Another area thoroughly examined is the process of documenting observations with examples, guidelines, and suggestions to assist in the actual process. In this chapter, the focus is on learning what to write and finding the appropriate ways to say it.

Few texts in the field of early childhood provide concrete information on the writing process, and even fewer introduce the perspectives of various students (all observers including mature students who have been away from school, new students from other countries, or learners with special needs, for example). This chapter will support not only educators currently practising in the profession but also beginning observers and writers of documentation.

pedagogical documentation

A shared documentation and pedagogical process intended to make visible the thinking, inquiries, and theories of children and others. It involves listening, observing, reflection, and analysis to prompt new and more complex learning and thinking.

WHAT IS OBSERVATION?

Observation continues to be one of the most important responsibilities we have as educators, for it helps to uncover what it is that we see and hear. Observation is functional, informative, and systematic. It is a foundational and cyclical process that involves watching, listening, and documenting children's learning and behaviour, as well as many other elements about children and the environment. Observers will document for a variety of purposes, which will be explored later in this chapter. Observation is also an action and process involving interpretation and reflection to understand and examine the behaviour of others, as well as what it is that we are seeing and hearing.

Since the last edition of this text, transformation has and continues to occur in observation and documentation practices within early childhood settings in Canada and around the world. For example, Westernized developmental theories dominated and influenced early childhood practices in Ontario and other provinces for many years, typically depicting the educator as the sole observer, knowledge keeper, and documenter of children's development for record keeping

objectify

Seeing only the development of children and their ability to achieve knowledge and skills (as per an assessment process). Children are not seen holistically and are often not viewed as competent and capable beings.

and assessment. Current practice and research infer that Westernized developmental approaches and theories are archaic and objectify children, and therefore are no longer considered the sole or preferred approach to observation in early childhood settings. Why do you think that might be? Current observational practices still value the development lens in understanding the potential of children, yet the influences of pedagogical documentation prompts observers to include other theories and perspectives from around the world in the process of watching and listening to enhance meaning and understanding. Advancement of technology and digital mediums has also enabled innovative and creative ways to observe and involve others in the process. New professional and quality standards, research and theories rethinking and valuing the image of children as competent and capable observers and beings, as well as changing needs of families and children are just some of the provocations prompting transformation in observation and increased understanding and use of pedagogical documentation in early childhood.

provocations

Inspired by Reggio Emilia, provocations are materials or experiences that educators set out to provoke children's thinking.

Looking to the future of the early childhood profession, the role of observation within pedagogical documentation remains significant. As we will examine in this chapter, observation, pedagogical documentation, and appreciative inquiry have the combined power to help observers understand and uncover the capabilities of children, their spirituality and values, their curiosity, inquiries, and wonderings in everyday moments, their relationships with others and with their environments, as well as the theories they have about their world. There is much to learn about the role of families in the observation process and about children, how and why children might utilize the materials available to them, and whom they trust and want to play with. Let's continue then our examination of Chapter 1 and all that observation can offer!

FOCUS QUESTIONS

1. Why is observation important?
2. What are the qualities that define a responsive and inclusive educator?
3. Describe the appreciative inquiry approach. How might it support observation processes in early childhood settings? How might questioning promote reflection and an understanding of the image of a child?
4. Pedagogical documentation is more than just observing. Describe the attributes of pedagogical documentation and why it is important.

5. Describe the many purposes for observing. How might observation and pedagogical documentation contribute to the quality of professional practice and early childhood settings?
6. What is family centredness, and why is it an important piece of the observation process?
7. Why is it important to understand culture, diversity, and societal change?

responsive

The act of responding with respect and intention to another's requests, needs, or situations; a pedagogy grounded in educators displaying sensitivity and responsiveness to others.

OBSERVATION: IMAGE AND ROLE OF THE RESPONSIVE, INCLUSIVE OBSERVER

In the early childhood profession, a responsive inclusive observer demonstrates a strong sense of self-awareness; an attitude of positivity, caring, and acceptance that permeates all aspects of observational practice; and an obvious respect and value for the individuality and uniqueness of self, children, families, and team. This particular text takes an approach that inclusion functions as an attitude, a process, and a concept and is not restricted to children with special needs, but instead encompasses all children regardless of culture, class, appearance, beliefs, lifestyle, sexuality, gender, age, family composition, religion, language, or other.

Responsive observers are attentive to and appreciative of the uniqueness and individuality of every child, taking care to note their interests, strengths, and abilities so as to respond in inclusive ways. They build relationships and a sense of community with all members of an early childhood setting or community and include every element of each child and family in all aspects of their observational practice. Responsive observation also involves attentively observing and developing curriculum that responds to and reflects "children's expertise, cultural traditions and ways of knowing, [and] the multiple languages spoken by some children" (Australian Government, Department of Education, Employment and Workplace Relations, 2009, p. 14; see also Pelo, 2006). Wisdom from Aboriginal Elders in BC teach us that: "every child is special; and every child needs to be treated with care and respect" (p. 6). It is therefore integral that our observation and documentation pedagogy reflects this wisdom, as this approach is a conduit to being a responsive and inclusive observer.

Lastly, the responsive inclusive approach involves engaging in an ongoing process of reflection, a process synonymous with appreciative inquiry. Schön (1983), a well-known author on the reflection process, consistently refers to paying attention as "hearing" or "seeing" what is before you. For our purposes, this would refer to hearing and watching what students say or do in the context of learning, essentially paralleling the observation process.

It is through observing, reflecting, and documenting that experiences are validated, shared, and open for interpretation and collaboration from all those involved (Chorney, 2006; Paige-Smith & Craft, 2007). Furthermore, "reflective practice is a form of ongoing learning that involves engaging with questions of philosophy, ethics, and practice. Its intention is to gather information and gain insights that support, inform and enrich decision-making about children's learning" or other elements of teaching or learning and then reflect on the changes necessary to improve practice (Australian Government, Department of Education, Employment and Workplace Relations, 2009, p. 13). As we examine further in subsequent chapters, this inquiry-based process "encourages educators to challenge their own assumptions and beliefs about early childhood education and practices" (McFarland, Saunders, & Allen, 2009, p. 506) and promotes dialogue with other professionals about the most meaningful ways to support children (O'Connor & Diggins, 2002; Pelo, 2006). Throughout this text, you will note continuous reference to responsive and inclusive practice. There is much to be learned about how to be responsive and inclusive in our professional practice.

inclusion

An attitude, a process, and a concept that accepts, respects, and embraces the individuality of any person regardless of ability, race, class, gender, language, ethnicity, age, sexual orientation, family, beliefs, values, or other.

Take a moment to reflect upon qualities you feel demonstrate a responsive inclusive approach. What is meaningful to you? Compare them to what has been discussed here—are they the same or different? Why?

REFLECTIVE EXERCISE 1.1

OBSERVATION AND APPRECIATIVE INQUIRY

appreciative inquiry

The practice of asking questions to enlist members of an organization in a collaborative conversation concerning positive change; prompts observers to query their practice and engage in processes that will assist in achieving positive change.

To be an attuned, responsive, and inclusive observer, it is also necessary to observe and listen to children using an appreciative inquiry approach. Essentially, appreciative inquiry asks the observer to demonstrate open-mindedness, appreciation, and positive regard for children. "The word appreciate is a verb that carries double meaning, referring to both the act of recognition and the act of enhancing value" (Whitney & Trosten-Bloom, p. 2). This inquiry-based process empowers the value of the voices and ideas of educators, children, families, and their community to co-create, co-research, and collaborate so as to prepare a holistic environment and a curriculum that is meaningful and mindful of the community they share. This approach encourages the observer to look beyond development, and to see children and others as competent, able, intuitive investigators, thinkers, and inquirers, capable of co-constructing new learning and confident in their ability to question new experiences. Observation and appreciative inquiry are integral components of pedagogical documentation and our observation cycle, a cycle we will explore in Chapter 2.

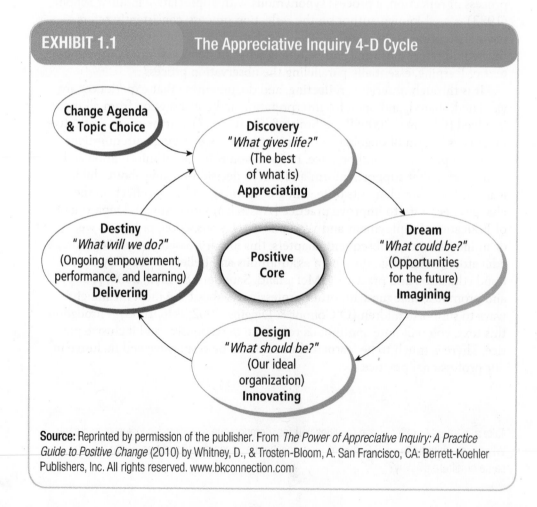

EXHIBIT 1.1   The Appreciative Inquiry 4-D Cycle

Source: Reprinted by permission of the publisher. From *The Power of Appreciative Inquiry: A Practice Guide to Positive Change* (2010) by Whitney, D., & Trosten-Bloom, A. San Francisco, CA: Berrett-Koehler Publishers, Inc. All rights reserved. www.bkconnection.com

Appreciative Inquiry: 4 Stages

Exhibit 1.1 presents the appreciative inquiry approach in four quadrants (known as discovery, dream, design, and destiny) as discussed by Whitney and Trosten-Bloom (2010, p. 6). In the first stage, discovery is intended to capture the strengths-based authentic inquiry resulting from dialogue and collaboration between those involved. The dream stage captures the possibility thinking, and the design stage prompts those involved to determine what it is that that they want to achieve. Lastly, the destiny stage is the celebratory stage—prompting those involved to celebrate successes and the socially constructed dialogue and collaboration that led to the new possibilities. Exhibit 1.2 illustrates how the appreciative inquiry approach was utilized with a group of children to understand how they learn. Each layer of the circle influences the other, leading to children learning about how they learn. Exhibit 1.3 applies the appreciative inquiry model to observation, and extends the limitations of observation to include and reflect the rich inquiry, questioning, and dialogue that is necessary to provoke new ways of thinking and doing.

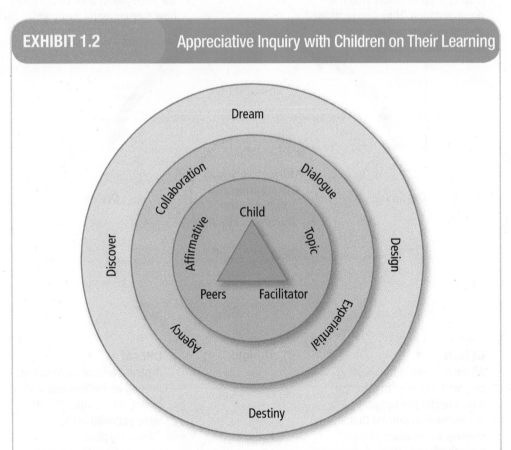

EXHIBIT 1.2 Appreciative Inquiry with Children on Their Learning

Source: "Appreciative Inquiry with Children on Their Learning." Davies, A. (2013). *Appreciating Learning: Children Using Appreciative Inquiry as an Approach to Helping Them to Understand Their Learning*, Figure 1, p. 4. Thesis, Master of Social Sciences (MSocSc). University of Waikato, Hamilton, New Zealand.

The collaborative nature between observation and appreciative inquiry enables the observer to document in a positive way. For example, in Exhibit 1.3, children, families, and educators converse about their affirmative topic, how they collaborate, how they arrive at their theories and hypotheses, and how they create their own narratives and stories. It is here "within the construct of the agentic child, children and adults both have power, which is negotiated as a critically conscious component of their relationship. The child is empowered through their relationship with the adult, who lends their power, strength and resources to the child, rather than imposing this upon, or doing for the child. The adult is also empowered and made knowledgeable, wise and influenced through the relationship with the child." (Sorin & Galloway, 2006, p. 19).

agentic

Introduced by Albert Bandura whereby the child is seen as a contributing being and shares equal power with the adult. Power is seen to be balanced and shared between the adult and the child.

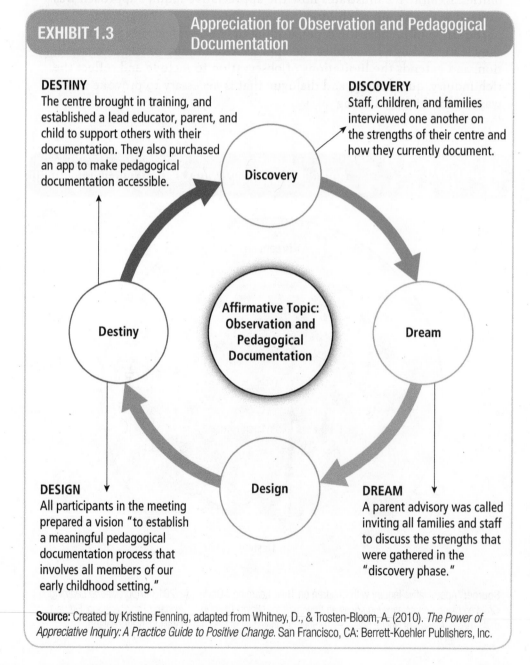

EXHIBIT 1.3 **Appreciation for Observation and Pedagogical Documentation**

DESTINY
The centre brought in training, and established a lead educator, parent, and child to support others with their documentation. They also purchased an app to make pedagogical documentation accessible.

DISCOVERY
Staff, children, and families interviewed one another on the strengths of their centre and how they currently document.

Discovery

Affirmative Topic:
Observation and
Pedagogical
Documentation

Destiny

Dream

Design

DESIGN
All participants in the meeting prepared a vision "to establish a meaningful pedagogical documentation process that involves all members of our early childhood setting."

DREAM
A parent advisory was called inviting all families and staff to discuss the strengths that were gathered in the "discovery phase."

Source: Created by Kristine Fenning, adapted from Whitney, D., & Trosten-Bloom, A. (2010). *The Power of Appreciative Inquiry: A Practice Guide to Positive Change.* San Francisco, CA: Berrett-Koehler Publishers, Inc.

Kristine Fehrung

▲ Take a moment to reflect upon the quotation by Sorin and Galloway on page 8. What is the quote inferring? How might or how could this educator apply the meaning of that quote to the children in this photo?

Appreciative inquiry is a lens that broadens our view of children beyond the developmental approach: it allows the observer to look at possibilities, listen with interest, and question with curiosity. Both adults and children deserve to be viewed as diverse human beings full of possibility, capable of contributing new knowledge to their world and who are appreciated for their uniqueness.

There is no doubt that appreciative inquiry has an impact on our perspectives and what we observe, how we interpret and reflect upon what we see and hear, and, finally, how we respond. These sound appreciative inquiry practices help educators to develop positive working relationships with parents and co-workers as well as transform all aspects of their practice. Educators familiar with this approach also recognize that it is comforting for parents to view how their children are demonstrating their learning and the theories they have about their world. This participative and strengths-based approach allows children to experience satisfaction and empowerment when listened to and gives them the opportunity to query, contribute to, and positively reflect upon how they are learning. This act of learning about how one learns is known as meta-learning/meta-cognition, and is a concept we will explore in later chapters.

meta-learning/meta-cognition

Self-discovery and learning about how one learns.

Questioning through an Appreciative Lens

Questioning, a valued step in the appreciative inquiry approach, "works on the belief that the type of questions we ask and what we inquire into will determine the kind of things that we find, and furthermore that these discoveries

reflective journal entry

The act of reflecting and documenting one's thoughts, theories, and ideas concerning critical learning experiences or events in a journal, book, or medium of choice. The intention is to promote deep critical thinking.

emergent curriculum

A form of curriculum development where educators follow the children's leads by observing their interests, skills, areas for improvement, and family and community cultures, and then reflect, document, and plan accordingly.

become the linguistic material, the stories, out of which the future is conceived, conversed about, and constructed" (Cooperrider & Whitley, 2000, p. 18; Davies, A., 2013, p. 24). Stories, questions, and inquiry are meaningful ways to connect human beings "to the past and the future" (Goeson, R., p. 2).

The Ontario Ministry of Education document entitled *Think, Feel, Act: Lessons from Research about Young Children* (2013) is an appropriate example of appreciative inquiry thinking and questioning. This document suggests that educators observe and reflect upon the following questions in Exhibit 1.4 every day in their professional practice.

The document *Understanding the British Columbia Early Learning Framework: From Theory to Practice* (2008) also employs an appreciative inquiry and questioning approach to help their educators observe and envision their view of children in Exhibit 1.5.

REFLECTIVE EXERCISE 1.3

Take a moment to appreciate the inquisitive nature of the questions from both provincial ministries in Exhibits 1.4 and 1.5. How does each example demonstrate the qualities of appreciative inquiry? Then, reflect upon their similarities and differences. Prepare a meaningful reflective journal entry on your responses to each of the questions. This will help to prepare your view of the child as it relates to what you are reading in this chapter and subsequent chapters.

play-based curriculum

A form of curriculum and learning based on the child's play interests and competencies, with its methodology reflected in journaling, documentation, and an educator's reflective practice.

Inquiry into the connections children make in their learning requires educators to move outside the thinking of curriculum as something educators "create" or "do." Being alert to and observant of daily occurrences, playroom experiences, and children's interests, language, and hypothesizing are just some of the considerations of emergent or play-based curriculum. Exploring the answers to those queries gives direction and meaning, focus to the observation and documentation, and ultimately drives the co-creation of curriculum by the children, families, and educators. Through keen observation, an educator sees the connections that the child is making on a daily basis. The documentation of those connections can provoke educators to engage in paradigm shifts concerning curriculum or other elements of practice to new theories and ways of thinking. In order to engage in this process, educators need to be prepared for these discoveries. This personal and professional "preparedness" will be examined closely in subsequent chapters.

Observation, inquiry, and questioning can also prompt educators to consider a number of contextual factors that affect children's learning, such as temperament, relationships, culture, environment, ability, family diversity, language, gender, development, philosophy and values, quality, and so much more.

Evidenced by the photos that follow, educators at the Bruce Peninsula Family Centre opened up a plethora of wonderings and possibilities that began with observation, and was further extended through questioning, inquiry, and pedagogical documentation. When we observe, as educators did at the Bruce Peninsula Family Centre, we open ourselves to possibilities. Take a moment to review the questions the children asked when shown the photo of the tree. These questions demonstrate their inquiry process. When a child asked questions about the wind, and another child shared her observations about what the wind did with the leaves at her house, it began a journey of investigation: Where do the leaves go? What happened to our trees?

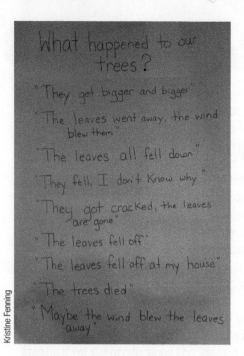

What happened to our trees?

"They get bigger and bigger"

"The leaves went away, the wind blew them"

"The leaves all fell down"

"They fell, I don't know why"

"They got cracked, the leaves are gone"

"The leaves fell off"

"The leaves fell off at my house"

"The trees died"

"Maybe the wind blew the leaves away"

Kristine Fenning

Kristine Fenning

OBSERVATION AND PEDAGOGICAL DOCUMENTATION

Inspired by socio-cultural theory, complemented by appreciative inquiry and the Reggio Emilia philosophy, pedagogical documentation is a fundamental, universal, and setting-independent approach to learning about children. It is also a process, a framework, a pedagogy, and an important component within the observation cycle in Chapter 2. It is a reciprocal responsibility of everyone.

Pedagogical documentation follows children's and educators' thinking and finds ways to make that thinking visible. It is a means of analysing what lies beneath the play experiences to find the questions being asked and the learning that occurs. It is a tool for educators to gather information to create meaning, but documentation is more than just the gathering of evidence . . . it is also the reflection on and analysis of the collection, and the presentation of that collection, in a way that makes the children's learning visible to the children, the teachers, and other adults. (Rinaldi in Wurm, 2005, p. 98; Fleet et al., 2011, p. 6)

If we think about the concepts of responsiveness, inclusion, and appreciative inquiry, it is easy to see the connection these concepts have to pedagogical documentation. We need to engage in collaborative dialogue and interaction, as well as use multiple theories, lenses, and documentation methodologies to appreciate and authenticate what it is that we are seeing and hearing, to ensure there are no preconceived ideas or judgements, and to validate there is no child or individual who learns and develops in exactly the same way. While observation and documentation for the purposes of assessment recognizes developmental stages, prerequisite skills, and skills to be developed, on its own it fails to appreciate the complex thinking and learning that children are capable of doing. Pedagogical documentation protects us from the need to be assessment focused and allows a process to evolve that is authentic and respectful of individuality and diversity. Everyone deserves to be listened to as well as have a voice in this process.

> Pedagogical documentation is grounded in a "pedagogy of listening"—that is, listening with all of your senses (Rinaldi, 2006), through collecting visual data (photographs, videotapes), audio data, and written notes for the purpose of understanding children's thinking in order to plan educational experiences for them, and as a reflective process for educators to understand their own role in the teaching/learning dialogue. . . . The intent is not to identify where children are at in the developmental process, and where they might be seen as deficit, but to remove those lenses that tend to blind educators from seeing the unique ways in which children construct their understanding of the world and ways in which they are actors in creating culture. (Dahlberg et al., 1999/2007; Tarr, 2010; Tarr, 2011, p. 13)

In this approach to observing and documenting, we also follow naturally the lead of the child and use a variety of observation methods to capture meaningful information and moments in time that reflect the how, what, when, where, and why of children's learning in their own unique and individual ways. Chapter 4 introduces a number of documentation approaches that embody the intentions and foundations of pedagogical documentation. Depending upon who the observer is and the purpose of the observation, each method can offer meaningful information to aid further inquiry, new provocations, and new learning possibilities. Whether you are a seasoned or a preservice educator, it is through collaboration that you will discover new and creative approaches to capturing the voices and thinking of children as they unfold.

The Ontario Ministry of Education (2012) in its Ontario Capacity Building series titled *Pedagogical Documentation: Leading Learning in the Early Years and Beyond* discusses how pedagogical documentation provides the tools that enable teaching and learning to transform in very authentic ways. Be sure to visit the strategies suggested in this document as they embrace the concepts of diversity, rights, shared understanding, ownership and accountability, and the voices of all in the observation and documentation process.

Pedagogical documentation also proposes that access to and engagement with observation tools be a daily occurrence, so as to engage children, families, and educators in documenting the learning of all within a classroom and to make learning visible. When this role is shared, the image of the child is broadened, our knowledge and understanding grow together, and experiences of others benefit all. See Chapter 2 for more on the topic of increasing accessibility to observation and documentation within the classroom.

Pedagogical documentation can result from and can also provoke questioning and inquiry-based practices. What gives pedagogical documentation meaning?—the inquiry reflected in the intention. If the inquiry or questioning techniques are authentic, contextual, and reflective of the children, their families, the staff, and the community, the observation and documentation will be meaningful and contextual. Educators are inspired to look at what they've seen a thousand times, whether it is a child getting dressed to go outside or a child washing hands. Embedded in these seemingly normal events are problems being solved, questions being asked, theories being posed, and basic concepts being explored. An example of an everyday experience is shown in Exhibit 1.6.

"I arrived home from my walk last night and was greeted by this most perfect arrangement at the front door. 'Who did this?' I asked. Well it seems that Ash was asked to put his shoes away and took the opportunity to tidy up all the shoes lying in the entrance-way. I would like to think that this has something to do with a propensity toward tidiness and order-liness. Mmmmm, maybe it has more to do with his ever-increasing preoccupation with matching and lining things up. Has he busied himself with things like this at the centre?"

Reproduced by permission of SAGE Publications, from Jocelyn Nana, Carr, M., & Lee, W. Learning Story 4.1. *Learning Stories: Constructing Learner Identities in Early Education.* Thousand Oaks, CA: Sage Publications, p. 67.

Why Are Observation and Pedagogical Documentation Important?

Observation and pedagogical documentation are the most important investigative and authentic tools we have to discover the world of young children. This statement, although true, does not have the same power in its meaning as the short story that follows:

> Isaac, a toddler (who loves butterflies) runs across the room, tips over a plastic bin, and scatters the toys on the floor. He flips the bin upside down and jams his index finger on the bottom of the bin, repeating intensely his word for butterfly, "Littlelittlelittlelittle." The educator sits down next to Isaac, looking and listening. She suddenly exclaims, "Take a look at this! The criss-crossing plastic on the bottom of the plastic bin has the shape of a butterfly! Good for you, Isaac, you found a butterfly!" Isaac looks pleased and now wants to show everyone in the room.

This story is about discovering a toddler's learning and thinking; it is also about the sensitive observation of a responsive educator. Observing young children and documenting their thinking and behaviour are considered essential practice in every early childhood setting. It promotes understanding and appreciation for the thinking and contributions of all learners, thus promoting transformation in the quality and equality of interactions, conversations, observations, documentation, and learning experiences created. Along with telling Isaac's story, observation shows us something about him and his educator, who listened, observed, saw the butterfly in the design of the bin's plastic bottom, and responded to his curiosity and delight.

WHY OBSERVE CHILDREN?

Understanding the reasons why we might observe is important, for it is the pedagogy that leads to meaningful observation. Before you preview the list that follows, make a short list of reasons why you would observe children. Are your reasons similar to those given in the next section?

Reasons for Observing Young Children

Making the connections between what we observe and understand is key. There are many reasons why observation is important to our professional practice. Following is a comprehensive list of some of the many purposes for observing within the early childhood profession.

To observe daily interactions and relationships between children and adults and between children and children. Interacting with others and building relationships are critical to a child's social emotional development, and to the building of resilience, trust, and attachment. Observing interactions and relationships enables the observer to understand how each child builds friendships or faces challenge, the theories and problem solving they use to deal with each situation, and their abilities to handle group situations. In group settings, children will hit and hug, yell and whisper; they learn to include and deal with exclusion. They struggle with conforming to other people's ideas and priorities while trying to express their own. Observations about these everyday occurrences are made even more significant when documented. Observations can be used as feedback to children about their interactions with one another. This practice of narrating what a child is doing, such as, "Are you feeling sad because Bridget took your Lego pieces, Josie?" helps children understand how they feel, how others may be feeling, or why certain events happened. Perhaps your feedback will help a child put into words what they are trying to express. If so, those observations will facilitate the child's social and emotional development. How does that make you feel? Observation and pedagogical documentation are great mediums to foster relationships as indicated in Exhibit 1.7.

To determine how children play, and manipulate materials and equipment. Educators are ever vigilant to what children say and do when they are playing, as well as how they invent new ways to play with ordinary objects or loose parts. This information tells them about how children learn, what they understand, their innovativeness and creativity, and how they feel about the materials and equipment in the room. Some children love to plunge elbow-deep into sand or water, yet other children will hold on to the very tip of a container so as not to touch the sand or water. Responsive educators can use these opportunities to learn more about how the child feels about gooey or squishy materials, for example.

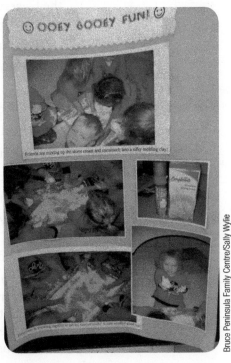

How children engage with materials can reveal a great deal about their problem solving, thinking, abilities, and interests. When educators listen, watch, and record children's play in an area such as a dramatic play centre, they may observe them with their dress-up clothes and hear their comments about the shoes or where they are going. From their dialogue, mannerisms, and inter-actions, they tell us about their home life, dreams, and frustrations. In turn, educators can expand these experiences by talking with the children, asking questions, listening to their answers, or prompting new ideas.

EXHIBIT 1.7   Fostering Reciprocal Relationships

Reciprocal relationships are cultivated through collaborative conversations using pedagogical documentation. Perspectives of children and youth, their parents and guardians, educators, and the broader community can be brought into these conversations for the purpose of furthering learning and connecting learners to their world.

Learning to Listen · Broader Community and Environment · Listening to Learn · Educators and School Community · Parents and Guardians · Children and Youth · Learning to Respond

Note: The graphic draws from Bronfenbrenner's ecological model of development as well as more recent work by Susan Fraser (2012) in *Authentic Childhood*.

For example, one morning, when Seth and Alexis set up their action figures in the construction area, they incorporated three large stuffed animals. One of the animals was a dog, and Seth said that was the "God-dog" because he was the biggest. Seth put him on top of the highest shelf so that "God-dog" could survey the figures on the floor. The conversation went like this:

Educator: Will God-dog be coming down on the floor?

Seth: Yes, he will come down later when we have the castle finished.

Alexis (looking up from stacking wooden blocks): No, Seth, he can't ever come down or he'll die.

Seth stood silently for a few minutes and then sat down, crossing his legs.

Educator: Do you and Alexis have to think about this some more?

Alexis: I think he can't come down.

Educator: What do you think, Seth?

Seth: Well, he can't come down now because we haven't started the battle. When the warriors start dying, he can come down. Then he can come down and get them.

Documenting the play of children is about looking and listening. As in the Seth and Alexis example, there are times to become part of the dialogue and times to be a spectator. "To be a good observer you have to suspend judgements . . . the idea is to learn the deeper meaning of what you are seeing. Observation combined with communication helps you seek out other

perspectives. The best way to communicate is to develop dialoguing skills. . . . A dialogue is a form of communication used to gather information, learn from it, and discover new ideas" (Gonzalez-Mena, 2008, p. 4). "Children begin to communicate ideas and questions while they are experimenting and investigating by describing materials they used, indicating a problem they might have had, or beginning to listen to their peers or offer suggestions to them" (Ontario Ministry of Education, 2010–2011, p. 16).

Documenting the play of children is also about taking note of your own attitude concerning play because it will shape what you "think" you see and hear. In addition to other's perspectives, take the time to reconceptualize play through a number of different lenses: culturally, philosophically, developmentally, and socially for example. Each lens holds significant implications for our practice, in our observations, interpretations, and reflections; in the relationships we create; and in how we talk and share information with families and teams, as well as for the types of responsive and inclusive actions we take in our design of early learning environments and planning for young children. These observations can also lead to new inquiries, new provocations, and new ways of thinking and wondering.

To appreciate and learn about children's growth, development, temperament, and interests. Using a variety of observational and pedagogical documentation methodologies is important in the process of learning about children. Each type of methodology or documentation approach will enable the observer to explore the specific interests, styles of learning, personality, knowledge, and skills of children. They will also learn that children develop at different rates in their own way. When young children are acquiring new skills, knowledge, and ways of figuring things out, you will see a wide range of competence during the learning process. They understand that documentation of Ahmed's questions, for example, is important. When Ahmed asked why snow has to be cold, this question indicates a keen interest in nature, a curiosity, and a desire to learn. Alternatively, an educator may note Kate's reluctance to sit on the carpet with other children. What are the reasons why Kate seems to shy away from this social activity?

Timing of the day, length of sleep, physiological and emotional needs, among many other reasons, can also affect children's behaviour, as well as how they learn, respond, and participate. These reasons illustrate the importance of keeping an open mind about the discoveries that unfold in any setting with young children. Just when you think Rebecca is mastering getting on and off low equipment or chairs independently and with ease, she surprises you by falling repeatedly while trying to climb over the sandbox ledge. Similarly, children react differently to different people, welcoming some with smiles and rejecting others by walking away. One day, the child says, "You can play," and another day, "No, you can't be here."

Take a look at the photo below. Observe this child's expression, body language, manipulation of the materials, and what has been created on the paper. What can be learned from this photo?

Woogies1/Dreamstime.com

In the photo within Reflective Exercise 1.4, we might learn that this child has a natural curiosity for mixing paint colours. As minutes pass, it might be observed that she is intently watching the paint drip or smear on her paper. Sitting closer we might realize that under her breath she is talking about making rainbows, and then through conversation she begins to theorize about how the colours are made. "Learning to explain represents an important part of children's discourse learning and gives them experience with how to construct an understanding of events and phenomena" (Gjems, 2011, p. 501). Together you then plan to explore rainbows in other areas of the curriculum as children join in the discovery.

To learn how to involve parents as co-observers and co-documenters in the process of uncovering how children learn and think.   Observation and pedagogical documentation provide opportunity for parent and guardian engagement. As partners and co-educators of their child's learning journey, parents want to know how their child is doing, what friendships they might have, how they feel throughout the day, and how well they are developing, among other things. As experts of their children, parents have vested interest in observations produced by all members of their learning community, and will have observations of their own to share in the process. "Parents who have become child observers get really excited about what they are discovering. As they share their findings with the teacher and the teacher responds by sharing observations with the parent, their relationship changes dramatically. They become true partners in education and care" (Beaty, 2006, p. 425).

To create pedagogy that informs a holistic image of the child, uncovers the thinking of children, as well as supports the child, family, and community in meaningful ways.   Pedagogy means the methods and practice of teaching. In other words, pedagogy is what you do as an educator of young children. This narrow definition actually is broad in its scope, casting light on an almost infinite array of teaching and learning possibilities. A pedagogical framework represents the ideas or core principles educators have that focus the practices within that framework.

pedagogy

The art or practice of a profession of teaching or instruction.

EXHIBIT 1.8 — Early Childhood Pedagogies and Frameworks

Prince Edward Island, Canada	PEI Early Learning Framework: Relationships, Environments, Experiences
	The Curriculum Framework of the Preschool Excellence Initiative
British Columbia, Canada	British Columbia Early Learning Framework
Saskatchewan, Canada	Play and Exploration: Early Learning Program Guide
Ontario, Canada	Early Learning for Every Child Today
	How Does Learning Happen? Ontario's Pedagogy for the Early Years
	The Kindergarten Program
Quebec, Canada	Meeting Early Childhood Needs: Québec's Educational Program for Childcare Services Update
New Brunswick, Canada	New Brunswick Curriculum Framework for Early Learning and Child Care
Northwest Territories, Canada	Integrated Kindergarten Curriculum: A Holistic Approach to Children's Early Learning
Ireland	Aister: The Early Childhood Curriculum Framework
New Zealand	Te Whāriki: He whāriki mātauranga mō ngā mokopuna o Aotearoa: Early Childhood Curriculum
Australia	Belonging, Being & Becoming: The Early Years Learning Framework for Australia

Exhibit 1.8 depicts some of the many examples available on the Internet of pedagogies developed by provincial ministries or licensure organizations in Canada and the world. Many speak to the pedagogies that guide professional practice, and introduce their image of the child.

REFLECTIVE EXERCISE 1.5

In pairs or small groups, explore the early childhood pedagogies outlined in each framework in Exhibit 1.8. Each framework can be located on the Internet.

- What is the view of the child according to each of the pedagogies/frameworks? What about the image of the family and educator?
- Using your answers to your reflections from Exhibits 1.4 and 1.5, do these frameworks resonate with your image of the child? Would they apply to children in your learning community?
- How might they be inclusive of Indigenous views of the child? Of newcomer views of the child?

The image of the child is not universal. "The view of the child is and ought to be has deep roots in the culture, society, and family values of the people involved. Because we live in a multicultural society, and the people we work with come from many different backgrounds, the images we hold of children

> **"Opening the Way"**
>
> First Nations, Inuit and Métis traditions are clear: children are a gift from the Creator, on loan to us from the spirit world. It is their birthright to inherit cultures whose central tenets for thousands of years focused on how best to nurture young ones physically, mentally, emotionally and spiritually. In too many communities, that knowledge of how to raise whole children has been interrupted by the fallout from residential schools and the lingering effects of colonization. Yet the underlying wisdom still exists, preserved in the memory banks and teachings of our Elders. And so too does the yearning on the part of parents for the kinds of cultural underpinnings that will anchor them and their children as they navigate their way through different stages of the life cycle. (National Collaborating Centre for Aboriginal Health. [2013]. *Messages from the Heart: Caring for Our Children*, p. 2.)

will reflect this diversity" (Fraser, 2012, p. 35). Observation, appreciative inquiry, and pedagogical documentation assist the observer to understand, appreciate, and inform their image of the child. Often observers may have preconceived ideas about a child; observation opens the door to seeing the child in a new way. When we watch, listen, and learn from children, the interpretations we formulate and the decisions we make will be impacted in a positive way. For example, observing, listening, and learning about First Nations, Inuit and Métis traditions opens our minds further to the image of the child in Indigenous communities as in the excerpt from "Opening the Way" above.

Considering the knowledge above as well as the teachings and philosophies from our Indigenous peoples regarding the Seven Grandfather Teachings and the foundations of the Four Directions, observation is of great significance to everyone so as to learn from the land, as well as from the stories and wisdom of others. To appreciate, respect, and learn about the meaning of the Four Directions and these teachings, please consult with your community Elder or Indigenous centre within your college, or visit online.

Alluded to in the excerpt from "Opening the Way" and in the following quote is the concept of spirituality, an important consideration in the holistic view of the child.

> It means different things to different people. For some, spirituality is about a sense of connection to the land, environment and the universe; for others, it is about religious philosophy and practices, or certain cultural or family rituals or ways of being that are regarded as sacred. For some people their spirituality is simply a way of connecting with people, and involves deeply held values about what is right and wrong and how one needs to conduct themselves. All of these and many more definitions of spirituality are important and valid. Spirituality is not something that can be captured through a set of activities or a curriculum. Nourishing children's spirituality is a two-way learning process between the child and the adult, and educators need to be careful not to impose their personal perceptions of spirituality onto children. Rather, they need to support children to discover what is important to them and to help them to reach their own understandings. (Tebyani, V. [March 2011]. "Nurturing Children's Spirituality." *Putting Children First*. Issue 37, pp. 11–13)

Observation is the portal that enables educators to see and appreciate the vital nature of spirituality in children's holistic development. Children are

Four Directions

In the medicine wheel are the mental, emotional, physical, and spiritual aspects of humanness; the four primary elements of earth, air, fire, and water; and the four stages of human life.

authentic in their inquiries, confident in their ability to question what they do and do not understand, and have a natural curiosity that leads them to new discoveries.

The learning we gain from observing requires planning for a sustainable meaningful pedagogy full of opportunity, resources, time, and space for all members to participate and flourish. It also values an action research and anti-oppressive approach whereby the stories of children, family, and communities are preserved, protected, and shared with others. We will explore more about action research and anti-oppressive approaches in subsequent chapters.

To inform curriculum and environmental design and make adaptations where necessary. Observing how children use, are influenced by, and respond to their environment is part of an educator's role. Integrating observation of the children within their environment, along with input from families, children, and their community will inform the preparation of new provocations, invitations, and curriculum co-prepared by everyone. Patterns may also emerge in the learning space indicating that certain changes may need to be made to create a new room design to accommodate heavy traffic, or more space for blocks and exploration of loose parts, for example. Please visit our extensive discussions in Chapters 6–8 as we connect our observations and pedagogical documentation to curriculum and environmental design.

To support early intervention. The team of educators, families, children and outside professionals engages in observation of children to proactively monitor the holistic and developmental progress of children in their care and to support children who may be experiencing challenges. Careful observation of young children is extremely crucial in identifying children who may need assistance, resources, or services from their community. Being aware of the role of early intervention is a focus of Chapter 7.

To observe the safety and well-being (social, emotional, and physical) of each child in the group. Taking the time to observe and record physical health or social/emotional behavioural changes enables educators to implement appropriate care practices for each child within the group. Take, for example, children arriving in the morning with their parents. Upon arrival, through observing, the educator may notice that Lauren, one of the preschoolers in the classroom, is tired, has a flushed face, and is clinging to her mother. Observing her behaviour and comparing it to how she typically arrives at her child-care centre—which involves smiling, running toward her peers, and quickly joining various play experiences—prompts a discussion with her parent. As she is examined by both the educator and the parent, they discover together that she has a fever and that her ears hurt. As a result, her parent takes her home. Not only does this decision allow Lauren time to recover, but it also prevents the unwanted spreading of germs among other children in the room. "A healthy start in life has a great impact on the well-being of children and throughout life, providing opportunities for children to develop the attributes and resilience needed to mature into healthy adults in our complex society" (Pimento & Kernested, 2010, p. 20).

Observing and documenting also provide the information necessary for other optimal health and safety prevention practices concerning a number of different elements of practice, including but not limited to helping children

action research

A cyclical plan for change involving the identification of elements of practice needing improvement and the questions, research, and reflection that will support the change.

anti-oppressive approach

Intended to reduce the potential for oppression and abuse of power between adult and child, and views children as capable and competent members of an early childhood community.

monitor

To check or test a process in a systematic fashion.

Duty to Report

Anyone who suspects with reasonable justification that a child is in need of protection are required to contact their Children's Aid Society to report information involving their suspicion.

cope with stress, child abuse reporting and Duty to Report procedures, protocols for lifting/carrying children, field trip considerations, and the appropriate supervision of children throughout the day. Is your field trip appropriate for your children? With supervision, do the rules within the classroom support the safety of the children? Watching to see if the children sit down before going down the slide or use their walking feet indoors ensures that the children are playing safely. Fortunately, observation of children's behaviours and appropriate follow-up can assist in preventing unwanted consequences. For example, if Matthew persists in sliding headfirst down the slide, he will be redirected elsewhere in the playground. Setting limits and following through means using your observation skills to see if the children are listening to directions and playing safely.

To expand professional roles, improve professional practice and pedagogy, as well as promote individual, group, and team reflection. As educators develop knowledge and skills in the role of educator–observer, they cannot help but be shaped by

what they learn and uncover. Through lifelong learning, not only do educators develop a professional body of skills and learning, but their personal attitudes, interests, and beliefs change and evolve as well. Working with children cannot help but change how and what you choose to observe and document but also how you see yourself as an educator within the context of child, family, and community.

Educators might also discuss their philosophy and practices not only to reflect together on their observations of children, the environment, and curriculum but also to reflect on their work together. Through reflective conversation, educators practise appreciative inquiry, expand their knowledge through others' perspectives, and develop abilities to think critically about the process of constructing a responsive environment.

Teams of teachers help each other gain perspective on the class, an individual, a time of the day. Observations can be a means of validating one teacher's point of view. By checking out an opinion or idea through systematic observation, teachers get a sense of direction in their planning. Such an assessment implies self-assessment. A team that looks at what their program is or isn't accomplishing and how their program may be affecting children values the reflective process and professional level of teamwork that goes with it (Gordon & Browne, 2007, pp. 204–205).

occupational standards

Standards in Canada that have been developed to define acceptable professional behaviour and the knowledge required for a particular occupation.

To maintain occupational standards. Occupational standards in Canada have been developed to define acceptable professional behaviour and the knowledge required for a particular occupation. Knowing what levels of occupational competence to expect from new hires and seasoned educators is integral to the maintenance of quality early learning and care. See Exhibit 1.9 for an example of a task and a subtask core competency. Be sure to go online for a more thorough and comprehensive review of the wide-reaching role that observation assumes in professional practice, remembering that expectations may vary from province to province and country to country.

Example: A.1. Facilitate the Development and Behaviour of Children

Context Statement

Early childhood educators facilitate daily experiences that support and promote each child's physical, language, emotional, cognitive, social, and creative development and behaviour using applicable observational tools while respecting inclusion principles and diversity issues.

Subtask A.1.1. Use a Variety of Observation and Documentation Techniques

Required Skills and Abilities	Required Core Knowledge
ECEs are able to a. document observations using a wide range of methods (e.g., notes, photos, videos) b. seek information from parents' observations of their children c. categorize observations into domains d. interpret observations e. communicate observations with team and families f. use non-biased language (e.g., open-ended sentences, non-judgmental terminology)	ECEs know 1. child development theories 2. effective communication skills to understand and interpret children's behaviours 3. theories and approaches about observation and documentation techniques

Source: Child Care Human Resources Sector Council, *Occupational Standards for Early Childhood Educators*, 2010, p. 11.

To build capacity and community through networking and the development of community partnerships. Building community within an early learning program requires its educators to engage in ongoing networking and partnering with team members, families, and outside professionals both within and external to the early learning field.

Networking within the community contributes to the well-being of children, families, educators, and the overall early childhood program. Educators working effectively as a team contribute significantly to the level of quality provided by the program. No one works in isolation, and early childhood settings are no exception. Staff cannot and should not try to be all things to all people. Staff must establish a network with professionals, agencies, and associations in their community (Pimento & Kernested, 2010, p. 44).

There is much to be said about observation and pedagogical documentation, and much of it will be found throughout the text. Historically and in educational environments, documentation has been seen as the "end game"—what we compile at the end of our observations. Yet, we see the value of documentation as a process—a means to learn, explore, and appreciate. Opening up possibilities with ongoing documentation supports appreciative inquiry. While observing and documenting, we can co-learn with the children while we investigate "in real time." Pat Tarr (2011) describes the process of documentation this way:

> The act of pedagogical documentation becomes a dialogue. The process of pedagogical documentation involves returning to the children, their images and their words to gather their insights, their confirmation, or their disagreement, in a shared dialogue so that the children's interest can be supported (p. 13).

Maloch and Horsey (2013) echo this sentiment:

> We hope that our students are inquirers—who make use of texts in purposeful ways to accomplish their own ends and answer their own questions—rather than "doers" of school tasks. That is, as they leave classrooms and schools, we hope for children to feel inspired to follow their own lines of inquiry, to move into and through the world as wonderers and learners. If the tools we offer in the classroom are grounded only in classroom tasks of focused inquiry but not embedded in a community focused on inquiring, children may leave our classrooms having learned fact, but not living as learners (p. 485).

Developing documentation, then, is about observing and recording authentic experiences as they occur with the intent of discovery, as well as creating curriculum and methods of sharing that information with educators, families, and communities. Whether the medium is a website such as Pinterest, an app, an online journal, print, or the notes of other educators, learning through observation and documentation continues the early childhood tradition.

OBSERVATION AND THE ESSENTIAL PARTNERSHIP

The best interests of the children bring families and educators into an essential personal and professional partnership. Sharing information from observations with parents is about creating, supporting, and nurturing relationships. These relationships are founded on a reciprocal learning process. Educators, like many other professionals, maintain a sensitive balance between providing a quality care service and responding within an emotional and personal relationship. Parents entrust their child to the educator's care, and the educators accept that responsibility with an attitude of mutual respect, trust, and confidence as noted in Exhibit 1.10.

child-sensitive

Attitudes, awareness, and practices that demonstrate care and sensitivity to the uniqueness of each child and his or her family and culture in a group setting.

> Showing respect means that programs and early childhood educators are child-sensitive, that is, they notice that children are unique, acknowledge this as important, and use this knowledge as a significant basis in planning the total program. "Respect" may be a more descriptive term than the frequently used "child-centred," which may seem rather one-sided or totally indulgent toward children. Respect demands responsiveness. (Gestwicki & Bertrand, 2008, p. 78)

Educators and families can become the

co-constructors of knowledge in partnership with the child, and with each other. As such, they should find new rhythms with which to be teacher and learner, parent and learner. Through their collaboration and respective perspectives, they can have a deeper understanding of the thinking child, and of the ways in which each child is a co-constructor of knowledge.

"These partnerships, not easily achieved, have to be founded on trust and confidence."

—Amilia Gambetti

Source: Courtesy of Child Care Information Exchange

Family Centredness

Family is a child's world, and as educators it is important to understand the value of family in children's learning. Throughout this text we place the family and child at the heart of what we do; they have much to offer. Family centredness can be defined as

a set of values, skills, behaviours and knowledge that recognises the central role of families in children's lives. It is sometimes described as working in partnership or collaboration. It involves professionals and families working together to support children's learning and development. Early childhood professionals who engage in family-centred practice respect the uniqueness of every person and family. They share their professional expertise and knowledge with families and at the same time regard families' expertise as valid, significant and valuable. (Kennedy & Stonehouse, 2012, p. 3)

When a child first begins a program, the sharing of information begins. The child's family is the first observer of the child; the family has much to share. Educators want to know from the parents what they can learn about the child and the family. The interest shown communicates respect and a willingness to learn and understand. Parents, in turn, want to know about the setting, the teachers, the program, and the policies. These initial exchanges and other daily practices strengthen bonds of trust and support.

Gaining knowledge about children from multiple perspectives helps educators ensure that programs also value the unique and diverse characteristics of the children's families and the communities in which they live. It's not a "one-size-fits-all" approach. In particular, programs should be reflective of the cultural and linguistic backgrounds of the children and families they serve, including those from First Nations, Métis, Inuit and francophone communities. (Ontario Ministry of Education, 2014, p. 18)

microcosm

A small representational system with the characteristics of a larger system: a little world.

Truly, the early years are the most opportune time for children and their families to experience acceptance outside the home and to develop respect for the diversity that exists within early childhood and early learning settings in Canada and around the world. Whether rural or urban, each setting reflects a microcosm of the community it serves. In that community, children thrive with opportunities for learning. Here is where children, staff, and family relationships grow, becoming more aware daily of one another's expectations, values, feelings, and priorities.

Every family is a complex unit that is also rich in diversity. Awareness of the diversity of family structures, ethnic backgrounds, and linguistic and cultural differences of the greater society means that educators are always challenged to create and respond to new ways of communicating with children and their families:

> In serving culturally diverse early learning and care families and communities, keep in mind that not all parents share the same ideas about how, where and when they should be involved in their children's schooling. Parents may also face barriers, such as limited time or limited proficiency in English. On the other hand, they, and their ethno-cultural communities, may represent substantial resources that schools can draw on to assist English language learners and to enrich the cultural environment for everyone in the school. (Ontario Ministry of Education, 2005, p. 44)

A child's family and culture influence all facets of a child's life. Acknowledging this fact is an important step in the exchange of learning between educators and families. Sharing information with parents is about a commitment to

- listening to and valuing the families of each child,
- recognizing that parents may have another point of view regarding their child, and
- working to create an open, meaningful, shared learning process.

The awareness that each child is unique in themselves contributes to an interest in the child and the family. When educators understand what families are trying to accomplish with their children, they can look for ways to support them.

Today, many children are cared for by one parent, grandparent(s), or extended family members. The child may be picked up and dropped off by a designated friend or relative. Throughout most of this text, the terms family and parent are used interchangeably. This reflects the reality that parents may not always be the primary caregivers as they struggle to balance other roles and responsibilities outside the family. This thought is echoed in many texts, in early childhood settings around the world, and in the views of various professionals: as the world changes, so does the configuration of the child's home life.

Culture and Transformation: Family and Child in Context

Earlier in this chapter, changes in the education and child-care profession around the world was discussed. Some of the changes were the introduction of new curriculum frameworks and directives from municipal, provincial, and territorial governments as well as philosophical changes in practice, to name a few. Other changes important to note are

- cultural and linguistic diversity in children and their families, particularly in urban areas;
- increased numbers of newcomer families to Canada; and the
- restructuring and administrative reorganization within organizations and government.

Why is it important to note cultural change and transformation? Change in society prompts transformation of ideas and practices in many different ways and causes the observer to continually utilize various perspectives to appreciate and understand what it is that they see and hear. Vygotsky's socio-cultural research on how children learn, for example, emphasized how thinking and thought processes can be scaffolded and transformed as a result of social interactions, collaborative learning, and dialogue. On the other hand, Bronfenbrenner's ecological model of development emphasizes the importance of understanding changes in a child's community (see Exhibit 1.7) to appreciate how community perspectives can transform how we observe, document, and learn from one another. Transformation can also mean a shift or altering of concepts and ideas regarding relationships in early childhood centres, or a new framework for developing curriculum. Recognizing change and that there are various theories that may help to frame what we see in order to respond appropriately and act conscionably is one of the foremost responsibilities of an educator today. As we explore the cycle of observation, we will look further at various theories that assist us in conceptualizing what we think we know and understand.

How are the values of an urban or rural early childhood/learning centre demonstrated in your practice? Whose voices are heard? What ways of knowing or seeing would be included in an early childhood setting in the Atlantic provinces, Saskatchewan, or British Columbia? What about Quebec, Nunavut, or Manitoba? How would the ideas and values of each community be reflected in its philosophy, procedures, practices, interactions, and, by extension, documented through observation? As referenced in Exhibit 1.11, the community plays a key role, fostering a sense of belonging for children and families.

Acceptance is a value that is part of Canada's diverse society. In early childhood, we must constantly ask ourselves if, through our attitudes and practices, we are creating a responsive atmosphere to meet the needs of our diverse

transformation

A process of profound and radical change that orients a person or organization in a new direction; a basic change in character or structure that bears little resemblance to the past configuration.

EXHIBIT 1.11 Fostering a Sense of Belonging

Opportunities to engage with people, places, and the natural world in the local environment help children, families, educators, and communities build connections, learn and discover, and make contributions to the world around them. It fosters a sense of belonging to the local community, the natural environment, and the larger universe of living things. As well, communities benefit from the rich experiences they have in learning about, with, and from children.

Source: Ontario Ministry of Education. (2014). *Professional Learning Resources.* "How Does Learning Happen? Ontario's Pedagogy for the Early Years" (p. 19). Retrieved from http://www.edu.gov.on.ca/childcare/HowLearningHappens.pdf.

Chapter 1: What Is Observation?

communities. For the most part, we are familiar with the obvious ways educators demonstrate their acknowledgment of new cultures in the playroom. Common practical examples may include culturally inclusive books, music, food, games, artifacts, family photographs, posters, and words of greeting and comfort in many languages, all of which are reflective of the learners within the room.

In the article entitled "Respecting Culture in Our Schools and Classrooms," Pearson (2006) uses the image of an iceberg to reflect the idea that some cultural indicators are visible at the tip, whereas a vast number are hidden below the surface (see Exhibit 1.12). How often have we noted and looked for examples of "the hidden iceberg"—the part under the surface? Do we acknowledge others' concepts of tempo of work, notions of leadership, concepts of beauty, approaches to problem solving, incentives to work? If we do acknowledge different perspectives, such as those noted under the iceberg's surface, how is that demonstrated in early childhood and early learning settings?

Another reason to investigate change is to gain new insights and to understand what we see and hear from a variety of lens and theories. From new insights, we can begin to appreciate anew the influences on children and their families and understand their perspectives. For example, we can learn from the article "Meeting the Needs of Refugee Families" (2007), when Freire says, "The immigrant child when he leaves his country has been part of a plan. . . . The youngster has had the

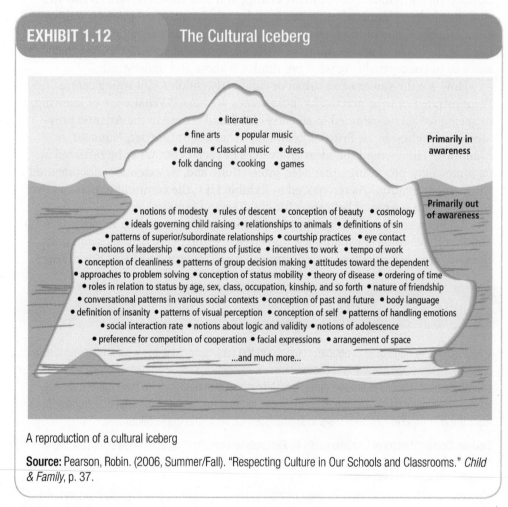

EXHIBIT 1.12   The Cultural Iceberg

- literature
- fine arts • popular music
- drama • classical music • dress
- folk dancing • cooking • games

Primarily in awareness

Primarily out of awareness

- notions of modesty • rules of descent • conception of beauty • cosmology
- ideals governing child raising • relationships to animals • definitions of sin
- patterns of superior/subordinate relationships • courtship practices • eye contact
- notions of leadership • conceptions of justice • incentives to work • tempo of work
- conception of cleanliness • patterns of group decision making • attitudes toward the dependent
- approaches to problem solving • conception of status mobility • theory of disease • ordering of time
- roles in relation to status by age, sex, class, occupation, kinship, and so forth • nature of friendship
- conversational patterns in various social contexts • conception of past and future • body language
- definition of insanity • patterns of visual perception • conception of self • patterns of handling emotions
- social interaction rate • notions about logic and validity • notions of adolescence
- preference for competition of cooperation • facial expressions • arrangement of space

...and much more...

A reproduction of a cultural iceberg

Source: Pearson, Robin. (2006, Summer/Fall). "Respecting Culture in Our Schools and Classrooms." *Child & Family*, p. 37.

possibility to dispose of his/her belongings, to say goodbye, to think of what type of precious things that he may want to bring like his toys for example or books" (p. 1). Furthermore, if we pause for observance of the experiences of Aboriginal families and children, we broaden our understanding of how "the well being of Aboriginal children and families has been disrupted and distorted by the process of colonization. Placement of children in residential schools led to the loss of language and culture, and prevented earlier generations from passing down traditional parenting practices" (National Collaborating Centre For Aboriginal Health, 2013, p. 3) and many other things. This is concerning; preventing further erosion of the identity and values of any family is a priority. Understanding the reality of just one child from any family should give us pause for reflection and learning. From the knowledge of one child's experiences, we may be better able to provide a program more responsive to the interests, strengths, and needs of the child and their family. Based on our observations and an appreciation of their experiences, networking in the community and taking the role of an advocate for needed family resources or services become part of our educator's role.

advocate

Someone who amplifies a client's voice, gives support, and pursues objectives according to instruction while empowering the client to self-advocacy.

When the care and education of young children are viewed as a collective of relationships, we can all become collaborators in creating a better world. Observation is the foundation upon which opportunities can be built with windows for new perspectives.

When documented and shared, these occurrences uncover or disclose something unique about that child. When shared with parents or families, they bring forth a family response and then, possibly, encourage them to share their observations. A treasured bond of communication has begun. We will continue to explore the important role of families in subsequent chapters as we explore ethics, various documentation methodologies, and early intervention.

monkeybusinessimages/Thinkstock

THE SPECIAL ROLE OF OBSERVATION IN DIFFERENT PHILOSOPHIES

Within Canada and other countries, different philosophies are practised in the early childhood profession. These philosophies, in turn, are reflected in the best practices or recommended practices, curriculum, and policies of each program. What is embedded in every philosophy is observation; it is generic in nature and independent of setting.

Observations do not represent a particular philosophy; they instead reflect a philosophy and practice of inquiry. Our practices should be

best practices

Based on or originating from evidence-based research and outcomes, these are ideal practices suggested by the early learning and care profession or other agencies or licensing bodies.

generic

Relating to or descriptive of an entire group or class; universal.

Chapter 1: What Is Observation?

EXHIBIT 1.13   Childhood Is a Social Construction

Pence proposed that

> childhood is a social construction—it varies over time and it varies across cultures and contexts. And as different peoples and parents around the world work to create appropriate care for their children, they do this differently—not just because the materials, environments and technologies are different, but because their understanding of children, who they are and what they can do, are different. And because of these inherent differences, when we speak of "quality care" there can be no single definition of what this thing called quality is, that there can be no single instrument or single method that captures it.

Source: Pence, Allan. (2006, Fall). "Seeking the other 99 languages of ECE: A keynote address by Alan Pence." *Interaction*, 20.3. Alan Pence, Professor, School of Children and Youth, University of Victoria.

High Scope

A curriculum model in which adults and children are seen as partners in learning. Through hands-on experiences, children can direct and scaffold their own learning.

Montessori school

A program employing the principles of Maria Montessori who believed and taught that children learn at their own pace, learn through discovery, and need to employ all five senses in exploring the world.

eclectic approach

A method of selecting what seem to be the best practices from various philosophies or programs.

emotional intelligence

Often associated with highly sociable, communicative, and motivated individuals who are able to easily identify with the needs and desires of others. These individuals are able to manage the dynamics of relationships effortlessly.

pluralistic

The idea that there is more than one method, philosophy, or pedagogy.

governed by a philosophy of what we believe about all aspects of our role, including but not limited to children, our views about childhood itself, our image of what an educator could be, and our values regarding relationships, families, partnerships, mentoring, sharing, and learning, including the willingness to change and transform as we continue to learn and discover. This text supports unequivocally the notion that there is more than one way to observe, document, and reflect upon the activity of young children. The tremendous variety of child-care experiences across Canada necessitates this flexible approach, as noted in Pence's keynote address at a national conference in Calgary, Alberta, in Exhibit 1.13.

Observation and documentation will take on more of a dominant role in some philosophies or practices than others. For example, settings that adopt a High Scope approach will use observations very differently from a centre that primarily uses a theme-based curriculum. The documentation developed from observations in a Reggio Emilia or an emergent centre will again be substantially different from the ways observations are used in a Montessori school or centre that has developed an eclectic approach to its early learning framework.

The influence of theories such as Howard Gardner's theory of multiple intelligence, Daniel Goldman's theory of emotional intelligence, and Jerome Kagan's research on personality types has made professionals in the field more aware of the need to pay particular attention to children's learning styles. Theories such as these influence program philosophies, the development of curriculum, teaching strategies, and documentation methods. Most crucial, however, is the development of an educator's beliefs and willingness to learn from the children. This willingness requires a commitment to observe on a daily basis, a subject we will explore in the next couple of chapters.

In a pluralistic, democratic society, educators of young children know they have valuable opportunities to promote social interactions and chances for social learning. Regardless of the philosophy or setting, discovering the uniqueness of each child is the greatest joy and challenge of every educator. Observation skills are the key to unlocking those discoveries.

1. Seeing and hearing the actions, conversations, and behaviours of others are natural components of observation. As human beings and observers of young children, we are fortunate to have observation as our primary investigative tool into understanding the world of children; their theories, their thinking, how they see their world why we do what we do. Like a chameleon, observation changes depending on its purpose and context for observing, and it reveals much about people, the environment, our curriculum, and our learning community. Observation is multifaceted as it is both a concept and a process, and is a methodology that can utilized by all members of a learning community (children, family, educators, community).

2. The image of the responsive inclusive observer is that of positivity, inclusiveness, and responsiveness, and an appreciation for the individuality of every child and learner. Engaging in reflection to support ongoing learning is a quality of being responsive and inclusive. From this approach, responsive, inclusive observers view children as competent, able, intuitive investigators, capable of co-constructing new learning and making meaningful choices in their play experiences.

3. Appreciative inquiry is an approach intended to engage all learners in possibility thinking. This approach promotes authentic questioning and inquiry, as well as participation from everyone in order to co-create and co-design new provocations, discoveries, theories, equitable learning opportunities, and interactions on topics of interest and value to those who are involved. Effective questioning prompts participants to reveal their thinking and knowledge to others, and promotes a positive strengths-based view of adults and children as equal partners in the teaching and learning process. Appreciative inquiry is an important approach to use in collaboration with observation and pedagogical documentation.

4. Pedagogical documentation is a shared documentation process (using a variety of methodologies) and pedagogy intended to make visible the thinking, inquiries, and theories of children. It is more than just observing; observation is only one component of this pedagogical approach. Pedagogical documentation involves listening to, observing, and reflecting upon children's inquiries, and then analyzing and applying the learning to prompt new learning, thus scaffolding and leading to more complex thinking.

5. The reasons and purposes for observing and documenting are vast. Taking the time to reflect upon the reasons and purposes for observing will promote meaningful use, application, and understanding of what is seen and heard. Review the many purposes for observing in this chapter.

6. In this chapter, we examined how important the relationship is between educators and children, parents and educators, and families and the community, and how when they all work together, they form a learning community. Listening to their voices contributes to a philosophy of transformation in observation and pedagogical documentation practices, which holds at its centre the practice of appreciative inquiry. Families know children the best; it is important to value and engage family participation and diverse perspectives in the observation and pedagogical documentation process, therefore supporting a culture of responsivity and inclusiveness.

7. Understanding culture, diversity, and societal change is important as it encourages observers to use various perspectives to inform their understanding of what is seen and heard. Whether it be culture, gender, spirituality, ability, or the many other facets of diversity, we must pause and reflect upon the voices of all families and children, and ask ourselves: how are we including the voices and perspectives of families in our learning community? Building relationships that support healthy and meaningful observation in every setting is necessary for authentic understanding of the uniqueness of every child, every family, and every learner.

For further application and understanding of chapter concepts, please visit http://www.nelson.com/student to start using NelsonStudy, our digital learning solution.

CHAPTER 2

PREPARING TO OBSERVE: ETHICS, RIGHTS, AND THE CYCLE OF OBSERVATION

Welcome to Chapter 2! This chapter builds upon the foundational concepts introduced in Chapter 1; it assists us in thinking about ethics and the rights of children, and it prompts us to explore how observers might meaningfully incorporate them into their observational practices. Examining the cycle of observation closely in order to navigate the many components and considerations within the cycle will assist observers in establishing a strong foundation of observation and pedagogical documentation, supporting the engagement of all participants—child, family, educator, and community. Let's begin to explore new territory, making new observational discoveries!

OVERVIEW

In Chapter 1, we discussed that as observers in early childhood, we have the privilege of learning from and with children, families, educators, and the community. It was also in that chapter that we looked at the multitude of purposes for observing. Understanding the frequency of observing in professional practice requires us to think about how we value and acknowledge the thinking and learning of others. Observation requires all observers to emulate an observational pedagogy grounded in integrity and ethics, as well as an ongoing commitment to respecting the rights, privacy, and confidentiality of those observed within all stages of the cycle of observation. Chapter 2 prepares the observer to conceptualize the "what" of observation such as "What ethical considerations must I think about before I observe?" and "What are the steps or components in the observation process?" We answer these and other fundamental questions by exploring how to build an ethical foundation for sound observational pedagogy throughout the cycle of observation, as well as reflecting upon how to promote the rights and voices of children and families in the observation and pedagogical documentation process. With the infusion of technology and social media (e.g., video, photos, email, websites, apps, Twitter, Facebook, blogs) as mediums that help observe, facilitate, document, and communicate the thinking of others, there has never been a more important time to execute ethical strategies and processes to reduce ethical dilemmas and bias we may possess or face so that we have the ability to protect our most vulnerable populations: children and families. As you explore each section of this chapter, think about how you might promote ethics in your early childhood setting and learning community so as to support a safe and secure environment for all participants.

integrity

Demonstrating the values of honesty, trust, fairness, respect, responsibility, and courage in our observation and documentation practices.

ethics

A set of beliefs or guiding principles one uses to understand the difference between right and wrong, and demonstrating these principles in our actions, words, and attitudes.

cycle of observation

This cycle, grounded in ethics, integrity, anti-oppression, family- and child-centredness, and responsive and inclusive values, outlines the many interactive and appreciative components of the observation process.

FOCUS QUESTIONS

1. Describe the importance of ethics as it relates to observation and pedagogical documentation. In what ways do the Code of Ethics and Standards of Practice relate to the observation of young children and pedagogical documentation?

2. Participatory rights theory introduces the role of power in observation as it relates to children. How might observers support children's participatory rights and equal voice in the observation and pedagogical documentation processes?

3. In what ways might we use our understanding of bias in observations to reduce the level of bias in our observations and documentation?

4. Social media has been described as a technology-assisted form of pedagogical documentation. In what ways might social media benefit the observation process, and what considerations might observers want to think about to reduce the concerns associated with this digital medium?

5. In what ways might consent, privacy, and confidentiality of children's information be maintained? How might parents and children be involved in this process?

6. What is the cycle of observation and how might it support observers who are engaging in the process of observation and pedagogical documentation?

ETHICS AND OBSERVATION

Observing and documenting as part of the cycle of observation does not guarantee ethical practice; it is the choice of the educator and observer to be ethical in the process. Pedagogical documentation introduces other ethical considerations and decision making that must take place when observing young children, and requires special attention at a philosophical, practical, and policy level. Let's begin first by understanding what it means.

Ethics may mean different things to different people; however, for the purposes of observation, ethics can be defined as "a way of thinking, acting and reflecting on how we see, speak and act and the effects of this for others. Ethics concern what is fair and unfair for people and they highlight what is fair rather than what is easy in how we live our lives. Ethics often distinguish between what a person believes is right or wrong" (MacNaughton, Hughes, & Smith, 2008, p. 43). Let's break this definition down, applying it to how we "see" within the observation process. The first sentence of the above quotation requires the observer to observe through a professional rather than a personal lens to ensure that the observation is not biased. Exhibit 2.1 helps us understand some of the differences between the two levels of observation: personal and professional.

EXHIBIT 2.1	Levels of Observation

Personal Level	Professional Level
• occurs in everyday personal life (outside of professional practice) • highly subjective, influenced by different aspects of your life (interests, family, friends, values and beliefs, opinions, education, etc.) and not always based on fact. These observations may not consider the effect on others. • often singular perspective	• used in professional practice • uses some form of structure depending on the type of observation • involves formal or informal professional training to understand how to document • consider theory, context, and fact (e.g., environment, socio-cultural, ability, development, appreciative inquiry, anti-oppressive approach) • subjective, yet framed using professional and positive language to promote objectivity and to allow for sharing with others. These observations should not contain personal opinions. • should state only what is seen and heard • may solicit multiple perspectives to inform and produce a holistic observation

Monkey Business Images/Shutterstock.com

Let's now explore a personal observation detailed in Exhibit 2.2.

Taking the time to reflect upon what we are observing in a professional way, and allotting the time that is necessary to truly listen, allow us to attain a level of appreciation and understanding of what is truly is seen and heard in a meaningful way as in Exhibit 2.2.

To be a good observer you have to suspend judgments. Only then can you begin to understand someone who is different from yourself and who operates out of another system. The idea is to learn

| EXHIBIT 2.2 | The Role of Observation in Early Childhood Development |

I once sat by a window looking out across the street at a man who was acting very strange. I could see him only from the waist up, but that was enough for me to know he was making extraordinary gestures and facial expressions. I opened the window so I could hear his words. I was even more mystified. The words coming out of his mouth were in a language I didn't understand, and they sounded very strange indeed. I watched this man for some time, trying to figure out what he was doing walking back and forth on the sidewalk making weird gestures and sounds. I had decided he was crazy and had begun to feel afraid when finally I stood up and saw the whole picture. There at the man's heels was a dog. Immediately everything made sense. Aha, he's training a dog, I said to myself. I would have figured it out sooner if this man had been of my culture and used the commands, facial expressions, gestures, and, especially, the words I was familiar with. I learned two lessons from this experience: (1) You have to see the whole picture to understand. (2) It's important to know the meanings attached to the behaviour.

Source: Gonzalez-Mena, Janet, *Diversity in Early Care and Education: Honoring Differences,* 5th edition. New York: McGraw-Hill Education, 2008, p. 31.

the deeper meaning of what you are seeing. Observation combined with communication helps you seek out other perspectives. (Gonzalez-Mena, 2008, p. 4)

Had this level of reflection not taken place in Exhibit 2.2, it may have prompted further misconceptions about what was seen and heard, and subsequently impacted the image of the person negatively. The levels in which we observe, speak, act, and document indeed have a direct impact on others.

As observation is a primary professional responsibility of educators, it is equally as important to understand the relevance of ethics as it pertains to the expectations of the early childhood profession, the observation process, and children's rights.

Code of Ethics and Standards of Practice

According to a 2017 report from UNICEF Canada, Canada ranks 25th out of 41 rich nations on children's overall well-being—a shift for the worse compared to the ranking of 17th out of 29 countries on the same scale in 2013 (UNICEF, 2017, p. 10). What do these results infer to us as educators and observers? They tell us that we have a significant role to play in not only how we co-create with children and families the safe and healthy environments necessary for them to thrive but also how we observe and document together. Following an established code of ethics and standards of practice encourages observers to be mindful when observing and documenting. Educators around the world are responsible for adhering to ethical and occupational standards specific to their role and, in this case, when observing children. In Canada, these standards are represented in different ways and with varying expectations and professional standards at different levels of government or licensing agencies—municipal, provincial/territorial, and federal. Exhibit 2.3 outlines some of the important ethical standards pertaining to educators across Canada.

code of ethics

Guidelines for responsible behaviour; principles and practices that guide the moral and ethical conduct of professionals in a field or discipline.

Heenal Shah/Shutterstock.com

Regulatory/ Governing Body	Document	Audience	Document Purpose / Relevance to Observation and Documentation
College of Early Childhood Educators (CECE)	Code of Ethics and Standards of Practice	Ontario: Registered early childhood educators	"The Code of Ethics reflects the profession's core beliefs and values of care, respect, trust. These beliefs and values guide RECEs in their practice and conduct with their responsibilities to children, families, colleagues, the profession, communities and society" (CECE, 2017, p. 5). The ethics are A. Responsibilities to Children B. Responsibilities to Families C. Responsibilities to Colleagues and to the Profession D. Responsibilities to the Community and the Public (CECE, 2017, p. 7). The standards are I. Caring and Responsive Relationships II. Curriculum and Pedagogy III. Safety, Health and Well-Being in the Learning Environment IV. Professionalism and Leadership V. Professional Boundaries, Dual Relationships and Conflicts of Interest VI. Confidentiality, Release of Information and Duty to Report (CECE, 2017, pp. 8–20).
Ontario College of Teachers	The Standards of Practice for the Teaching Profession and the Ethical Standards for the Teaching Profession Professional Advisory: Maintaining Professionalism—Use of Electronic Communication and Social Media	Ontario: Certified elementary school teachers	The purpose of the Standards is • to inspire members to respect and uphold the honour and dignity of the teaching profession • to identify the ethical responsibilities and commitments in the teaching profession • to guide ethical decisions and actions in the teaching profession • to promote public trust and confidence in the teaching profession (Ontario College of Teachers, n.d.) The Ontario College of Teachers also have an ethical standards document, and their ethical standards are known as "care, respect, trust and integrity" (n.d.). The Professional Advisory Report "is intended to help Ontario Certified Teachers (OCTs) understand their professional boundaries and responsibilities in the appropriate use of electronic communication and social media" (Ontario College of Teachers, 2017).

Name	Type	Applies to	Description
Northwest Territories Teachers' Association: Code of Ethics	Code of Ethics	Northwest Territories: Teachers	"To ensure high standards of professional service the Northwest Territories Teachers' Association (NWTTA) Code of Ethics sets out general policies or guidelines for Association members" (Northwest Territories Teachers' Association, n.d.).
Early Childhood Educators of British Columbia: Code of Ethics	Ethical Principles and Standards for the Early Childhood Profession	British Columbia: Early childhood educators	"This code articulates the principles and standards of practice endorsed by ECEBC. Members of ECEBC undertake, as a condition of membership in the association, to incorporate them into their practice. ECEBC advocates the voluntary acceptance of these principles and standards by all early childhood educators, both members and non-members" (Early Childhood Educators of British Columbia, 2008, p. 2.).
Early Childhood Development Association of PEI	Code of Ethics	Early childhood educators in Prince Edward Island	"This code of ethics contains the principles by which members of the Early Childhood Development Association of Prince Edward Island adhere to while working with children" (Early Childhood Development Association, 2017).
Manitoba Child Care Association	Code of Ethics	Manitoba: Early childhood educators	"The MCCA Code of Ethics represents agreed upon values, principles, and standards of practice for those who have chosen to work in the field of early childhood education in Manitoba" (Manitoba Child Care Association, 2011, p. 1). It is intended to provide a framework in which to support educators in their ethical decision making.
Nova Scotia Child Care Association	Code of Ethics	Nova Scotia: Early childhood educators	"The NSCCA Code of Ethics provides guidelines for responsible behaviour as an Early Childhood practitioner. These Code of Ethics provides consideration that is needed to refer to when making ethical decisions" (Nova Scotia Child Care Association, 2014).
Newfoundland and Labrador Teachers' Association	Code of Ethics	Newfoundland and Labrador: Teachers	This code encompasses principles aimed at providing teachers with guidance regarding behaviours and actions associated with ethical behaviour.

Sources: College of Early Childhood Educators. (2017). *The Code of Ethics and Standards of Practice for registered early childhood educators in Ontario;* Ontario College of Teachers. (n.d). *Ethical Standards;* Ontario College of Teachers. (2017). *Professional Advisory: Maintaining Professionalism— Use of Electronic Communication and Social Media;* Early Childhood Development Association of PEI. (2017). *Code of Ethics;* Early Childhood Educators of British Columbia. (2008). *Early Childhood Educators of British Columbia: Code of Ethics;* Manitoba Child Care Association. (2011). *MCAA Code of Ethics;* Nova Scotia Child Care Association. (2014). *NSCCA Code of Ethics;* Northwest Territories Teachers' Association. (n. d.). *Code of Ethics.*

Oji-Cree educator and artist Bruce K. Beard creatively depicted the ethical standards associated with the Ontario College of Teachers. Take a look at the four posters below, which represent their standards known as *Care*, *Integrity*, *Trust*, and *Respect*. What might they be communicating about ethics and how might they relate specifically to observation? Once you have taken a moment to reflect, visit Ethical Standards—Anishinaabe Art Posters located on the Ontario College of Teachers website.

Oji-Cree Artist, Bruce Beardy and Ontario College of Teachers

Oji-Cree Artist, Bruce Beardy and Ontario College of Teachers

Oji-Cree Artist, Bruce Beardy and Ontario College of Teachers

Oji-Cree Artist, Bruce Beardy and Ontario College of Teachers

Evidenced in Exhibit 2.3, ethics may be more or less explicit in professional practice as not all provinces have a code of ethics. If you were to replicate this exhibit with ethical standards documents and regulating agencies pertaining to where you practise, what would it look like? What ethical standards do you feel are important?

Educators in Ontario early childhood settings are expected to register with the College of Early Childhood Educators and follow the Code of Ethics and Standards of Practice in order to practise as registered early childhood educators. Elementary school teachers also have a regulatory body called the Ontario College of Teachers, which has created a set of ethical standards with the teaching profession. These ethical standards reflect the commitments and actions educators embody in their professional practice.

College of Early Childhood Educators: Code of Ethics and Standards of Practice Poster

Code of Ethics and Standards of Practice

For registered early childhood educators in Ontario

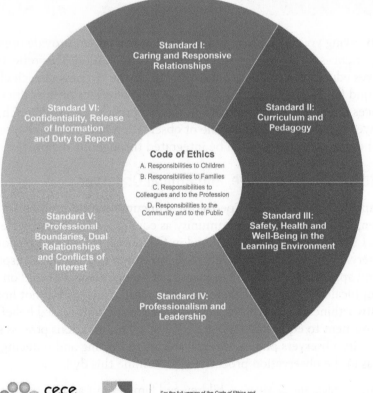

Standard I:
Caring and Responsive
Relationships

Standard VI:
Confidentiality, Release
of Information
and Duty to Report

Standard II:
Curriculum and
Pedagogy

Code of Ethics
A. Responsibilities to Children
B. Responsibilities to Families
C. Responsibilities to
Colleagues and to the Profession
D. Responsibilities to the
Community and to the Public

Standard V:
Professional
Boundaries, Dual
Relationships
and Conflicts of
Interest

Standard III:
Safety, Health and
Well-Being in the
Learning Environment

Standard IV:
Professionalism and
Leadership

For the full version of the *Code of Ethics and Standards of Practice* (2017) please visit the College's website at **college-ece.ca/standards**.

Source: College of Early Childhood Educators. (2017). *Code of Ethics and Standards of Practice*. Retrieved from https://www.college-ece.ca/en/Documents/Code_and_Standards_Poster_EN.pdf

A centre posts its code of ethics to indicate that the staff and the centre support the values and principles laid out in the code. More importantly, the staff are stating their intention to work toward fulfilling these tenets on a daily basis. These principles apply to everyone who is involved at the centre, including you, the educator.

Observing young children and interacting with them provide opportunities for experiences to evolve and for meaningful observation. This reflective process gives educators a chance to uncover the distinctiveness of each child. Does this sound familiar? In what ways do your code of ethics or the ethics of other provinces relate to the appreciative inquiry approach discussed in Chapter 1? As we begin to explore the cycle of observation later in this chapter, think about how a code of ethics can be integrated throughout the process.

The Responsive, Inclusive, and Ethical Observer

In Chapter 1 we learned that pedagogical documentation promotes parents, children, educators, and the community as equal partners in the cycle of observation. Like the expectations outlined in Chapter 1, this shared responsibility for observing requires all observers to demonstrate inclusiveness, responsiveness, and appreciation for the uniqueness of others. Here we build on this philosophical approach to include ethical qualities such as but not limited to trustworthiness, mindfulness, anti-oppressive and anti-biased beliefs, and a commitment to equity and integrity. While all observations possess some subjectivity, observers play an integral role in addressing and reducing power and bias in the observation process. Let's examine this dynamic.

Power, Observation, and Children   Children and families put a lot of trust in those observing them to ensure their right to privacy and protection, and to feel assured they are being observed without bias. Like trust, power and authority are naturally associated with adults, and this is evident in the relationships between children and adults. Participatory rights theories proposed by Smith (2002) in the article titled "Interpreting and Supporting Participation Rights: Contributions from Sociocultural Theory" prompt us to think about how this power dynamic influences children's participation in decision making, as well as how children may automatically assume that adults are the knowledgeable ones "in charge".

> Ideas about what are right, normal and proper relations and ways of being with children for oneself as an adult have a long and shifting history that influences if and how we listen to and respond to children. . . . How we see and understand the child in relation to the adult in specific institutional roles and contexts informs whether and how we consult young children. It guides the ethics of our consultations with children. For instance, if we see the adult as more knowing and more capable than a child, then we as adults will consult a child quite differently than someone we see as more knowing and more capable than ourself. (MacNaughton, Hughes, & Smith, 2008, p. 32)

This brings us back then to how we view children and their participation as learners. To help us with this exploration, Shier (2001) has designed a five-level model outlining how adults might support the participatory rights of children. This model connects well to Vygotskys's socio-cultural theory in that children benefit from social participation in their learning community, and more specifically from observation and documentation that involves them. According to Smith (2002), Shier's model has five levels as outlined in Exhibit 2.5.

As we will explore in the children's rights section of this chapter, supporting an anti-oppressive approach and promoting children's decision making and participatory rights are important components that enable children to demonstrate their competence, knowledge, and skills. Anti-oppressive practices require observers to relinquish and share power within relationships, and require a concerted effort from everyone in order to be mindful of what might be occurring in the moment.

REFLECTIVE EXERCISE 2.2

Take a moment to reflect upon Exhibits 2.5 and 2.6. Based on your experience, where do you see children's participation and leadership in settings familiar to you? Think about each component of Shier's model—in what ways are children listened to in your setting? How might they express their views or have their views considered? How are they involved as co-partners in decision making? Reflect upon the questions below in relation to Shier's model. How might we alter our paradigms of practice to support it?

EXHIBIT 2.5   Shier's 2001 Model of Children's Participation

1. Children are listened to.
2. Children are supported in expressing their views.
3. Children's views are considered.
4. Children are involved in decision-making processes.
5. Children share power and responsibility for decision making.

Sources: Shier, H. (2001). "Pathways to Participation: Openings, Opportunities and Obligations." *Children and Society, 10,* 110; Smith, A. (2002). "Interpreting and Supporting Participation Rights: Contributions from Sociocultural Theory." *International Journal of Children's Rights, 10,* 76.

| EXHIBIT 2.6 | How Is Children's Participation Determined in Your Setting? |

Who determines:

- When it is time to wake up?
- When it is time to eat breakfast?
- What to wear?
- When to put on outside clothing?
- When to brush one's teeth?
- Where to sit on the bus or in the car?
- When naptime will be?
- What decisions need to be made about the curriculum and schedule?

- When to go outside to play?
- What theories, inquiries, or hypotheses to explore?
- When to wash hands for lunch?
- Where, how, when to display or keep documentation?
- When to use the washroom?
- Where and when to sit for snack?
- How to resolve conflict?
- What provocations or invitations to prepare in the setting?
- Other?

mindfulness

The ability to be in the moment in a non-judgmental way, while being aware of context, feelings, thoughts, and actions.

In addition to understanding power within our relationships with children, mindfulness expects observers to also be cognizant of one's feelings, biases, and beliefs impacting what is seen and heard. With the shift toward more visual technologies and documentation methods, children may feel coerced or oppressed when visibly or verbally confronted by cameras, photo documentation, or other visually oriented observational tools. Several strategies to promote children's participation and observational competencies can be found later in this chapter.

ZoneCreative/iStockphoto.com

Understanding Bias and Anti-Bias in Observation and Pedagogical Documentation   Once you begin observing and interacting with young children, attitudes toward learning, perceptions of equity, and responsiveness develop. Each decision you make, such as whom or what to observe, is a personal choice and is, therefore, subjective. As we will explore later in Chapter 5, even if two people observe the same child, very different information can and will be recorded.

When educators of young children are asked if they have a favourite in their group, they often say, "Yes." Human nature is such that we simply prefer some people to others. Being aware of a bias—positive or negative—is the first step in treating all children fairly and professionally. In your role as an educator, you should be perceived by children as someone who is just and reasonable; their trust in you as a nurturing, caring adult depends on it. Being or becoming a just and reasonable educator is primarily about relationships, ideals, and values. Yet there are many practices that enhance that notion in any child-care setting:

- Document your observations in a manner that is respectful, inclusive, and professional. See Exhibit 2.8 for an example.

- Use descriptive language that clearly captures the essence of your observations. Chapter 3 will support understanding of observational writing and the importance of first person language. This also includes consideration of preferred pronoun references to children in our observations.
- Share and compare your observations and documentation, and discuss your reflections with the children, their families, or colleagues at your school or centre.
- Bring in outside resources, and continue to invite others to observe and document. Children, families, and community members offer wonderful perspectives about what can be learned from observation, and offer unique insights into new curriculum, provocations, and invitations.
- Maintain motivation and accountability. Observation is a privilege, and a window into understanding and appreciating how children learn and think. If your setting is struggling with consistent observations, initiate communication with others to address it.
- Be aware of your biases. Take the time to observe and document through the eyes of the children and families in your classroom.

We all bring to our professional practices our unique personality, attitudes, culture, philosophy, and background or life experiences, as noted in the areas of diversity shown in Exhibit 2.7. The circle diagram outlines a number of aspects of diversity within the human population; however, it is not exhaustive. Size, nationality, ideals

EXHIBIT 2.7	Diversity and Areas of Bias

Source: Adapted from Hall, N.S., & Rhomberg, V. *The Affective Curriculum: Teaching the Anti-bias Approach to Young Children.* 1/e. © 1995 Nelson Education Ltd. Reprinted by permission. www.cengage.com/permissions.

governing child raising, and other elements of diversity like those outlined in the cultural iceberg in Chapter 1 could expand this list. Every one of these components will influence your perceptions of children and how you view their thinking, learning, and actions as well as how you interact and work with children, families, your team, community, and numerous other elements of professional practice.

What are your values, perspectives, and beliefs concerning each of the above areas of diversity and bias? Although we are trained to be caring, professional, and objective in our observations, we cannot remove all elements of bias, but we certainly can look at strategies to deepen our self-awareness and how our backgrounds and experiences influence how we teach or educate. "Because beliefs and biases influence what we choose to ignore or act on, it is important for teachers to reflect on their family values, how they were raised, and what behaviours they view as acceptable or not acceptable" (Chen, Nimmo, & Fraser, 2009, p. 3; see also Marshall, 2001). For example, if educators believe that children should have free choice to do whatever they like, then their appraisal of certain behaviours will be quite different from that of an educator with plenty of rules for everything. When we begin to understand our values and beliefs, we enhance our ability to reduce subjectivity. Furthermore, this awareness can assist in avoiding the superficiality of a "tourist curriculum" as well as support in-depth understanding and increased sustainability of learning about respect for diversity for children and adults alike (Derman-Sparks & Edwards, 2010). Being aware of our biases or judgmental errors in our observational practices or assessment approaches is the first step in addressing them. We will explore common forms of bias that may occur when using other types of assessment methodologies later in Chapter 3.

Ethics: The Image and Rights of Children in Observation and Pedagogical Documentation

We build here upon the image of the child established in Chapter 1 with our ethics lens. We turn our attention first to the United Nations General Assembly who adopted the Convention on the Rights of the Child in 1989. The convention lays out principles to protect the rights of all children of the world, set out in 54 rights and optional protocols. Children have the right to be heard, to recognize they have rights, to express themselves, and to be recognized as knowledgeable and competent. As educators and observers, we have a moral and legal obligation to children. They do not vote, and their voices are rarely heard on topics like

tourist curriculum

This approach trivializes cultural diversity, such as by organizing experiences only around holidays or food, or by bringing it up only on special occasions and then having nothing further to do with the culture.

biases

Preconceived ideas or attitudes (personal or philosophical) that affect objectivity; prejudice.

Santypan/Shutterstock.com

globalization, economic disparities, and social issues, and yet they are the ones who will inherit the consequences of adult decisions. Children hold the knowledge to understand, participate, and have their views considered in decisions affecting their lives, while considering their age and maturity (see Exhibit 2.9). "Whether or not they can verbally articulate their rights, children experience the presence or absence of rights viscerally in their everyday lives, and they have the capacity to express these experiences and understandings through the images they make and the stories they tell" (Greenwood, Fowler, Graham, Boulton, & Hall, 2016, p. 21). Based on the UN Convention on the Rights of the Child, "compliance with Article 12 is therefore an ethical, legal, and moral imperative (Lundy, 2007) and mandates that all children must be involved in decision-making processes on matters that concern them. This is a non-negotiable and permanent human right afforded to children" (Harcourt & Sergeant, 2011, p. 423). As responsive, inclusive, and ethical educators/observers, we have a responsibility to uphold this principle by applying it to our observational practices.

EXHIBIT 2.8 'K' and the Sneaky Spiders

'K' and the Sneaky Spiders

It had been raining for several days. "K" went outside every day in the rain, running over to the trees and logs to see where the spiders and insects had gone. "K" had observed several days previously that there were holes in the logs and trees that allowed insects and extremely tiny spider babies to go in and out of. Today the rain had finally stopped and "K" was sharing her questions and wonderings prior to going outside:

June 15, 2018
4.1 years

"I wonder if there is too much water in their house."

" Did-ed they have to hide under the log from the rain?"

"Where did the green bugs and the sneaky spiders go?"

Just prior to going outside, "K" gathered a clipboard to document her discoveries. "K" invited her educators to take photos and co-participate in theorizing about how "the baby spiders sneaked out of their hole without the mommy spider." "K," you discovered that water didn't enter the holes because they were on the side of the tree which meant the water wouldn't stay because of gravity. Your idea that 'the rain wouldn't make a puddle because the tree and logs were on a hill' led you to discover that the ground was dry in the areas you examined. "K," you came up with ideas like 'the mommy spider was out building a web to catch food' which you explained was because 'she was too busy to watch her babies.' Your second theory included that they were 'told to go out and practise building their own webs.' Just as you were about to leave the tree, you discovered a large spider (with the same body markings) that had created a web on the plants beside the tree. How might you figure out if that spider is the mother? We look forward to hearing about your research about how spiderwebs are created and for what purpose!"

Co-authored by "K" and Ms. C.

Photos courtesy of Kristine Fenning

Source: Kristine Fenning

Listening to children also applies to other contexts. For example, as a keen observer of young children, you are also in a position to support the voice of a child who is abused, neglected, or in harm's way as it is your duty to report. Please see Chapter 7 for details.

When you walk into many early childhood settings, you will see on the wall a copy of the UN Convention on the Rights of Children. It is posted for all to see, to remind us of our important role in encouraging expression, making sure we listen carefully and deeply, and responding in an inclusive, positive manner to support children through understanding their culture and home life's context and relevance.

Visit the websites of the Canadian Child Care Federation/Fédération canadienne des services de garde à l'enfance and UNICEF Canada for more

---

EXHIBIT 2.9   The Views of the Child

The views of the child must be "given due weight in accordance with the age and maturity of the child." It is not sufficient to listen to children. It is also necessary to give their views serious consideration when making decisions. Their concerns, perspectives and ideas must inform decisions that affect their lives. However, the weight to be given to children's views needs qualifying. It must take into account the age and maturity of the child: in other words, the child's level of understanding of the implications of the matter. It is important to note that age by itself does not necessarily provide guidance as to the children's levels of understanding.

Source: Lansdown, G. (2011). *Every Child's Right to Be Heard: A Resource Guide on the UN Committee on the Rights of the Child General Comment No. 12.* London, England: Save the Children UK, p. 23. Retrieved from http://www.unicef.org/french/adolescence/files/Every_Childs_Right_to_be_Heard.pdf

on this subject. As you examine these resources, think about how you as an educator might use observation to support the tenets and principles they describe.

Valuing Children's Identity in Observation and Pedagogical Documentation

Children should always have the right to share their voice and perspective on their developing identity. Children should also have a voice in how images taken of them are interpreted and documented. Who is to say that the educator or the parent's interpretations are correct? Who is giving power to the child's interpretation of the learning taking place? These questions are worth your consideration. As you continue to reflect upon ethics in your role, think about putting yourself in the child's place. Would you as a future adult want to have these images shared and viewed by others? What are the rights of the child in this case? Putting yourself in the position of the child, having your behaviour, actions, feelings, interests, and needs documented continuously without permission, would be an unnerving feeling. How would you feel if everything that you said and did on a daily basis was made visible to others? Would you want to be constantly under this perceived surveillance? Exhibit 2.10 introduces two children whose photos have been placed on a

perceived surveillance

Being aware or thinking that one is being watched and documented in a variety of ways (e.g., photo, video, hard copy documentation) all the time; lacking privacy.

EXHIBIT 2.10   **Placing Children's Vulnerabilities at Risk**

This first photo to the left is of a 15-month-old child who is obviously in distress. Someone in the moment witnessing this and taking this photo might infer the child has come from the home centre in their classroom, and the observer took the photo not realizing the child was in distress. The observer's purpose for taking the photo was to document the thinking and conversations that were occurring between this child and their peers.

This second photo identified here is of a 12-year-old school-age girl who is inside the classroom feeling visibly upset. The observer taking this photo may be witnessing a number of things. One possibility might be that the girl is taking some time for reflection, while another observer may have spoken to the girl afterward only to find out that she was bullied by two peers sitting behind her for the entire day and is feeling very isolated.

stock photo website for purchase on the Internet: a 12-year-old girl whose photograph was taken when at elementary school and a 15-month-old child in a child-care setting. Take a few moments with a peer to view the photos in Exhibit 2.10. If an observer had taken these photos for pedagogical documentation, would they be a violation of ethics? If so, how?

What can we learn from the photos in Exhibit 2.10? We can learn a number of things. The first is that a camera put in the face of a child elicits feelings—and in the two situations, both children are experiencing distress of some kind. We also learn that there are times when we can take a photo and when we cannot, and that the technologies we use to document the thinking and learning of others have the potential to introduce surveillance concerns (e.g., cameras, videos). "Educators inherently have an ethic of care to treat students fairly, with respect and with dignity. Vulnerable groups require additional consideration, including those who are socially, economically or politically marginalized, including the elderly, children, those with disabilities or mental health considerations. When sharing documentation, special attention should be paid to ensure that vulnerable people are not negatively represented and/or impacted" (Ontario Ministry of Education, 2015, Capacity Building Series, p. 7). This particular quotation alerts us to the concerns in using photos like those in Exhibit 2.10. While intended to highlight concerns regarding use of photos like these (even if we are unable to identify the individuals), the mere insertion of these photos into this textbook warrants concerns from authors of this text for the reasons stated here. Such photos should not be taken of children for it exposes their vulnerability and places them further at risk. Children should be permitted to experience their feelings privately and should be given the right to consent before photos are taken. What other reasons can you think of why these photos might not be appropriate for sharing or use?

In upcoming chapters, we will look at important questions and queries observers must consider before documenting children no matter the methodology chosen. Used all the time, technology-assisted documentation has

> the potential to bring about changes to the spaces children inhabit. They may for example change the way children conduct their day-to-day activities, build relationships with others and come to an understanding of who they are and the world they live in. The question is, what is the exact nature of these changes, and is it possible to identify any situations where an increased surveillance presence might be to a child's detriment, perhaps inhibiting rather than enhancing childhood experience? (Rooney, 2010, p. 344)

This is an interesting question, as it is important that the observer considers the implications of documentation on the trust, safety, security, privacy, and confidentiality of those being observed. A 15-month-old like the one in Exhibit 2.10 trusts the adult enough to seek out for comfort, yet at the same time their vulnerability is being documented. Is their trust in the adult being violated?

Promoting the voices of children in all aspects of the observation cycle is an important way in which to support children as their identity grows and evolves. Using appreciative inquiry to empower children to participate and

EXHIBIT 2.11   Consulting with Children to Promote Their Voice

In what ways have children been

- recognized as meaningful contributors and citizens in the room with participation rights in all aspects of the observation process? In what ways does this continue to occur?
- asked for their consent daily? Regularly? Prior to images taken?
- asked to have their learning documented?
- involved in deciding what to document and when the observations would take place? For example, have they had the opportunity to participate in deciding which images to use for daily communication, webbing, documentation panels, portfolios, etc.? Have they been given the rights to select the images that are used and to deny those that violate their privacy or show them in a less positive light?
- involved in leading or sharing the observation, documentation, and interpretation processes of their own learning?
- invited to review and/or assist in preparing the written narrations of what took place and the meaning-making process (interpretations)?
- informed about how their learning will be interpreted by others or who will be reviewing their documentation to interpret the learning taking place?
- informed about how the information will be used, where it will be stored, and for how long? Images that are stored online or in some apps may be subject to clauses that indicate images stored no longer belong to those that posted them. Knowing the implications of where images are stored are extremely important.
- afforded the opportunity to be anonymous and to not have their faces depicted in photos or images?
- asked about which artifacts represent significant learning moments or experiences for placement in their portfolio?
- asked for consent by an adult who comes to the child's level to ensure there is not a height difference, thus equalling the power relationship between adult and child?
- advised that they can withdraw their participation at any time in being documented or in documenting their own learning?
- asked about how they wish to be referred to in their documentation (re: pronoun preferences). Has a conversation taken place with children and their families to clarify their preferences?
- prompted to discuss observations and interpretations with their families to allow them to feel in control of what is shared and communicated?

Source: Kristine Fenning

share their voice can be done in many ways. Exhibit 2.11 explores a number of examples for reflection.

Many of the questions in Exhibit 2.11 require significant reflection, discussion and collaboration, and planning within a team (educators, children, families, and community) to promote meaningful learning.

Ethics, Technology-Assisted Pedagogical Documentation, and Social Media

Some may say that social media has changed the way children and adults communicate with one another as habitual use of digital/online social communities continue to rise. It has certainly transformed educator abilities to communicate and build relationships with children and families, as well as make the thinking and learning within the early childhood classroom visible in real time. "The collaborative capacity of social media tools make them an attractive and

social media

Social networking digital mediums (e.g., websites, apps, blogs, etc.) that allow users to communicate and share information in various forms (e.g., photos, videos, music, private messages/texts).

useful tool for users who desire 'synchronous (real-time or near real-time)' or asynchronous interactions" (Cheung et al., 2008, p. 694; Yost & Fan, 2014, p. 36). For early childhood settings, social media has become a common documentation methodology to elicit communication, participation, inquiry, questions, and reflection from its community of learners (parents, children, community, and educators). Facebook, Instagram, Pinterest, blogs, websites, and various apps and forums are common digital tools for building pedagogical documentation communities of practice. We will explore examples of each of these as we discuss various forms of pedagogical documentation in Chapters 4 and 5.

To understand the influence and interaction of social media with pedagogical documentation in early childhood and early learning settings, let's examine a research study that explores social media impact. Yost and Fan (2014), in their study titled "Social Media Technologies for Collaboration and Communication: Perceptions of Childcare Professionals and Families," explored the ability of digital technology to promote social dialogue with children and families regarding how children learn. Using interviews as their data collection method, these researchers were able to obtain information regarding the reasons for and against adopting social media. The reasons can be found in Exhibit 2.12.

EXHIBIT 2.12	Participant Perceptions of Influential Factors in Adopting Social Media
Reasons for Adopting Social Media	**Reasons against Adopting Social Media**
Interview Responses from Directors, Educators, and Parents in Order of Preference	Interview Responses from Directors, Educators, and Parents in Order of Preference
<ul><li>communication<ul><li>– engagement with others</li><li>– maintaining connections</li><li>– keeping up to date</li></ul></li><li>convenience</li><li>confidentiality</li><li>flexibility</li><li>design and structure</li><li>access to computers</li><li>access to networks</li><li>receiving useful information</li><li>age</li><li>cultural factors</li><li>preference for written formats</li><li>being able to access sites at work</li></ul>	<ul><li>personal/individual preferences</li><li>time</li><li>a lack of current I.T skills</li><li>design and structure</li><li>access to networks</li><li>age</li><li>socio-economic status</li><li>difficulties associated with maintenance</li><li>language barriers and cultural differences</li></ul>

Source: Adapted from Yost, H., & Fan, S. (June 2014). "Social Media Technologies for Collaboration and Communication: Perceptions of Childcare Professionals and Families." *Australasian Journal of Early Childhood*, *39*(2), 36–41; originally from Cheung, K. H., Yip, K. Y., Townsend, J. P., & Scotch, M. (2008). "Health Care and Life Sciences Data Mashup Using Web 2.0/3.0." *Journal of Biomedical Informatics.* Vol. 41, pp. 694–705.

We can learn a number of things from the pros and cons of social media adoption in the Exhibit 2.12. For example, being able to share information and communicate in real time is an added bonus. Knowing that families have competing priorities, communicating children's thinking through the day reduces the need for communication at the end of the day when families are eager to get home. This could, however, be seen as a barrier to developing face-to-face relationships for those that are unfamiliar with technology or for those who lack access or the skills to use trusted computers for communication and sharing of children's learning. Take a moment to reflect upon the list in Exhibit 2.12 with a colleague or peer. Do you agree with the pros and cons? Can you think of others? What strategies would you use to address them?

Many children even at a young age will possess a strong familiarity and knowledge base with technology, and often will engage with it in a variety of ways. Knowing the vulnerabilities of young children highlights just how important it is for all observers to understand the ethical expectations and implications of posting images of children online. Many may simply "click" and post on Twitter, Instagram, and other social media domains without consideration of those being surveilled or photographed. Social media options and usage change all the time, so much that licensure and regulatory bodies for early childhood settings have not caught up with their advancement, nor have many been able to address the implications of the relationship between social media and pedagogical documentation such as but not limited to privacy, confidentiality, ethics, and rights of children. This may also be due to lack of knowledge regarding the reach, capabilities, benefits, and detriments of social media upon those observing or those being observed. As one peruses the left side of the same chart in Exhibit 2.12, it is easy to understand the benefits of using social media to augment pedagogical documentation. The "real time" convenience of being able to engage contributions and responses from parents, children, educators, and the community in building and scaffolding knowledge, extending inquiries, and provoking new thoughts all at the click of a mouse is quite appealing for many.

REFLECTIVE EXERCISE 2.3

Review and reflect upon the checklist below. Have these components been considered in the program you are in? Have you considered them previously? In what ways? If not, what inquiries and questions do you have? Take the time to develop a plan with your peers and colleagues to ensure your learning community is safe and protected, and to set the stage for safe usage of social media.

SOCIAL MEDIA CHECKLIST FOR TECHNOLOGY-ASSISTED PEDAGOGICAL DOCUMENTATION

Social Media Reflective Checklist for Technology-Assisted Pedagogical Documentation	Action Plan *Questions? Inquiries to pursue? Items to discuss with your team? Next steps?*
Have policies been developed to address ❑ use of centre or school devices only— avoiding use of personal devices that can blur the lines between personal and professional information and posts;	

(continued)

❏ social media–approved sites (password-protected sites with individual family passwords and access only to their child's information are recommended. Families would not be permitted to share their passwords or information.). This includes verifying with quality assurance or licensing agencies to ensure the necessary protective features are in place;

❏ ongoing consent for families and children (signed disclosures by families and children for posting online; ongoing consultation with children regarding the creation, use, and posting of any information or images) as well as written agreements that indicate areas for children to provide their own consent;

❏ appropriateness of photos or videos to maintain the integrity and dignity of those being observed (e.g., avoid faces or identifiers in text or visuals, consider location, use terms like "Child A" if other children are in the post, use positive and first-person language [Chapter 3 will explore these terms]);

❏ requirement that group photos be shared only with families and children who have provided consent;

❏ how images will be posted and used (e.g., not for downloading or sharing with others); and

❏ how to maintain safety, privacy, and confidentiality of posts and images—note that no information or image is ever completely private on any social media site (e.g., a simple screenshot overrides any protective features on a site, blog, or app)?

Has access for children and families been considered?

❏ Do they have Internet access?

❏ Are they familiar with how to use electronic devices?

❏ Are they familiar with the social media forums chosen by your setting?

❏ Is language or any other element of diversity a barrier? Can families and children document visually or in their language?

❏ Are there varying fonts, backgrounds, and voice-to-text features?

❏ How will families who do not wish to participate in digital documentation be accommodated and respected?

Social Media Reflective Checklist for Technology-Assisted Pedagogical Documentation	Action Plan *Questions? Inquiries to pursue? Items to discuss with your team? Next steps?*
How will the digital forum be maintained and managed?	
❑ Who will do this and how?	
❑ Where will information and images be stored? How will they be secured?	
❑ Who determines the images that are used?	
❑ Who will ensure personal information is not used?	
❑ Who will investigate and communicate copyright? (Knowing who has rights to the information and images posted is extremely important to know and understand.) Giving credit to the author for information being shared, pinned, or tweeted is necessary.	
❑ Who will address violations of ethics?	
❑ Who will determine the forums to be used?	
❑ Who will ensure passwords are in place for every user?	
❑ Who will ensure security and virus protection are up to date?	
Other considerations?	
❑ _____	
❑ _____	
❑ _____	

Source: Kristine Fenning

The checklist in Reflective Exercise 2.3 is not exhaustive. Understanding how children's learning and thinking can be made visible using social media in a safe and secure way is a priority. More information related to online use can be found in Chapter 4. Government legislation, standards of practice, and our profession expect all observers to be ethical both inside and outside of the classroom—our community depends on it.

ETHICS: CONSENT, PRIVACY, AND CONFIDENTIALITY

Consent, privacy, and confidentiality require a specific focus from observers as depending on where you practise and the pedagogical documentation chosen (online or hard copy forms), there may be varying expectations from government legislation and regulations, licensing agencies, and those directly involved in the actual observation and pedagogical documentation process.

Professional Responsibilities and Consent

Part of being a qualified educator involves adhering to confidentiality when documenting and sharing information about children. Ethical standards require that student–educators sign a Pledge of Confidentiality stating that the student will not discuss the events of the centre or the persons involved. Similar confidentiality assurances are required by provincial/territorial law to ensure that the privacy of information on children and their families held in centre files will be respected by all who work or interact with the child and family. Educators must sign such an assurance indicating they understand and agree they will hold all information in confidence, as well as abide by their own code of ethics and regulating bodies.

Part of a postsecondary early childhood program is an orientation that involves the discussion of field placement or practicum. Fundamental to that orientation is the discussion of your role and responsibilities while attending an early childhood or early learning setting. This orientation will include the important procedures regarding consent and confidentiality. Compliance with your postsecondary policies of consent and confidentiality and those of the early childhood setting you will be attending is mandatory.

As well, each province and territory, through the appropriate government ministry, sets out standards and guidelines regarding consent and confidentiality for qualified educators to follow. Visit your provincial/territorial website for details of the administration of online and hard copy children's records.

Policies and procedures recommend a system for exchanging information between the parents/guardians and the centre. "Records are covered by legislation dealing with privacy and an individual's access to information. A record is defined as almost any form of information, including letters, daily logs, case notes, memos, drawings, videotapes and computer files. Therefore, a record includes all agency records, from the most informal to the most formal" (Valentino, 2004, p. 14). Agency, school, or organization policies and procedures are guided by legislation such as this and noted in a licensed centre's parents' manual or office documents. In addition, federal legislation, such as the Freedom of Information Act and the Bill of Rights, must be considered as this legislation guarantees confidentiality and the rights of the individual. Each licensed early childhood setting must follow the advisories but may interpret how the consent forms it uses will be phrased. Exhibit 2.13 illustrates recommendations from the Ontario Ministry of Education *Child Care Licensing Manual* in conjunction with the Child Care and Early Years Act 2014 regarding how to store and protect information about children.

Note the reference to the posting of pictures to digital forums such as Facebook in Exhibit 2.13. Taking the time to read the fine print on every

EXHIBIT 2.13

Ontario Ministry of Education Child Care Licensing Manual

Each licensee should have a policy describing the types of information that will be collected and the purpose for collecting and storing such information. Information includes written records, as well as photos and videos of children.

The policy is to align with the following protection of privacy principles:

1. Information collected should be the minimum needed to serve the purpose of the service provided.
2. The right of every child and family to privacy should be recognized and protected to the greatest extent possible.
3. Parents are to have access to their child's records and should be informed of who may have access to the child's records on an internal basis (e.g., staff, volunteers, bookkeeper).
4. The appropriate informed written consent of a parent should be a requirement prior to the release of personally identifiable information to third parties. This includes the release of any information through social media (e.g., posting pictures to Facebook).

The written consent of a parent must be obtained before a child's personally identifiable information is released to an outside researcher and/or a child participates in any research project conducted at the child care centre (Ontario Ministry of Education, p. 135).

Source: Ontario Ministry of Education. *Child Care Licensing Manual*. (2018). Copyright Queen's Printer for Ontario, 2018. Reproduced with permission.

app or website used to store c hildren's information is a necessary step in protecting their privacy. Be sure to review the social media checklist for technology-assisted pedagogical documentation in Chapter 4 to be well informed.

Centres will have separate consent forms for each child. Some children, if they are enrolled in two different programs, will have specific consent forms. The consent form gives the centre permission to receive and transmit information from one centre to the other.

Whether you are a student–educator or a new educator, you should be made fully aware of the centre's policies and procedures before you begin your new position. Make sure to be advised as to what information you may access and what records and files are strictly confidential. If this information is not forthcoming, it is your responsibility to ask so that you are apprised of the policies and procedures. Parental permission must be obtained prior to any research (observation) being conducted on a child.

Exhibits 2.14 and 2.15 provide visual examples of typical consent forms: Authorization for Release of Information and Authorization for Exchange of Information.

With a colleague, peer, or your team, use Exhibits 2.14 and 2.15 (or one of your own) to create a new consent form that includes the child's voice.

REFLECTIVE EXERCISE 2.4

EXHIBIT 2.14   Authorization for Release of Information

This form may be used to exchange information when the child is attending more than one program. Please complete and sign this permission form to allow this exchange of information.

    I/We give permission to ABC Nursery School and Canadiana Public School to exchange information about my child. This consent form covers the time period from September 7, 20____, to June 20, 20____.

Name of Child	Date of Birth
Signature of Parent/Guardian	Date
Witness	

Source: Courtesy of Sally Wylie

EXHIBIT 2.15   Authorization for Exchange of Information

This form authorizes a professional from the child-care centre to obtain information on a child.

    I/We hereby authorize ABC Nursery School through its representative

_____

(Supervisor/Director)

from any educational, social, and/or medical authority on

Surname	Given Names

I/We hereby further authorize ABC Nursery School to convey to any educational, social, and/or medical authority information on

Signature of Parent/Guardian	Date
Witness	

Source: Courtesy of Sally Wylie

Children's Consent   Exhibits 2.14 and 2.15 do adhere to the legal requirements of most early childhood settings; however, if we apply our participatory rights theory and appreciative inquiry approach to the consent process, these consent forms lack something. What might that be? Yes, of course—the child's voice and rights. It is important to understand that the frequent eye glance or response of a child smiling to a photograph being taken does not imply consent. It raises the question whether what we are capturing is truly informed consent or whether the child has simply resigned themselves to not having a voice in the observation and documentation process. While parental consent may imply legal consent in the eyes of the law, it fails to address children's rights under the UN Convention of the Rights of the Child. How do we truly know when a child is giving informed consent? Is the child aware of how the information collected will be used or why it is being used? Are they informed as to what is being shared and has the child and family provided input? Are they aware of who will be viewing the information? Do we understand the impact of documentation through technology and social media on children, the quality of their play, the environment, and what it is that we see and hear? How might children participate in designing these consents? These questions require our attention.

Hard copy permission forms are one way to promote child consent or assent to being observed and documented. We know, however, that children may have difficulty comprehending the true intent of paper-based consent forms. Children or others who are being observed can become informed in other ways as to what is being documented, how their learning and thinking is being documented, and how the information will be used, kept, and stored. It is very important that children understand their privacy and confidentiality rights, their rights to participation or withdrawal, and how their knowledge and competence will be made visible. Let's explore some of these ways. Take a moment to reflect upon the scenarios in Reflective Exercise 2.5. How might you support these children to understand the consent process?

REFLECTIVE EXERCISE 2.5

▲ The photo above was taken by the parent of a child by the name of Aurelie, a four-year-old new to your classroom this week. Aurelie is the child to the right playing in the sand with your colleague Charmaine. You have learned from this child's parent that Aurelie has a profound hearing impairment and possesses an expressive language disorder. Her parent indicates she is mostly nonverbal, and uses some sign language. You have obtained written consent from her family to document this child's thinking and learning; however, you are unsure how to respect and support this child's participatory rights in the pedagogical documentation process. You need to come up with some daily strategies to obtain Aurelie's consent and assent—what ethical strategies could you use?

(continued)

▲ Meet Sanoh, a two-year-old child who has just started in your room. Sanoh has never been in a child-care centre before. Sanoh speaks a few words in Korean, and does not yet communicate in English. Sanoh's parents possess limited English. You want to support the family and child in settling into your environment, and you want to begin the pedagogical documentation process. The family has signed the written consent form, but you are concerned they did not understand what they were signing. You need to implement strategies to ensure informed consent from the family and the child as well as to engage them as active participants in the process. What ethical strategies could you use?

To support comprehension of consent and assent regarding pedagogical documentation processes, younger children or those with special or diverse needs may benefit from child-centred consent and assent approaches. Some of the ways to support children like Aurelie and Sanoh might include

- taking the time to build a trusting relationship by engaging children at their level, showing interest in what they do—this could be through observing and commenting on their interests and strengths, and listening to what it is that they see and hear. Co-documenting and making decisions together on full-room observations enabling the child to feel valued and empowered is important;
- conversing and sharing information in single words or short sentences;
- using approved sign language or symbols for children to understand and use;
- communicating information in larger fonts and using background colours for visual clarity;
- using real photos of items, materials, experiences, and interactions to communicate intent;
- providing ongoing access to child-centred materials to document their own learning (see Chapter 3 for examples);
- having sensory-based options available to support children's self-regulation, and their ability to communicate and process information;

- using audio software (Chirbit, Google audio, voice recorder apps, etc.) to explain pedagogical expectations, participation, consent, and use of observations—allows for revisiting of this information at their leisure;
- providing voice-to-text software or other software that allows for children to communicate in their language through technology or audio/visual images on a tablet;
- providing videos or social stories in their language that demonstrate what consent means and what it looks like. This would also involve examples of children not providing consent with discussion as to why they might not want to be observed. See Exhibit 2.16 for an example.
- reviewing documentation completed on an ongoing basis and asking the child how they feel about the documentation, their interpretations of what

social stories

Descriptions (which include photos) of an everyday social situation written from a child's perspective to assist children in preparing for and managing upcoming changes in their day.

EXHIBIT 2.16 — Social Stories and Pedagogical Documentation

▲ I take the school bus to go to school.

▲ On the bus, someone might ask to sit next to me.

▲ If I say no, the person might be sad. Everyone has the right to sit anywhere.

▲ If I say yes, they will sit and maybe I can talk to them about school.

The above images are just a portion of a possible social story for a child who may be using school bus transportation for the very first time. New experiences can elicit a variety of feelings and questions for individuals. Social stories can be changed and adapted to suit any child. It is recommended that educators consult with sources on social story development to support comprehension for children (e.g., real photos versus abstract pictures).

took place, and how they want the documentation to be made visible (or not). "Young children need to know how and where their words and work will be used and distributed and to know that they will be used for no other purpose unless consent is given. Consulting with care is not about child's artwork and words being positioned as 'cute' and a form of 'decoration' for advertising events, website, invitations or book backgrounds" (MacNaughton, Hughes, & Smith, 2008, p. 38);

- moving away from adult predetermined agendas for documentation—and promoting child and family engagement to determine how they want to document; and
- having ongoing conversations with children to allow for processing of their own thinking and development of new inquiries. Children need to be consulted throughout every day should they choose to withdraw their participation from observing or documenting. Not everyone wants to be observed or surveilled every day as we all need our space to think, wonder, and play authentically.

Office and Digital Files: Safe Storage of Documentation

Every licensed early childhood environment maintains its records according to a set of ministry expectations and policies unique to each setting. All licensed early childhood settings have office files that must be maintained. The office files are kept in the main office or supervisor's office in a secure, locked cabinet, or they may be digitized and stored on a mainframe computer. Typically, office files will contain such information as medical records, referral forms, intake information, and financial records. Only licensed educators, administrators, and parents have access to these files. Parents and guardians will have access only to their child's file. In addition to the ethical considerations discussed previously, it is necessary to also consider how sensitive child information is transmitted to families. Email transmission of child information poses concerns as many servers face breaches and subsequent access to this information. It is important that families who prefer email transmission of information be informed as to the risks of using that digital option.

Settings choosing to store information digitally on a computer or tablet should consider encryption or password protection. Should online or social media be the method of choice for tracking or storage, consider strategies outlined in this chapter and Chapter 4 to ensure protection, confidentiality, and privacy.

Getting Permission for Observations

If you are a student not yet practising in the profession, ensure that parents and guardians are aware of any observations you may complete on their child while you are a student–educator. This is often done through a permission letter of some kind. It is recommended that an introduction be given stating your name, the name(s) of your instructor(s), and the purpose of the observations. If this introduction is in letter form, it could be shared with the centre supervisor, involved staff, and the parents. You will find examples of permission letters online. If you are a practising educator in an early childhood setting, requirements of your setting for permissions to observe would be outlined in the centre, school, or agency policies. Not all settings will require a letter in their exchange-of-information procedures, but parents do like to know who is in the room with their child and need to know what information on their child is obtained or exchanged.

Whether you are a student–educator or a seasoned educator, be sure to explain to parents/caregivers that observations are part of your studies or role. If the parent wishes to read your observations when you are in a student capacity, it is important to consult with your professor first, as student observations and interpretations are opportunities for practising and learning and are not intended for authentic entry into a child's portfolio. Student observations and interpretations must be vetted and approved by the supervisor or director, as the observations and interpretations may require rewording. While employed educators have permission to use name or centre identifiers within their setting, students do not have the same authority or ability to use real names of children or settings. This is to ensure confidentiality of information gained and used for learning purposes. As a student, it is important to remember not only to transmit written information to parents only with the approval of the educator or supervisor in charge, but also to be aware of and follow the agency's policies and procedures regarding consent and confidentiality.

Ethics places value on the participation of children, enabling them to make active decisions in all aspects of the cycle of observation. This means that children are to be provided the opportunity to participate in the inquiry, observation, documentation, reflection, interpretation, response, and collaborative stages as they have much to offer. By viewing the image of the child as we have in a different way, we see that children have the right and the ability to be co-observers, co-researchers, and co-educators in our early childhood settings.

OBSERVATION REVISITED

Now that we can appreciate and understand the importance of being an ethical observer, we can apply our ethical approach to observing within the cycle of observation. For observation, watching and listening are at the top of the list, for the observation process allows observers to document children's thinking, learning, voice, and so much more. Observation expects that observers utilize all senses such as smell, touch, and taste to aid that learning even further. For example, if we were asked for our observations on a bakery, we would probably comment on more than just what we see: we would remark on the wonderful aroma upon entering the bakery and certainly describe the tastes!

Educators will tell you that their observations are much more than that. Since young children communicate much of what they think and feel through their bodies, educators also have to develop the expertise to understand the intent and purpose for behaviours. This infers that they need to interpret what children are communicating through their behaviour or the actions and the sounds/words they use, reflect upon their intent and purpose, and then convey or share that information in a variety of ways for a variety of purposes. The process of observing can refer to the actual observation you are making on a specific child at a certain time, or it can refer to the entire lifelong practice of observation. This idea will be further solidified as we explore educator development in subsequent chapters. In those chapters, we will explore the evolution of reflective practice and the honing of one's skills, and come to see just how integral these are to the

EXHIBIT 2.17   Learning about Jerimiah

An experienced educator for five years now, today in my classroom, I experienced something for the first time. I had never really taken the time to see the world through a child's eyes, to allow the child to communicate to me through his actions the decision making that was taking place. Let me explain.

Two months ago, we had a new preschooler by the name of Jerimiah. Jerimiah had no siblings, and both he and his family were new to Canada within the last six months. Our centre was the first place of contact for this family. As Jerimiah began to settle into our program, I began to notice that he played on his own most of the time, humming and talking to himself in a very low tone as he interacted with materials in the room. Two weeks after starting our program, Jerimiah began pushing other children as they crossed his path, or at times he would be observed running up to a child to push him down. Educators at first were seeing only the visible behaviour of "pushing," and often were responding only by stopping him to tell him "no pushing." At the time, we were missing the key communication of what Jerimiah was trying to tell us.

With his parents, we agreed to begin observing and documenting Jerimiah's play and movements within the room. We took the time to listen and then interpret what we were seeing, and we were amazed by what we learned. We discovered that Jerimiah frequently gravitated toward materials in the classroom that could topple over. We saw musical instruments on shelves pushed to produce sound as they fell on the floor. We saw a child excited by his decisions and the sounds of these materials as they fell. We learned that he would smile when a child fell and began crying. Why was this information so important? Taking the time to view Jerimiah as a competent learner in the room was the key to seeing beyond the perceived "negative behaviour" constantly discussed and identified by the educators in the centre. Jerimiah was communicating his fascination with sound and movement. He wasn't meaning to hurt others—their tears and response to him were what he was fascinated with. He was focusing on the connection between when he pushed and the reaction he got—cause and effect. Making this important realization prompted our team to rethink how we view children. We were caught up in the "behaviour" and we weren't listening. Once we determined what his behaviour and actions were communicating, we were able to respond with learning experiences that allowed him to engage with cause-and-effect actions in a more appropriate way. By doing this, the pushing of children stopped and peers began initiating interactions with him. Our children also began a new inquiry into sound and movement with Jerimiah leading our learning journey!

Source: Courtesy of Kristine Fenning

process of observing young children. When developing observation skills, learning with, about, and among others always takes place along the way, even for an experienced educator, as mentioned in Exhibit 2.17.

As observers, what have we learned from Jerimiah's educator? What were some of the words used? Listening, interpreting, seeing, competent learner, cause and effect, documenting, reflecting, experiencing, inquiry, and, of course, observing. These words are those used by a reflective educator who viewed Jerimiah in a new way, engaging actively with the child and family and colleagues to uncover why Jerimiah was pushing other children.

It is a useful example of the kinds of interactions, problem solving, and communication that are practised by responsive educators within an inclusive learning environment. Fortunately, to appreciate from a holistic perspective the thinking and stories of children, the beauty of everyday moments in time, as well as context and environment, early childhood settings will provide a multitude of opportunities to engage observation skills.

Subsequent chapters will introduce the many observational methodologies available for use, and Chapter 4 will help us to navigate the differences between observation and pedagogical documentation as this understanding is necessary in order to develop sound observational pedagogy.

THE CYCLE OF OBSERVATION

To appreciate all that the cycle of observation has to offer, it is important to begin conversations about observation with children and families upon enrolment. Depending on the philosophy, the pedagogy of the setting, and the community of learners, this process may look different from setting to setting. The cycle itself is complex yet it is authentic and natural in its evolution. Orienting a family and child, however, to observation and the purpose of pedagogical documentation is a necessary first step, as it sets the stage for equality and collaboration, and it communicates the message that there is appreciation for all voices and perspectives as well as for individuality of thought. Exploring together how children and families can become co-observers, co-documenters, and co-educators in the room is an ongoing priority as discussed earlier in this chapter. These conversations and ongoing engagement promote an observational culture that embraces all perspectives, and one that fosters deep mindful listening and inquiry. Listening is one of the most important aspects of observation and is a component within the cycle; it means that the observer attends to the child and, by doing so, demonstrates value and respect for the child's voice. Listening gains a broader perspective, as shown in the photo and in Exhibit 2.18. As Wilson (2014) reminds us, "active listening makes those around us feel appreciated, interesting, and respected. Ordinary conversations emerge on a deeper level, as do our relationships. Listening with intent may in fact reduce misunderstandings and we always learn more when we listen more than we talk" (p. 232).

Wiarton Kid's Den/Sally Wylie

Understanding the importance of listening prompts us to now take a look at the components of the cycle.

"'Through careful listening, [teachers] are better able to spontaneously support and challenge a child to extend his thinking' (Gandini & Kaminsky, 2004, p. 9). Documentation is seen as 'visible listening. . . . To ensure listening and being listened to is one of the primary tasks of documentation . . . as well as to ensure that the group and each individual child has the possibility to observe themselves from an external point of view while they are learning. Your attention sends a message to a child that what they do has value and meaning (Rinaldi, 2001).'"

Source: Browne, Kathryn Williams, & Gordon, Ann Miles. (2009). *To Teach Well: An Early Childhood Practicum Guide*, NJ: Pearson, p. 72.

The Cycle of Observation as an Interactive Process

The cycle of observation, as we see it, is not a structured, prescriptive formula for observers, but rather an interactive and ongoing process involving a team of others: parents, community professionals, educators, and children. It involves the gathering of multiple perspectives in all components.

As with observation itself, the cycle of observation is also setting-independent and is an essential part of all inquiry. It is ongoing and self-rectifying, meaning that it is a vibrant process that provides an approach without a set time frame and prescribed outcomes.

Exhibit 2.19 illustrates that there is no specific or single entry point in the cycle, as observation is organic and responsive in nature and may not continue always in a natural sequence. The observer may begin at any point of the cycle because observation occurs all the time in any philosophy.

Let's explore each component from the cycle of observation in Exhibit 2.19 to understand its significance within the cycle.

self-rectifying

To set right; correct. To correct by calculation or adjustment.

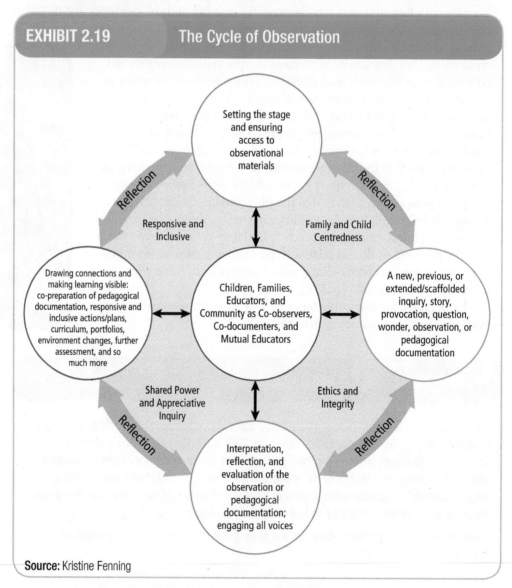

EXHIBIT 2.19   The Cycle of Observation

Source: Kristine Fenning

Setting the stage and ensuring access to observational materials to promote collaborative and co-shared observations and pedagogical documentation

Engaging all members in the observation and documentation process requires the creation of a sustainable observational culture and pedagogy. Pedagogical documentation is intended to be a shared reflective learning experience, rich with education and dialogue, and accessible to all. It is necessary to collaborate with all participants in a setting to discuss how each might contribute, and

Dinosaur Desert

Child: Peter A.
Age 3.3 Years
D.O.B.: October 29, 2015

Courtesy of Scotia Plaza Child Care Centre

Today I overheard you Peter with your friend Child C manipulating the dinosaurs in the sandbox while raising your voices to make roaring sounds "RARGH". The sounds were convincing as you made others look at your dinosaurs when they roared. You mentioned to Child C that it was important to have places to get shade in the desert for your dinosaurs so that they didn't burn their skin. Your idea to put the magnifying glass close to the skin of the dinosaur to show the redness of the skin was a good idea to confirm what you were communicating to your friend. It was very interesting when you placed the driftwood in the sandbox, for it immediately created shadows in the sand that you noticed. "Look at how tall my dinosaur is and how little yours is Child A" you exclaimed. We can certainly add the coloured lights you asked about to the sensory table tomorrow so that you can explore your ideas further regarding how to alter the shapes of the dinosaurs in light. It was an exciting discovery when you created what you called "spine bones" for your dinosaur using the different loose sticks you brought from another area in the room and attaching them to the backbone of your dinosaur.

Child C was asking you Peter how you knew your dinosaur was a meat-eating dinosaur. Child C was interested in your theory because he demonstrated curiosity by asking you why you said "you dinosaur only eats plants" Child C is looking forward to you bringing your dinosaur encyclopedia tomorrow to explore why his dinosaur can't eat meat.

Peter's response:

"Tomorrow we are gunna check to see who can make their dinosaur even bigger. We have some good ideas to make the dinosaurs purple. I think it will make them look really cool."

Curriculum or Environmental Extensions/New Provocations:

Peter plans to retrieve the light board tomorrow to experiment with the theories he presented today. Child A plans to document her experience tomorrow with photographs to show how she can make the dinosaur's skin colour change. What other extensions or provocations might you make in this instance? How might you become a play partner or co-documenter in the experience he is planning? What might you do to promote further inquiry and documentation from the children?

explore why observation and pedagogical documentation is important. Chapter 3 explores various strategies in which to build a shared and collaborative observational pedagogy so that all members can make their learning visible together.

A new, previous, or extended /scaffolded appreciative inquiry, provocation, question, wonder, observation, or pedagogical documentation

Inquiries, provocations, questions, wonders, observations, or pedagogical documentation can originate from a child, a parent, an educator, or a community member. As we learned in Chapter 1, there are many purposes for observing, and understanding these reasons assists us in drawing connections to what it is that we are seeing and hearing.

scaffolding

A concept developed by Lev Vygotsky, who stated that an adult will scaffold, or put in place, a form of assistance, whereby a child gradually develops the ability to do certain tasks without help.

Appreciative Inquiry and Questioning Appreciative inquiry and questioning are not only integral values in the cycle but also vital threads throughout the cycle of observation. Meaningful inquiry takes time, the ability to be mindful, and a commitment to having no preconceived thoughts or agenda. As the cycle evolves, it often includes questions or provocations that invite reflection and evaluation to build intentionality in learning. This appreciative inquiry approach, involving reflective observation and an interactive, ongoing process, is a positive framework of informed, responsive, and inclusive practice and the central focus of this text.

Inquiry is a major component within the cycle and maintains its momentum. The most important action a team can engage in is the process of inquiry through the acts of pausing, listening, and questioning. For example, before documentation begins, fundamental questions can be asked by any member of the learning community. The questions below represent some of the many types of inquiries that might take place:

- What type of environment (social, emotional, cognitive, physical) do we wish to create with children and their families?
- What behaviours or values must I demonstrate to create or maintain this environment?
- How are children involved in observing and the creation of pedagogical documentation?
- What theories are children emulating in their play or what wonders and inquiries do they wish to pursue? Why?
- What are our beliefs and values about learning? Children? Families?
- How will the documentation reveal our learning?
- What kinds of questions will our documentation reveal? How might they provoke new and/or extended thinking processes?
- How will self-reflection be valued or promoted within the day?

The discussions involving these kinds of questions prompt everyone to listen to others and examine the beliefs of others and themselves. Once observers begin to ask, listen, revisit, challenge, and reflect, divergent ideas begin to emerge that move the group from where it was to where group members would like to be—a new space. This process is not necessarily easy, but whatever the perceived challenges might be, the will to problem solve and construct creates a positive, responsive climate in which respect and nurturance can thrive and ideas can grow. With answers come new questions.

The process of inquiry invites change. Openness to change and the predisposition to change are key in creating alternative change in practices.

predisposition

The act of predisposing or the state of being predisposed; previous inclination, tendency, or propensity; predilection, such as a predisposition to anger.

EXHIBIT 2.20 — The Lens of Observation in a Holistic Approach

When beginning the observation process, you may not have a specific purpose in mind or may not be sure of a focus. Often when we form new questions or areas of inquiry, we are led to different types of observations, and thus we become more holistic in our approach. Where do you begin? Perhaps you might be wondering about

- what makes each child unique. How does each child express themselves? In what ways would an infant use body motion to communicate?
- the theories that children use and apply to understand the environment and world around them. Children are competent learners and educators and have much to share;
- how children interact with others socially. Play-based observation yields the most amazing discoveries of children, from infants to children in kindergarten. Would the social play of two-year-olds be different from that of five-year-olds? Is the social development of children from different cultures obvious during play? How do friendships develop? How do children deal with antagonistic peers? When a new child joins the group, how are those patterns of play changed?;
- how spirituality and voice/power is or can be shared, promoted, and respected. Revisit Chapter 1 for a spirituality discussion as well as query various early childhood philosophies online to determine how spirituality exists in different settings;
- a child's attachment to his educators and caregivers or perhaps to peers. Play-based groupings of children offer opportunities to examine play partners, relationships, and attachments. How are attachments formed? There are other types of observations that can be conducted—many of which are explored in Chapter 5;
- a child who is new to the centre and/or country. What might you learn about the child's culture, language, and beliefs? Add to that exciting opportunities to learn about a new culture and language, find out about community resources for the family, and develop a relationship with the parents; or
- a child who might benefit from extra support or who might be struggling in an aspect of her or his development. Perhaps the parents have approached you for help because they are concerned about their child. All children may have a time in their developmental pathway when they need some type of support due to the challenges they may be facing, behaviourally, developmentally, or for reasons beyond themselves. Through observation, you can find out which current abilities this child has, which skills require further development, and perhaps even which influences are affecting the child's overall progress. Chapter 7 will introduce us to the various types of professionals who may join the team to assist in supporting a child with diagnosed or undiagnosed special needs within the early childhood setting.

What would questions look like in an observation cycle? Questions offered in Exhibit 2.20 illustrate some possibilities.

Exhibit 2.21 gives a visual of the key words representing essential ingredients of the observation cycle. In the diagram, you'll note the interplay between the key words representing an equitable exchange rather than a hierarchy of who/what is most important.

The words in Exhibit 2.21 combined with the guiding words in Exhibit 2.22 illustrate the dynamic nature of the cycle of observation.

For example, guiding words such as *perception* and *inquiry* referring to children and community professionals could mean that children have inquired about what people do in the community.

Kristine Fenning

EXHIBIT 2.21   Observation Cycle: Key Words

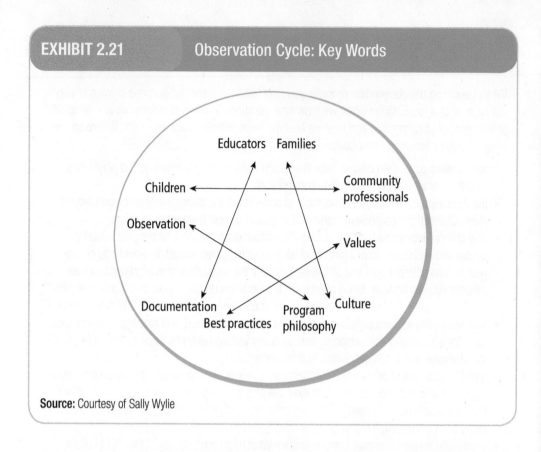

Source: Courtesy of Sally Wylie

EXHIBIT 2.22   Observation Cycle: Guiding Words

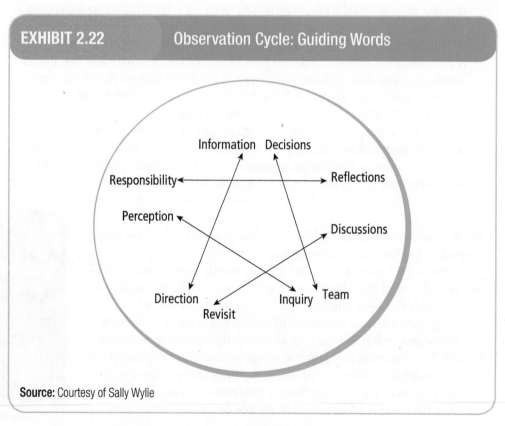

Source: Courtesy of Sally Wylie

Perhaps some of these professionals in the community loom larger than life, such as a firefighter or a Royal Canadian Mounted Police officer patrolling the park on his horse.

Having the children meet these professionals in their environment provides an opportunity for inquiry from both points of view. Observations from that real-life interchange form a basis for curriculum, talking points in the community, and inter-relationships, to name but a few possibilities.

Through dialogue and collaboration using guiding words such as those found in Exhibit 2.22, this reflective process becomes transformational; the team (often consisting of the child, educator, parent/guardian, and, possibly, others) creates and directs the process leading to new possibilities. This process could then prompt discussions from the educators, who revisit the event with further documentation.

If the decision is to represent publicly what was learned, those involved will determine the format of representation. Will the documentation be presented as a documentation panel, a binder set up in the foyer, an article in the school newsletter, or a PowerPoint presentation to inform the board of directors, parents, and municipality? How will information be conveyed or transmitted?

Ultimately, through inquiry, the process may lead the team toward making other types of decisions. Examples of other decisions may include, but are not limited to, inquiring further if the children wish to revisit their theories, build upon past hypotheses, or, perhaps, extend upon their play ideas, planning, or school work of the previous week.

Following the ebb and flow of questions, discussion, and reflection, where might this process lead? Including the children and involved adults allows the shared process to proceed without a scheduled time frame or outcomes driving the process; it is ongoing, vibrant, and transformational. This process involves the children, their work in all forms, and the possibility to revisit the process and work created as well.

Questions, when formed as "What if" or "I wonder" questions, are intended to stimulate thinking, hypothesizing, problem solving, and curiosity. Questions associated with reflection are not intended to test knowledge but rather to prompt learners to query what they see and know, and to collaborate and build knowledge. Questions like those in Exhibit 2.23 can range from basic questions, such as educators asking themselves in the morning, "How will I continue to document the children's interest in the differences of textures?" to divergent questions such as "What are the ways we will display the documentation of the preschooler's ideas about water?" or to critical questions from children such as "Why do caterpillars turn into butterflies?" These pedagogical questions reflect the thinking of appreciative observers and learners who are transformative in their approach to learning.

Interpretation, reflection, and evaluation of the observation or pedagogical documentation through engagement of all voices

Chapter 3 will explore interpretation processes and considerations depending upon the observational methodology chosen as they may require different styles of writing and preparations. With interpretation comes active reflection throughout the cycle as it allows for authentic movement between and among the cycle. Active reflection engages educators, families, and children in inquiry-based thinking and further observation, leading to discoveries, new provocations, and actions that lead to and connect with the next component of the cycle.

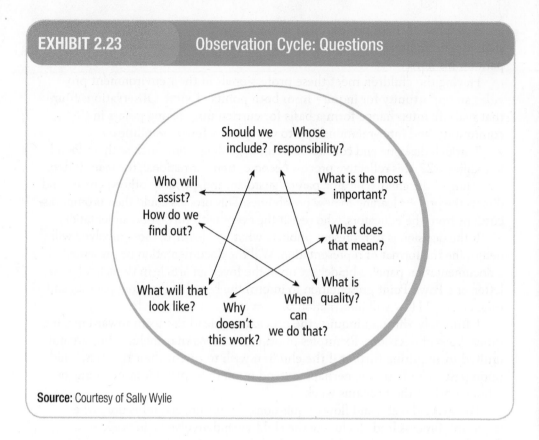

EXHIBIT 2.23 Observation Cycle: Questions

Should we include? Whose responsibility?

Who will assist?

What is the most important?

How do we find out?

What does that mean?

What will that look like?

Why doesn't this work?

When can we do that?

What is quality?

Source: Courtesy of Sally Wylie

Schools and early childhood settings support reflection and interpretation for all participants as a vital part of their pedagogy and professional practice. We have all heard of planning time. What about reflection time? Is the reflection process valued? How is the value of it represented within the day? Perhaps that question, if posed at the beginning of the cycle of observation, would have an influence that would be felt throughout our practice. As Hughes (2005) states,

> One of the greatest contributions from the educators of Reggio Emilia is the promotion of discussion, reflection and examination of beliefs and values that are translated into teaching practices (New, 2000). When teachers are serious in their study, they optimize the opportunity to question and to examine the underlying principles of this approach and apply their understanding to their own unique early childhood education program. (p. 49)

Roger Greenaway confirms what educators of Reggio Emilia are communicating, and outlines very simplistically in Exhibit 2.24 why we as educators need to reflect upon our experiences and actions.

The curiosities of children lead them to engage in self-reflection and reflection naturally. Approaching children with "I wonder" questions will prompt discovery of many answers, hypotheses, and solutions to simple everyday moments and sometimes complex problems. Each component of the chart holds meaningful learning; reflection is the lens to new possibilities. You will find extended conversations, additional information, and examples of self-reflection and reflective questioning in subsequent chapters.

EXHIBIT 2.24   Why Reflect?

Adds meaning to experience.

Offers **support**—providing a safe place to celebrate successes and work through failures without fear of judgment.

Develop **observation skills**—maintaining more awareness during/after experiences.

Get unstuck—stop repeating the same cycles and move forward.

WHY REFLECT?

Exploring **means of self-expression.**

Show that we **care about others' experiences,** want to hear about them, learn from them, and celebrate!

Empowerment—helps develop tools and ability to take charge of own self-development and learning.

Gain **new perspectives**—opportunity for growth, understanding the bigger picture, and developing empathy.

Source: Gans, K. (2017). *A Practical Guide for Forest School Leaders (or Anyone, Really!) to Facilitating Reflection in the Outdoors*, p. 5. Retrieved from http://docs.wixstatic.com/ugd/8dd281_d349c3026468 4c9f99940d7a8e754812.pdf

Drawing connections and making learning visible—co-preparation of pedagogical documentation, responsive and inclusive actions/plans, curriculum, portfolios, environment changes, further assessment, and so much more

As observers, we are fortunate to have the opportunity to reflect upon what it is that we see and hear in order to make meaning and draw connections from our observations. While making learning visible is a significant focus of pedagogical documentation, information and meaning gained from observing and documenting can inform other aspects of early childhood practice.

This text carefully examines each of the outcomes and components of the cycle in various chapters as there are a number of possibilities that can result from drawing connections and making learning visible. Various methodologies in Chapters 4 and 5 make visible the learning of children in different ways, and allow for the creation of inclusive actions and plans co-created by the team (child, educators, family). Curriculum, portfolios, the environment, and assessment are all explored in Part 3 of this text. Observation is undoubtedly the most powerful resource and tool we have as educators to inform every aspect of our early childhood practices.

Collaboration from all team members (child, family, educators, community)

Evidenced through this text so far is the expectation that all team members are involved in all aspects of the observation and pedagogical documentation process, and for the cycle of observation, the expectation is no different. Voices and participation from all educators and learners are welcomed in all facets of the cycle. This collaboration, as we will see in upcoming chapters, may vary depending on the methodology or documentation chosen. Take a look at the example in Exhibit 2.25. Tomi, the boy in the striped shirt, collaborated with his educator to prepare the photo narrative response. This response not only reflects collaboration between Tomi and his educator Ingrid but also reflects how connections can be drawn from documentation prepared.

Name: Tomi

Date: November 1, 2017

Written by Ingrid and Tomi

It was the near the end of the afternoon play period when I approached Tomi to engage in some reflective dialogue about his day. Tomi mentioned there were some photos on the tablet taken by peers of him engaged in block play. The image seen here is the one Tomi selected for his portfolio. When Tomi shared the photo he selected, I responded with, "I wonder what you were thinking about as you were building with the blocks. Can you tell me about it?" This provoked Tomi to verbally narrate what had taken place.

"Child A and me were buildin fun slides and climbers for our Star Wars guys. The tower I am building here was like a mountain for them to climb cuz robots can only climb them if they have wings. Even robots with wings can't get em cuz I builded a cave on the top to protect them. The cave fitted two people so Child A had to build a house to protect the others."

Ingrid's question: "How did you know how to build the caves and houses? How can you be sure the people will be safe?"

Tomi's response: "I squished the people together and made sure the blocks went around their bodies to protect their heads. Child A used wood and lego cuz the wood was stronger. I pretended they were more safe in my cave cuz it was made of rock and robots have a hard time blasting rock."

REFLECTIVE EXERCISE 2.7

With a peer, prepare an educator response based upon what you see and have learned from Tomi. What have you learned, and how might you involve Tomi in building upon this learning? How might this inform curriculum? Materials within the environment?

A foundation based on ethics and integrity, family- and child-centredness, anti-oppressive approaches and shared power, appreciative inquiry, responsiveness, and inclusiveness

Each of these values and concepts has been explored extensively throughout the text and more specifically in Chapters 1 and 2, as all are equally important. Starting Chapter 2 with extensive examination of ethics as it relates to observation and pedagogical documentation portrays ethics as a core value of one's observational practices. Without ethics, we place children and families at risk with the documentation being prepared. Emulating these values throughout the cycle of observation and in all observation and pedagogical documentation is necessary for a multitude of reasons. Why are each of these concepts so important within the cycle of observation? Exhibit 2.26 illustrates a practical example of the cycle of observation applied to everyday professional practice.

For further variations of the cycle of observation and applications to assessment and curriculum, be sure to read subsequent chapters in the text.

For the month of May, children at our early childhood setting were actively engaged and curious (in many rooms) about flowers, plants, and vegetables, and in particular how they grow.

Adding to this were the curiosities of other children who were fascinated by the properties of water: what it could be used for, how it helps things grow, how it helps our bodies. During reflection time, several children indicated that they had conversations with their families about their gardening experiences at the centre, and that they wanted their families to participate in the growing of a vegetable garden.

Ensuring opportunities for documenting and reflecting, responding in a family- and child-centred way, and documenting and making visible

the learning and thinking of children are all components of the cycle of observation that led to the community gardening experience occurring. Educators, families, and children were provoked by the observations and documentation made from the curiosities of children when they were gardening.

The photos depicted here in this exhibit were transformed into photo narratives that were used as a documentation panel on the window closest to the gardening space chosen. This prompted many discussions to occur at arrival time of families.

Several parents approached the educators to organize an evening of gardening and tilling of the soil. Subsequent collaborative experiences have been planned to eat the vegetables that will have grown in the garden!

---

1. Ethics is a necessary component of professional practice to address at the practice, policy, and philosophical levels in order to protect and preserve the rights of children and families in the observation process. All educators, no matter where they practice, are expected to adhere to their code of ethics and/or standards of practice. These are intended to guide educators in all aspects of practice and outline expectations regarding observation and pedagogical documentation.

2. As responsive and inclusive educators, it is important to be mindful, trustworthy, anti-biased, and anti-oppressive in our observational practices. Appreciating the natural power imbalances that may occur between adults and children enable those who collaborate with children to ensure their decision making and participatory rights in all aspects of the observation and documentation process.

3. Chapter 2 explores a number of strategies to do this.

4. Understanding and respecting all aspects of diversity is an important step in reducing bias. Being aware of these biases and reflecting upon each one to ensure we are being fair and equitable in our observations is one strategy amid many explored in this chapter. Seeing children as competent and contributing beings also reduces bias as it promotes the inclusion and recognition of their rights in the observation and documentation process. This is a moral and professional obligation for educators, as children deserve to be treated with dignity, and to have their identity and voice valued and respected.

5. Social media is transforming the observation and pedagogical documentation process in a multitude of ways. While there are a number of benefits and concerns associated with technology-assisted observation and documentation, observers can implement a number of strategies to ensure safe and positive use of social media mediums. Consent and assent of children must be considered on a daily basis, as children deserve to be consulted and be involved when observers want to document and make visible their learning. Observers are responsible for ensuring that those being observed be given the right to choose whether or not to be documented and surveilled. Children's privacy and confidentiality must be respected at all times.

6. Consent, privacy, and confidentiality are mandatory responsibilities of all observers at all times. All persons who work with young children must ensure that they have procedures in place to obtain consent and to ensure privacy, confidentiality, and safe storage of all information collected—whether in hard copy or digital forms. Daily consent processes for children, password protection, and encryption are just some of the many strategies discussed in Chapter 2.

7. The cycle of observation is a natural and authentic process involving a number of interactive components such as inquiry, questioning, observation, pedagogical documentation, reflection, and making connections. This cycle applies to any setting and philosophy and is intended to support observers in making meaning from observation and in co-creating pedagogical documentation all in efforts to make learning visible.

LEARNING TO DOCUMENT THE ACTIVITY OF CHILDREN

Several first-year early childhood education students are loading their books and papers into their backpacks. Their first class of the day is Developing Pedagogical Documentation Skills. They have been in class for an hour; for the second hour of class, the instructor has directed them to the child-care centre to conduct their first observations of children. "What are we supposed to be doing? I don't get it," says Karyn.

"I don't know for sure, but we're going down to the child-care centre to watch the children play," replies Janelle. "If you ask me, I think it will be boring watching the kids run around. I don't know what we're going to do exactly—she said we'd be writing down what we see the children doing. Sounds easy to me."

When the students arrive, they are instructed by the professor to write down what they see and hear the children do. Some are asked to do a group observation, while others observe individual children within the group. Later, the class regroups in the staff room at the child-care centre to discuss what they had learned. The professor asks, "Beginning with the students who observed the group of children, please share with us what you learned today, what you experienced, and what you are now wondering about. The following are some of the comments:

- "The children were all over the place. Two children were using sticks to mix a potion, while another child was taking photos of tiny eggs stuck to a plant in their garden. I couldn't figure out why the child wanted so many photos of the egg!"
- "When I was watching the same three children, I heard the little boy say he was taking photos because he wanted to see if the egg was going to hatch into a butterfly. I was amazed that a child that age understood how butterflies develop! Then he ran to the educator to show his photos and the educator replied by asking more questions of the child. The child replied back saying he needed to look at the chrysalis! Can you believe that?!"

The professor pipes in: "I overheard the educator with that same child ask him, 'Why might the eggs be stuck to the plant? What will your next inquiry be? How will you know when it becomes a chrysalis?'"

The professor directs their attention to the other group of students who were watching another child playing alongside a group of children in the playground. The professor then says, "Tell me about your wonders, your findings, and what you documented, answering the same questions as the other group."

- "I couldn't believe what a child does in the span of a few minutes!"
- "There was so much going on, with children talking to one another, and so I didn't know what to write down."
- "When I looked down to write and then looked up again, my child had moved from the sand area over to an area with a bunch of sticks, and I never saw him go!"
- "I saw a child adding a photo and some scribbles to a circle diagram on the outside window with a marker, and he was talking to some other children about what he had built with the wooden nature blocks. I saw the educator then ask that same child about what he had written on the wall. The educator called it their 'learning web', and then added their own piece of information underneath the child's scribbles. I thought that was really interesting."
- "What are we supposed to do with these observations now?"
- "I can't read mine! I couldn't write words down fast enough."
- "I couldn't think of the right words. I didn't know what to call some of the toys they play with, and I couldn't think of words fast enough to describe what she was doing."

As the discussion continues and students try to read what they had hurriedly written down, they comment on how much they had actually recorded. If more than one student had watched the same child, they continue comparing observations. They talk about how interesting it was that when three people had observed the same child, each person picked up on something that the others had not.

We've been listening. Whether you are a preservice educator, as in the example above, or a seasoned educator in the profession, observation and pedagogical documentation are not as easy as they seem. The journey of discovering what interests a child, what a child learns, and what a child loves doesn't stop there. You will be on the same journey, learning about yourself, your biases, and your ability to problem solve your way through questions and reflections, while coming to appreciate your own unique skills and discoveries. We've anticipated some of your questions and hope in this chapter to provide topics that will enlighten and expand your knowledge.

OVERVIEW

Chapter 3 ends this first section with guidelines and ideas about how to involve everyone in the cycle of observation, looking at ways to increase access and shared responsibility for observation and pedagogical documentation. This chapter and this text are unique in that writing and the actual writing processes are discussed for all students and preservice educators. In this chapter, you will discover how language usage and the words we use matter, in addition to examining how the use of first person language supports an appreciative perspective. Observational writing can be very exciting!

Whether your documentation represents a few lines that accompany photographs or comments attached to a chart or a narrative, there must be congruence between what was observed and what is documented. As you observe and document, you will begin to understand how writing is also a process of discovering your own and others' thoughts about how children learn and about the image of a child.

narrative

The describing or telling of an event involving characters and setting; a story.

This chapter will also introduce the important step of interpretation and reflection, a process involving making sense of what has been seen and heard. This step is necessary in developing our understanding of children, our environment, and our practice, and responding in a meaningful way. With observation and reflection come the values, images, bias, knowledge, and perceptions of the observer. Understanding the various forms of bias that might influence our perceptions cannot be overlooked.

This chapter will be most effective when used in conjunction with opportunities to observe. Over time, opportunities for application will help you grow in skills and confidence. It is through documentation that educators can construct new learning starting with a blank page. Let the writing begin!

FOCUS QUESTIONS

1. Participation in the cycle of observation expects shared responsibility for observation and pedagogical documentation. How might an observer create an observational practice that includes everyone?

2. What might be the necessary preparations for preservice educators if considering observing in the community?

3. Discuss the role of descriptive language in the writing and documenting process, and describe what "people-first" language infers. Why do the words we use matter, and what might be some of the strategies that new observers could use to build confidence, comfortability with the English language, and meaning in their observations and interpretations?

4. Describe behaviour, internal conditions, and characteristics. How might each of these components influence our inferences, and what roles do development and other theories play in the observation and pedagogical documentation process?

5. What are interpretations and why might they be challenging to write?

6. How might we use our understanding of bias in observations to reduce the level of bias in our observations and pedagogical documentation?

SETTING THE STAGE FOR THE CYCLE OF OBSERVATION: INCREASING ACCESSIBILITY, SUSTAINABILITY, AND SHARED RESPONSIBILITY

Reflecting back upon Chapters 1 and 2, we learned that observation is an important responsibility of all educators, regardless of their setting or philosophy. We also now know the value of having all members of a learning community participate in the cycle of observation. Opportunities to observe young children and to practise documenting their thinking and learning are fundamental to developing the complex abilities and skills needed to co-create pedagogical documentation. Seizing daily opportunities to observe promotes a natural approach to gathering the information needed to interpret, reflect, and respond in an inclusive way.

Being able to capture and provide open-ended opportunities for observing, wondering, questioning, inquiring, interpreting, and responding requires us to create a sustainable and meaningful observational practice that is sensitive to the rights of those being observed, that addresses situational barriers within

a setting, and that promotes access and engagement from all participants. This foundational pedagogy should include planning how observation and documentation can occur within the context of one's day as well as purposefully planning for accessibility to a variety of digital and hard-copy materials and technologies that support the creation of pedagogical documentation. Dialogue and discussion between all members of a learning community is necessary to determine what materials best suit this access and engagement, how to plan fiscally and responsibly for the purchasing of the materials necessary, and what pedagogical documentation will look like for their setting. Materials and actions that empower and encourage shared responsibility, equal voices, and participatory rights ensure a thriving inclusive environment for everyone. What materials could be made accessible to children, parents, families, and educators for observing and documenting? Take a look at Exhibit 3.1 to see how one centre created a culture of inquiry and observation.

Wiarton Kids' Den/Sally Wylie

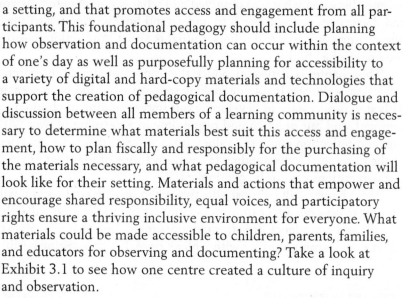

EXHIBIT 3.1	Engaging All Observers

Tony, a full-day kindergarten early childhood educator, and Liz, his elementary school colleague, have worked together now for just over one year. Their administration had introduced the new changes for the kindergarten curriculum, one of which was a strong emphasis on capturing the play and learning of children in the room. "How are we ever going to be able to document the experiences of every child in the room?" Liz asks Tony as they are preparing for the children to arrive. "I've been thinking about this a lot, and I have an idea," Tony replies.

"We should create an observation centre in our classroom." Liz asks, "What do you mean?" As the children started entering the room, Tony explains, "At the end of my shift when the children go home, I'll show you."

The end of the day comes and their transformation begins. Throughout the day, Tony had gathered a number of materials, bins, and an extra shelf for the classroom. Knowing they have space close to the door of the classroom, Tony and Liz talk about placing a variety of observational materials on the shelf for parents, children, students, and educators to use to self-observe or to observe the experiences and wonderings of others in the room. The materials include

- clipboards;
- assorted paper—lined, blank, scraps, sticky notes;
- pens, pencils, crayons, and pastels;
- file folder sticky labels;
- mini-whiteboards and erasable markers;
- mapping sheets/visual photos or diagrams of the classroom for easy documenting by children;
- paper with areas for photos and printed lines for narratives/messaging;
- paper with basic webs for drawing or writing what was seen/heard and to connect to concepts/inquiries, etc.;
- two cameras with photo and video functionality (with visual instructions/steps available that explain how to use the equipment effectively and safely);
- one tablet with documentation apps (in the cupboard above the shelf for signing out and using) (the technology had been purchased through the parent advisory board)
- digital devices that allow for voice-to-text software—to assist children or those who are unable to write while observing (they can voice prompt text to be written through these apps)

To make this a shared experience, Tony and Liz organize a night for discussion around the following:

- purpose of this new space, opening up dialogue regarding how everyone could participate in the process of making learning visible in the classroom—including a discussion about what pedagogical documentation means and the various reasons for observing and documenting
- children's rights in the pedagogical documentation process, inviting discussion about consent and confidentiality from children—not just their families—on a daily basis
- increasing the materials available, exploring how additional cameras and tablets could be purchased for use—developing a financial plan for the processing of photos, the purchase of electronic photo frames and televisions with slide shows of what occurred in the day; how to develop their own pedagogical documentation and social media policy and plan for documentation
- how to include pedagogical documentation as a prioritized part of their everyday experience—considering time, ratios, responsibilities, safety, training, teamwork, etc.
- how to create children's portfolios (see Chapter 6 for more information)

Pedagogical documentation is a shared responsibility within the cycle of observation and requires a commitment from all participants. Before long, children, families, and educators are all contributing transformative documentation of children's learning for children's portfolios, digital photo frames in the classroom, communication boards within the classroom, and documentation panels for the halls.

Source: Kristine Fenning

With a partner or colleague, develop a plan that would support the staff, families, and children in Exhibit 3.1. If you were a part of their learning community, in what ways could you support the building of a sustainable practice as well as address some of the concerns they had in making it a part of their everyday practice? What steps, materials, money, or resources would be needed? What social media considerations do they need to think about when integrating pedagogical documentation with digital forums for their centre (see Chapters 2 and 4 if you need help)? How might the whole team be supported and ultimately successful with this new pedagogical documentation adventure?

For the cycle of observation and pedagogical documentation to be truly sustainable, it must be adopted as a priority at a philosophical, policy, and practical level by all participants. This includes being prepared, organized, and systematic at times, making it a part of one's day rather than "on top" of one's responsibilities, and having a plan for making learning visible. Plans must also include the who, what, where, when, why, and how of observing and documenting, and should consider training needs to assist those in understanding the many facets and benefits of pedagogical documentation. Communicating with one another as well as sharing your enthusiasm for your role in the process is beneficial for everyone to see. This engagement promotes understanding and adoption of meaningful observational pedagogy at a philosophical level, and it promotes discussion of observation and documentation policy expectations that are fair, just, and reflective of your learning community. Declare your "wonders" publicly, relish in the discoveries of others, practise, research, and learn about pedagogical documentation in your community (municipally, nationally, internationally, etc.), and collaboratively form new inquiries that will continuously lead you and your families, children, and community to new discoveries enjoyed by all.

LEARNING TO DOCUMENT AND UNDERSTAND WHAT WE ARE OBSERVING

Having an observational and pedagogical documentation plan with access to a variety of materials available to document is a great start! Let's turn our attention now to the writing process. As we explore the rest of this text, we will learn that there are many different styles of observational writing, each with their own complexities, steps, and transformative qualities. Even writing a simple shopping list requires a series of steps such as

1. deciding what you need at the store and why you need it—your purpose,
2. making a list—format,
3. writing the items down—documentation,
4. checking with others—teamwork, and
5. remembering to use the list! Observations are meaningful only when they are used!

The purpose of this brief, real-life example is to demonstrate that even a shopping list is not simple. There are steps in the process of this familiar task. Writing observations in a clear, descriptive narrative relies on similar steps:

1. Determining the purpose through appreciative inquiry, while including others in that conversation
2. Choosing a format or method to suit the purpose or spontaneity of what you are attempting to capture and make visible
3. Documenting your observations
4. Consulting with others while sharing your observations and reflections

This basic comparison illustrates the steps required for purposeful writing no matter how simple the task. The purpose of this chapter, therefore, is not only to make visible for the observer the necessary steps to follow within the observational writing process but also to clarify what an effective observation involves.

The Writing and Documenting Process

Initially, many students find developing the skills to effectively document and record their observations challenging. Some struggle with appropriate ways to write down what they think or feel: "The way we say things when writing our observations is not how we'd say them in regular conversations, so we find it sort of clumsy to try to write like that." This chapter examines why it might be "clumsy to try to write like that." One of the most direct ways to begin is to find out why writing observations is initially a challenge.

While we know that all observations possess subjectivity, various types of observational methodologies require us to document in a factual way, based on what actually occurred. Factual writing is about using nouns, verbs, adverbs, and adjectives in a clear, concise way. The following are some of the reasons why learning this skill is challenging:

- using a descriptive vocabulary for detailed writing
- having to observe and record simultaneously
- navigating the English language particularly if English is a second language
- being unsure about what to actually observe and record
- being unsure of how to compose the observation
- recognizing that discovering how to express your thoughts in writing in a professional manner is a multifaceted skill
- lacking confidence in current writing skills
- being unsure of the nuances of each type of observation and understanding their purpose

Being proficient in documenting clear observations, interpreting children's behaviour, and creating documentation that is inclusive, respectful, and meaningful is expected of all responsive educators. This complex process begins with focusing on starting the documentation process, learning the guidelines for consideration while observing, and laying the groundwork for determining the use and purpose of information we are gathering, such as including it in a portfolio. We hope that as a result of our comprehensive approach, readers will continue to use this text throughout their professional career.

Preservice Educator/Observer Guidelines in the Community

Once you have had opportunities to observe, either in an early childhood setting or through the use of online clips, you will have begun this amazing process of discovering the world of children. Fortunately, the foundation has been laid for

Observing from a distance; not involved with the children.

unobtrusive

Blending with the environment so as not to stand out; inconspicuous.

us in Chapters 1 and 2 to understand the multitude of purposes (the whys) for observing as well as the important ethical considerations that observers must employ throughout the cycle of observation to ensure the safety and dignity of those being observed. Exhibit 3.2 outlines some of the many guidelines that preservice educators must consider when embarking upon the observation journey or when preparing pedagogical documentation within an early years' setting.

EXHIBIT 3.2	Preservice Guidelines for Observing in Community Settings: The WHYS, WHENS, WHERES, WHOS, WHATS, AND HOWS
Guideline	**What to Consider**
Talk with educators/staff and supervisor/principal about the purpose for the observation (WHY).	• Explore expectations, policies, and procedures. • Ensure adherence to ethical protocols. • Share and discuss your observational/pedagogical documentation needs/expectations/goals—WHY do you want to observe and document?
Consider timing and how long the observation will be (WHEN), and location (WHERE).	• Consider schedules of those in the setting—for meetings/conversations. WHEN is the most appropriate time for you to observe and/or ask for help/to answer questions? Depending on the purpose for the observation, WHEN is the best time to conduct the observation to pattern or learn the information you need to know? Are there challenges to this observation taking place and, if so, what are the solutions to overcoming the challenges? • Perhaps the team (child, other educators, family) may want to co-observe—plan for this to occur. • WHEN is the best time for the child to be observed considering the purpose for the observation? • WHERE is the observation taking place? Note the location in the essential information or in the context of the observation depending on the requirements of the observational methodology or pedagogical documentation used.

Choose a child to observe (WHO) and the type of observation/documentation you wish to do (WHAT). Consider (HOW) to involve the perspectives of others, including the child's voice, in the process.	• WHO is going to be observed?
	• WHAT is the purpose for observing the child chosen? Is it a child new to the setting? A child who is quiet and keeps to themselves? A child whose new inquiry interests you? Do you want to learn about a child's development? The child's spiritual connection to their environment? A child who has invited you to participate in co-observing? Chapter 1 introduces many more reasons—be sure to take a look!
	• Consider (WHAT) biases you may possess and implement strategies in which to reduce this bias (consider strategies in this chapter that look at Forms of Bias in Our Observations and Interpretations).
	• Follow confidentiality and consent processes with the child/family/centre and consult Chapter 2 for strategies.
	  – Protect integrity of information collected/employ confidentiality procedures with digital/hard-copy information/ensure anonymity of child/those observed. Be sure to also check with your educational setting regarding the storing, use, and transportation of information used for assignments/class.
	  – consult with the centre and family regarding the use of pronouns (he, she, they, names for e.g.) in your observations. Observers in a student capacity are encouraged to use terms like "Child A, Child B" for observations to protect privacy of information being used for post-secondary school purposes. For registered educators in the child's environment, the use of a child's real name (or otherwise indicated by the child and family) in their own observation is appropriate.
	• Look at how to facilitate child and family participation.

Guideline	What to Consider
Be a spectator or participant.	• **Spectator approach**—involves selecting an **unobtrusive** location to observe from a distance to see the big picture. This approach also means the educator has time to reflect upon what is observed as well as to document the observations without interruption. Documentation may be recorded during the observing process or may occur as a post-observation process. As preservice educators, this is typically the mode that may be employed. With additional experience, the participatory mode may be most realistic. • **Participatory mode**—if observing using this approach, be sure to plan HOW to manage observing while engaging with the children at the same time in a safe way. Determine if hard-copy or technology-assisted observational tools will be used for documentation. This mode is most common in early childhood settings. Children in responsive inclusive settings will appreciate and participate in the documentation process to help co-inform understanding of their learning and to make their learning visible.
Record the information needed for the observation/pedagogical documentation methodology chosen.	• Each setting might have different ways of recording and formatting essential information (e.g., variations might be (1) only the child's first name, (2) initials, (3) a fictitious name or initials, or (4) simply "Child A"). When working or employed in the field as a registered educator, you will use a child's real names, both first and last, as the information is housed only in the school, centre, or agency. • Determine HOW dates for the observation will be documented as each setting may record it differently. Is it month/day/year or day/month/year? This is important as it impacts how the age of the child is calculated. • WHAT other information is needed? Time? Location? Name of observer? Is a title needed? (e.g., learning stories may have titles and other information needed while anecdotal observations may not require the same information).
Prepare the necessary materials needed (HOW).	• Determine HOW you wish to observe—for example, are you using a pen and sticky note to jot notes, are you preparing a learning story and therefore documenting through photos (thus needing a camera, tablet, or other device), or perhaps you are completing a language sample and are using audio app software on a tablet? Ensure accessibility to and understanding of use of the materials in advance to accommodate those who wish to participate in documenting with you. • Determine the expectations of the methodology chosen as it will determine HOW to go about observing. • Determine if shortcuts or short forms will be used during documentation. For example, • LH = left hand A = alone CP = Cooperative Play MIN = minutes • Once the observation has ended, update the shorthand or abbreviations with additional context and information in order to capture all meaningful information.
Record dialogue and context (WHAT).	• Use **direct quotations** if documenting the exact language of the person being observed (see Exhibit 3.3 for an example). If unsure of what exactly has been said, **paraphrasing** may be appropriate. Paraphrasing means that you are summarizing or putting into your own words the gist of the child's conversation. For example, suppose that a four-year-old girl is sitting at a table painting a picture. While she paints, she says, "You know what, last night I watched TV until really late, and then my mom said it was time for bed, so I went upstairs and then I had to brush my teeth and get ready for bed, but I wanted my mom to read me a story and so she did, and then I still wasn't tired and I asked if she'd read another one, so she read me another one." Obviously, writing down all she said would be exhaustive, but paraphrasing captures what she said in the following manner: "Nina talked while she painted. She talked in sequence what she did last night, ending with her sharing that her mother read two books to her before she went to sleep."

Guideline	What to Consider
Rewrite your observations (WHAT).	• Once you've finished your observations, rewrite them so that not only you can understand what you've written but others can as well. Go back over your notes and rewrite what is needed, or expand on key words and phrases while they are fresh in your mind. The longer the time that passes between the initial observation and the rewriting, the more that will be forgotten. • A student wrote, "I found it helpful for me to put little reminders on my rough notes for things that really stick out. I also tried to write my good copy as fast as I could after the observation so that it was all fresh in my mind."
Use key words or descriptors.	• Rewriting your notes is the perfect time for considering descriptors. Descriptors act to strengthen the meaning of the action. A descriptor enhances the meaning of the original word used. There is a difference between changing a word from "walked" to "shuffled" and to actually interpreting the gist or essence of your observation. To illustrate this point, note the examples in Exhibit 3.3 and content in the rest of this chapter. • The key words or descriptors will not only assist in remembering what you saw and heard but also remind you how he ran or how she smiled. They can be seen as "interpreting" the observation, which, arguably, may be true. But more importantly, descriptors are clues when rewriting to remind the observer: "He ran quickly to retrieve the soccer ball". or "Her smile slowly grew larger as she watched the balloon rise higher."
Reflect, Interpret, and Respond.	• Reflect upon WHAT was seen and heard. • Consider and involve the perspectives of others (note that different methodologies may involve more participation than others). – Dialogue with the team to explore HOW this could happen and what considerations need to occur. – Involving others aids in examining WHAT theories might have been used by the children. Explore multiples lenses to understand what has been seen and heard. • HOW will the observation be used? Is it to inform curriculum? A new provocation or invitation? For contribution to a portfolio? A storyboard, documentation panel, or digital forum?

Source: Kristine Fenning

participatory mode

Observing simultaneously while engaged or interacting with children or within the environment.

direct quotations

When exact words have been used in another source and are supported with quotation marks to indicate the exact phrasing selected.

paraphrasing

To say the same thing but in other words; a restatement; to give meaning in another form.

The information in Exhibit 3.2 may seem overwhelming; however, experienced educators will say that it becomes easier with time, learning, experience, and collaboration from all team members. Exhibit 3.3 is an example of a learning story prepared by an experienced educator, supported by the voices and participation of Tomas and his family.

EXHIBIT 3.3	Learning Story: Tomas and his Doll

Tomas had brought his doll to the centre today, and eagerly runs toward his teachers in the morning with smiles while holding the doll above his head. Earlier that morning, Tomas's parents, Kate and Mojgan, had informed the centre of the arrival of their newly adopted daughter, Madalina. His educators listen to Tomas as he shouts, "That's my baby, MY Madalina." Tomas proudly carries his doll, Madalina, inside his zipped sweatshirt, walking over to peers smiling with raised eyebrows, and is observed several times in the morning pulling the baby out from

descriptors

A word or phrase that characterizes an idea or item; the adjectives used to rate the items of a rating scale continuum.

his sweatshirt and saying, "My baby came out." Tomas is determined to bring Madalina outside to experience the playground. He responds quickly to his educator's request to put Madalina in his cubby while he is going outside with the words, "Madalina come outside. I watch her in garden." His educator understands Tomas's purposeful intent and permits him to take Madalina outside. He saunters toward the garden, kneeling just before the wooden base. He positions the doll a first time only to have the doll fall over into the dirt. He brushes the dirt off the doll, this time bending the legs more toward a 90-degree angle to the torso of the doll, and slowly places it in front of him in the middle of the piece of wood. The doll seems to remain balanced on the wood—and Tomas quietly says, "Yeah!" He notices that the doll's hair is pulled up and tied atop its head to reveal the stitched hairline of the doll. He splits the hair on the forehead of the doll with both hands flat on the head, and he is overheard saying, "Dere, dere, you ok Madalina." He pauses. The strands begin to come out of the elastic in the doll's head and Tomas uses his pointer finger to push them back into the stitched holes.

Tomas's comments and new inquiry:
"Dere, that's what I said (pointing to the photo)."
"That's me!! My baby play outside. She felled down. Baby hair dirty. I fixed her. Baby all better now. I get new diaper and clothes to clean her."

Kate and Mojgan's response (Tomas's Moms):
"Tomas—it seems that you are so caring toward your new baby. She has the same name as your new sister! You are going to be a great big brother. We might need your help bathing her because you seemed to really help to clean your baby. We are very proud of you!"

Educator A's response:
"Thank you for giving us permission to document your time with your baby today. It was so interesting, Tomas, to watch you take care of your baby. I noticed that you were able to balance the baby on the wood so that you could help her better. You were so focused on helping the baby for most of the outdoor time. You knew what to do when the baby was dirty. You said you wanted to find more clothes for the baby—let's plan together to find more clothes and baby items to help your baby to play and have fun. Let's also put this story and the photo in your portfolio as you pointed out to us today."

Source: Kristine Fenning, Sally Wylie

Courtesy of University of Toronto Child Care on Charles Street

THE ROLE OF THE OBSERVER AND LANGUAGE USAGE

In the role of educator–observer, you will become reacquainted with language usage—verbs, adverbs, nouns, pronouns, and adjectives—and how language will become a powerful tool in your oral and written communication.

Remember our examination of the meaning of observation in Chapter 1? *Observation is functional, informative, and systematic. It is a foundational and cyclical process that involves watching, listening, and documenting children's learning and behaviour in a meaningful way, as well as many other elements about children and the environment. . . . Observation is also an action and process involving interpretation and reflection to understand and examine the behaviour of others, as well as what it is that we are seeing and hearing.*

Watching, listening, and documenting children's learning and behaviour in a meaningful way implies active participation in the cycle of observation, and infers that this information will be accessible, useful, and written in an inclusive, responsive manner and is intended to be shared with others. As part of a sensitive, caring team, educator–observers learn to recognize the importance of oral and written communication skills in the early childhood profession.

Adapting Your Communication Style in Early Childhood

Adapting your language with children will represent a shift in your communication style. Finding the words children understand challenges us to look beyond the words we normally use, to rethink concepts, and to reframe them in words children can relate to. This does not mean talking down to children or using baby talk: it means talking to children differently from the way you talk to your peers. For example, if you tell a toddler, "Bring that over here," you might get a blank stare. Why? Children need concrete descriptions. Because toddlers do not understand what "that" refers to or where "here" is, rephrasing the sentence using concrete descriptors will clearly convey what is expected: "Joey, bring me the ball." Another example to illustrate how understanding was achieved through rephrasing took place in a kindergarten setting. When asked if a young girl could draw a picture of a woman, she replied, "No."

When the same request was made, but with different words, "Can you draw a picture of your mommy?" the girl responded with a smile and began to draw immediately. Adapting language or rephrasing using concrete words or descriptors makes a big difference in the process of communication (written or verbal) with young children.

Instead of the casual conversations you engage in with peers, you have to think through not only what you are going to say to children but also how you will say it. Instead of saying, "Hey, you guys, stop throwing sand on the floor," you will need to use the children's names rather than slang and state your expectations positively: "Aisha and Maribeth, let's keep the sand in the sandbox. We can throw the beanbags and balls instead when we get outside." Adapting your language and monitoring your messages are a critical part of developing your communication skills in early childhood.

What does this adaptation of language in the learning environment have to do with observation? Being aware of language usage with young children, we communicate using key words that are descriptive yet concise. When we conduct observations, we also use key words to focus on what is important. Our adaptation of language influences the way we look for, listen to, and document information that is relevant. We begin to use meaningful words with children, and we write down these words when observing them.

Using Descriptive Language

Let's examine now the very simple building blocks of language: verbs, adverbs, nouns, and adjectives. Here is where we can begin to build strong images in our observation and pedagogical documentation, starting with ordinary words such as "walk" and "talk":

- alternative verbs for *walk*: *amble, stroll, saunter, clomp, stomp, march, strut, stride, toddle*
- alternative verbs for *talk*: *whisper, state, declare, speak, converse, utter, shout, murmur*

Each word creates a different mental image—think of the difference between "limping" and "marching." Verbs are action words. Sometimes we can get enough action out of a word so that we do not need any other words to get our meaning across. However, if we need to qualify a verb further, adverbs are very handy. Many adverbs in the English language end in "ly." Some examples are *hastily, happily,* and *brilliantly.* These words add meaning to the action, for example, "walked heavily" or "lightly" or "quickly." Adverbs make the action come alive to help others see what you have seen. For example:

- adverbs for walk: slowly, heavily, carefully, briskly
- adverbs for talk: slowly, sharply, haltingly, surely

Using imaginative and descriptive language gives us new words and the ability to further our understanding. Adjectives are words that qualify nouns. Nouns are words that name a person, place, object, or idea. Young children begin learning language word by word, and a baby's first word is usually a noun. Adjectives state the attributes or qualities of a noun—for example, *big, yellow, fuzzy.* Adjectives perform the same function with nouns that adverbs do with verbs. Adjectives clarify what we are talking about. For example, instead of just a chair, we could have a highchair, a small chair, a lounge chair, a rocking chair, or a folding chair. Instead of a puzzle, we could have a single-inset puzzle, a floor puzzle, or a multiple-inset puzzle.

A clear description of an item (noun and adjective) helps illustrate for the reader what the child sat on or played with. This object could have a direct influence on the child's behaviour. For example, if four-year-old Nadia takes a five-piece, single-inset puzzle off the shelf, sits down, and begins taking it apart, she will probably have no difficulty in putting it back together. But if she takes a thirty-five-piece, multiple-inset puzzle off the shelf, you will likely see a different set of behaviours. Defining the kind of puzzle or contextual information gives us clues and helps us understand Nadia's difficulty—or lack of difficulty—with the puzzle. These words serve to clarify for the reader a child's response to materials in the environment.

Let's experiment with some words and descriptors in Reflective Exercise 3.2. Remember that when documenting observations, it is important to describe what was seen and heard rather than what you "think" may have been seen and heard.

Original Words	Descriptive Words (Descriptors)
• poured water in bin	• slowly tipped the pitcher to dribble water into the bin
• sat in middle of teeter-totter	• edged their bottom back using their hands to balance their body in the middle of the teeter-totter
• put yellow chips on the yellow square	• glanced side to side to discriminate between colours as they sorted the yellow chips from the coloured chip pile into the yellow square
• spoke to peer in the sandbox	• whispered with a smile, "I built a castle" to Child A.

Let's pretend you have just observed this child playing and have just taken the photo below. Using the Internet, a dictionary, or resources available to you, prepare a sentence or two that describes what was seen and heard using descriptive words. Remember, however, that your descriptive words must be accurate, factual, and should not exaggerate or inaccurately represent what was actually occurring. Then share and discuss with those around you.

AnSyvanych/iStockphoto.com

As we will soon learn in the next few chapters, depending on the type of documentation chosen, the words used will reflect whether you are documenting while the observation is occurring or whether you have decided to document after the observation is finished. If an observer discovers that documenting while observing is difficult, then perhaps they might prepare the documentation following the observation. For others, they may document during the observation with shorthand or key words but then elaborate following the observation. The key words or descriptors will not only assist in remembering what you saw and heard but also remind you how the child ran or how they smiled. They can be seen as "interpreting" the observation, which, arguably, may be true. More importantly, descriptors are clues when rewriting to remind the observer: "Jagger ran quickly" or

"Hudson's smile grew slowly in size." Do not add descriptors just to make a lot of words—make the words count and be meaningful. Does exchanging words while rewriting change what was originally written? Adding descriptors to what you write is acceptable providing that the essence of the observation is not changed.

Do you see why using descriptive language is important in the process of documentation? The environment also influences the activity of young children. Children who have experience with loose parts and materials, for example, would have the opportunity to practise the appreciative inquiry approach, thinking about possibilities and ways in which they could construct and create based on their imagination and use of these pieces. Puzzles that are missing pieces, torn books, and broken toys also influence children's play and behaviour but in a very different way. In using descriptive words such as "torn" and "broken," clear images are conveyed, helping the reader understand the consequent behaviour of a child—for example, "He picked up the torn book and quickly placed it back on the shelf." Noting that the book was torn and that the child placed it quickly back on the shelf is an important observation. It speaks to the child as much as the environment. As Mark Twain once wrote, quoted in the article "People First Language" by Kathie Snow (2010), "The difference between the right word and the almost right word is the difference between lightning and the lightning bug" (p. 1).

People-First and Person-Centred Language: The Words We Use Matter

We build here on our learning from Chapter 2 with a focus on people-first and person-centred language. The words we use, the images we share and discuss, and how we communicate about and with others MATTER throughout the cycle of observation by supporting an ethical, responsive, and inclusive approach, and promoting an appreciation of every child and family as unique and competent in their own right. People-first language can be defined as "the philosophy and practice of referring to an individual first rather than referring to a disability and then the person (e.g., the disabled or autistic person) when writing and speaking in order to minimize bias or stereotypes" (Snow, 2005; West, Perner, Laz, Murdick, & Gartin, 2015, p. 17). Exhibit 3.4 offers some examples of this approach.

People-first language has been typically applied to individuals with special needs; however, if we apply this approach to different areas of diversity

EXHIBIT 3.4	People-First Language
Avoid Using Words Like . . .	**Using the People-First Language Approach**
Glenn is a fetal alcohol syndrome kid.	Glenn has been diagnosed with fetal alcohol spectrum disorder.
Jerry is an out-of-control problem child because he purposely hits others when he is mad.	When he feels frustrated, Jerry will use hitting to communicate. Jerry has yet to consistently use his words to communicate his anger.
Jaspreet is mentally challenged and has mental problems.	Jaspreet has bipolar disorder and requires some support to manage the changes in her moods.

(see Exhibit 2.7), we discover that it is equally as important to be appreciative of the strengths and qualities of all individuals including and beyond ability. Observers need to be cognizant of the words they choose to use to avoid stigmatization, oppression, categorization, and the negative influences upon the identity of others. The impact of words we use might not be immediately evident as in the case of gender for example. Gender Schema Theory and Developmental Intergroup Theory posit that gender categorization can occur as a result of a variety of influences within the social environments that surround children (including but not limited to educators, parents, families, peers). Applying this to the observation process, this can then impact pronoun usage in our documentation. Taking the time to consult with children and their families regarding people first language and their preferences for pronoun references are important considerations. Observers also need to be aware of all areas of bias, they need to avoid imposing their values upon others, and they need to observe and listen to understand the unique narratives of others. These considerations also pertain to our own calls to action as observers appreciating and working with Indigenous peoples. According to Article 15 from the *United Nations Declaration on the Rights of Indigenous Peoples* (United Nations, 2008), "Indigenous peoples have the right to the dignity and diversity of their cultures, traditions, histories and aspirations which shall be appropriately reflected in education and public information" (p. 7). We hold an important responsibility to foster relationships with all people, and to recognize that the words and terminology we use matter. For example, the University of British Columbia, in its document *Indigenous Peoples: Language Guidelines*, encourages people to look closely at how we communicate with others and to reflect meaningfully upon why terminology matters, as in Exhibit 3.5.

EXHIBIT 3.5	Why Terminology Matters

In the history of relationships between the Canadian institutions and Indigenous peoples, terminology has often been deployed in ways that have been damaging to communities. The terminology used in public discourse has rarely been that actually preferred by Indigenous people, who most often refer to themselves by the traditional name of their specific group. Using the best terminology in any given situation is not just a matter of being politically correct, but also of being respectful and accurate. The plural "peoples" can be used to recognize that more than one distinct group comprises the Aboriginal population of Canada. In some contexts, "Aboriginal people" may seem homogenizing, or seem to refer simply to a collection of individuals. In contrast, "Aboriginal peoples" (plural) indicates a broad group that includes a number of separate Aboriginal populations.

For the purposes of style, it is acceptable to use "Aboriginal people" when referring to separate Aboriginal populations, or in contexts in which the scope of reference is clearly aggregated, and then conversely to use "Aboriginal peoples" in contexts in which a recognition of multiple communities, or the diversity of communities, is helpful. The subject and context will determine which is more appropriate (e.g., news article vs. an official report). In any case, the key is to be consistent, or to have a clear logic in each choice. (pp. 5–6)

Source: The University of British Columbia. (2016). *Indigenous Peoples: Language Guidelines.* Retrieved from http://assets.brand.ubc.ca/downloads/ubc_indigenous_peoples_language_guide.pdf

To promote understanding of appropriate language and terminology that not only reconciles meaningful relationships with Indigenous peoples but also respects their communities, please reach out to the Elder(s) of your community.

Semantics and Pragmatics

Before children attend Grade 1, they have already acquired the grammar, semantics, and pragmatics of their first language. If children have been in child care, nursery school, or home care, educators have been their first teachers, along with parents/caregivers and other family members. Being in a caring, nurturing environment where children are included in conversations or are told stories promotes language development. Children learn that language is giving and receiving—a most social endeavour. Social interactions, particularly those between adult and child, are the most important influence on language development in young children.

Semantics is concerned with the meaning of words. Although words are learned, so too are other forms of communication that often accompany these words: tone of voice, facial expression, and body language. Conversations with people we know tend to be full of body language, sounds, intonations, facial expressions, and code words that have meaning within that social group.

To clarify the meaning of semantics, here is an example: the word "mummy." It is one of the first words a very young child learns and says. Yet look at the powerful meanings in that one word:

- "Mummy!" Translated: "I want the person who feeds me."
- "Mummy?" Translated: "I'm in my room. Where are you?"
- "Mummmyyyy!" Translated: "I miss you and I want to go home!"

That one word is so powerful, but by itself it is just a word. The tone, strength, and meaning of the word are what is important. Discovering the meaning behind the word is necessary in order for the observation to convey the appropriate message.

Social interactions give rise to the use of language in a social context—pragmatics. In social settings, the child learns how they will use language as a means of communicating socially with others. "Hi" and "Bye" are two of the earliest forms of social communication that families and educators model for young children. Waving bye-bye and saying the words convey a strong social message. Greeting people with a "Hi" uses language as a social conveyance. For children to achieve understanding and use of language, there must be a high degree of adult participation and understanding of the language-learning process.

semantics

The studying of the meaning of language; the relationship between words (symbols) and what they refer to, and how these meanings influence behaviour and attitudes.

pragmatics

Dealing with events sensibly and realistically in a way that is based on practical rather than theoretical considerations.

meddelveld/iStockphoto.com

Documenting Observations: A Unique Style of Writing

Writing what was seen and heard requires a unique style. It is not like writing an essay or a term paper, where a topic is chosen, researched, and then composed by the tried-and-true stages of successful essay writing. Many books, courses, and workshops exist for people who are interested in writing a successful essay, a good business report, a technical manual, a romance novel, or a short story. Yet few resources exist that guide educators/observers in developing the appropriate writing skills needed for documentation, summary reports, and forms typical

summary report

A report that presents the substance or general idea in brief form; summarizing; condensed; the compilation of the pertinent factors of an educator's notes that is shared with the child's family.

Chapter 3: Learning to Document the Activity of Children

of the early childhood field, such as those available online. This text, and particularly this chapter, attempts to address this need.

Lecture Note Taking versus Observational Writing

How is lecture-based note taking similar to writing rough notes during observations? In one way, the process is similar because while taking notes in class (electronic presentation/smartboard/whiteboard notes), you are simultaneously listening, watching, and writing.

Lecture notes represent important academic information. During lectures, students typically receive hints about headings, grouping of information, and examples to illustrate main points—guidance and cues that are helpful when assimilating new information. Lectures provide shortcuts that are used during note taking, such as how to highlight certain terms and organize important points within your notes. You are familiar with this process.

While observing young children, there are no such guides or examples (of what to write) or cues (how to write it). Learning how to observe and co-construct meaningful pedagogical documentation, as well as to decide what is relevant to document and what is not is a highly personal process with varying perspectives. Observations will indeed look different from observer to observer due to varying perspectives and methodologies chosen for documentation. To illustrate this point, refer to the four examples of different observations of the same child in Exhibit 3.6.

Rough Notes and Rewriting: Reproducing Thoughts

The process of writing rough notes of observations and then rewriting them is more than a skill; it is a process of discovering thoughts. Exhibit 3.7 offers an example of how a student used her rough notes to reproduce her thoughts into observations that are meaningful and easily read.

This student's rough notes demonstrate what they recorded during the observation. When the student had time to copy the rough notes and reflect on what they had written, the student was able to clarify the meaning. Repetition and practice allow us to become better at not only knowing what to write down but also using key words to express our thoughts. The more you practise, the more efficient you will become at conveying clearly what you have observed.

An educator wrote, "I scrambled trying to write down everything that was happening. However, when I wrote my good notes from my rough notes, I recalled more details when I was rewriting."

The first few observations engender uncertainty of what to look for and what to write. With guidance and opportunities to observe, write, and rewrite, students gain skills. As one student wrote, "I found writing from rough notes to good copy very rewarding. Observing made me become aware of looking at what a child does in their play at the centre. Observation is an eye opener!"

Writing with Confidence

Good writing takes time, reflection, the ability to analyze and critique, the willingness to redo what has already been done, and the courage to self-evaluate. It also requires willingness to make visible your observations to others in order

EXHIBIT 3.6 Comparison of Four Observations: Putting the Baby to Bed

Kristine Fenning

Educator, Observer 1: Riyanne had glanced between three blankets on the picnic table for use, and carefully selected the yellow blanket for her baby. She wandered over to an open area, squatted down, and placed the blanket down with both hands on the ground. She pushed the blanket outward to spread it out. Laying her baby in the middle of the blanket with both hands, she proceeded to pull each side of the blanket inward and over the baby's stomach "to put her to bed." She then carried it around in both arms for the rest of outdoor time.

Riyanne, Observer 2: "Dat's me. I'm the mommy. Duh baby was cold because she had a bath. Now baby won't cry because it's warm. I need to find her some clothes. I couldn't find any outside."

Educator, Observer 3: "Riyanne, you were observed today thinking about how best to wrap up your baby. This thinking was evident as you first placed your baby sideways on the blanket and tried to wrap her up. You discovered there wasn't enough blanket to put on the baby and so you opened the blanket up further and placed the baby in a different position on the blanket. You smiled as you realized that there was enough blanket to pull up from the bottom and from the sides with both hands as the baby became snuggled up in the blankets. You then shared your success with your peers who glanced at your baby in the blanket."

Parent, Observer 4 (at the end of day reflecting upon the photo and the observations in this exhibit. "Riyanne, you took care of the baby outside today just like a mommy would. The photo shows how careful you were in wrapping up the baby to keep her warm. You covered up all baby body parts as you mentioned you needed "to put her to bed".

EXHIBIT 3.7   Example of Rough Notes and the Good Copy

Child A
D.O.B: July 3, 2017
August 22, 2018
Age: 13 months
Time: 10:10 a.m. – 10:15 a.m.
- walked independently over to the tunnel
- first held the top in left hand and peeked inside
  to see Child B – they both giggled when
  seeing each other
- both hands on tunnel
- slid hands down, squatted and fell forward
- now on hands and knees, crawled around
  back of tunnel
- began banging with right hand, looked up
  and squealed with a smile at Child B

Reflections/Interpretations

Kristine Fenning

Kristine Fenning

Name: Child A
D.O.B: July 2, 2017
Time: 10:10 a.m.–10:15 a.m.

Date: August 22, 2018
Age: 13 months
Observer: Educator A

Child A walked independently one foot in front of the other from one side of the room over to the tunnel near the wall. As Child A neared the tunnel, he placed his left hand on the top and leaned forward to tilt his head downward to look inside the tunnel. There he discovered Child B; both giggled as they looked at one another. Child A remained standing with both hands on the top of the tunnel. Child A's hands began to slide down the side of the tunnel. As they slid down, he began to bend his knees into a squat and he fell forward. He is now on his hands and knees. He crawled forward and around the back of the tunnel. As he entered the tunnel, he began banging the bottom of the tunnel with an open hand. Within seconds he looked up and squealed with a smile as Child B began entering the tunnel.

Reflections/Interpretations:

- Child A is able to respond to others with squeals and smiles indicating happiness.
- Child A seems to enjoy being near peers as he initiated peeking at Child B (almost as if he was playing peekaboo).
- Child A seems to be able to move about the room independently through crawling and walking.

For provocation: This reflection utilizes a developmental lens. If we were to look at this same experience through other perspectives, how might this observation and reflection look different?

to invite them into the observational experience. For some observers, writing is not a comfortable or desirable exercise; in the case of a child writing the observations, they may have to use a methodology that involves less writing and more visual components. Writing may not engender confidence because of lack of familiarity or understanding, or a history of previous struggles.

Students in a continuing education night class suggested that a lack of confidence was a bigger issue than the actual writing process: "I found it to be very difficult. I wasn't sure of myself. I wasn't too certain about what was expected. This was my first assignment in many years, so I agonized whether I was doing it right or not." From a mature student point of view, "doing it right" or "not sure what is expected" are common concerns as they might feel they have forgotten how to study. Other students who have identified themselves as having diagnosed learning needs requiring writing supports will need to obtain consent (from those who own the devices and from those being observed) to access and use approved audio recording devices to assist them in capturing what is needed. Fortunately, pedagogical documentation affords observers the opportunity to use digital devices, apps, and other digital mediums to capture and/or assist their documentation. Colleges and universities will have learning centres, tutors, accessibility, and English as a second language supports where students can access free resources, workshops, and the help they need to build their skills and confidence in observational writing practices. There are many supports available—be sure to reach out for help!

Translation and Documentation

For student observers who have recently immigrated to Canada or students who are now returning to school after a period of adjustment in this country, another layer is added to the writing process: translation. Students will often write rough notes of their observations in their own language without the initial concerns with grammar, spelling, or semantics (or both languages, as in Exhibit 3.8). They will then translate them and rewrite them in English. Some may also develop a word bank to assist with ongoing word retrieval, while some students might engage in conversation with others to discuss what was seen and heard and to negotiate meaning where needed.

Students write in their own language while making rough notes of observations because they can think and write faster in their own language. They have said that even finding the right words to capture what they are observing is easier in their own language. This, however, takes extra time. Later, when rewriting into English for the good copy, a student has more time to reflect on the right translation, consult an English/other language dictionary, or use a thesaurus. Internet resources are available to assist with translation while students are online.

Self-Evaluation: Revisiting Reflective Practice

When several sessions of observations have been completed, take a look at the documentation you have written. This is a natural component of the cycle of observation. Ask yourself,

- Can I read what I have written?
- Did I use any shortcuts, abbreviations, and key words?
- Did my observations include the people who were involved with Child A?

EXHIBIT 3.8   Rough Notes: Spanish and English

Child's Initials: DR

Parece que sabe bien que con la pintura pueda hacer su marca en el papel.

It appears he knows that with the paint he can make markings on the paper

5.2 Holding and Using Tools
- making marks
- scribbling

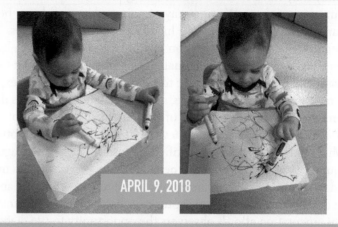

APRIL 9, 2018

APRIL 26, 2018

DR seems to enjoy scribbling or making marks on the paper. He uses his palmer grasp to hold the markers and make scribbles. He enjoyed dipping his fingers in paint and making a mark on the construction paper. He may be wondering how the different materials can make a mark on the paper. We wonder if he makes the cause and effect connection while using the different materials. He would benefit from activities that further engage him in scribbling or making a mark and making connections between the markings or scribblings and his actions.

DR appears to be active and engaged. He uses different materials and explores them through his body, mind and senses which is the goal of engagement, one of the four foundations of HDLH.

He is also displaying expression, one of the other four foundations of HDLH. As he uses the paint and the markers he is creatively communicating with us.

Reflection—It was great to see DR engaged and willing to explore the different materials. It gave us an opportunity to examine our practice and think of more ways in which we can provide more creative, and meaningful exploration for him and the other children in our care. We are currently working on trying to incorporate more sensory activities within all areas of the learning environment.

Child's Initials: DR

Le gusta tocar la pintura.

He likes to touch the paint

5.3 Tactile Exploration
- touching

APRIL 18, 2018

Courtesy of Jabin Carrasco

Take a moment to reflect upon this exhibit. As you begin to explore different types of methodologies in Chapters 4 and 5, what aspects of pedagogical documentation are evident in this exhibit? As pedagogical documentation can look different from observer to observer, what would you keep the same or what would you do differently?

- Did I include contextual information?
- In what ways have I involved the child?

You will see a difference between your earlier observations compared to the ones you have currently completed. What has changed? As a lifelong learner, your ability to evaluate your own progress is crucial to your learning. Develop a willingness and ability to evaluate your current skills against your former skills. Only you know where you started with your observation skills and how much you have learned and developed in this area. As can be seen in Exhibit 3.9, self-evaluation and critical reflection provide feedback that focuses on self-constructed skills and knowledge. Those questions play an important role in developing the habit of reflection. Becoming aware of what questions to ask and reflecting and acting upon the answers are part of the pedagogy of observing, listening, and establishing a practice of personal inquiry.

The ongoing learning begun in the process of observing young children and documenting their experiences leads both students and experienced educators to gain insight not only into the pedagogy of documentation but also into their personal and professional beliefs and values. For examples of self-reflective and personal inquiry checklists, consult with your course professor and see those available online.

EXHIBIT 3.9 Reflective Practice from Australia

Reflective practice is a form of ongoing learning that involves engaging with questions of philosophy, ethics and practice. Its intention is to gather information and gain insights that support, inform and enrich decision-making about children's learning. As professionals, early childhood educators examine what happens in their settings and reflect on what they might change.

Critical reflection involves closely examining all aspects of events and experiences from different perspectives. Educators often frame their reflective practice within a set of overarching questions, developing more specific questions for particular areas of enquiry.

Overarching questions to guide reflection include the following:

- What are my understandings of each child?
- What theories, philosophies and understandings shape and assist my work?
- Who is advantaged when I work in this way? Who is disadvantaged?
- What questions do I have about my work? What am I challenged by? What am I curious about? What am I confronted by?
- What aspects of my work are not helped by the theories and guidance that I usually draw on to make sense of what I do?
- Are there other theories or knowledge that could help me to understand better what I have observed or experienced? What are they? How might those theories and that knowledge affect my practice?

A lively culture of professional inquiry is established when early childhood educators and those with whom they work are all involved in an ongoing cycle of review through which current practices are examined, outcomes reviewed and new ideas generated. In such a climate, issues relating to curriculum quality, equity and children's wellbeing can be raised and debated.

Source: *Belonging, Being & Becoming—The Early Years Learning Framework for Australia.* (2009). Commonwealth of Australia.

EXAMINING THREE BASIC CONCEPTS IN THE OBSERVATION PROCESS: BEHAVIOUR, INTERNAL CONDITIONS, AND CHARACTERISTICS

In an earlier discussion, we explored the personal and professional observations of educators, stating how our experiences, culture, communication, and diversity all influence our perceptions of what we see and hear. In the context of examining how we observe and document, we've introduced three basic concepts that all observers should consider as they endeavour to portray the children in their care in an equitable fashion. The three concepts to examine are behaviour, internal conditions, and characteristics.

These concepts may look different depending on the methodology chosen. For example, learning stories (described in future chapters) are written in a unique style that includes subjective, interpretive words within the body of the text; there is no clear separation between the observations and the subjective feelings and ideas embedded in that story. Anecdotal records, however, require a style of writing that separates interpretive words from the body of the observation to further support objectivity in the observation portion. Chapters 4 and 5 will introduce these and many other methodologies.

Searching for a Definition of Behaviour

An operational definition of behaviour is helpful so that everyone understands what behaviour means. A clear definition should be easily read, said, understood, and remembered. Behaviour has been defined as "anything that can be seen, heard, counted, or measured" (Cartwright & Cartwright, 1984, p. 4). While this definition is over 30 years old, its accuracy is still intact. Here we see the influence of the behaviourists, with the words "measured" and "counted"; these words sound very scientific. In this text, our focus is not on promoting this image of educators/observers counting behaviours, although there is a use for precise measurement, as we will see in Chapter 5. We are interested, however, in coming to some kind of understanding of what behaviour is so that as this understanding broadens, we can see how important it

is to separate what we actually see or hear from our conjecture. To assist in this understanding, let us begin by imagining the following behaviours:

- stamping feet
- tilting head down
- swinging legs
- sucking thumb
- running in circles
- blinking eyes

Just a few words like these make it possible to visualize a child doing these things. Can you visualize a toddler running in circles like in the photo here?

Susan Sheldon/Dreamstime.com

Is it possible, then, to make a basic inference about how the child might be feeling or thinking if this was seen? What words would you use? What about a kindergarten child swinging his legs under a table? What does that say to you?

Young children express themselves with their bodies. They reflect their learning and feelings not only with their eyes and ears but also their bodies. When toddlers try things out, they practise over and over until they master whatever it is they are trying to do. Young children explore and discover their world using all their senses to understand concepts of over and under, round and soft, sticky and squishy. If we can observe a toddler's behaviour as he climbs in and out of a cardboard box, puffing and grunting, and tugging at a box, we can witness this intense learning that takes place. When the educator says to Jacob, "Can you climb out of the box?" and he does, Jacob's behaviour tells us that he has learned what the word "out" means, and he can follow that one-step direction. Five-year-olds love games and pretend play. They, too, learn with their whole being. As adults, we often forget how important the process of discovery truly is for children.

Since young children communicate much of what they think and feel non-verbally, it is even more important to be aware of this "silent talking" to best understand what each child is "saying." You cannot see sadness, but you can hear crying. You cannot see imagination, but you can hear a child in the dramatic centre telling another child to "make some dinner for the baby" or watch children race across the playground making horse noises such as "neigh, neigh, neigh".

On the basis of Cartwright and Cartwright's definition of behaviour (1984), sadness and imagination cannot be behaviours because we cannot see them. Behaviour is something that can be seen or heard. We can see a child crying. We can hear a child proclaim, "My dinosaur is sad today." We conclude from these behaviours that sadness and imagination exist as internal states.

Internal Conditions

Internal conditions are unobservable, internal states of being that are cognitive, emotional, or physiological. Some examples of emotional conditions are disappointment, pleasure, fear, happiness, distrust, apprehension, excitement, and frustration. Some cognitive conditions are thinking, problem solving, and remembering.

Physiology refers to the body's functioning, taking into consideration physical condition, for example, being tired, energetic, or achy. Physiological

inference

An opinion based on given data or assumptions; judgment.

Take a moment to reflect upon the words below to differentiate if they are either behaviours or internal conditions:

- ❑ jumps with two feet
- ❑ sad
- ❑ happy
- ❑ falls down

- ❑ frustrated
- ❑ hungry
- ❑ thinking
- ❑ snapping fingers

REFLECTIVE EXERCISE 3.3

Chapter 3: Learning to Document the Activity of Children

conditions refer to internal states that cannot be directly observed, such as a sore throat or a headache.

Five of these words are internal conditions—sad, happy, frustrated, hungry, thinking. Consider the word "frustrated": what would you need to see or hear in order to infer that a child is frustrated? If you describe the behaviour using such words as "yelled and threw the puzzle on the floor" or "sighed heavily" or "mumbled, 'I just can't do this puzzle. I'm so upset,'" you might conclude that the child seemed frustrated. Can you see or hear "said," "stumbles," and "painted"? Yes. What about "hungry"? That is a physiological condition because it is an internal state that is not observable. If you were hungry, how would other people know? You would probably tell someone, or you might point out the grumbling sounds coming from your stomach. How might an infant express hunger? Internal conditions will prompt the externalizing of behaviour in many ways such as a child asking for something to eat if they feel hungry, a child screaming out loud if they are in pain, or a child slamming a door if they are angry.

This is why observing young children is so important. Much of what we do as responsive educators and observers is not only to assist them in having their wants and needs supported but also to capture their thinking, interpret and co-reflect upon what they are "saying," and assist them in making sense of their world. The educators also need to clarify to other adults involved how they arrived at these conclusions. Responding to and communicating with an infant who appears upset involves many vital skills, including relaying that information to the parent or caregiver.

Characteristics

Characteristics are a little different in that they are repeated patterns of behaviour or sets of actions or traits that distinguish an individual from others. For observation purposes, the term "characteristics" will not refer to physical traits or characteristics, such as brown hair or blue eyes, but rather to behaviours specific to characteristics or traits of personality (some may also call them attitudes). Characteristics can also refer to a predisposition to behave in certain ways. What is a characteristic of a good friend of yours? Some examples (which often will reflect descriptive adjectives) of characteristics could be

- easygoing
- affectionate
- adventurous
- considerate

The above characteristics can be described as positive attributes of a person. There are many characteristics, however, that people may use to negatively describe someone such as "lazy," "rude," "unruly," and "bossy." As observers, we have a responsibility to ensure that we do not engage in descriptive language that places children in a negative light, but rather maintain an appreciative, positive, and strengths-based approach to describing characteristics about children.

The Three Concepts: How Are They the Same/Different?

Behaviours are different from characteristics and internal conditions. Behaviours can be seen or heard and, in some cases, measured or counted. Characteristics and internal conditions must be inferred. An inference is a logical conclusion based on given information or, in this case, on groupings of behaviour. In other words, you would have to observe the behaviour in order to make an inference. Inferences add personal judgment. An inference adds another dimension to the observation so that now your observations have created the possibility to ascribe a characteristic to a person or to surmise that some internal condition is occurring. For example, if a child is crying on the bus, we infer that "the child is upset" as an internal condition. On that same bus, we look around and form immediate impressions about others on the basis of their behaviour. We observe a man move over to make room for a pregnant woman on the bus and think, "He's a considerate person." We have learned to use our background knowledge and accommodate new information to make inferences. Let us see if we can analyze the three concepts discussed thus far in Reflective Exercise 3.4.

Indicate which of the following are behaviours, internal conditions, or characteristics:

- ❑ breaks toys
- ❑ nervous
- ❑ pushes wagon
- ❑ easygoing
- ❑ patient
- ❑ sore throat
- ❑ affectionate

REFLECTIVE EXERCISE 3.4

   "Breaks toys" and "pushes wagon" are behaviours as they can be seen. "Sore throat" is an internal condition because it cannot be seen. "Nervous" could be a condition (that is, how you are feeling, but no one is aware of it) or it could be a characteristic of someone: "She's a very nervous person." "Easygoing" and "affectionate" could be characteristics. "Patient" could be either a condition or a characteristic. Take a moment to reflect on the picture that follows here—what behaviours might be occurring in this particular moment? What about characteristics and internal conditions?

Characteristics and Labels

What is the difference between a characteristic and a label? Children learn to classify people, things, and events to bring meaning to their world. In the process of ordering and classifying things such as zoo animals, types of cars, or varieties of flowers, children further classify things into categories of "like" and "don't like." As adults, we continue this process. We affix personal values to them. Some people, things, and events are valued or are more important than others. When we value people or things, we ascribe positive value and describe

Wiarton Kids' Den/Sally Wylie

them in positive ways. When we ascribe negative values and describe in negative ways, we are labelling. Labelling is often used to describe someone in a demeaning manner. Great care must be taken to define the characteristics of a child in a positive manner and to avoid assigning negative labels. Check out the examples in Exhibit 3.10. Can you think of other examples?

When interpreting a young child's behaviour, be as thoughtful yet accurate as you can when discussing what was seen or heard in order to make reasonable interpretations about that behaviour. For example, imagine that Anthony is gazing out the window at the rain. You observe him tracing the drops of rain with his finger as they trickle down the window pane. What inference could you draw from this one observation? Is he sad, curious, daydreaming, or just waiting for his dad? When you reflect upon what Anthony may be feeling or thinking, or perhaps engage in dialogue about what he is feeling, you are being a considerate, responsive educator.

This entire process, certainly when engaging in the act of reflection, also causes us to revisit our conversation in Chapter 1 about observation, pedagogical documentation, and the appreciative inquiry process. It also prompts us to examine the importance of viewing children as able and confident learners, as well as how we can phrase our communication about children in a responsive and inclusive way. Children are children first; they deserve to be treated, and their behaviour discussed and documented, in a dignified and respectful way.

labelling

To attach a term or phrase to a person or thing that classifies or characterizes him, her, or it.

EXHIBIT 3.10 — Characteristics and Labels

There is a fine line between describing people in terms of their characteristics and negatively labelling them. Listed below are some words that have negative connotations. Other words are offered as alternatives. Can you think of others?

Label	Alternatives
• impulsive	• may act before they think
• aggressive	• assertive in speech or actions
• antisocial	• prefers doing things independently
• competitive	• committed to winning
• insecure	• yet to develop the confidence to . . .
• bossy	• directs others
• irritable	• feeling upset or bothered by something

Source: Kristine Fenning

Drawing inferences from one situation can often prompt a great deal of reflection. For example, let us assume you just walked into the ABC Early Learning Centre. As you enter the preschool room, you observe Milena screaming at the top of her lungs and hitting Sladjana over the head with a doll, and the educator running toward them. What would you infer from this? Suppose that after things settle down, you find out that Sladjana took Milena's favourite doll from her cubby, the doll she had just received as a birthday present. When you talk to the educator, she remarks that she has never seen Milena act that way before. Now what do you think? Do you still maintain the same impression of what you initially saw?

When examining the behaviour of children, we need to reflect upon many variables before we arrive at conclusions. Remember to not only capture the beauty of everyday moments but also to establish a systematic practice of observing children on a regular basis to capture their learning, their joys and interests, the things that seem to challenge them, and the ways they problem solve. Be sure to involve children, family, and other educators in the process, as well as be familiar with a wide range of appropriate observation methods. Ensure your documentation is meaningful, and be creative in making children's learning visible. Judiciously observe and document what you saw and heard in a way that is meaningful to share with others.

Variables Influencing Behaviour

There are a number of variables that may impact children's experiences and behaviour including but not limited to time, environment, and situations. All educators could tell you many stories of how time changes how children experience or perceive their day. Although young children may not understand time and are not aware of schedules in the strictest sense of time, they do experience what went before or what happens next, and children will tell you after snack, we go outside, or when we come in from outdoors, we eat lunch. Changes to the day will have an impact on the behaviour of some children and how they experience novel or unusual events.

Consider the behaviour of preschoolers starting junior kindergarten in September. Will their behaviour or their experiences of their day change by the following April? By then, they will know the routines, schedule, and expectations, and will have made new friends. Those children who cried for their parent probably won't be crying anymore. Many children who appeared shy initially will be chatting busily with their friends. Children display subtle and overt differences from one time frame to another—from morning to afternoon, or even hourly or daily! Consistent routines at certain times of the day help "set" children's internal clocks. The beginning of the week versus Friday afternoon also makes a difference in the behaviour of some children. Some children are just like adults in that some are "early birds," whereas others are "night owls." Ironically, time is one of the main variables of behaviour, yet it is a concept not totally understood by children. Identifying with children's experiences helps us understand better how time influences their lives.

Changes in the environment, adult expectations/provocations, or situational circumstances will elicit changes in the behaviour of young children, in how they act or react. For example, educators know that children often behave differently when taken out of a familiar early childhood setting. Children who find themselves in an unfamiliar situation may become shy when they are usually outgoing, while others may become more confident when they are usually shy. This is all the more reason to keep an open mind about the discoveries that unfold in any setting with young children. A change in circumstances at home or school may also prompt a change in how children respond, act, feel, or think. Sometimes when a child is unsure of something or is challenged by something developmentally, they may react in a different way.

Why mention these variables? Change creates change, and it is incumbent upon the responsive educator to be aware of all the children in the group in terms of what excites them, what interests them, and what seems to cause a child who is accustomed to acting in certain ways to suddenly change behaviours. These changes can signal anxiety, illness, excitement—a host of behaviours that flag the educator's attention and create an "aha moment," sparking curiosity in the educator and interest in what those changes may mean.

These variables and others remind us that behaviour varies at different times and in different settings or situations and will influence the accuracy and depth of your inferences. Recording patterns of behaviour gives us the information we need to understand and reflect upon the children's growth and progress, appropriate curriculum, teaching strategies, and the environment and allows us to talk professionally with the parents and caregivers of the children and other professionals. Being aware of the subtle or overt changes in the child's life is the responsibility of all educators.

THE DEVELOPMENT LENS: ONE PERSPECTIVE

Understanding how children learn within the context of child development is an important role of the educator. Here we discuss how understanding development is helpful to interpreting what is seen and heard; as we read further into Chapter 4, we will see how important it is to also look beyond traditional Westernized theories in order to explore the multitude of theories children use to explore their world around them. This allows observers to expand the strengths/needs lens to include other aspects of a child's being such as identity, spirituality, community, and so much more.

Child development is an important lens when interacting and collaborating with children, as well as when sharing information with parents. Using a variety of observational methodologies enables observers to appreciate and recognize the unique variations in development demonstrated by Rachel in the following example:

> Rachel, a 14-month-old infant, was a curious baby who enjoyed moving herself around the infant room to grasp at the toys available on the shelves and to seek comfort from the teachers. She began crawling at 10 months and began pulling to stand at 11 months. However, instead of moving from crawling to walking, Rachel would scoot her bum backwards and forwards by bending her knees and using her feet to propel herself in the direction where she needed to go. When prompted by her teachers and parents to walk, Rachel would cry and sit down on the floor. This happened repeatedly until one day at home time, her mother

shared her concerns with the educators about Rachel's resistance to walking. While in discussion, the team explored how all children develop and grow at different rates and noted that Rachel had found "her" way to move around and assert her independence. Hinging on Rachel's interests, together her parents and room teachers tried a new approach. Instead of having all the materials she enjoyed at a level requiring her to simply sit on the floor, they decided to place her favourite musical materials on the wall in front of mirrors, which required her to pull to stand and to practise her balancing. For Rachel, the new discovery of her favourite toys on the wall became a pleasurable time for her while standing, and within four weeks' time, Rachel was standing independently and beginning to take steps!

Infant educators strive to create a nurturing environment for them based on their observations of what the infants enjoy, how they thrive, and generally how they are developing. Reflecting upon their observations of each child in the group encourages educators to find new ways to facilitate relationships with families, handle infant interactions and attachment, expand curriculum possibilities, and so much more.

Principles of Development

The principles of development are beliefs about how children grow and develop. "To include everyone, early childhood settings must encourage healthy dialogue about the principles and shared beliefs that relate to inclusion, diversity, and equity" (Ontario Ministry of Children and Youth Services, Best Start Expert Panel on Early Learning, 2007, p. 11). Some principles have been founded on decades of child studies and/or have resulted from a base of research, observation, and discourse. One such example is Early Learning for Every Child Today: A Framework for Ontario Early Childhood Settings (ELECT; Ontario Ministry of Children and Youth Services, Best Start Expert Panel on Early Learning, 2007). This framework, introduced in 2007, was intended to further promote quality early childhood pedagogy in Ontario. Now also referred to as the Ontario Early Learning Framework, ELECT includes a continuum of development for children from birth to age eight. Seven years later, How Does Learning Happen? Ontario's Pedagogy for the Early Years was introduced, building on the learning that took place since the publication of ELECT, and capturing the critical importance of relationships and the foundations of Belonging, Engagement, Expression, and Well-Being. The How Does Learning Happen? document builds on and works collaboratively with the principles of ELECT. Those principles originating from the ELECT framework are as follows:

1. Early child development sets the foundation for lifelong learning, behaviour, and health.
2. Partnerships with families and communities strengthen the ability of early childhood settings to meet the needs of young children.
3. Demonstration of respect for diversity, equity, and inclusion are prerequisites for honouring children's rights, optimal development, and learning.
4. A planned curriculum supports early learning.
5. Play is a means to early learning that capitalizes on children's natural curiosity and exuberance.

Wiarton Kid's Den/Sally Wylie

6. Knowledgeable and responsive early childhood professionals are essential to early childhood settings. (Ontario Ministry of Education, 2014, p. 10)

Organizations will often highlight their guiding principles, stating how these principles guide their practices as an organization.

Governments may also illustrate the principles that guide the curriculum for all areas of the country, such as those developed by the Ministry of Education in New Zealand. Te Whāriki is the New Zealand Ministry of Education's framework for early learning. The curriculum policy statement emphasizes the learning partnerships between parents, children, and teachers, and posits holistic development as one of their guiding principles:

- The curriculum should reflect the holistic development of children.
- The empowerment of the child should be a key factor (Maori principle).
- Family and community links should be strengthened.
- Children learn through responsive and reciprocal relationships. (New Zealand Ministry of Education, 1996)

REFLECTIVE EXERCISE 3.5

When examining the principles of New Zealand's framework and the principles from Ontario, what becomes apparent is their similarities, but also their differences. What similarities would you expect to find? What might some of their differences be? What other inquiries might you make about these two documents as they pertain to development?

domains

A sphere of activity or function; psychology; area (for example, cognitive and gross motor are areas of development).

pincer grasp

A grasp whereby small objects are picked up using the thumb and forefinger.

palmar grasp

A grasp whereby the tool or utensil lies across the palm of the hand with fingers curled around it, and the arm, rather than the wrist, moves the tool.

dexterity

Skilled physical movement or ease of use, typically relating to the hands.

Domains of Child Development

Areas of development represent groupings or domains of similar, related behaviours, skills, growth, or attitudes that typically occur in a predictable pattern. For example, the fine motor developmental area includes such skills as pincer grasp, palmar grasp, dexterity, and coordination of fingers. How these groupings are determined and how and why they are organized depends on a variety of factors, and the discussion of those variations goes well beyond the scope of this text.

The reasons for a particular terminology are embedded in the philosophy or practices of that philosophy, and these will also vary from country to country. Be prepared for these distinctions as you progress with your academic courses. As a professional educator, you will be expected to be aware of the jargon and terminology associated with your professional field of study.

When reflecting on your documentation, the areas of child development can be a guide or framework to interpret or give meaning to what you have just observed. For example, if you observed three-year-old Gulad in the construction and block centre, you would want to document what you observed in some meaningful way (see Exhibit 3.11). Chapters 4 through 6 will introduce a myriad of observational and pedagogical documentation possibilities to capture the learning and thinking of children. In some instances, such as when wanting to draw some inferences about a child's abilities in one area of development,

EXHIBIT 3.11   A Snapshot of Gulad's Development

Gross Motor

- jumps with two feet over a two-foot-high tower
- squats in front of the shelf while reaching to lift large block off the shelf

Cognitive

- builds a "garage and racing speed track" and pretends he is a race car driver
- theorizes about speed and how to angle the blocks to go faster

Fine Motor

- steadies large blocks with two fingers on one hand to balance the tower
- draws and cuts out one large green circle and one large red circle for stop lights

Socio-emotional

- takes turns with peers while building a tower
- seeks out peers for help

Speech and Language

- initiates conversations with peers: "hey wanna build with me?"
- makes various car sounds such as "vroom, beep beep"

educators may choose to construct a profile or portfolio which collates developmental information from various observations and pedagogical documentation to discern the kinds of skills and knowledge a child possesses such as in Exhibit 3.11.

Rates of Development

Children not only go through phases of what they like to do, but they also develop according to their own rate of development. For example, one toddler in a group may be pointing at things and imitating sounds with a vocabulary of only 20 words, and yet another toddler in the same group may be labelling objects and using abbreviated sentences and have a vocabulary of over 50 words. This variance in behaviours can be attributed to a wide variety of factors, such as experience, temperament, expectations of family and culture, and environment.

Norms and Developmental Guidelines

The Ages and Stages maturational approach to child development was popularized by Arnold Gesell who believed that all children mature through certain sequential developmental ages and stages; yet he was also concerned that people would see norms or age expectations as necessary milestones rather than guidelines. This caveat is instructive even today as parents often want to know if their child is progressing on target.

Using any developmental or sequential approach or guidelines can be helpful in explaining behaviour, but should be a guide rather than a prescription. All children develop at their own rate and learn about the world through a variety of ways including but not limited to their unique family, friends, culture, and child-care environment. Observing children is part of appreciative inquiry, asking questions such as, "What are the expectations of the parents and their culture?

guide

To direct the way with the implication being that those following will benefit.

caveat

A warning or specification of conditions that must be considered before taking action.

What patterns do families value in their children? What traits are encouraged or discouraged?" Whose perspective is revealed when observing and making assumptions about a child's development? Pedagogical documentation encourages all perspectives to be included and promotes a holistic understanding of children's thinking, as well as the consideration of multiple ways of making learning visible.

Understanding development and what it is we see children doing takes time, practice, and frequent engagement in appreciative inquiry. Then we can make sense of what it is we are seeing, plan how we might support children in their next stages of development, and think about what we might provide within our environment to stimulate development in a particular area.

Where might pedagogical documentation fit, then, in our journey to understanding development? Pedagogical documentation, as explained in Chapter 1, is about documenting with the holistic image of the child rather than focusing on specific domains. Yet, understanding developmental areas and how they inform our understanding of a child's growth and development is important, especially when just beginning your career in early childhood. "Pedagogical documentation invites us to be curious and to wonder with others about the meaning of events to children. We become co-learners together; focusing on children's expanding understanding of the world as we interpret that understanding with others" (Wein, 2013, p. 2).

DEVELOPMENT AND CONTEXT IN DOCUMENTATION: EXTENDING BEYOND WESTERNIZED THEORIES

Human beings are naturally curious, and are driven to use unplanned or purposeful theories or questions in their everyday lives to explore their "wonderings," to make decisions, and to understand the environment and world that they live in. They will theorize about a variety of things throughout their day. For example, an educator may theorize why young infants fear strangers or how children come to possess complex knowledge around certain subject matters. Children may wonder why germs are invisible, why their stomachs grumble when they are hungry, or why thunderstorms make so much noise. Our world is full of wonders; theories will guide us to new discoveries! What do you theorize and wonder about?

For many years, many educators integrated only developmental theory (from theorists such as Vygotsky, Erikson, and Freud, for example) into their interpretations and understanding of what it was they were seeing and hearing from children in order to gain understanding of how they learned as well as their strengths and needs. Running records and anecdotal observations are two solid examples of observational methodologies from Chapter 4 that utilize the developmental approach to understand strengths and needs, as well as, for example, sequence, rates, stages, and patterns of development. These methodologies and theorists are still valid and useful in professional practice, and, when paired with pedagogical documentation, enable and equip observers with the skills and tools with which to query and understand further. Pedagogical documentation, however, moves us beyond solely developmental theory and provokes us to expand beyond Westernized developmental theories to understand how children think and learn and to ensure the acknowledgment of all voices when making learning visible. Exhibit 3.12 outlines this point.

EXHIBIT 3.12   Beyond Developmental Theory

As we all know, one event may be viewed differently. For example, an observation of two children playing in the sandpit can be framed through different theories. We could use maturational theory, seeing the children developing in ages and stages in their ability to manipulate the sand and the equipment. Or we could see a social event, and frame the play through socio-cultural theory, explaining their conversation and play as socially constructed. We could also see it from post humanist theory, where the sand and equipment are active agents upon the children. Or we could see gender theory in action as the children delegate roles in the play according to gender, "you be the mummy". . . . It's also important to note that at any one time multiple theories are in action, and so the above scenario might be written with all theories identified. (Fleet, Honig, Robertson, Semann, & Shepherd, 2001, p. 20)

Source: Fleet, A., et al. (2011). *What's Pedagogy Anyway? Using Pedagogical Documentation to Engage with the Early Years Learning Framework.* Children's Services Central. Marrickville: New South Wales.

INTERPRETING OBSERVATIONS AS PART OF THE WRITING PROCESS

What Are Interpretations?

Interpretations are our subjective responses to what we have observed. In our daily lives, we are inundated with information. We constantly make observations of people and events around us and spontaneously assign a value to these observations. We have all developed strategies to navigate our way through our busy lives based on our observations. We have become experts at making spontaneous judgments about people, places, or things as we observe them.

Whether we realize it at the time or not, and whether we like it or not, we respond to our environment with a personal judgment: like/dislike, trust/distrust, accept/reject. We may accommodate new information or reorganize it to align with other experiences. This process happens spontaneously and quickly. We have learned to form quick impressions and make hasty interpretations of events or people, partly to compensate for the sheer volume of information in our environment. In our personal lives, we order and classify many experiences, events, and people based on values that are uniquely ours: good or bad, important or trivial. While we filter the daily mass of information, we build our own eclectic views, keeping/discarding information and incorporating new experiences into our existing beliefs. No wonder our initial observations of children will include words or phrases that refer to our thoughts or feelings.

Interpretations are reflections upon what was seen and heard. The very nature of reflection implies a pause for thought, whether that reflection happens at the time documentation is being entered on a tablet or later, after the observation has been written. Interpretations, like reflection, suggest that these thoughts are more than a quick, judgmental response, but rather a pause to consider what something means, its relevance, or its relationship to something else.

interpretations

Subjective responses to what is observed; personal or professional judgments or beliefs.

accommodate

To bring into agreement, for example, adapt new information to previous knowledge.

Interpretations also have their own unique style of expression. Words such as "seems," "perhaps," "as if," and "appears" are used to indicate that interpretations are speculative and subject to personal bias. These and similar words convey the tentative nature of interpretations. They are not the truth—they represent only our best efforts to explain what is meaningful about what was seen and heard within the observation.

As educators of young children, we should pause and reflect, asking the question, "How will my views affect others?" We need to communicate professionally with colleagues and families or caregivers to share our perspectives, not dictate them. This means accommodating the viewpoints of others, including the children: discovering what they find relevant, and why. What aspects of the observations were meaningful to families? How did the children interpret and reflect upon their learning? Including the child(ren), other educators, and families is about inclusive communication and developing responsive relationships.

How we portray a child in writing is an immensely important professional responsibility. This applies not only to the child but also to their families, the context of the observations, and the early childhood environment, which includes the staff, policies, and procedures of that setting. Our perception is tightly woven into the practice of pedagogical documentation.

Where perceptions and professional practices converge is in the interpretations or reflections of what is observed, and this is especially true in the documentation. That is why we have included in this chapter conversation about these concepts:

- sharing responsibility for observing and documenting
- language usage including person-first language
- development, theories, and context
- the writing process
- the differences between behaviour, internal conditions, and characteristics
- forms of bias in observation

These and other concepts do influence interpretations. When you read about "interpretations" in Chapters 4 and 5, you will already have an understanding of what interpretations mean, and also what has gone into that understanding, including bias, internal conditions, characteristics, behaviour, language usage, ethics, and professional standards.

Among many other characteristics, we bring to this reflection our values, images, bias, knowledge, and perceptions. Writing interpretations can be even more challenging than writing observations; with interpretations there is also a process to follow. As observers, it is important to

- analyze the observations;
- interpret what the child did or said, considering multiple lenses with which to understand what has been seen and heard (including but not limited to socio-cultural theory, ecological theory, child psychology, child development, and the child within the context of her environment);
- frame your inferences using inclusive language and a person-first, positive, and professional approach;
- reflect upon what has been documented and what your interpretations are inferring;
- share your observations and interpretations with an appreciative inquiry approach, inviting others to wonder and interpret what has been observed,

adding the perspectives of children, parents or guardians, and other educators; and

* remain open-minded to other possible interpretations

Practice in observing and documenting the thinking of young children will change not only how we see things but also how we express what we've seen. For example, a novice observer might say, "Sarah was so smart because she placed all five shapes into the shape sorter by herself." A more experienced observer may say in a short narrative, "Independently, Sarah carefully problem solved for 10 minutes turning, twisting, and repositioning the square, rectangle, circle, oval, and octagon shapes into the shape sorter. She demonstrated her theorizing of size and shape in order to rotate and flip each piece using both hands until she found the correct hole for each shape to fit in." Do you see the difference between the two statements?

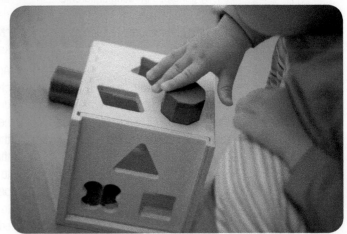

When observing and documenting children's behaviour, you'll need to accommodate new habits of observation that invite change in your professional practice. For example, you will learn to observe first and then interpret. You'll begin to separate those two processes. Separating what we see from how we think or feel about the person or event is exactly the opposite process of what we have spent a lifetime learning to do. For additional practice with interpretations, be sure to visit NelsonStudy.

Variations within Interpretations

Interpretations for some methods, such as anecdotals, participation charts, and running records, are meant to be in third person; they are not intended to reflect first-person narrative, as in the case of learning stories. Familiarize yourself with the various methods and take time to understand the role of interpretations in each observational approach. The cycle of observation reminds us of the importance of reflection as an integral part of the interpretation process. It also reminds us of the importance of ethics; therefore, let's turn our attention now to the types of bias that can influence our observations and interpretations.

FORMS OF BIAS IN OUR OBSERVATIONS AND INTERPRETATIONS

Every decision we make within the cycle of observation, such as whom or what to observe, is a personal choice and is, therefore, subjective. As we've discovered in Chapter 2, ensuring the presence of ethics in our observations and all aspects of the observation and pedagogical documentation process is difficult but critically essential. To further maintain integrity in our professional practice, it is important to reflect upon different types of observational bias so that strategies can be put into place to minimize their influence. Exhibit 3.13 examines each type and provides an example for understanding and application.

EXHIBIT 3.13　　Types of Observational Bias

	What It Is	Example
Leniency Bias	• Common • Overly generous in rating children's actions and behaviours • Child may be favoured or seen as the "teacher's pet."	• An educator rates a child in the achieved column for building a stack of 10 blocks. When asked for their evidence of this occurring, the response of the educator was, "Kaden is so cute and smart—I didn't see it but I just know she could do it."
Severity Bias	• Common • Negative bias toward the child (e.g., child is labelled as a trouble maker for their behaviour). There is no obvious reason, yet the bias exists.	• An educator learns from another educator that the new child in the room had numerous conflicts with other children in the toddler room. Now in the preschool room, the new educator sees an isolated moment of the same child throwing a toy across the room. The educator concludes that the child is a "problem child" without taking the time to observe and understand what may have been happening in the moment. The educator observation seems to be negatively influenced by information from another educator.
Central Tendency Error	• Associated with new educators—may be due to lack of experience or lack of knowledge of development theories, among other reasons • Inability to express and understand what is seen and heard • All children evaluated/observed in the same way and uniqueness of each child is not noted	• A child with leg braces has not been credited for the "ability to run and change directions without stopping." The child with the leg braces will run and pivot on one foot in order to change direction. This child's unique approach to this skill should have been noted and credited.
Expectancy or Logical Error	• Lacks systematic observation of all areas of a developmental domain to understand a child's skills • Assumptions or expectations about two seemingly related behaviours not based on direct observation	• Child uses their feet to pedal and propel a bike forward—the assumed conclusion is that because the child was able to do this, they must then have age-appropriate gross motor skills. The error is that not all aspects of the gross motor domain have been observed to draw this conclusion.
Observational Drift	• Common error in the observation process—differences in defining what to observe • May include inconsistencies in the type of observational method used to collect information on the target behaviour • Lacks inter-rater reliability (the extent to which two or more people rating the same behaviour will yield the same results).	• Educators are asked to observe and document "children sharing" in the room. Each educator forms their own idea of what it is they are observing. One educator notes in the assessment tool only the sharing of ideas between children and does not identify achievement of that skill, while another educator notes only the children sharing materials and grants achievement of that skill on the assessment scale. The educators did not discuss prior to observing the examples of sharing they were going to document that would provide evidence of "children sharing," and each documented according to their own perspective. They "drifted" with their own interpretations of what sharing is.

Bias or preconceived ideas can lead to erroneous assumptions about a child. Bias can lead to a focus on the child being the problem rather than a focus on discovery, which includes the educators, environment, or other factors. If the child has already been identified as "a problem," then the likelihood of that perception remaining is quite high. One of the perceptual errors of human nature is to see what we believe rather than believe what we see. Being proactive, rather than reactive, in observing children and their environment expands the early childhood educator's attention to all behaviours, not just those that are problematic. Keep this in mind.

Another form of bias is called cultural bias. It occurs when people of one culture make assumptions about another culture. These assumptions could pertain to beliefs, values, and practices. People who demonstrate this type of bias interpret and judge events and circumstances in terms particular to their own culture. People with a cultural bias see through the narrow lens of only their culture. In early childhood settings, becoming acquainted with children and families from many different cultures helps us all better understand one another, so the lens is widened to embrace more clearly the visions of many. An example of efforts to combat cultural bias and cultivate a culturally responsive classroom is found in the article "Culturally Responsive Classrooms: Affirming Culturally Different Gifted Students" (Ford, 2010). This article is based on experience in the United States, but it raises questions such as, "Are teachers eager and enthusiastic about working with students who are different from them culturally?" and discusses culturally responsive teaching and how to create a culturally responsive learning environment.

In her book *Diversity in Early Care and Education: Honoring Differences*, Janet Gonzalez-Mena (2008) states,

> You can't remove from your cultural framework the ways you relate to children and guide their behavior, plan a curriculum, set up the environment, handle caregiving routines, and carry out parent education. Your behaviors are determined by what you consider normal, which can be influenced by your race, ability, social status, income, sexual orientation, religion, age, and/or the messages you've been given about yourself in regard to these aspects of your background and identity. (p. 14)

Becoming aware of personal bias and judgmental errors is an important step in identifying and dealing with attitudes that influence the children and other adults with whom you work. This process is essential if we are to become educators who demonstrate sensitivity and inclusivity, engage in appreciative inquiry, and show a fair and professional approach in all aspects of our relationships with children, their families, and the community.

cultural bias

The action of interpreting what one sees by the values, beliefs, and principles attributed to one's own culture.

culturally responsive

The act of being respectful toward others and using and incorporating knowledge of another's culture, beliefs, values, and approaches to learning to be both response and inclusive.

CHAPTER REFLECTIONS

1. Shared responsibility and participation in the cycle of observation requires consultation with all participants to discuss the meaning of observation and pedagogical documentation. Discussion regarding access, materials and resources needed, types of methodologies, as well as how the information might be used are necessary considerations.

2. There are a number of steps to consider as non-registered preservice educator observers in the community to protect the vulnerability of children and families, to support children's participatory rights, and to adhere to setting and profession expectations considering observation and pedagogical documentation. It is also important to know which approach to observing will be used (spectator or participant) as well as which methodologies will be used. Considering the WHY, WHEN, WHERE, WHO, WHAT, and HOW questions will allow for thorough exploration of responsibilities when observing, documenting, reflecting and interpreting, and responding.

3. Understanding the importance of written communication skills in the documentation process is part of being a responsive, ethical, and inclusive educator observer. The descriptive language we use influences and clarifies how others see and understand an observation, it provides context, and it should be factual when making learning visible (rather than what we think is occurring). Words influence how children are seen and heard, and influence how we refer to children in our written and oral communications. Understanding that a child is a child first before their special need is important in appreciating the uniqueness of every individual. Rewriting observations, self-evaluation and reflection, as well as ongoing practice helps observers to increase confidence and meaningful observational pedagogy. English as a Second Language observers might consider writing in their own language first and translating as a second step. Exploring strategies to engage children to document is also necessary.

4. Behaviours can be seen and heard, and are necessary for the observer to draw inferences and conclusions regarding characteristics and internal conditions. Traditional Westernized developmental theories still hold value to the observation process; however, pedagogical documentation provokes observers to also consider other theories beyond a strengths/needs developmental approach to explore and make visible in a holistic way how children think and learn.

5. Interpretations are reflections upon what is seen and heard, they can be prepared by all members of the learning community, and their structure may vary from methodology to methodology. Interpretations are more complex in that they require a particular process to follow in order to reduce bias.

6. Bias influences how and what we document. Being aware of the various forms of observational biases enables observers to promote fairness and professionalism in their documentation, avoiding misconceptions and assumptions being formed about children.

MEANINGFUL OBSERVATION AND AUTHENTIC PEDAGOGICAL DOCUMENTATION

Part 2 clearly guides observers in their examination of pedagogical documentation methodologies intended to capture the spontaneity of children's wonderings and actions as well as those methodologies that may have a specific purpose. The methods found in these two chapters are inclusive; they can be used with all children. Each method discussed has application to the appreciative inquiry process and the cycle of observation introduced in earlier chapters, giving breadth to the understanding of pedagogical documentation. Any documentation, with the intent to be meaningful, requires ongoing reflection on, inquiry into, and responses to what we are seeing and hearing. Engagement with educators, parents, and children is part of this process.

The purpose of Part 2 is also to provide a variety of pedagogically sound observational tools from which to choose, considering which one would be most appropriate for a philosophy, a set of practices, a population, or an intent. Exhibits within Chapters 4 and 5 include the innovative work of educators and children that exemplify the notion that through observation, observers can co-construct new knowledge and understanding. This can be achieved through the use of a multitude of hard copy or technology-assisted documentation methods such as videos, audio, learning stories shared through social media (e.g., Twitter and Instagram), or documentation panels profiled at parent nights or through online classroom blogs, for example. Chapter 4 methodologies would be used for recording unanticipated behaviours, wonderings, curiosities, and questions so as to discover something new or uncover something unknown. Other methods in Chapter 5 such as checklists, ABC analysis, and behaviour tallying and charting assist the observer in discovering or targeting specific skills, knowledge, experiences, or events.

All methods in each chapter require us, the observers, to pause, reflect, and question the purpose of our observation. Like in previous chapters, when we ask ourselves a number of questions such as why we want to observe, what we want to observe, as well as when and where we want to observe, we are more likely to be led down a path of meaningful observation and documentation.

In Part 3 of the text, discussion of the application and compilation of documentation will include topics such as portfolio development, development of curriculum through documentation, and observer as pedagogical leader. This Part 3 section will build on knowledge of the methods presented in Chapters 4 and 5.

Rob Hainer/Shutterstock.com

CHAPTER 4

OBSERVING AND DOCUMENTING SPONTANEOUS THINKING AND BEHAVIOURS

Paired observations were not uncommon for the educators of six-year-old boys and cousins, Sebastian and Rocco, since they were inseparable. Their parents had provided permission for their names to be used in each other's portfolio. One Monday afternoon, Sebastian and Rocco raced to the block centre at their before-and-after-school program as soon as they walked in the door, running fast past the educator who had just welcomed them in. Sebastian had just gone with his family to see Old Fort Henry on the weekend and was talking quickly the minute he arrived at the classroom. As he ran past the educator who was calling his name for attendance, he raised his voice and shouted, "I want to build a cannon just like the one I saw at Fort Henry. I can't talk right now, I gotta get the blocks fast! Rocco, you comin'?" Rocco nodded his head and quietly ran after Sebastian. As Sebastian ran, he jumped in mid-air with both feet and landed with his whole body lying on his side on the floor, both feet stretched out touching the block shelf. "Phew, I'm safe," he said in a quiet tone to Rocco, who came to sit beside him. Rocco sat with his bottom on his heels and bent his back and head forward as he crouched down behind Sebastian. "That's how I do it in baseball so they don't put me out," Sebastian whispered to Rocco. Rocco remained silent, just looking at Sebastian. Rocco reached up to the highest shelf to pull out the bin of Tinkertoy blocks. He picked up a tube and a circular block, one in each hand, and put them together, repeating the same action until he had a metre-stick length of tubes and blocks all put together. "There, mine's ready," said Rocco to Sebastian, who was lying beside Rocco and facing him. Rocco pointed to his creation, which he had placed on the floor between them. "That's not gonna work," replied Sebastian, who had sat up to begin creating a triangle of blocks on his own. "Here, it's gotta be put on this thing so that it can go over the wall to reach the battleships." Sebastian picked up Rocco's creation, pulled off several block lengths, and then attached it to his triangle of blocks. "There, now you watch for the enemy while I get some blocks to build our fort," whispered Sebastian to Rocco as they both peered through the rectangular hollow block, pointing their creation out toward the room. Rocco nodded his head up and down and watched Sebastian as he rolled over to the shelf to begin construction of their fort.

Observational methods that capture unexpected, spontaneous imaginative play such as that of Sebastian and Rocco are like fishnets cast out to sea—you never know what you may catch. This open method of documenting spontaneous behaviour is flexible and unstructured. It suits the catch of the day: unanticipated behaviours, everyday moments, and the spontaneity of children's wonderings.

open method

Records or methods used for unanticipated behaviours and thinking.

Unanticipated behaviour means unexpected, unpredictable, or unknown moments of the day and children's natural behaviour and curiosity. Part of the excitement of unanticipated events or behaviour is the element of discovery and inquiry, and part of the excitement of discovery and inquiry is doing something new, uncovering something unknown, or having to respond unexpectedly. It also means being open to learning possibilities and listening to children. Developing new relationships and perspectives with how we know, view, and document children opens the door to creating meaning from what we observe. Being open to the possibilities of what you may see and hear, being ready with the appropriate methods in which to record those times of discovery, and engaging in shared reflection with families, children, and other educators are key strategies to becoming a responsive observer.

Educators will tell you that unanticipated behaviour in the classroom is a daily occurrence. Children, by their very nature, are spontaneous, and their behaviours and responses are unpredictable. The uniqueness of each child will be reflected in the observations and, ultimately, the documentation created and the decisions made. As Turner and Wilson (2010) describe,

Documentation is not just a technical tool, but an attitude towards teaching and learning. Gianni Rodari (1996) urges us to consider that everyday things hide secrets for those who know how to see and hear them. In this sense, documentation is an essential tool for listening, observing, and evaluating the nature of our experience. We need to be clear about this mental habit, this cultural attitude, rather than simply focus on the technical or professional practice of documentation. (p. 6)

Assuming this attitude and making the choice to be a reflective and responsive observer requires understanding of all observational methods and pedagogical documentation. This chapter is the first of two chapters that will describe various observational methods that are used to document the experiences and learning of young children. In this chapter, the featured types of records are:

- anecdotal records,
- running records,
- photographs and text,
- documentation panels,
- learning stories,
- audio/digital voice and sound recordings,
- video recordings, and
- technology-assisted pedagogical documentation (such as those above) augmented through social media forums such as, but not limited to, blogs, Twitter, and Instagram.

The first two methods—anecdotal records and running records—are methods historically used by educators to observe young children. These records still have significant value to the early childhood role and profession and, as such, will be discussed at great length in this chapter. The other methodologies listed above—photographs and text, learning stories, documentation panels, audio recordings, video recordings, and social media applications—challenge and bring forward our observational practices to look at new ways in which we can observe young children and engage all perspectives within our learning community. While most records within this chapter demonstrate the practice of separating objective information from subjective interpretations of that information, the purpose and intention of pedagogical documentation may transform this traditional paradigm of thinking, wondering about, observing, and documenting in new and different ways.

FOCUS QUESTIONS

1. In what ways do the unique features of each methodology align with pedagogical documentation?
2. Describe how interpretation and reflection may vary within each methodology. Why might this occur?
3. Photos introduce a visual element and role to several methodologies in this chapter. How might photos augment and support those methodologies?
4. In what ways are anecdotals and learning stories different?
5. How might the learning story approach empower and promote the Indigenous perspective?
6. What is technology-assisted pedagogical documentation and how might social media technologies align with pedagogical documentation?

ANECDOTAL RECORDS AS PEDAGOGICAL DOCUMENTATION

One of the most well-known recording methods in early childhood education is the anecdotal record. Anecdotal records capture spontaneous behaviour as it occurs. When the educator documents a child's learning experience, they are telling a real anecdote. While we know that no one method will ever be completely objective, anecdotal records are intended to be as objective and accurate as possible when recording what has been observed. Historically this methodology has been used to record developmental and contextual information that allows for eventual interpretation of a child's strengths, achievements, and needs. The roots of anecdotal records extend back to the 1800s when Jean-Marc Gaspard Itard, a French physician, wrote of the extreme behaviours of "the Wild Boy of Aveyron." Piaget's observations are another example of anecdotal roots as his observations led him to conclude that children develop different constructs of learning at different ages and stages. Anecdotal records have been a valuable tool in establishing the difference between popular thinking and legitimate investigation. What we know now, however, is that anecdotal records have unique features that envelope pedagogical documentation approaches. Let's take a look.

> **anecdotal record**
>
> A narrative form of observation, a word picture, a description so clearly written that when read, the image of what is seen and heard immediately comes to mind. Anecdotal records capture spontaneous behaviour as it occurs.

Purpose and Unique Feature

Anecdotal records have traditionally been described as an objective word picture, a description so clearly written that when read, the image of the child and the learning moment or learning experience immediately comes to mind. An anecdotal record could consist of a few lines, or a paragraph or more, depending on what spontaneous or unanticipated situation is being observed. Anecdotal observations can originate in many ways; they could be written by the educators, self-reported, documented by children to highlight their learning or created by parents as co-observers.

Anecdotals can follow the appreciative inquiry process and the cycle of observation as they create a moment in time, prompt further inquiry, inform planning and curriculum development, prompt extensions of play experiences, or become the basis for many other decisions made by the team (including parents and children). An anecdotal record is written in narrative form; it is a description of what the observer saw and heard (see Exhibit 4.1). While no observation is without subjectivity, documenting only what is seen and heard is intended to support more of an objective approach. These characteristics allow this methodology to be considered a form of pedagogical documentation as it has the capability of making learning visible.

The key feature of anecdotal records is their flexibility; they can be used to record and narrate the behaviour and thinking of children in any setting, within any philosophy or set of practices, and under any conditions. All you need is paper or a sticky note, and a pen/pencil, or perhaps a laptop, tablet, documentation app, or any electronic device to begin your observation.

> **key feature**
>
> An integral or central part or component of something.

Format of Anecdotal Records

Anecdotal observations can be presented in different formats, as this method is considered flexible, open-ended, and spontaneous. As seen in Exhibit 4.1,

EXHIBIT 4.1   Robert Discovers "Sticky"

Anecdotal Observation

Common essential information here

Name of Child: <u>Robert</u>   Age: <u>22 months</u>   Date of Birth: <u>July 5, 2016</u>

Date: <u>May 8, 2018</u>   Location: <u>Toddler Playroom</u>   Time: <u>9:35–9:38 a.m.</u>

Robert drops his jacket on the floor and runs to the creative shelf upon arrival. With his full left hand he selects a glue container, and with his right hand he picks up a bowl full of stickers. He turns around and drops them abruptly on the table in front of the shelf. He shifts his body again to face the shelf to select a large basket of loose parts that includes large buttons, miscellaneous puzzle pieces, and remnants of Scrabble pieces. He returns to face the table, glances in front of him, and notices the glue leaking onto the table. He touches the glue with his right pointer finger and then begins pinching the glue between his thumb and finger bringing his hand close to his eyes. He continues to watch the glue create strings between his two fingers. He then moves his right hand back to the basket full of loose parts and places his finger with glue onto a small round button. The button sticks to his hand and he smiles. He glances up moving his eyes and head from side to side reaching his right hand outward and upward with the button still sticking to his finger. No one responds. He looks back down, and with his left hand, he then places his palm in the pool of glue on the table, raising his hand slightly to watch the glue drip back onto the table. As the educator remarks from across the room, "I see the glue is sticky, Robert," he raises his eyebrows and sticks his hand into the pile of buttons in the basket. Seconds later he raises his hand opening his eyes wide. "What happened, Robert?" said the educator. He turned to where his teacher stood sticking his hand high in the air. His smile grew widely, and he squealed a high-pitched "OH" sound. He hand was covered in numerous colourful buttons.

Notice in the body of the observation —it is only what is seen and heard

Interpretations

Use of *seems or appears* indicates it is a personal interpretation.

It **seems** that Robert is able to engage in both solitary and onlooker play as he stands at the table interacting with the materials on his own while glancing at his peers around the room. He appears to demonstrate interest in exploring the materials as well as repeating his newly discovered experiment of buttons sticking to glue on his hand. This was exhibited by beginning with the initial exploration of the sticky properties of the glue, leading to one finger and then a full hand exploring the material. His excitement for his discovery of glue and **"stickyness"** was displayed through the raising of his eyebrows and smiles, and as he responds nonverbally by looking at the educator.

This experience connects to the **ELECT social domain skill (1.4)** and *Communication, language, and literacy* **(3.1)** as Robert connects through space to his educator across the room through his facial expressions and nonverbal communication skills (eye contact, raising of eyebrows, and smiles).

Historically, anecdotal interpretations have typically identified developmental information and a child's strengths/skills to be further developed. Note, however, they can also explore theories tested by children, interpretations created by the children/family, and connections to new provocations, references to a curriculum framework, extension of experiences, and expansion of curriculum.

New provocations/extensions of this experience:

In the afternoon Robert brought the educator to the creative area once again. Together Robert, his educator, and other peers began to pull out other sensory materials to determine if materials would stick to them as well (water, mud, and paint). This was extended and documented further as days progressed and further discoveries were made with other sensory materials.

simply noting the date, the age of the child, and the essential information is all that is needed to begin the observation process. Anecdotal observations within the early childhood environment are natural observations, that is, events or experiences that happen spontaneously in familiar surroundings. Using anecdotal observations in informal settings captures everyday moments and behaviours that are unanticipated.

In the example of Robert's play in Exhibit 4.1, the observer wrote what actually occurred. The observer began their observation by jotting down notes of what was seen and heard. Later, during their reflection time, the observer transformed the jotted notes into an anecdotal observation written in past tense. Even with such brief episodes, we can learn a lot about Robert. The familiar setting, combined with the open-ended style of the anecdotal observation, means that the observer could take advantage of free playtime to document the spontaneity and behaviours of children.

Observer notes should be transcribed at the earliest available time and used to inform the anecdotal observation when the time permits. Developing shorthand or abbreviated forms of writing often assist this process. Robert's educators transcribed their initial rough notes soon after writing them, noting key words such as verbs, adverbs, and adjectives. Their purpose for observing was to gather information about Robert's interests and overall thinking and development as he was new to the classroom. As we learned previously, the systematic recording of children's behaviour involves investigating strategies for efficient ways to document observations.

Although the focus of documentation is primarily on the children, their environment or setting is of particular importance. The open-ended style of an anecdotal observation recorded in a familiar environment includes contextual information.

When you record your observations of children and adults, make sure to include appropriate references to other children, adults, and the environment while remembering the considerations of confidentiality and ethics from Chapter 2.

The observation of Robert in Exhibit 4.1 represents not only the first part of the anecdotal observation (the factual account of a child's learning, thinking, and experience) but also the interpretation and the response or extension of the experience. The actual observation could stand alone; it could serve to provide others with a written account of this event. Typically, however, like in Exhibit 4.1, an observation is accompanied by an interpretation. What do you notice about the interpretation that is different from the observation section in Exhibit 4.1?

Anecdotal Interpretations

Interpretation plays a role in all open-ended types of records that capture unanticipated behaviour. As discussed in Chapter 3, for many methods of observation in this book, interpretations are professional reflections upon what we see (the factual descriptions of events and behaviours) and what we hear. They are intended to reflect upon what was learned about a particular observation and are not intended to be definitive in their singular form. When we observe a child over time, we are able to see patterns and repeated demonstration of knowledge and skills and, as such, are able to draw more meaning and conclusions when we integrate this information with the perspectives of

contextual information

Relevant information from the environment that directly or indirectly influences the behaviour of a child; information that helps explain or give meaning to a child's behaviour.

parents and children on the same information. Remember that your interpretations and reflections rest on your observations, and your observations achieve significance with your interpretations, reflections, and wonderings.

As we review the interpretation section in Exhibit 4.1 and recall what we learned about interpretations in Chapter 3, we see the importance of

- considering the context of the learning experience, development, as well as the thinking and interests of the child. This includes language examples where possible;
- phrasing interpretations as "it seems" or "it appears" to indicate that information being discussed is based on one observation only, and therefore would not be representative of patterning or multiple observations to indicate mastery of a skill/domain of development;
- avoiding the use of first person and keeping the information in third person; and
- providing opportunities to children, parents, and educators to interpret and talk about what is seen and heard, supporting increased understanding of how a child learns and what might be appropriate supports or curriculum to assist each child in furthering their development and unique identity.

Let's turn our attention to another example now in Reflective Exercise 4.1.

patterning

Determining the repetition or recurrence of behaviour. Common behaviours of individuals can be easily patterned through the integration of information gathered from various observations and documentation tools.

REFLECTIVE EXERCISE 4.1

Examine the anecdotal observation below. Describe the characteristics that define it as an anecdotal observation. Then prepare an interpretation using your knowledge of interpretation considerations.

Emin Kuliyev/Shutterstock.com

THREE-YEAR-OLD PAYTON IN THE DRAMATIC CENTRE

Anecdotal Observation

Name: Payton Mercer   DOB: August 5, 2015   Date: August 19, 2018

Time: 9:00–9:03 a.m.   Location: Preschool Indoor Playroom

Observer: Xinyu

Payton runs quickly over to the dramatic centre, where she confronts Child A standing at the play sink pretending to wash dishes. "That's mine," says Payton to Child A. She grabs two of the red dishes with one in each hand and rushes over to the table, where she drops both bowls and picks up the pretend smartphone. She says, "Hi, Nana, I come now," while she taps the screen with the palm of her hand and returns the phone to her ear. "Goo-by, goo-by," she says, and drops the phone on the table, twirls around, and runs out of the dramatic centre.

Let's debrief the Payton example a little bit. First, in the essential information section at the beginning of the observation, the last name of the child was included. Proper names of children should be used only by the registered educator in the room. For observers not yet registered or qualified (i.e., if you are a preservice educator), the real name of the child should be kept confidential. The use of "Child A" is appropriate so as not to disclose the identity of the other child. The language examples provided give insight into the context and accuracy of the expressive language abilities of the child. What else can you gather from the observation? What can you gather from the child's use of the pretend phone?

Interpreting Expanded Observations

When observations describe the quality of the behaviour, reasonable inferences can be made from them. This is true even with expanded observations, which include multiple observations of one child from different settings, during different times, from other observers or educators and, as a result, will include multiple examples of behaviour, thinking, and learning. With a variety of anecdotal observations of a child, you would be able to net some meaningful information inclusive of behaviour, language, and so much more—all of which would offer more opportunities for reflection and interpretations. Although quantity is no substitute for quality, expanded anecdotal observations will allow you to see more behaviours that are similar or related and to see patterns that you might say are characteristic of that child. When educators observe with intent, they begin to see into the surface behaviour of a child to ask questions about what it means, as stated in Exhibit 4.2. This process reframes our role, influences our practice, and changes how we observe.

expanded observations

Multiple observations of one child from different settings, during different times, or with other observers and, as a result, will include multiple examples of behaviour.

EXHIBIT 4.2	Rethinking the Role of Observation in Early Childhood Development

Through careful and intentional observation and critical reflection educators can begin to see children differently, as capable learners who are continually constructing knowledge and theories. Rather than deciding what children "need" to know, we can begin to see what children already know. If we begin to view children as competent and capable, as continually researching the world and how it works, then new ways of being with children emerge, new ways of thinking and doing in our practice. If we reframe how we see children, we then need to reframe our role; instead of transmitters of knowledge, we become co-constructors of knowledge. If we observe children carefully and intentionally, we can begin to ask different kinds of questions about what we see. (p. 4).

Source: Atkinson, K. (2012, Fall). "Pedagogical Narration: What's It All About? An Introduction to the Process of Using Pedagogical Narration in Practice." *The Early Childhood Educator, 27*, pp. 3–7.

Interpretations as an Evaluative Function

Observations compiled over several days or weeks demand a more complex set of skills and increased depth of interpretations. As discussed earlier, interpretations compiled from multiple observations involve discussion, making comparisons, analyzing, and reflecting. What makes this kind of interpretation different from interpretations previously mentioned? Interpretations based on expanded or multiple sets of observations usually take on an evaluative function. This evaluative function could be part of an overall assessment process, as described in Chapter 7.

Adapting Anecdotal Records

As previously discussed, due to the flexibility and open-endedness of the anecdotal methodology, various adaptations to the format can be made, such as those found online. The observer can check off whether or not the observation was remembered or live, as well as whether it was a natural or a contrived observation. Contrived observations refer to those that are staged by the educator, researcher, or play therapist. The majority of references to observations made in this text are about natural observations, that is, events that happen spontaneously in familiar surroundings. Can you think of an example of when an educator would want to stage a contrived observation? One example might be when an educator sets up a small group of children at a new experience to explore how the children interact socially and conversationally with one another. Deliberately setting up this situation might allow that educator to see who assumes a leadership or communicative role and who might be a good fit to help new children adjust to the classroom. Or, perhaps their intent might be to provoke other children in the group to role model language for another child in the group.

Structurally, anecdotals typically start with the observation first with the interpretations/reflections to follow. The cycle of observation discussed in Chapter 2 captures interpretation as an integral part of the observational process. Other anecdotal records have the observations and related interpretations in column form, side by side, displaying the observation and then the interpretation in left-to-right sequence. This format has the advantage of making connections between the two columns relatively easily. The location of the interpretation section comes down to observer preference. Take a moment to reflect upon the qualities and characteristics of the brief anecdotal in Exhibit 4.3 based upon what was observed in the photo.

Considering your learning thus far, what anecdotal elements are included? As anecdotal writing can be either an individual or a shared writing experience (thus building a holistic and robust understanding of a child), if you were another educator or Child E's parent co-writing this anecdotal with Michael, and together you discussed what you each saw and heard, what perspective might you offer that is the same or different?

Regardless of which format is used, the focus is the recording of unanticipated behaviour. Not having a preconceived idea of what to look for keeps the windows of perception open to numerous discoveries. Just the process of wondering opens our eyes to a new lens of opportunity. As noted in Chapter 1, appreciative inquiry is exactly that: wondering, considering, and questioning our pedagogical practice. With an open-ended method like anecdotal observation, we might wonder what to document in the classroom on any given day. We most likely wonder what significance our observations have on developing curriculum, what to share with parents, or how to make public in the community what we have discovered about how children think and process their

contrived observations

Observation that is prearranged for a specific purpose in a formal and informal setting.

play therapist

A therapist or consultant who specializes in working with children in a play-based environment to assist with their social, emotional, or communicative development.

natural observations

Observation that is recorded as it happens within a familiar environment.

perception

An intuitive judgment often implying subtle personal bias; insight.

EXHIBIT 4.3   Child E's Water Play

Name: Child E _____   DOB: _____   Age: _____

Time: 10:35 a.m. _____   Location: Wet Sensory Bin _____   Observer: Michael C. _____

Child E is exploring and selecting a variety of large and small containers in the wet sensory bin with his left hand. He does this by repeatedly taking turns scooping and pouring water from one container into another, bending down to look at the water as it fills the new container he has selected. He then grasps the sponges, places them in the water, and then squeezes the water into the containers using his right hand to grip and squeeze the water out of the tiny pieces. Child E was engaged for 10 minutes in this experience.

Courtesy of Michael Carlucci

Interpretation and Reflection:

It appears that Child E could be wondering about the amount of water that it takes to fill the containers that are different sizes. He could also be wondering how it is possible for the sponges to soak up the water, which then can be squeezed out into the containers as he repeated this action several times.

Based on this observation, it appears that Child E is thinking about pre-measurement and capacity skills. While he may not yet know the exact quantity of water that each container holds, he may be beginning to think about how containers of different shapes and sizes can hold varying amounts of liquids like water.

As a way to extend Child E's learning, we could introduce containers that are varied in size and shape in order to determine his understanding of capacity. We could also include sponges of different shapes and sizes to establish whether or not that plays a role in how much water they can hold. As a further extension, we could provide funnels and strainers as additional tools for exploring liquids. Additionally, we could switch the coloured containers for clear ones, and add food colouring to the water. This would lend itself to the exploration of opposites. To reinforce use of different tools, we could incorporate turkey basters as another vessel for transporting water and other types of liquid.

Source: Michael Carlucci.

What questions might you ask Child E to extend and make visible his learning and thinking?

world. For example, an educator might wonder why a child was jumping up and down and running around in the playground, only to discover the child was chasing her shadow after spending time indoors with their new inquiry about shadows on the shadow boxes. For the whole morning they had wondered together about shadows asking questions like

Kristine Fenning

- why is my shadow short sometimes? and
- why does my shadow get bigger than me?

They had engaged other children in the preschool room about the subject of shadows, and, before long, the educator and the children were adding colour paddles, using different intensities of light, and eventually making room on the walls to create shadow art. They were also wondering how they could take pictures of their shadows, and while all that wondering was going on, the educator documented the entire adventure until they hung it on the wall for all to see. Seen here is a photo of their beginning inquiry about light, using prisms to change the colour they see.

Documenting information only to learn more about the child reduces bias on the part of the observer, and that is an advantage for everyone. Paradoxically, the anecdotal observation may be one of the most biased types of records because of the strong role given to personal interpretation. Could this be both an advantage and a disadvantage? Check out additional detailed examples of anecdotal observations as well as the advantages/disadvantages chart in NelsonStudy to answer the above question and other wonderings about this methodology.

Combinations and Adaptations

Anecdotal observations can be combined with many other pedagogical documentation methods, such as learning stories and participation charts. A participation chart (see Chapter 5) targets particular behaviours and does not include a narrative or anecdotal record. Yet educators often like to include a comments section for contextual information or for information about the child that does not "fit" in the chart but is still highly relevant. Combining or adapting certain methods to include the narrative of the anecdotal record is a common practice. The methods in Chapters 4 and 5 can be easily adapted to include an anecdotal section.

Perceptions and Cultural Inferences

Before we go any further, let us re-examine the notion of subjective influences in anecdotal observations. Although we try to be as equitable as possible, some subjectivity is bound to influence our observations. Writing a "sly smile" is different from writing a "winning smile." An "awkward-looking walk" is laden with perception, isn't it? A few words placed here and there can make a difference between a child being perceived as assertive and confident and being perceived as aggressive and bossy. Reading too much into an observation that may be based on inexperience or misunderstanding can bias our observation and potentially portray that child as someone quite different from who they really are. Reading too little into our observations can also mean that although we have clear, factual observations, we will not be able to use them to their full advantage by providing insight and perception into the child's behaviour, experiences, or learning, thereby losing the potential for better understanding.

As noted throughout this text, Canada is a diverse, multilingual society, which is reflected in group settings where not only children and their families but also educators and staff represent a microcosm of this society. How could differing cultures affect how a child's behaviour is perceived? In what ways could we involve our entire observation team in collecting more information that truly reflects the uniqueness of each child?

An understanding of diverse backgrounds, cultures, and lifestyles helps educators be in tune with their children and families and be open to differences even in a common routine such as naptime, as illustrated in Exhibit 4.4.

Being aware of a child's home culture, the dynamics of the children within the group, and your own bias helps you understand how to interpret a child's behaviour in ways that are reflective, meaningful, responsive, and inclusive. As discussed in Chapters 2 and 3, being aware of your own biases is a good starting point when writing in a fair manner about your observations. As you observe, how will you maintain a professional approach, ensuring that your values, reactions, and biases aren't projected onto others?

EXHIBIT 4.4	Basic Routines and Cultural Sensitivity

When observation and cultural sensitivities are discussed, most often the focus is on environment, curriculum, or documentation of children's free play or activities at learning centres. Yet we know that throughout many basic daily routines, observation continues to be part of an educator's mind-set and practice. Naptime is one of those routines for infants, toddlers, or preschoolers.

During enrolment, family practices regarding naps and naptime are part of the supervisor's interview. Communication about this routine is important so that staff can discover rather than assume the values and practices of families, particularly newcomer populations in Canada.

Consider this story of a family-centred program where, one afternoon when the children were napping, a child woke screaming. This scream could not be comforted by the educator, and another staff member ran down the hall to get his mother. Mother and child sat on the cot together, not saying a word. The child was immediately comforted. He stayed in his mother's arms until he fell asleep again. Later it was discovered that this child had experienced separation and war in his country of origin. He did not like the darkened room.

What do we learn from this? We cannot assume that basic routines are common to everyone, nor can we assume that every family practises naptime in the same way. Seeing how the child acted and reacted, and learning from the mother–child relationship and discussing what happened, the centre made adaptations. Soft lighting was introduced in an area of the room. An educator sat with the child until he fell asleep. If there were days he could not sleep, he was encouraged to participate in quiet activities with the other non-napping children. An awareness of family experiences and documentation of what is learned enhances professional sensitivity, responsiveness, and knowledge. It is through observation and pedagogical documentation that we are able to reconceptualize and question why we do what we do.

RUNNING RECORDS AS PEDAGOGICAL DOCUMENTATION

Purpose and Unique Feature

The running record documents a child's learning experiences in the narrative and, as such, is similar to the anecdotal observation. The main purpose for using a running record is to focus on a child and record the child's learning experience over time and in present tense. There are many reasons why an observer would wish to conduct a running record, such as documenting the social interactions of a child with peers, logging the verbal exchanges of one child with adults and other children, or noting the physical efforts of a child with special needs to maintain safe mobility within a busy room.

The unique feature of the running record is that it is chronological in nature, a series of observations in a sequence: minutes, hours, days, or weeks. This open-ended approach to collecting information on a child over time requires dedicated observation time and considerable commitment. A running record generally focuses on a child at one or more moments for short time frames, or it may be used throughout the day. Documentation could occur from the morning until the child leaves the centre, perhaps every day for weeks or even months. In many instances, the observer should be a non-participant in the playroom. As educators rarely have the opportunity to devote hours of time solely to observing one child, outside resources could be enlisted to conduct this function. Centres that have access to a resource educator or consultant are fortunate that they can call upon this professional for assistance in this process.

Format of Running Records

This method records the thinking, learning, and behaviour of those being observed as they occur. Observers are encouraged to use shorthand with this as well. The narrative may be recorded in detail or captured as a sketch of events with minor details to be filled in with more description after the events. Some may infer that this method is similar to a sports game or a sports commentator role because details happen in bursts/sections throughout the event/experience. The reason for the documentation will, in effect, determine the number of entries and their detail.

What should be the length of a running record? No set number of days or number of entries per day is recommended, as it depends on the purpose of keeping the record and many other variables.

What else could be included in the running record? When formatting the running record, an observer could include the learning experiences frequented or a description of the setting or the adults and children involved. Some observers may include a running time element to indicate at what exact time of day a particular event, behaviour, or experience occurred as it may give insight and context to a situation. The actual formatting of the running record would include the variables that are relevant to the purpose.

Let's take a look at John, who in Exhibit 4.5 was referred from a behaviour clinic to a community program.

EXHIBIT 4.5   Example of Running Record

Child's Name: <u>John</u>   DOB: <u>February 3, 2015</u>   Age: <u>3</u>

Observer(s): <u>Aline</u>   Date(s): <u>March 15, 2018</u>

The setting: <u>Free playtime indoors in the morning (11:15–11:45 a.m.)</u>

Observations	Comments
Child J runs around corner into room. Yells "Hi, guys!" Stops, looks, runs over to water play, dashes both hands in water (still has winter coat on), splashes until educator removes him.	Appears excited to be in the program—is only his second week.
Runs to easel and stops, grabs brush, smacks brush on paper, laughs, runs to dramatic centre.	Appears eager to try things as he runs to experiences.
Pulls truck out of B's hands, J yells, B laughs, J pulls harder at truck, glances at educator, drops truck.	Perhaps still enthusiastic about everything new—as J stays only briefly at the easel.
J is screaming, indicating verbally that he does not want to go, while walking toward the door with his educator. Educator is gently holding on to his hand. Children are lining up at the door.	J has yet to become familiar with transitions as he is new to the program.
Volunteer now walks with J in the hall. J is doing the talking and smiles when glancing at the volunteer.	Providing the walking support appears to calm J. J's talking relates to the transition at hand, and J smiled in response to the volunteer.
Cloakroom. J is talking fast to K (another child). about a TV program: "Did you see Marvel yesterday? It was so cool!" K responds by adding information about what they saw the characters do in Marvel.	J appears to seek out social friendships and conversations and is able to carry on a conversation about the same topic as a peer.
Runs to other end of playground when parent arrives, and declares he does not want to leave. J begins to cry and sits on the ground with legs crossed and arms across his chest.	J appears to enjoy being in child care (states he does not want to leave) and seems to need support transitioning to go home. Discussing a transition plan with the family would be a priority.

The example in Exhibit 4.5 illustrates briefly the sequence of events, the behaviour that was documented, and the comments. The comments show that the observer makes brief notes that are open-ended and speculative. The pages and pages of similarly recorded observations that must be presumed to continue would yield a wealth of information. Perhaps then, after days or weeks, patterns could be identified, strategies developed, and resources identified for John during this transition to the community program. While Exhibit 4.5 is developmental in its focus, running records have significant potential in that all observers can document beyond the developmental approach. All observers can partake in the documenting, revisitation, and interpretation of the information gathered to collaboratively respond, co-provide new provocations and invitations, or extend the learning taking place.

To report on J's progress during this transition from one program to another, a running record was required. The running record appears to be appropriate in the short term. Running records can also be created to record the dynamics of a group of children, such as in Exhibit 4.6 with Tabitha, Hanna, Meghan, and Cassidy. In Exhibits 4.5 and 4.6, the educators had reasons for their observations that were compelling enough to take the time to learn. Most early childhood settings, however, simply do not have the capacity to conduct these intensive kinds of observations regularly; therefore, running records are the exception rather than the rule.

EXHIBIT 4.6	Running Record for a Kindergarten Group of Children: Observation

Date: <u>July 15, 2018</u>   Centre: <u>ABC</u>

Time: <u>Afternoon Outdoor Play (2:00–3:00)</u>   Observer: <u>Karen</u>

Children/Ages: <u>Tabitha (6), Hanna (7), Meghan (6), and Cassidy (6)</u>

- Tabitha, Hanna, Meghan, and Cassidy spent over 20 minutes today shouting out to the open air around them, "We are monkeys, we are monkeys" as they hung and climbed up on the monkey bars in the playground.
- Tabitha and Hanna identified themselves as the mom and dad and could be overheard trying to feed "bananas" to the baby monkeys known as Cassidy and Meghan.

Kristine Fenning

- Cassidy was observed stating, "Let's pretend we are in the zoo and a whole bunch of people are coming to pay money to see us."
- Tabitha responded quickly, "Yeah, we could put on a show!"
- The girls set to work, each moved their arms and legs, one after the other, climbing up on the ladder up to the top bar, and then they hung and moved on the bars in ways they wanted to move for the show that they were going to put on.
- The girls shared their ideas back and forth, and they also paired up to hold hands and do movements together for a paired performance.
- Meghan shouted loudly, "Ladieeeeeeeeeees and Gennnnnntelman, welcome to the silly monkey show!"

(continued)

- Hanna interrupted: "Wait, we haven't collected the money yet."
- Cassidy responded, "I'll do it," and dropped down from the monkey bars to the areas in front, whereby she reached forward with her hand several times in front of her toward the open space, putting her hand in her pocket each time. "There, I collected one hundred dollars. That should be enough to feed all the monkeys in the show," she said.
- "Okay, now let's start. WELCOME TO THE SHOW," shouted Meghan.
- "Oooo, ooo, ahhh, ahh," the girls began shouting out loud. Each girl began moving, making a variety of faces, repeating the sounds they each made. Meghan and Cassidy were holding hands and letting their bodies hang from the bars for 30 seconds, and Hanna began flipping her body backwards while the bars were behind her knees, allowing her to hang upside down. Tabitha kept hanging by one arm, with her other arm scratching her armpit.
- "That was awesome!" piped up Tabitha. "Yeah, let's do it again tomorrow," shouted Meghan.

Educators have learned that observation plays a key role in understanding each child as well as discerning the dynamics of the group. It is through observation that educators are more equipped to understand and appreciate the diversity within our learning environments, enabling the co-creation of responsive and inclusive environments. To learn more about the advantages and disadvantages of using running records and to view other examples, refer to the resources and chart in NelsonStudy.

PHOTOGRAPHS AS PEDAGOGICAL DOCUMENTATION

Photography as a form of visual literacy and communication can be traced back to at least 150 years ago, when the photographic process evolved enough to allow for public use. For years, photos have been used to document history, societal changes and trends, innovations, milestones, and human behaviour. Technology is changing at an ever-rapid pace, and we find ourselves having access to a multitude of technological tools transforming the way in which photos can be taken, adapted, used, communicated, and shared. Staying abreast of technology changes and its presence in observation and pedagogical documentation is an important responsibility of the educator.

What we also know is that every moment of everyday people use visuals (photos or real experience) for a variety of reasons; let's explore then the relationship between photos and pedagogical documentation.

Photos in early childhood have most often been associated with the Reggio Emilia philosophy, an approach known for its authentic commitment to documenting the learning journey of children, and for capturing the image of the competent and thinking child. Photos are powerful in their ability to transcend all early childhood philosophies and perceived language barriers in order to bridge cross-cultural communication. Observation through photo documentation prompts pedagogical inquiry, further observation, interpretation, and the co-construction of new knowledge and questions for all learners including children, educators, and families. Let's take a moment to practice documenting using photos as in Reflective Exercise 4.3.

Analyze the photo and anecdote here. How might this photo be shared with this child's family and how might the family participate in the photo documentation? Pretending that you are the educator taking this photo, prepare an anecdote of your own, and compare yours to those of your colleagues. How are they similar or different? In what ways might this collaboration benefit your perspective?

Kristine Fenning

Note: Child A had examined from afar this pop-up farm toy several times today. As Child A watched others interact with the toy, she began to crawl towards it. Her first two attempts while on her knees involved gently patting her right hand on the top of the toy in several different areas. Nothing happened. Child A then decided to sit on her bottom for one last attempt. This time she pulled the toy with both hands onto her lap. With several minutes of touching different pieces, poking with her fingers, and banging with both hands on the doors of the toy, the doors popped open to her amazement! Child A squealed with delight!

Purpose and Unique Feature

Familiar to many educators are the photos of family members, pets, special toys, and objects from home posted visually in places around the classroom such as in a child's cubby, portfolio, or in spaces low enough on the wall for the kisses and smiles of infants and toddlers. Photos of family members help ease children's stress at being away from family for the first time and are often very supportive in transitions between home and child care/school. Together, educators and parents might also be seen making books of personal stories and photos for each child to build connections to past experiences, learning, events, people, and the classroom. These purposes still hold validity; as educators, we recognize how important it is for children to see themselves within their learning environment as they engage in their journey of constructing their identity. For others, photos serve a further inclusive purpose which is to function as visual communication tools for individuals with special needs. To fulfill these and many other purposes, many educators will keep their camera or tablet ready upon parent request to record their special moments. Taking a picture of a young child intensely involved in problem solving a science experiment or collaboratively playing a game with peers are just some of the many wondrous moments worthy of revisiting and reflecting upon—there is much to learn!

Photos and pedagogical documentation are a rich source of learning—of developing memory for past events and sequencing of time and of becoming aware of shared experiences with others such as friends and family. "Parents can readily follow the development of project work and group interests using the photo information supplied. Through teacher modelling, they learn how to use the photos as a tangible memory prompt for their child. Selecting one photo and asking a specific question will elicit a fountain of information from their child" (Walters, K., 2006, p. 5). Photos appeal to children and parents alike, providing opportunities for paired or small-group discussion and reflection.

The tablet or camera can also be used for other specific purposes. As Luckenbill (2012) points out, "The camera can document children's interests and patterns of behavior, assisting caregivers in following the children's lead. The camera/video camera can pinpoint environmental stimuli and caregiver behavior patterns that may be triggering problematic behaviors" (p. 31).

Providing opportunities for this inquiry and reflection, and responding to children's interests and actions promotes a responsive and inclusive approach. Understanding the impact that educators have upon children, interactions, and the environment is worth examining so that we might continue to improve all aspects of our observational practice, a concept we will explore further in Chapter 8. Using a camera to understand our impact upon children's behaviour and interactions with others is a great tool for team discussion and reflection so as to improve our building of relationships and resiliency in all learners. Engaging multiple perspectives to reflect upon visual documentation communicates to children, families, and educators that all learners are valued, knowledgeable, capable, and competent in their ability to learn. Photographs open the door to inquiry and the sharing of perspectives.

Format of Photographs

Photos make children's learning and other forms of documentation visible. Like a chameleon, photos can absorb the power, richness, and vitality of what is going on around them, and they have the ability to stand alone or be adapted or paired with other forms of documentation to aid a specific observational purpose. Formats will vary for a variety of reasons, including photo combinations with other methodologies, early childhood settings who have preferences for certain documentation methods, and purpose of observing, to name a few. For photos to truly tell the story of what is taking place in that moment, reflect upon the considerations shared in Exhibit 4.7.

Let's examine the role of photos with other forms of documentation and text to further assist our inquiry.

Pictorial Combinations: Photographs and Text

Explored later in the learning stories section of this chapter is the realization that the photograph and text do more than answer the question; they may illustrate visually and narrate in print the event, the inquiry, or the thinking that occurred.

EXHIBIT 4.7   Photo and Photo Documentation Considerations

- Taking frequent photos often reduces the tendency of children to pose; however, be sure to balance the frequency of photos with the concern of "surveilling" children, as discussed in Chapter 2. Posed photos should only be used if children wish to document something they have made, perhaps photos of friends or family they want to share, proud moments, and so on. A balance of photo and photo/text combinations assists in ensuring a more comprehensive approach to authentic representation of the image of a child and his interests, thinking, and abilities.
- Ask ongoing daily permission from children as to whether photo documentation can actually take place. Ensure that a separate consent form has been signed for sharing and communication of photos in a digital, web-based app and/or hard copy format—it is important for families and children to understand how photos will be used. Examples of consent forms are available online. If children refuse to be documented, it is important to respect their wishes.
- Involve children and families in taking photos and creating documentation of their thinking, learning, and work as well as reflecting upon their own learning when looking at the photos at a later time. See Chapter 3 for ideas on how to promote access to documentation tools.
- Ensure photos are protected from use by others. Identity theft and long-term implications of having images and personal information online are real concerns. Be sure to also become familiar with the UN Convention on the Rights of the Child in relation to visual documentation.
- The better quality of camera or technology device, the better it is for photo quality.
- Get down to the level of children to understand and capture the essence of the experience at their level. This position also aids in reducing the perceived "power" in the situation between photographer /observer and child.
- Use natural light as it captures the authenticity of emotion and context in a photo.
- Have children select the photos to be used in making their learning visible. Having a conversation with children prior to taking any photos might also lend power to the children to decide when photos could/should be taken or which photos they feel are worthy of capturing their thinking.
- Take photos of meaningful moments and context—know your purpose for taking the photo(s). Ask yourself, Whose needs are being met for taking the photo?
- Have the camera or technology device accessible to all members of your learning community for taking photographs.
- If trying to capture the emotion or authenticity of a child's thinking or emotion in a moment, focus on the expressions of the child's face. Be sensitive and responsive to ensure children are being portrayed in a positive light.
- Capture moments as they unfold naturally to show evolvement of a moment in time.
- If capturing groupings of children, follow all required permissions and confidentiality processes as well as duplicate the documentation for all who were in the photo.
- Consider photo documentation of various aspects of practice including but not limited to relationships, interactions with the environment, manipulation of materials, new inquiries and questions, and social interactions.
- Establish a process that prompts organization and use of photos from a device rather than photos sitting on a USB or SD card. Photos of experiences or children's thinking lose their meaning if simply left on a camera or downloaded without purpose.
- Use photo apps or computer programs that allow for cropping and the addition of text or narrative. Common Apps and programs such as HiMama, Pic Collage, Educreations, StoryPark, iCanProgress (Ontario Edition), and Showbie can be found online. Be sure to familiarize yourself with the strengths

(continued)

and limitations of each app and read about their confidentiality and copyright protection. Chapter 2 also outlines social media considerations worth revisiting.

There is no doubt from the above list that in pedagogical documentation, photographs hold meaning. Framing what we see in a context we want to communicate requires some thoughtful reflection. What other considerations or suggestions can you offer?

They provide opportunities for parents, children, and educators to make further inquiries and to respond. Adding a page on which anyone can respond is an inclusive practice. That documentation promotes co-learning involving, in this case, the key participants: educators, children, and parents. Photographs have become teaching tools that capture in unique ways the activity of young children as they play and learn. Margot Boardman (2007) notes in the article "I Know How Much This Child Has Learned. I Have Proof," "Educators indicated that using digital cameras facilitated children's reflective thinking processes: It was good to show other children [the digital photos as a follow-up to the initial learning experience], as they can explain and talk about what was happening and what they were doing in the photos and so you got a lot more information out of this" (p. 61).

Digital technology has given us the ability to economically use photographs with greater flexibility than before. Several good pictures out of many can be chosen for their strong visual images that capture a particular behaviour or event. These photographs can then be further enriched with narratives, such as the narrative found in Exhibit 4.8.

EXHIBIT 4.8   Jurassic Park

Jurassic Park plans were designed today by the combined ideas of Child J, Child A, and Child C. Child J said that his friends Child A and C became "excited when they saw his dinosaur from home" at the snack table in the morning. "I told my friends about the Jurassic Park movie I sawd with my family so we wanted to make our own." They all raced to the block area to start their shared project. Child A said that "tall blocks were needed so that the dinosaurs couldn't climb out of the cage." Child C identified on her plan that "circle blocks were better because they could float like islands which was safer." As their ideas evolved on paper, Child J began pulling together the ideas of Child A and Child C suggesting that they "use the circle blocks as islands for the meat-eating dinosaurs who are afraid of water so that they don't kill the plant-eating dinosaurs on the blocks of land."

Kristine Fenning

Child A came up with the idea on day two that they need to have bars made of metal to surround their park because "his dog chews wood and therefore dinosaur teeth would crush their wood ideas." That began the two-day long building of the park using nails, hammers, and wood pieces from the outside forest area. Their Jurassic Park has now become a daily resource/material used by many different peers in the room and has spawned many new discussions of meat eating versus plant eating, healthy versus junk food, and many more questions for investigation!

What do these photographs and narratives tell us? Visual imagery can be complemented by educators and/or parents adding significant written commentary, as in Exhibit 4.8 above. Note in Exhibit 4.8 how the text enables the story portrayed in the photograph. Text accompanying photos can be varied in length and can be written in the narrative by the parent, the child, or educator. We will see later in this chapter how one child in this photo documented his own learning about this experience digitally using a tablet.

Visual Communication and Children with Extra Support Needs

total communication

An approach using as many kinds of communication as necessary for a child to understand an idea or concept, for example, sign language, hearing aids, pictures.

Visual communication with pictures and text embraces the concept of total communication. Photos are used to assist all children to understand what is taking place in their day. This helps children to self-regulate and reduce anxiety about new experiences and aspects of their day. Photos have been particularly effective with children who require supports to communicate. Photos can be pointed to, looked at, named, and used as a visual means of communication. Children with special needs might use pictures of learning materials or toys in a personal photo album to show what they would like to play with. Their photos can also represent meal choices, functional items they need, or experiences in which they wish to engage. The pictures are supplied and organized by family members, teachers, and professionals. To provide this kind of pictorial aid, these people must be aware of the child's interests, likes and dislikes, needs, and skills. Carefully observing any child who might benefit from visuals will give the educator clues about what pictorial aids would be most useful and appropriate. Ongoing monitoring will also be necessary to make sure the choices are significant, relevant, and helpful to the child. Go online and visit Pinterest or other apps and websites for examples of communication photo boards used with children.

Photographs and Other Documentation Methods

Photographs can also be formatted with other documentation approaches, including but not limited to mapping, webbing, documentation panels, and learning stories. Using photos on a mapping diagram either in hard copy or on a tablet can assist the documenter in visualizing the areas frequented by the child or children being observed. Positioning photos within a webbing diagram on a whiteboard in the classroom enables children, families, and educators to respond and contribute to the interests, inquiry, and learning taking place. This can be accomplished through additional discussion, the addition of new materials, the rethinking of curriculum, or written comments to extend the thinking or perhaps stimulate new questions and inquiry for exploration.

Photo Documentation: Possible Ethical Dilemmas

Chapter 2 first introduced us to the ethical conversations we need to have with fellow educators, families, children, and communities regarding the observation and documentation process. Often it is perceived that the photos we take are nonintrusive; however, this is not the case. If we take a moment to first think critically about ourselves as human beings and educators, it is easy to recognize that as adults we might not be comfortable in having our own photos taken and then used on Facebook, Instagram, and Pinterest. What if someone took or posted a photo of you without permission? Have you consulted with the children regarding having their photos taken? Have you taken a moment to reflect upon the privacy laws guiding the practice of taking photos with your cellphone or tablet? What if the photos were misused? Sent to the wrong email address? Lost or stolen? What about photos being downloaded onto apps or websites for viewing?

Pedagogical documentation is about appreciating what we see, and this requires attention to ethics. As Lindgren (2012) insists, "Further discussions need to occur about ethics and what it means for children and adults to produce pedagogical documentation, and particularly when using visual technology" (p. 337–338). This is particularly true when photos are used to communicate learning through social media. When using the social media platform, how are you ensuring confidentiality, integrity, and appropriate use of the images shared? In what ways have families been consulted? To answer these questions, be sure to review the ethics conversations in previous chapters. In Chapter 2 we discussed ways in which to promote confidentiality with the storage of visual media—be sure to revisit that conversation as well. Articles, legislation, and ethical resources for educators in early childhood settings are available online. To learn more about the advantages and disadvantages of using photographs, consult the chart in NelsonStudy.

DOCUMENTATION PANELS AS PEDAGOGICAL DOCUMENTATION

Realizing the importance of photos, we also come to appreciate that they are just one medium that can formatted for the purposes of documentation panels. Documentation panels chronicle the learning and thinking progressions of one or more children in a visible and meaningful way. Visually they allow the viewer to understand, value, and appreciate how learning and inquiry occurs, grows, and becomes more complex for a community of learners. "Documentation panels are different from bulletin boards or art displays because they are explicitly designed to function as a communication tool" (Tarini, 1997). They are more meaningful than traditional bulletin boards because they are created to facilitate understanding of the complexity of children's project work and the learning which results (Helm & Beneke, 2003). "One feature distinguishing documentation panels is that the representations of learning featured become more detailed as the children learn more about the object or phenomenon under study" (Kline, 2007, p. 73). This learning might come in the form of posing or testing new theories or hypotheses, taking risks and problem solving, or in the decisions made.

documentation panels

A panel that displays the ideas and feelings of a child or group of children through artwork, photographs, and text.

Purpose and Unique Feature

Documentation panels are intended to invite communication, conversation, and reflection by all participants; this includes those preparing the pedagogical documentation for the panel and those viewing it. This methodology is authentic in nature as it is not premised on developmental norms, stages, or developmental frameworks, nor is it intended to be used as an evaluative function against some form of assessment criterion. Often associated with a project-based approach, documentation panels are responsive in nature, engaging children of all abilities and backgrounds in the investigation of new inquiries, ideas, questions, and wonderings. In a study conducted by Mehmet Buldu titled "Making Learning Visible in Kindergarten Classrooms: Pedagogical Documentation as a Formative Assessment Technique," the potential of pedagogical documentation, specifically documentation panels, was realized. Exhibit 4.9 explores many of the strengths and challenges of this approach, and allows for reflection upon the merits of documentation panels as a formative assessment technique.

There is no question that documentation panels promote the value of play and of children's thinking, leading to increasing understanding and value placed on children as co-educators and co-constructors of new knowledge. Documentation panels are a valued methodology in building equity in the relationship between adult and child as all perspectives are valued equally.

Format of Documentation Panels

Selected, prepared, and co-created by one or more observers (including children, families, educators, and community), documentation panels may be composed of a variety of methodologies and presented in a variety of authentic ways. Their large-scale nature is intended for viewing and visibility, questioning, or additional contributions of other perspectives. They are often placed on a variety of surfaces, including walls, display boards, whiteboards, electronic devices such as digital photo frames, or movable room dividers. Recommended to begin on a blank slate, observers may prepare documentation panels that include artifacts such as the following:

- a combination of artwork or illustrations;
- photos of creations or actual 2D/3D sculptures with captions/text;
- anecdotes and narratives, transcriptions of conversations;
- a mapping of hypotheses, investigations, questions, theories, and wonderings;
- a group or individual experience or moment in time;
- a telling of a story or timeline;
- a collaborative mural; and
- a depiction of interconnecting relationships, or narrations of an individual or group journey of discoveries.

The list above is not exhaustive as documentation panels take many forms. Every child is unique, as is their thinking processes. Providing authentic opportunities for children to explore their interests and subject matter of importance to them engages them in ways that empower them to demonstrate and communicate their knowledge in different ways. No one child learns in the same way—documentation panels assume that every child is a competent learner and subsequently can demonstrate that knowledge collaboratively and communicatively.

formative assessment

Evaluation that can be done at any point for reasons identified by the team. Through discussion and reflection, the team can make changes as the process evolves.

artifacts

Objects that are representative of a culture and are made by a human being, typically an item of cultural or historical interest.

PEDAGOGICAL DOCUMENTATION AS A FORMATIVE ASSESSMENT TECHNIQUE

TEACHERS

Contribution

- Awareness
- Self-reflective
- Partnership/Collaboration
- Informs practice
- Guide for instruction
- A basis for modification
- Help with planning
- Source for new strategies
- A way to exchange ideas
- Child perspective
- Child's thought process
- Means to reach parents

Challenges

- Time-consuming
- Difficult to observe and teach simultaneously
- Lack of equipment and material
- Too much to document
- Requires extra effort and attention
- Change in typical behavior
- Lack of parent presence

CHILDREN

Contribution

- Self-awareness
- Self-confidence
- Motivation
- General improvement
- Probe thinking
- Peer assessment
- Collaboration
- Building relationships

- Scaffolding
- Interest in learning
- Sense of ownership
- Sense of power
- Pride in their own work
- Self-assessment
- Community of learners
- Involvement/Participation

PARENTS

Contribution

- Dialogue
- Collaboration
- Awareness
- Support
- Opportunity to connect
- Ideas to use at home
- Connection with school

Value of Pedagogical Documentation for Children

- It scaffolds children's learning
- It creates a community of learners
- It increases children's participation, motivation, and interest in learning
- It increases children's self-awareness

Value of Pedagogical Documentation for Parents

- It increases parents' awareness of their children's learning experiences at school
- It increases dialogue with school
- It educates parents about effective practices and ways to support children at home

Value of Pedagogical Documentation for Teachers

- It informs teaching.
- It is a self-reflective process.
- It creates a professional learning community
- It increases dialogue and communication with parents

Challenges of Pedagogical Documentation for Teachers

- Lack of parent presence to view the documentation affected the documentation process itself as well as the value of it.
- Lack of equipment, material and financial support might make the construction of the documentation panel process difficult.
- Documentation process requires time and effort.
- Children change their typical behaviour when they are aware of recording.
- It is difficult to fit all the data into one documentation panel.
- It is difficult to remember to document the interactions while teaching.

Source: Buldu, M. (2010). "Making Learning Visible in Kindergarten Classrooms: Pedagogical Documentation as a Formative Assessment Technique." *Teaching and Teacher Education, 26*(7), pp. 1439–1449. Elsevier Ltd.

Interpretations are a component of documentation panels in that reflections and responses to what has been seen, heard, and documented are then also commented on by the person preparing the artifact as well as by those reviewing the items on the panel. Format of the interpretations are the same as learning stories in that they are not free of subjectivity but rather include responses that may reflect a number of considerations including but not limited to new questions that hinge on the inquiries of those being observed, comments on language and context of the situation, comments on skills and knowledge demonstrated by the learner, storied responses to prompt new inquires and hypotheses, as well as developmental information.

Documentation panels, as seen in Exhibit 4.10, require thoughtful planning and collaboration to promote their authentic intent and to minimize potential barriers in their implementation.

REFLECTIVE EXERCISE 4.4

Take a moment to reflect upon Exhibit 4.9. Together in teams, explore how a learning community composed of educators, parents, children, and community members might overcome some of the perceived challenges identified in that exhibit.

To give documentation panels some context, let's also look at an example in Exhibit 4.10.

EXHIBIT 4.10   The WE ARE Project

We asked the children in ELH about their talents. We discovered that we are talented in different ways. This is a snapshot of the "We Are" project. The children brainstormed all of the things they are.

We are...
artists
writers
scientists
gardeners
builders
a team
friends

Can you find all of the things "we are" based on our representations?

Documentation is an essential part of daily learning and exploration in early years programs. Capturing children's thinking and representations gives us a window into their creative, thought, and learning processes. Documentation becomes "pedagogical" when it is shared and interpreted with children, families, and colleagues. My own experience documenting has evolved and continues to evolve by ensuring that children's voices are evident and that they are given multiple opportunities to revisit and interact with the documentation.

(continued)

Photos by Sergio Pascucci

The We Are Project was sparked by a school talent show. Spring, traditionally, is a time when schools put on concerts for families. At the time, the school was putting on a talent show. Inspired by Reggio Emilia, the "image of the child" is always foremost in my mind. If we believe that children are "competent, capable of complex thinking, curious, and rich in potential and experience" (Kindergarten Program, 2016), then we must remember that ALL children have talents. This led to a rethinking about participating in the talent show and to consider alternatives that would be more developmentally appropriate for our kindergarten children. The talent show sparked a conversation about our own talents, and the We Are Project was born.

As children play, learn and represent throughout the year, I find myself "labelling" what they're doing. When they design and build, they are architects, engineers, and designers. They are readers and writers, artists and sculptors, scientists and teachers. When the children were asked what their talents were, they said, "We are artists, writers, scientists, gardeners, builders, friends . . . a team."

By June, we had a room full of documentation and children's representations. We selected drawings, paintings, writings, and photographs to demonstrate the children's talents. The documentation was displayed in a way that would invite families, teachers, and children to easily move around the documentation, to make their own observations, to ask questions, and to re-visit the learning. Watching the children engage with the documentation was a reminder that they truly are the protagonists of their learning. As they revisited the documentation and the artifacts that they included, they shared their learning with each other.

When children engage with documentation, they provide us with opportunities to gain deeper insights into their learning as they reflect on their own processes and learning experiences. As part of co-constructing our own learning as educators, children's interactions with documentation can further guide us as the children continue to make their thought processes visible through their conversations with each other. Observing and listening allow us to further interpret the documentation so that we can better respond to them in creating invitations and provocations that will extend and challenge them.

Source: Sergio Pascucci, Teacher

For additional examples of documentation panels, be sure to visit the NelsonStudy site.

When co-creating documentation panels, there are a number of considerations in panel design. These considerations include but are not limited to

- a title that provokes thought and makes visible to the reader the purpose of the documentation (and includes connections to curriculum/inquiries);
- transcribed responsive inclusive language and text that is person centred and error free (grammar/spelling) where possible;
- a variety of mediums/artifacts that communicate the complexity of thought and action from children;
- contributions that are authentic in nature—actual artifacts from all learners in the classroom (including their thoughts, interpretations, comments, conclusions, questions, theories, etc.);
- a readable font that reads from left to right; and
- a focus on the documentation rather than on competing backgrounds.

REFLECTIVE EXERCISE 4.5

What other considerations can you think of? Take a few moments to visit examples of documentation panels on Pinterest, Twitter, or other digital forums. Based on what you see, what other considerations might you add to the list above?

Documentation panels often serve as provocations for meaningful conversations at arrival and departure times or during planned community nights within an early childhood setting. Having these panels available regularly for children to discuss, review, interpret, reflect, and evaluate their learning and inquiries with families and others supports the creation of a responsive, inclusive curriculum and environment that is reflective of its learners. See other examples of documentation panels available online.

LEARNING STORIES AS PEDAGOGICAL DOCUMENTATION

learning stories

A narrative approach incorporating the feelings, actions, strengths, needs, and interests of a child or group of children.

Learning stories, originally created by Dr. Margaret Carr and colleagues in New Zealand, continue to gain momentum and recognition in Europe and North America as a pedagogical narrative approach that documents children's learning, theories, individuality, and competencies as well as multiple points of view. Dr. Carr initiated her research in 1998 with a group of early years educators to determine the effectiveness of an "assessment story approach" as part of the New Zealand curriculum. These teachers "storied" their observations on paper, as digital technology was not yet available and computers were not readily accessible to most teachers. It was this research and the addition of many new articles and books on the topic of learning stories that led Dr. Carr's research to become popularized around the world. Her leadership in this area has led to the examination of this method as a way to engage and reflect upon the perspectives, voices, cultures, and languages of children, their families, and educators within their communities.

Learning stories are the most malleable of all of the methods discussed in Chapters 4 and 5, as their narrative feature can accompany many different types of observational methodologies to make children's learning visible. Rooted in socio-cultural theory, this particular methodology also challenges the traditional developmental approach to documenting only developmental achievement or non-achievement.

A situated/socio-cultural viewpoint looks at knowledge and learning not primarily in terms of representation in the head, although there is no need to deny that such representations exist and play an important role. Rather, it looks at knowledge and learning in terms of a relationship between an individual with both a mind and a body and an environment in which the individual thinks, feels and interacts. (Carr & Lee, 2012, p. 5)

As stated in Exhibit 4.11, this theory proposes that children are to be viewed as beings connected to culture (self and societal), to family, and to their diverse communities (child care, family, friends, where they live and play, etc.). Learning stories can accompany artwork, photos, work samples, interview notes, videos, and documented conversations, among other methods. This methodology is not setting-dependent, as it lends itself to many types of philosophies and curriculum frameworks, including Reggio Emilia, Emergent, Maori, Te Whāriki, the Ontario Early Learning Framework, and approaches based upon appreciative inquiry, responsiveness, and inclusiveness.

Purpose and Unique Feature

Although written, interpreted, and formatted somewhat differently around the world, learning stories are a unique narrative approach that combine a number of traditional elements, including observation, interpretation/reflection, analysis, and a responsive plan or next steps. Some may argue that learning stories

---

EXHIBIT 4.11   Learning Stories and Pedagogical Documentation in Nunavik

Many educators, policy makers, and program consultants working in Indigenous communities suggest that many mainstream assessment tools are culturally inappropriate, meaning that elements in the testing, including both the instruments and the processes, do not make sense to the person being tested because, for example, the language or pictures used are not familiar or have meanings inconsistent with local knowledge (Rowan, 2010b). In Nunavik, where 90% of children speak Inuttitut (Duhaime, 2008), an assessment tool in English or French is unsuitable because these languages are not the language of the children and families in the community. In Nunavik images of farm animals and city buses are out of place—they are unfamiliar and therefore not recommended for use with young Inuit children for assessment purposes.

Pedagogical documentation, or learning stories, supports practices of communication, reflection, and action, thus it holds great potential to contribute to the development of stronger, fairer, more just relationships among families and communities in Nunavik (Rowan, 2010b).

Source: Rowan, C. (2011). *Exploring the Possibilities of Learning Stories as a Meaningful Approach to Early Childhood Education in Nunavik* (master's thesis). University of Victoria, pp. 19–23. Retrieved from https://dspace.library.uvic.ca/bitstream/handle/1828/3483/Rowan_Marycaroline_2011-1.pdf?sequence=1).

paradigm shift

To have a sudden change in perception, a change in a point of view, of how you see a set of assumptions, concepts, values, and practices that constitutes a way of viewing reality.

have prompted a paradigm shift from the traditional anecdotal style of observation to a forward-thinking, pedagogically sound way of documenting, storytelling, capturing a moment in time, and making learning visible. There are a number of elements that differentiate traditional documentation from learning stories that will be examined within this section.

Learning Stories offer a thoughtful and reflective window into a child or children's learning as this learning happens and how these stories attempt to describe unique experiences or moments that cause teachers to pause, wonder or consider a particular event. At their best, Learning Stories inform future curriculum paths and directions, serve as assessment in children's portfolios, develop into invitational and engaging democratic documentation, are gathered into classroom journals and can be quickly reformatted to email to families as a newsletter. (Kashin & Jupp, 2013, "So What Is a Learning Story?" para. 1)

How might the learning story in Exhibit 4.12 inform curriculum for Ethan? How might this be used as a portfolio entry? What has been learned

---

EXHIBIT 4.12   Ethan's New Purpose for Our Dump Trucks

Exploring a New Purpose with Our Dump Trucks

Yesterday Ethan had been talking about the dump trucks that kept passing by our playground to dump sand into our new nature playground being built. When he came into the classroom, he immediately went to the bin of toy trucks and was pushing them along on the shelves in the room saying "vroom, vroom." Painting at the easel soon caught his eye, and he sauntered over to the easel with a truck in each hand and began to put the wheels of the truck into the paint on the tray, and then in broad side-to-side and diagonal strokes he made these patterns on his paper. As he did this, colours on his paper began to mix and change. Immediately he shouted to Louisa his educator, "COME!"

Louisa's Reflection: "Ethan, you were purposeful with the marks you made on the paper with your trucks. It was interesting that you knew the tires on the trucks would make different patterns. You were also quick to notice that when colours mix, they create new colours, and you were excited to share your new discovery with me! I wonder what would happen if you tried other colours tomorrow—what colours do others make when mixed together?"

Ethan's Reflection: "I went up and all around with the truck. I maded these tracks and maded the colours like dat. Daddy's four-wheeler maded tracks in the mud too."

Parent Reflection: "Ethan loves mud exploding all over his back when we go through the mud puddles. I can tell he was trying to recreate our recent trip to Algonquin Park here in his picture. We will have to put this picture alongside the photo of us covered in mud!"

Source: Kristine Fenning

EXHIBIT 4.13

EXHIBIT 4.13 — Storytelling as a Traditional Aboriginal Teaching Tool

First Nations people share important knowledge, culture and traditional lessons through the telling of stories. It is through the telling of stories and legends that First Nations people preserve what is most important to them—language, traditions, culture, and identity. Stories are used to provide a sociocultural and historical account of the community knowledge from elders to youth, ensuring its survival with new generations. (Fixico, 2003)

Through narrative we develop a deeper understanding of the social world—of how others think, why they behave the way they do, and the implications people's actions hold for others. The stories we share of our life's experiences are shaped, in terms of content and organization, by the stories others tell us within our culture. When we share stories of our life with others, we cast ourselves as both narrator and protagonist and we entertain a range of plots, characters, and stories to explain why people do what they do (Bruner, 1991)…. Thus, by representing events, narratives necessitate reflection and analysis, requiring us to interpret and make meaning of experience (Nelson, 2003). As such, narrative is a powerful tool for socialization (Miller, Wiley, Fung, & Liang, 1997) and an effective way to transmit cultural knowledge, values and beliefs (Campbell, 1988). (McKeough et al, 2008, pp. 5–6)

Source: McKeough, A., et al. (2008). "Storytelling as a Foundation to Literacy Development for Aboriginal Children: Culturally and Developmentally Appropriate Practices." *Canadian Psychology, 49*(2), pp. 148–154.

---

from this information? How might his family be further involved in this experience and new learning?

Exhibit 4.12 and other examples online also showcase various structures of a common learning story. Exhibit 4.12 also models in a very visible way the appreciative inquiry process and strengths-based approach, as well as its ability to capture the context of the experience. "Children's voices . . . are included . . . in the creation of their own narrative accounts, using visual elements and a variety of textual forms, and communicating within a framework of active listening, inviting children to be skillful communicators, rights holders, and meaning makers" (Clark et al., 2011, p. 6; Burke, 2012, p. 6). A learning story presents a framework much like the cycle of observation in which the child, parent, educator, and community function as co-educators and co-learners, each playing a role in questioning, prompting, dialoguing, wondering, and scaffolding new learning for the other. Through a sociocultural lens, learning stories enable children to revisit real events, memories, theories they have tried, problems they have solved or are facing, social relationships, contexts, and situations. In doing this, children are more apt to experience feelings of mastery, achievement, pride, and confidence; generate new cultural and community identities and knowledge; and build upon their language and relationships.

Format of the Learning Story Narrative

How we document a learning story is influenced not only by our philosophy of teaching and learning but also by the images we create of children. When we take the time to reflect upon each child as a unique individual with their own strengths, talents, abilities, interests, and rights, we are more apt to practise the appreciative inquiry approach within the cycle of observation and wonder how we might capture that child's "story" in a thoughtful, positive, responsive, and inclusive way. Learning stories can be visually portrayed in a variety of ways, such as in traditional hard copy printed photos and accompanying narratives; through documentation panels on walls; in storybooks prepared by children narrating their own learning journeys; in blogs, tweets, or video vines (footage of 15 seconds or less); and on webbing boards/visual mapping boards outlining photos and narratives scripted by educators, children, and families. The flexibility and open-ended nature of this "storied" approach allows for multiple interpretations of the same story and, in fact, invites other perspectives to interpret what took place.

Let's now break down a learning story into story development stages.

Section One: Capturing and Developing the Authentic Story

- The story is written in the child's home language or language of choice, recognizing that the main audience of the story is the child. The story must be authentic and culturally relevant.
- Characters of the story are identified, including who is being storied, as well as the context of the situation or event.
- Descriptions of what took place in the story are narrated, including the thoughts, feelings, and conversations/language heard. Unlike anecdotal records, where additional details allow the reader to re-enact the actions of the observed, learning stories do not capture every single detail. The story might also include questions and observations from multiple observers. Be present and mindful in your story—create a rich picture of words.
- Stories may take place in one moment or over several days or months. This includes adding more photos or text as needed to communicate the story that unfolded as well as subsequent stories that follow as a result of the initial learning story. The addition of multiple perspectives contributes to the building of relationships between home and child care/school.
- First-person narration is permitted to reflect the perspective of the person telling the story, and to provoke others to comment, reflect, and become engaged.
- Stories are written and told by everyone including the child—allowing for the child's voice.
- Learning stories have a title that captures or reflects the content within the story.

Section Two: Reflecting upon and Interpreting the Learning to Make Meaning

- This section follows the learning story. This portion not only interprets the learning that took place, but also links the learning to curriculum frameworks or learning outcomes used or practised by the setting/observer.
- This section should include an area that invites interpretations and perspectives of others, including the child, parent, and educator. Incorporate comments that are meaningful to the children who were observed and that reflect their thinking.

Section Three: New Provocations, Possibilities, and Extensions of Learning

- This section discusses how the learning might be extended or scaffolded to lead to other opportunities for learning.
- This section should also have an area to invite the interpretations and perspectives of others, including the child, parent, and educator.
- Consider how this story will be communicated. Will it be on a wall or in a digital photo frame? A documentation panel? Perhaps in a digital or hard copy portfolio? Or perhaps on a wonder board? What about on a classroom website/blog or in binders that reflect inquiries within the room? The possibilities are endless.
- How might this learning be connected to curriculum or to new inquiries, questions, or investigations? How might this learning prompt reconceptualization of thinking, practices, and ways of doing and being?

wonder board

A board (whiteboard/wall) used to document the wonderings of children, and to prompt new inquiries/ foster creative thinking.

For more information or examples that explore and present templates for learning stories, please visit websites such as Pinterest, Instagram, the Aussie Childcare Network, and classroom blogs as outlined later in this chapter.

As identified above in the structure of a learning story, the style and expectations of a learning story—narrative writing and forming interpretations/reflections—are quite different from those of other observational methods. Less structured and more "storied" in approach, the interpretations and reflections of the observer are included in the narrative of the learning story simultaneously at the time of recording, contrary to the discussion in Chapter 3 of how interpretations are formed and written. In methods such as anecdotal observations and running records, interpretations are separated from the observation to heighten objectivity, they are written following the observation, and they use language that posits the skills, knowledge, and behaviour which might be visible in a particular observation. Learning stories, however, invite outside perspectives of the child, family, or educator to comment on the learning story in an interpretive way. Exhibit 4.12 also illustrates these qualities. It is in that exhibit that the child interprets his own experience in the photo of the artwork and presents it to his parent, who has a complementary yet entirely different perspective on what was being communicated through the artwork. Exhibit 4.14 presents characteristics of a learning story as well, and demonstrates yet another way to present learning in a storied approach. For each of the examples, what are the implications for documenting children's learning if the perspective of the observer is included in the observation? Take a moment to reflect upon the pros and cons of the methods of observation. Based on your learning in Chapter 2, what strategies were used to promote an ethical approach?

Certainly, a goal of being an effective educator is to ensure objectivity and ethics in our observations and documentation. These can exist within the learning story approach, as observers can employ a number of the strategies discussed in Chapter 2 to support objectivity in observations and interpretations as much as possible. Remember, there is no method that is fully objective—all methods require interpretation at some level and, as such, are subjective in their approach. It is again important to think about how the child or children have been involved in documenting their experience or event and whether they have been consulted to provide approval for documentation of their learning. Involving the children helps them to develop an awareness of how they learn.

EXHIBIT 4.14   Learning Story

exploring and celebrating families, heritage, and culture

We have been working on our self-portraits. Our first attempt was using fine black marker and white paper. A copy of the drawings were sent home last week for families and friends to enjoy!

self-portraits
& the art centre

The self-portraits were truly amazing! Each one is very special in its own way. The children took such care drawing their faces, noticing the differences and similarities between them. They used a mirror to look deeply at their faces, admiring their eyes, shape of their ears, and the rich colour of their hair. One student even counted his teeth!

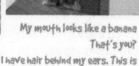

My mouth looks like a banana
That's you?
I have hair behind my ears. This is
the way I usually look.
My hair goes down to my ears.
You should put spots on your face.
It will look just like you.
That's the neck.
I have cheeks. Oh! I forgot my ears.
I have a huge head and a tiny body.
I'm going to have to look in the
mirror to copy myself. I need
teeth.
Look at my hair!
I have glasses on. My hair is long
and messy.

What are the children learning while they are drawing or making their collages? What are their OWN theories of learning?

- The children are noticing same and different characteristics in their features (math connection).
- They are beginning to or furthering their appreciation of themselves as individuals (personal and social development).
- Some have observed that they look like their family members.
- They are thinking about the materials that they chose to make their self-portraits.
- What material makes the best hair? What colour are their eyes?
  What should they use to make their nose?

Lakehead
Public
Schools

Laura Hope Southcott
2012-2013

Source: Hope Southcott, L. (2015). "Learning Stories: Connecting Parents, Celebrating Success, and Valuing Children's Theories." *Voices of Practitioners, 10*(1), pp. 33–50.

EXHIBIT 4.15   Promoting Objectivity in Learning Stories

- Continue to use "it seems" and "it appears" to communicate to the reader of the narrative that this is one perspective on what is seen (in the photo, video, art sample, etc.) and is not necessarily the perspective of all who view the documentation. While this is not a requirement of the approach, it is a strategy to evidence that interpretations are subjective and may reflect personal bias.
- Use evidence from the observation to support the narration: "It seemed you were really proud of the cupcake you made today as you were clapping your hands, smiling, and showing your cupcake to all your friends."
- Co-author the learning story with the child, parent, or other educator who saw the experience or event take place. This will bring together multiple voices to inform a holistic perspective.
- Try to avoid using words such as "good," "great," and "wonderful" to qualify level of achievement or demonstration of skill, as they run the risk of implying that a child has mastered a skill or a set of skills based on only one demonstration or little evidence, or that one child's thinking is more superior than another. Avoiding these terms does not imply that a child is not these qualities; it merely implies that mastery is evident with repeated demonstration of a skill and that discussion with all co-educators and co-learners (child, family, and educator) about all the knowledge, theories, learning, and skills evident or demonstrated over time is important for accuracy in our reflections and in our conclusions.

While no methodology is ever free of subjectivity, there are strategies to promote as much objectivity as possible in our writing. Visit the discussions in previous chapters in addition to the strategies outlined in Exhibit 4.15 to assist you. What other strategies can you think of?

Take some time to review the online examples that compare and illustrate objectivity, ethics, and different styles and formats of the learning story approach. Some styles more than others may reflect your philosophy or setting.

Technology-Assisted Learning Stories

Technology devices continue to enable opportunities for learning stories to be created digitally. According to Carr and Lee (2012),

> Digital story-telling by young adults has provided eloquent reflections of the views of self that the teller wishes to tell, and for the very young, the ease of digital photography has provided new ways of contributing to their own assessments; taking their own photographs, being able to "read" assessments, and setting up visual cues for remembering after the event. The new information communication technologies enable Learning Stories to document both vividly and quickly the range of multimodal pathways and affordance networks that have always characterised the early childhood educational environments (p. 36).

For these reasons and others, many centres are digitizing their learning stories for remote and in-centre access to learning stories. Parents, educators, and children can conveniently access and upload new stories or comment on older ones when at home or at the centre. This approach promotes real-time discussions of children's learning as it occurs, and leads to the co-development of responsive curriculum and planning to further support the interests and

Kristine Fenning

development of children. Permissions for electronic documentation need to be obtained separately from hard copy permissions due to accessibility.

Observers who are keen to document learning stories directly on their computer can access various e-portfolio sites (discussed in Chapter 6) or other learning story programs such as Storypark, Educa, and Kinderloop, all of which are protected and accessible by families to add documentation. Note that password protection is very important for digital and technology devices when saving photo and digital media. In addition to the passwords on the app sites, think about password protection for opening the devices being used for documentation as an extra protective feature. While this text does not endorse any one product over another (for reasons that settings and observers must select approaches and technologies reflective of their environment), Storypark lends itself to a more open-ended learning story approach that is not defined by a particular framework or curriculum. It also allows the creator to add learning tags reflecting the Ontario Early Learning Framework to uploaded stories. Educa is more specific to the New Zealand curriculum framework yet is adaptable to fit other approaches as well. Kinderloop also allows educators to post digital observations for parent access to updates of their child's day and experiences. Be sure to consult with other apps if they pertain more specifically to your curricular framework. To learn more about the advantages and disadvantages of using learning stories, consult the chart in NelsonStudy.

AUDIO/DIGITAL VOICE AND SOUND RECORDINGS AS PEDAGOGICAL DOCUMENTATION

audio recording

A way of recording sound waves, such as spoken voice, singing, instrumental music, or sound effects.

aural

Referring to hearing or concerning the ear.

Hard copy audio recordings or voice recordings have been part of the early childhood educator's repertoire of educational tools for decades. Educators have always known that sounds are important to young children in sorting out the aural world. Children love to listen to themselves and others sing and talk on recordings. Do you remember the first time you heard your voice recorded? Most people's reaction is one of stunned amazement, followed by, "That's not me. That's not what I sound like!" We know the reasons why we sound different on a recording, but children generally do not. This is a great opportunity to ask questions, generate discussion and inquiry, and explore with them how our ears function and what sound is, and to expand the subject to include animals' ears, animal sounds, and so on. Children also love to identify themselves and their friends on recordings and take pride in participating in recorded singsongs, whether just for fun or for a special musical event.

This text's definition of observation includes "watching and listening." Sounds can tell us much. In familiar surroundings, the sounds you hear will be enough; you do not have to look around to confirm what you heard. Children who live in rural Saskatchewan or northern Manitoba will learn different auditory cues than children who live in downtown Vancouver or Halifax. Sounds are part of a specific environment. Think of the sounds in the playroom that are alarms for educators: sudden crashing sounds, cries, and screams. Educators can tell you quite easily, "The group is louder today than usual" or "They're very quiet; it must be Monday morning." Experienced educators will observe with their ears as well as their eyes to gauge the mood or feeling of the group.

Purpose and Unique Feature

This methodology engages a number of pedagogical documentation principles, as it enables the authentic audio gathering of real moments, conversations, and communication, attuning the listener only to the auditory components of the experience. For example, when on their own or paired with another methodology, recordings have the capacity to capture many unique experiences happening within a learning environment, including role playing and conversations between children in the dramatic centre, children narrating a story as they look at pictures in a storybook, a bonding moment between an adult and child, and much more. Children, families, and educators are able to use these recordings for revisiting, reflecting, interpreting, and discussing what took place, why something was said, and what thinking might have been occurring, and experience new inquiries as a result.

There are a multitude of purposes for audio/voice recording. Audio recordings can be used effectively to capture samples of children's communication or speech and language. A parent, a speech pathologist, or an audiologist might be interested in a profile of sounds that may further clarify the patterns of a child's speech and language development.

Audio recordings can also serve as a temporary substitute for writing. An educator could conduct a one-on-one interview with a child for a variety of reasons. When writing is not feasible at the time or is not fast enough to keep pace with what is occurring, audio recordings are a viable option.

Kristine Fenning

▲ This is a follow-up to the beginning creation of Jurassic Park. Here Child J is audio and video documenting stage one of the park building with his peers. Later this day Child J shared with the class his collaborative plans, and played the audio description of his creation.

Format of Audio/Digital Recordings

Audio/voice can be recorded in a variety of ways using digital technology devices. For many years, the simple hand-held voice recorders commonly used for interviews had been an option for many educators. This approach required the observer to audio record and write simultaneously, or later transcribe the recordings on paper. While any observer has the ability to transform audio to handwritten or word processing formats, many no longer choose this option as a result of the technology available. Recent digital technology has enabled audio recordings to be transformed even further with the variety of apps and programs available online to users around the world. New digital programs enable the production of hard copy audio notes into digital form as well as provide access to digital resources that enable the observer to voice record and then digitize the notes simultaneously. This saves the observer a significant amount of time in transcribing the information.

With the proliferation of smartphones and tablets, as well as new digital hand-held devices, recording audio has become quite easy. Depending on the type of device, particularly if it has a removable secure digital (SD) card, programs may use individual SD cards with different children so that the documentation can stay in audio form for future listening and reflecting upon with children and their families. Certainly, a strength to keeping the documentation in digital form is that this reduces the amount of paperwork, but keeping it digital isn't always the best use of information if it's not organized properly for storage and communication with others. The tricky part for most educators is the time needed for the transcription of data.

Depending on the type of recording device used, educators may need to transcribe and interpret the audio recordings immediately following the observation so as to remember the context of the situation being recorded. Interpretations could also be made while the recording is taking place; it rests with observer preferences. Take a moment to think about the relevance of understanding the context of an audio or voice observation. Why might it be important? New apps and assistive and online programs as discussed in the photo documentation and learning story sections would be of significant assistance in recording and documenting audio or voice. With a Livescribe pen, observers are able to write and record at the same time using special lined paper and the pen to take notes. The pen itself records the audio/voice while the observer makes notes. Observers are then able to connect the pen to a PC or a tablet and transform the notes into digital form. Many apps and programs, such as Dragon NaturallySpeaking or Evernote, allow you to record the language or audio straight to a word or working document for easy formatting into a document ready for printing, sharing, or including in a child's portfolio.

Digital audio/voice recordings aided by a voice-to-text program can also assist any observer who finds it challenging to simultaneously listen to and document audio of a child or group of children. Programs and technological aids like those identified above also create opportunities for English-language learners to document in their first language and then use the audio recordings to enhance in English what they may not have been able to translate.

As a final important note regarding format, no specific structure is defined for interpretations of audio/digital recording. Interpretations may be done after the recording (like an anecdotal or running record), or they may be interwoven into a storied approach or response to what was heard.

Audio/Digital Voice Recordings and Children's Portfolios

Having the capacity to replay audio for clarity, reflection, and understanding assists in ensuring accuracy of information gained on a child or group of children to contribute to their online or hard copy portfolio. As with video recording, audio and voice recordings in digital form allow children to listen to and reflect upon what they were saying or perhaps how they resolved a situation and the language they used. Eliciting a child's perspective on their own audio recording gives further insight into the questions we might ask to prompt further inquiry, as well as into the other knowledge and skills the child possesses. This inquiry

Livescribe pen

The Livescribe is a ballpoint pen with an embedded computer/software application and digital audio recorder. It records what it writes on digital paper for uploading/synchronizing to a computer.

may prompt further questioning and reflection by the child and inform curriculum planning by the child or educator based on what was discussed.

Take a look at the online audio exhibits, which include portfolio entries and transcriptions as narratives for a wall exhibit demonstrating the questions children had on a particular day in their classroom. Examples to practise writing in quotations the conversations happening between children are also available online.

To learn more about the advantages and disadvantages of using audio/digital recordings, refer to the chart in NelsonStudy.

VIDEO RECORDING AS PEDAGOGICAL DOCUMENTATION

It is well known by those who coach sports teams that using visual methodologies such as video playback assists the team and individual players to reflect upon past plays, new strategies, and their role in the team to enhance their future success. The use of video playback is no different for early childhood education. As a pedagogical documentation methodology, video recording provides a unique opportunity to watch children, listen to them, understand their thinking, as well as appreciate how learning and knowledge might be demonstrated in different ways.

video recording
An electronic capture of both the audio and visual aspects of what is seen and heard.

Purpose and Unique Feature

Video recording in the classroom, in its use and application by children, parents, and educators, poses numerous opportunities for revisiting, reflecting upon, interpreting, and discussing observations made on video. In Exhibit 4.16, we see that Enoch changes his image and perspective of Child A as a result of introducing and using a video camera in his kindergarten classroom. In this example, Enoch learns the importance of providing opportunities for children to build and scaffold their own knowledge by using video recording as a process to capture what they know and understand.

He also learns how video can be used as a way to communicate children's learning to others, as well as to reflect upon and assess what they don't know and want to learn more about. These new insights serve to support his understanding of how children learn. The multi-purpose application and format of video recording is further reflected in Bullard's (2010) ideas and his reference to the video recording of George Forman:

> George Forman has labelled video recording "a tool of the mind" (1999), an aid for reflection for both teachers and children. It is easier for children to consider their thinking when they are not also engaged in the action. As children watch themselves participating in different interactions and then reflect upon them, they might also see the incident from another child's point of view. Once used only to record special events in the classroom, video cameras are now small enough and affordable enough to be used to document everyday events. Video cameras with foldout screens allow children to watch their activities immediately after they happen and to discuss them with a teacher. (p. 296)

Video capture, of course, is not limited to video cameras. Many centres are now using tablets or smartphones to capture video footage as a result of their

EXHIBIT 4.16   Video Recording as Relationship Building

Enoch, a kindergarten educator, recently attended a session on pedagogical documentation with his peers. In this session, they had discussed the idea of using video as a way to prompt inquiry. Intrigued by this session, Enoch and his team member Rebecca decided they would place some pretend video cameras in the classroom for the children as a provocation. They were pleasantly surprised with what they saw and heard. On one occasion, Enoch was able to capture a narrative of two children discussing how delicate the camera was, where to place their eyes, how to ensure the strap was around their neck, and how it "was so expensive."

The time soon came for the real video cameras to arrive. The children were squealing with delight as Rebecca opened the boxes. Concerned about the expense of the cameras, Rebecca raised her eyebrows, put her finger to her mouth, and stated, "Hmmm, I'm really confused on how to use this camera and how to take care of it so that we have it for a very long time in the room. Can any of you help me to understand how I am going to be able to remember?" One child piped up, "READ THE INSTRUCTIONS, SILLY!" Rebecca chuckled in response. "Oh yes, that is a good idea. But I'm not sure I am going to remember all this information." The same child replied, "Let's make a poster of the rules of the camera and how to take videos. That will make sure everybody will remember." "I think that will really help everyone, Child A. Would you like to prepare this, Child A?" asked Rebecca. "Yeah," responded Child A. Over the next three days, Child A recruited his father to video record him talking about how to hold the camera in different positions and where to store the camera. He also asked another boy in the classroom to help him to print photos of his video to put on a poster board. Rebecca and Enoch ensured that Child A had the materials he needed when required.

Child A soon completed the project and selected where to place the poster, as well as where and how to store the camera. Quickly, Child A became the "expert" in camera care and video recording as other children consulted with him about the new video they had on their classroom computer. As each child played his video, Child A would stop it at different points to ensure that his peer was imitating exactly what he was showing on the video. As Enoch sat down with Child A and his father to reflect upon Child A's experience, he learned just how significant this opportunity was. Child A's father discussed how touched he was that the educators in the room trusted his son to put this together, something he was not used to experiencing. Child A's eyes widened and he smiled. Enoch said, "Child A, we were very fortunate to have your help. In what ways have you been the educator in helping our class?" As the conversation continued, Child A elaborated for 15 minutes on all the ways it would help others and how he would continue to be of assistance in the room. It was at that moment that the image of this child and the relationship he had with this child changed for Enoch. Given the opportunity, Child A had become the educator, the researcher, the documenter, and the inspiration for new ways of knowing and learning.

Source: Kristine Fenning

portability and multi-purpose usage. Video recordings, then, have two very distinct and important elements: they combine the visual aspects of photos with audio recordings. In early childhood settings, video recordings can enrich learning and awareness for all involved—from parents to educators to children.

Video recording can serve a number of functions, including but not limited to the following:

- Educator self-awareness. Educators constantly analyze their interactions, relationships, and all aspects of their practice. Video is viewed as a powerful tool to support educator learning because of its unique capability to capture the elusive classroom practice for later study (Borko et al., 2008, cited in Zhang, Lundeberg, & Eberhardt, 2010). Video recordings allow educator–researchers to replay classroom events and notice aspects of classroom situations that they are too busy to notice during the act of teaching; as a teacher–participant said, "You see things that you don't realize in the heat of teaching" (Zhang et al., 2010, p. 3).

- Curriculum planning and implementation. Video captures a large volume of information regarding children's interests, where they prefer to play and with whom, their engagement in each aspect of the learning environment, and the interactions that took place, among many other elements. This information could be used to inform future planning; to prompt discussion between educators, children, and families regarding planning; and to enhance educators' abilities to meet the needs of the children.

- Environmental design and the lay out of the day. Video recording enables the examination of different elements of the physical environment (e.g. inclusive of routines, outdoor and indoor play, transitions etc.), and the possible influences on children's behaviour and actions. This would include everything from the availability and accessibility of equipment and furniture to items on the wall, levels of natural light, and developmentally or culturally relevant materials. Video can provoke new possibilities and ways of doing things in our environment and practice.

- Modifications and adaptations. Monitoring of modifications and adaptations helps ensure that they are effective and appropriate. This video-recorded information could help outside professionals who are supporting a particular child or group of children or the educator and family who are looking at ways to scaffold children's learning, therefore recognizing each child's individuality. To further enhance the discussion between parents and educators, videos have the capacity to document electronically a child's developmental journey and variations in development.

- Children's self-assessment and connectedness to the world. As in Enoch's experiences with his group of children, videotaping can be used by children to inquire, reflect upon, or demonstrate their learning. "When young children reflect, they build skills like remembering, questioning, investigating, explaining, translating, sharing and revisiting. . . . Reflection is a valuable part of anything we want to teach preschoolers—self-regulation, conflict resolution, planning, even literacy" (Foley, 2015, p. 21). In fact, children of varying ages are able to record their own thinking, narrate it if they choose to do so, and implement corrections or new ways of thinking if through their self-assessment they determine there are other ways to achieve a goal or conquer a challenge.

> Video will more likely capture how the child deals with and solves problems in real time; the decisions, false starts, corrections, and clever strategies that exemplify the child's intelligence in action, as opposed to a simple check list for what the child can or cannot do. Such an orientation to the child will improve the teacher's ability to enter the child's mental world, support the child's thinking, provide constructive provocations, and raise the child's consciousness of his or her current assumptions about how the social and physical world works. (Forman, 2010, p. 32)

It is an authentic approach for children and students to embrace, share, and connect their knowledge, feelings, and emotions not only to their own learning experiences but also to the learning experiences of others within their own classroom or anywhere in the world. Children can also use this methodology for peer review, offering opportunities for collaborative feedback by fast forwarding or rewinding portions of the video. Using video technology as a platform to express one's connections to learning can be a very affirming and positive experience.

- Educator–parent interviews, online parent engagement, and making learning visible. Videos can be used to record special events or brief clips of children engaged in inquiry to share with parents as part of a digital portfolio, a classroom Twitter feed, or even on a blog. During parent meetings or parent get-togethers, videos can provide an amazing provocation for dialogue about the importance of play, child-initiated thinking, hypothesizing, exploration, mastery, attachment, language, and independence, for example. By watching the video in person or online at their convenience, parents are able to appreciate and become a part of their child's day, which may have been invisible to them before for various reasons. Setting aside time for parents, educators, and children to view video clips together encourages communication and can be an interesting starting point for dialogue. The immediacy of a video recording available on an tablet, digital photo frame, or computer helps those watching to see first-hand and respond spontaneously. Parents who may not feel comfortable sitting with an educator at a desk with written communication might find viewing a clip of their child at play with an educator a more comfortable experience. For families whose second language is English, videos allow for the integration and use of their first language to explore and explain what has been seen and heard in the video. In some centres, remote access video streaming can be obtained via the Internet (by password) and is a viable option for families wishing to see their child in action within their classroom without having to be physically present with their child.

Format of Video Documentation

At first, it might seem unnecessary to discuss the format of video documentation when traditionally, the format of videos has simply entailed watching a "movie" of a memorable event or experience in video form, captured on DVD. While this may be one way of viewing video, it is limited in its scope when applied to early childhood education and pedagogical practice. The multi-purpose, unique features of video have resulted in a transformation of formats, viewing capabilities, and pedagogical applications of this methodology.

Depending on the video app, site, or program used to format video footage, video can be transferred to MP3 or MP4 formats on USBs, SD cards, or chips for portability and viewing on laptops, tablets, and mounted wall screens, to name a few. They can be formatted and zipped for easy uploading or downloading onto password-protected websites for virtual viewing.

Understanding that this methodology has the capability to be mass distributed or shared with more people than just the child and family, it is important to revisit and reflect upon the confidentiality and ethical implications associated with visible documentation outlined in earlier chapters. Prior to using this video methodology, it is imperative that educators think about "ethics and what it means for children and adults to produce pedagogical documentation, particularly visual technology" (Lindgren, 2012, p. 338). Video recording or any electronic transmission of documentation through formats such as social media (Twitter, Pinterest, Instagram, or Facebook, for example) requires a separate and distinct permission form, stating exactly where and how the videos will be used and accessed, to be signed by a child's parents or guardians. Examples of ethical considerations and questions, as well as a special permissions letter for video recording, are available online.

As with the other methodologies in this chapter, it is important for the observer to interpret and reflect on video documentation. Interpretations can be prepared in the same format as interpretations for anecdotal observations, or they may be as simple as capturing word for word the verbal interpretations being made of the video by the child and/or the parent and educator. Interpretations can be captured via hard copy in a child's portfolio or file, or they can be filed electronically in a child's digital portfolio. The knowledge gained from this interpretation process can then be used for further inquiry, curriculum planning, or a multitude of other purposes.

Video Recording with a Specific Purpose: Socio-emotional Development

The area of socio-emotional development in young children has been highlighted in current literature, along with other topics, such as redefining diversity, special needs, resiliency training, health and development, and brain research. This is not to say that the social and emotional development of children is a new topic but, rather, that it is new in light of the changes in families, the reordering of social structures, advances in technology, changes in social communication strategies, stresses upon children and families, and socioeconomic factors. These effects and many other variables require educators to challenge themselves to re-evaluate their perspectives, strategies, and curricula in order to support all children effectively. A primary example of the use of video with socio-emotional context can be found in the article "Show Me Again What I Can Do: Documentation and Self-Determination for Students with Social Challenges" (Cox-Suárez, 2010). This article speaks to the use of video documentation by educators who are assisting children in Grade 7 who were diagnosed with pervasive developmental disorder to self-assess themselves in social interactions. One intention was to assist the children to use their reflections and conversations regarding the video footage to further grasp the strengths of social strategies they were using, as well as to think of other ways in which they might invite a friend to play or respond appropriately to social conversations. One child, named Johnny, "grew to depend on these visual images as a visual reminder of his abilities particularly when he felt too frustrated to continue on any given day" (Cox-Suárez, 2010, p. 26).

This video was also transformed into video social stories that Johnny could revisit frequently to independently self-regulate and build his self-confidence. Video in this particular circumstance also enabled the educator to do some self-inquiry and reflection, resulting in better strategies that they and other

social story

A simple description of an everyday social situation written from a child's perspective. The stories can help a child prepare for upcoming changes in routine or learn appropriate social interactions.

educators and support staff could use to assist Johnny and other children within their classroom.

As researchers, psychologists, and educators research and discuss socio-emotional development, it is no wonder that they have used video in early childhood to learn more about the importance of social relationships and to understand the role of play in the child's social development. There is no doubt that using this methodology can assist us in learning about the complexities of social expectations and circumstances for any child or individual.

Is Video Recording an Effective Method?

When video recording, there is a planning process: decisions have to be made in terms of ethics and use, purpose of use, time, cost, resources, responsibility, and management. The technical aspects of obtaining and setting up apps or video-editing programs, as well as the actual editing, maintenance, repair, and storage of any mechanical or electronic media, can be an involved process if this is a new experience. Once understood and mastered, however, video capture and downloading can be quite quick, efficient, and easily accessible for viewing, interpreting, and application.

As with every method of observation, evaluating whether or not this is the most effective method for the purpose or event is a major consideration. The information from this type of documentation must still be interpreted, reflected upon, and compiled with other information. (Using media-assisted documentation does not mean that educators escape their responsibility for interpreting and communicating that information.) When video is used meaningfully, the outcome can be quite positive, profound, and transformative for all involved. To learn more about the advantages and disadvantages of using video documentation, consult the chart in NelsonStudy.

ONLINE/TECHNOLOGY-ASSISTED PEDAGOGICAL DOCUMENTATION

Pedagogical documentation methodologies combined with online technologies continue to expand and transform the way we observe and learn about and with children, families, and early childhood environments. Many educators around the world are now experimenting with blogs, Twitter, and Instagram as a way to connect with others. These social media applications amid many others (like Facebook and Pinterest) are enabling children, families, and educators to document and share their learning, make their learning visible, communicate about resources and research they have prepared or discovered, and co-construct new knowledge with others by inviting new perspectives. Rapid changes in technology also continue to spur development of new apps and ways in which to document, and when we reflect upon their relevance to pedagogical principles, their value becomes increasingly evident.

As we examine social media approaches, we remind you to think about ethics and technology once again, as it is important to continue ensuring confidentiality, respecting the rights of children and families, and being aware of how information is accessed and used.

Let's begin our discussion by examining a few of the common social media forums that are used by educators in the profession. Marlina Oliveira from Richland Academy in Richmond Hill, Ontario, orients us to the potential of social media to augment pedagogical documentation in this way:

> Social media is the new medium for sharing information. Articles, research, images, notifications of events, and much more can be distributed and reviewed instantly with your team. Material can be collected and shared daily; by the hour, the minute, the second. In a Reggio inspired learning environment, the teacher is seen as a co-learner and researcher. Having current, relevant, authentic and useable information available and accessible for teaching and learning is a huge benefit to their work, to their classroom, to the children and the learning community. (Qtd. in Kashin, 2013, "On the Relationship between Social Media and Leadership")

We begin our examination of social media forums with that of blogs.

Blogs

Blogs are online forums on websites that house ongoing commentaries and information on topics of interest to registered members or anonymous visitors depending on access parameters. There can be one or more blogs on these sites depending on the purpose and intention of the site. Blogs are a viable option for keeping historical entries of classroom projects, individual accomplishments, videos, and vines of excerpts recorded by children and adults reflecting learning taking place, special memories, and much more. Blogs are also known to support global citizenship as opportunities for dialogue, building knowledge, and the sharing of perspectives from students, practitioners, families, and educators. "Posting work at the unfinished stage allows the community to look and listen to student thinking, effectively opening classrooms to the community, to other teachers, to parents and to the world. Inviting other educators, parents and students to comment on student learning is initially frightening but can have significant benefits towards building a community of learners and improving teaching and learning in the classroom" (Helling, 2015, p. 2). Posts may consist of a variety of pedagogical documentation methodologies such as anecdotals, photo narratives, learning stories, videos, and audio clips.

Let's apply this information then to Exhibit 4.17, a blog created by Rebecca Versteeg (a Grade 2 teacher) and her class from Ontario. Rebecca uses a number of interesting strategies to engage families, children, and visitors in following new inquiries of the children in the classroom as well as celebrating and communicating student voice and accomplishments. This blog can be accessed online simply by entering in the title.

There are many excellent blogs like the one in Exhibit 4.17 that can be used or designed for early childhood purposes. While this text will not endorse

EXHIBIT 4.17   Team 2 Eagles Blog

Rebecca Versteeg on Blogging:

I maintain a classroom blog, and I attempt to post daily. In addition to this, each of my students has their own blog, which they understand is a space to share what they are learning at school with the whole world. My expectations for content and frequency of blog posts are different for each student based on my own assessment of their understanding. These expectations increase in scope and complexity through the school year to match student growth in language and communication skills. All students can document their learning in any subject area with a photo. Most are expected to apply what I have taught in our language lessons by writing an appropriate explanation of the photos they share. Some are even able to identify their own next steps when they conference with me to publish their work.

Student blogs are also an excellent way to address the "metacognition" expectations. These appear at the end of each language strand, and, while I do not have research to back this up, these are frequently and heavily overlooked by most classroom teachers. Until I discovered blogging, I was guilty of doing the same: careful to cover all of the overall expectations, and not always making time for the metacognition specifics.

The Zoe interview below is an example . . .

Instagram and Twitter: My primary reason for using Instagram and Twitter is that I recognize the value of both as professional tools. These have become places where I connect with other educators to gather ideas and inspiration, ask questions and share my own experiences as teacher of digital natives. I have made many connections and seem to have acquired lots of followers on both accounts, and none of these are my current students or class parents. Former students who are old enough to have their own Instagram and Twitter accounts were the first to follow me on both platforms. (This is the other reason why I keep it up—to model how easy it is to write and share something meaningful and appropriate!)

Almost all of what I share on both my Instagram and Twitter accounts is taken directly from a post on my classroom blog. The blog itself is something that engages 100% of my students and families daily. It is the only tool I have found that is so consistent and so much positive feedback.

(continued)

Rebecca Versteeg's conversation with Zoe, a Grade 2 student, regarding blogging:

Rebecca: What is your favourite thing about blogging?

Zoe: I like it because you can tell the world about your day and how it went.

Rebecca: How does the Team 2 blog help you learn?

Zoe: It helps because you can read someone else's learning. If you are away from school you can look up what you missed. It is good that you type your post in front of the class on the Smartboard before you publish it because then the kids can see how to get to the dashboard and all posts and put media in. I like finding mistakes before you publish. I'm learning to edit my posts like that before I submit them.

Rebecca: What do you notice you've improved at?

Zoe: I'm better at putting my photos in and taking good ones. I'm better at writing sentences. I can read everything on my blog now. I can compare my work from the start of the year to now. I want to make my own grade 2 book about my blog someday.

Rebecca: Tell me about the post.

Zoe: This is a great post because I can see everything I did that week. I didn't have to write on my blog about this very much because my picture shows everything. I'm way better at photos now.

Rebecca: Do you want to know what I think about what you said?

Rebecca: I like your blog as much as you do! It helps me be a better teacher. I can look at your posts and see what you understand. I can

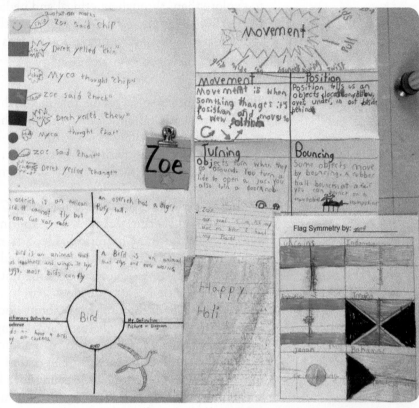

see what things are important to you. When I read your posts and look at your photos, it helps me understand what you need to learn next and what I can teach you. I noticed how much better you are at photos now too. Remember this? It was your 8 or 9th post. What a difference!

http://edublog.amdsb.ca/myblogzoe630/2017/10/12/my-bot/

Final Remarks from Zoe on the main post at the beginning of this interview:

"This is all the best work I got done at school that week. I did a lot of stuff and even though I didn't write about it, when I look at the things I can remember what I had to learn for all of them. I like that I made a collage so you can see a bit of everything. I remembered to show things that I did not just all the books I read and papers I got with information written by teachers."

Authors: Zoe (Grade 2 student) and Rebecca Versteeg, Teacher

any one blog design forum over another, common ones include Blogger, Edublogger, Weebly, WordPress.org, Edmodo Blog, Animoto for Education, and Squarespace.

There are a number of early childhood blogs worth reflecting upon for ideas on how to profile pedagogical documentation in authentic ways. It is recommended to visit different sites to find ideas on what reflects your learning community. To review class blogs on the Internet, go to the site called Edubloggers Class Blog List on your search engine. Review the list of class blogs using the content from this chapter and Chapter 2. You are encouraged to explore them through an ethical and pedagogical lens. An alternative is to go to your NelsonStudy resource to complete the evaluative exercises on online forms of pedagogical documentation such as blogs.

Twitter

Twitter is another social media tool in which educators, children, and their families are sharing their learning through the use of a tablet, smartphone, or other communication device. With a 140-character maximum for tweets, Twitter allows for the sharing of learning in real time, subsequently allowing the recipient to share in the inquiry and perhaps reciprocate a question or query immediately.

In the same blog forum (Edubloggers Class Blog List), is evidence of early childhood settings/classrooms experimenting with Twitter exchanges as they tweet out new inquiries, videos of experiences, learning, and threads of information of interest to their preferred contacts. To find threads of interest relating to pedagogical documentation, users can simply communicate via specific hashtags or do a search with key terms that they feel describe their pedagogical beliefs about documentation and how children learn. With this social media tool, any learner is able to add a short text in a timely fashion for parents to read about the learning taking place. Essentially, a trail or history can be created that supports the scaffolding of topics of interest or points of learning for children, the building of ideas, and the recalling of past learning. Parents are able to participate and become informed of what their children are doing throughout the day. There are many examples in Canada and around the world whereby Twitter has been interconnected with a password-protected blog or website for the purposes of sharing and co-creating pedagogical documentation. Be sure to visit the examples available through social media.

Instagram

Visual documentation methods are synonymous with these social media websites. Instagram has taken educators and those in the early childhood community to a new level, permitting the sharing and use of visual documentation methods and environmental design amid other topics related to early childhood that have been prepared by children, families, and educators around the world.

Not recommended as an individual documentation forum representing confidential portfolio artifacts, Instagram does allow users to post photos and videos (less than 15 seconds) as well as examples and exhibits of documentation to inspire others. This site is helpful in assisting users to build and create environments, explore new curriculum ideas, network with others who have similar philosophies, and follow only the subjects, inquiries, or wonderings of interest to them. Users also have the ability to set parameters allowing only specific users to be able to follow their posts, however it is important to note that online information is never truly private. Users of the internet, computers, and social media can still access content that some feel has been protected from public consumption (e.g. screen shots, accessing through someone else). Use strategies when posting that utilize ethical considerations to protect anonymity. More information regarding the application of Instagram to pedagogical documentation is available online.

Social Media Tips, Safety, and Considerations

Evidenced by blogs, Twitter, and Instagram, these social media tools are transforming the way many educators can document, considering the complexities and business of the educator role. Facebook and Pinterest are other examples of social media that are used for pedagogical documentation purposes but not discussed in this text. Pinterest in particular houses a number of pedagogical documentation examples used by educators all over the world. These and other tools allow educators to search the history of their pins, tweets, blogs, and so forth, for evidence of children's learning to support portfolio development, report cards, or term evaluations, for example.

In addition to recognizing and appreciating the benefits of social media for augmenting pedagogical documentation, it is equally as important to note the possible harmful or negative implications if not used appropriately. Social media posts that fail to meet program policies, licensure, program standards, or the UN Convention on the Rights of Children, for example, should not be permitted. Exhibit 4.18 outlines recommendations for educators and those considering documenting through any form of social media. Unfortunately, there is not enough peer-reviewed research in the education community that truly captures the longer-term benefits or concerns of blogs and social media. That said, the information listed in Exhibit 4.18 prompts reflection for everyone.

The list in Exhibit 4.18 is not exhaustive. It is likely there are many other considerations worth discussing with your classrooms or early childhood settings that would be appropriate considering your learning community.

peer-reviewed research

Articles/research that are reviewed by experts in the field for authenticity in the subject matter.

> One's digital footprint and online presence is a real concern for many. If you were an educator about to embark upon experimentation with digital and online pedagogical documentation, think about how might you set it up, what you might do to involve others, as well as how you might ensure adherence to the list in Exhibit 4.18. Have you consulted with your licensing and regulatory bodies or your standards of practice for the profession concerning online pedagogical documentation? Prepare a journal entry with a reflection upon the queries in Exhibit 4.18 and present your views to your peers. Do they feel the same? Why/why not? How might you come to agreement?

REFLECTIVE EXERCISE 4.6

- Create a protocol for posting that might include
  - rules in this exhibit as well as others derived by the learners and families involved;
  - language that is appropriate/not appropriate; and
  - guidance on how to post and policy that posting by families is restricted to posting only on their child or on the group learning.
- Establish a password protection system that is individualized for each family or those who access it.
- Consider first names or initials only when posting and avoid posting faces. Consult with children and families as to their preferences concerning pronoun usage.
- Verify with your quality assurance or licensing services and agencies to ensure that the appropriate steps have been taken to adhere to early childhood standards and expectations in the online community.
- Obtain permissions from families for online posting—ensure informed consent for parent or guardian and child is provided. For children, this consent should be for every image or item posted. Do all families have the ability to post? If they don't, how will this be supported?
- Request that those posting must give credit to the author of information being shared, pinned, or tweeted.
- Before any post, consult with those in the photo or video to ensure they are comfortable with what is being posted.
- Consider the digital footprint of young children as they grow and develop. What is posted online may stay there forever.
- Consider children's input and thinking about the posts you are making. Do they place them in a positive light? What are the implications of the photo, documentation, video etc. later in life for the person? For example, how might it impact employment, self-esteem, beliefs, and values (e.g., spirituality, religion, culture), concerns like custody issues, and/or overall psychological, mental health and well-being? Could your posts be subject to possible cyberbullying for the child in the present or future? How will you know?
- Eliminate the potential for the image to be misused or used inappropriately by non-approved persons.
- Ensure that children are fully clothed and in their natural environments, taking care not to disclose the location of the child/setting.
- Make sure posts from children require input and final approval from the owner of the blog site.
- Comments need to be positive and person centred, and should relate to the post in question.
- Consider how to maintain anonymity (e.g. blurring faces, not using faces at all, avoiding use of real names etc.)

CHAPTER REFLECTIONS

1. Evident in the purpose and unique features for each method was the importance of observers understanding the intent of each method prior to engaging in the process. The open-ended and flexible nature of many methodologies in this chapter enables the recording of unanticipated and spontaneous actions and behaviours of young children as they investigate, wonder, and test their theories about their world. Each method allows the observer to utilize an appreciative inquiry approach, seeing the image of the child as capable and knowledgeable due to the authentic nature of each methodology.

2. Introduced first in Chapter 3, interpretations have traditionally followed the observation section of the methodology used such as in anecdotals and running records. While this is still valid, and allows for additional perspectives to be added, other pedagogical documentation methods such as documentation panels and learning stories encourage interpretations either along the way and throughout the documentation experience or post-observation when opportunity for dialogue and reflection upon the experience can occur. Variation in interpretations and reflections will occur based upon the purpose and intention of each method. Be sure to review and practise each method to understand and appreciate the reflective and inclusive nature of each methodology.

3. Photos introduce a visual element to many methodologies in this chapter. Photos have the properties that capture the interests and inquiries of children, allow those reviewing the photos to be able to build memory, recall, as well as scaffold their learning. Photos provoke new questions and inquiries and invite others into the experience as if it was still occurring. Photos also serve as a communicative tool for children with special needs and can be used with technology-assisted approaches to be accessible online. These and other reasons position photos to easily augment the intentions of pedagogical documentation.

4. Both anecdotals and learning stories are positioned to capture the spontaneity of children's learning and thinking. There are many components that makes them different. One difference is that anecdotals are intended to portray to the reader a word picture that clearly and factually outlines what was seen and heard. Readers of an anecdotal would be able to picture exactly what took place, and interpretations often focus on a developmental approach. Learning stories are different in that they stem from a socio-cultural point of view and possess a photo and storied approach. Multiple perspectives are invited as part of the observation process, and often will include interpretations and reflections as part of the observation process. Children are viewed as connected to their community and, as such, would be invited to include their perspective in the story. For more information, please review the anecdotal and learning story sections of this chapter.

5. The storied nature/narrative approach of the learning story aligns with the storytelling traditions of the Indigenous peoples. Storytelling is an integral element of the Indigenous perspective as it enables others to appreciate the stories of one another, it communicates what is most important to them (i.e., language, culture, identity, spirituality), and its authentic approach prompts deeper learning and appreciation for the individuality and identity of each person. It is recommended that readers become familiar with Indigenous resources and materials available in their community to support their appreciation and learning about the Indigenous perspective.

6. Blogs, Twitter, and Instagram are some examples of technology-assisted/social media methodologies. Each of these methodologies are intended to support other forms of pedagogical documentation in making children's learning visible and accessible for reflection, discussion, and additional learning. If choosing to document using these approaches, it is important that observers familiarize themselves with the social media considerations within this chapter as well as the information in Chapter 2 and Chapter 3 so as to protect the confidentiality and rights of those observed. Online documentation prompts the observers to think about digital implications and their digital footprint.

CHAPTER
5

OBSERVING AND DOCUMENTING TARGETED BEHAVIOURS

Three-year-old Sonja is in your preschool room. She frequents various areas of the room each day, is known to sit quietly at art zones of the room and engage with scissors and pasting materials. She takes risks to try a variety of tasks in this area, and most often will sit on her own intently with her attention on the task at hand. Your team members report she responds to one-step direction requests, and during transitions, she quickly responds to requests to use the washroom, put her coat on, line up to go outside, and, subsequently, wait for the playground check to be completed. She is not known to need guidance to comply with safety in the classroom but, rather, follows the educator to the next part of the day. In fact, Sonja is so quiet that the educators struggle in engaging Sonja in documenting her learning or engaging her in new or extended provocations based on her interests. Interestingly, when asked, the team struggled in recalling Sonja's experiences and movements during the day.

Children like Sonja in Exhibit 5.1 are not always noticed because they are independent and self-reliant. They can go through the day without drawing attention to themselves. Children who are shy, reserved, or content with their own company can be overlooked in a lively classroom of young children. As educators, we have an important responsibility in knowing how we can engage and support all learners like Sonja and others; let's continue our examination of observational methodologies that can help us to ensure that no child is overlooked.

EXHIBIT 5.1 Participation Chart

Name: Sonja   DOB: July 3, 2016   Age: 3

Observer: Afton   Date: July 27, 2019

Zones and Learning Centres	Monday	Tuesday	Wednesday	Thursday	Friday
Dramatic centre	✓✓✓	✓✓	✓✓	✓✓✓	✓✓
Listening centre (audio books on DVD with headphones)	✓✓✓	✓	✓	✓✓	✓
Creative area (Sonia added spiders on Thursday afternoon for Friday's playroom experience.)	✓	✓✓	✓✓✓✓	✓✓✓	✓✓✓
Projects area	✓	✓✓	✓✓	✓	
Spiderweb inquiry					
Flowers in our garden inquiry		✓			
Construction centre with blocks and manipulatives		✓	✓		
Light board centre with colour prisms, cubes, and various materials	✓✓	✓✓✓	✓✓	✓✓✓	✓

Comments: Sonja was observed standing daily at a distance from her peers who were examining the spiders on their web on the windowsill. When encouraged to move closer, she would quietly step back and walk away. Additional new creative materials (paints, sparkles, loose parts) were added to the art centre each day, which appeared to sustain her interest in that area more as the week progressed.

Curriculum provocation: Sonja was asked on Thursday if she wanted to add anything to the creative shelf. She selected assorted pretend spiders from the science cupboard and placed them on the creative shelf for Friday. As soon as she arrived on Friday, she went to the creative shelf to select pretend spiders off the shelf and placed them in paint to make dots on her paper. Peers began to observe Sonja's new inquiry and soon joined beside her making their own spider creations. Peers were observed talking to Sonja about her painting to which she would nod and smile and respond quietly. Sonja's decision to add spiders as a creative prompted additional engagement from Sonja (*How Does Learning Happen*, 2014, p. 12) as she began a new inquiry with others making spider foot designs and mixing various paint colours.

Considering this new interest for Sonja, how do you think the participation chart might change over the next week? What about a curriculum response or new inquiry? What have you learned? How might this information be used for discussion with Sonja and her family?

Pedagogical documentation methodologies like those in Chapter 4 would provide an authentic look into Sonja's interests. Introducing other methodologies like a participation chart in this chapter would provide additional information on all the children in the group. Participation charts such as the one in Exhibit 5.1 would provide insights into preferred zones or areas of the room, inquiries drawing attention, and more information about where Sonja spent her time each day.

This chart provides an at-a-glance visual of the learning centres or zones of the classroom that Sonja frequented. Questions like those in Exhibit 5.1 arise when we observe and reflect. What other provocations might extend her learning in this area?

OVERVIEW

Chapter 4 used the analogy of the fishnet cast out to sea "catching" information and experiences through documentation. Those Chapter 4 narrative methods represent an open-ended method of recording observations of unanticipated behaviours. Not surprisingly, closed methods like the ones we are about to examine are used to document preselected behaviours, contextual factors, use of the environment, or social dynamics, to name a few. This chapter groups together a second broad category of observational tools preselected by the observer that may be used to record a variety of "targeted" aspects within an early learning environment, as well as targeted behaviours exhibited by a child or group of children.

The featured types of records discussed in this chapter are

- checklists,
- rating scales,
- behavioural tallying and charting,
- ABC analysis,
- participation charts,
- profiles,
- pictorial representations,
- sociograms and ecomaps,
- mapping, and
- webbing.

These types of records do not have the storytelling characteristics of the narrative but, rather, are precise, brief descriptions that are easily recorded as single words, diagrams, marks, codes, or point-form notes. These closed methods are specially designed to encompass the "I wonder why or how . . ." inquiry approach in a different way, thus enabling the observer to catch and reflect upon specific information.

The narratives in Chapter 4 are different from those in Chapter 5 in that the methods we are about to examine require some preparation and reflection before they are used. While these methods may not be the trending methodologies in observation practices today, they still hold significant purpose in understanding, examining, and appreciating how children think, act, and learn. When given opportunity for reflection by children, families, and educators, these methodologies have the potential to be pedagogical in nature. This leads us then to examine how these methodologies can aid our ability to support, guide, and nourish the inquiries and development of young children.

As we reflect back to the cycle of observation introduced in Chapter 2, it is easy to see the connection these closed methods have to the cycle and the appreciative inquiry approach. Using appreciative inquiry in the application, implementation, and reflection components of these methodologies assists educators to participate as co-inquirers, to query and understand the behaviours/skills/events seen, and then to respond to their findings in a supportive and inclusive way. As you reflect upon each methodology in this chapter, think about its relationship to pedagogical documentation. Does it align well with pedagogical documentation or might it be complementary in some way? How might we involve everyone in the process?

FOCUS QUESTIONS

1. In what ways might each observational tool be adapted or used to inquire about children or aspects of your practice?

2. Describe how the purpose and design of these methods differ from those of the methods discussed in Chapter 4.

3. In what ways might each methodology benefit our understanding of how children think, learn, and develop?

MAKING DECISIONS

Methodologies in this chapter require the observer to select a purpose for the observation. In addition to this consideration, following are other possible queries and decisions to consider:

- How might we determine the behaviours to observe?
- In what ways can we define those behaviours clearly and in such a way that anyone using the form will have the same understanding of what those behaviours are?
- How might we decide, if applicable, which symbols to use: numbers, check marks, or specific descriptors?
- How would the observer consider the diversity of the group: age ranges, children who require supports, individual personalities and beliefs, or social dynamics, for example?
- How might we ensure equity, fairness, and an anti-bias or anti-oppressive approach in all methods?
- In what ways could we consider environmental factors that influence how children act, including space, equipment, and materials?
- In what ways could we design our methods to gather contextual information to assist in understanding the behaviours and skills seen?
- How might we involve our team (including the family) in the inquiry, design, and implementation aspects of the observational process?

OTHER CONSIDERATIONS

Making choices about which descriptors to use or how to ascribe certain symbols to represent some kind of evaluation is a complex task. Even defining the behaviour to be targeted and monitored is a challenge. For example, if "sharing" is the targeted behaviour, educators may interpret sharing in a variety of ways. Some educators may refer to sharing in relation to learning materials, whereas others may consider the sharing of space, ideas, or friends to be more relevant. If the educators have different ideas about what kinds of sharing are important to observe and record, then the information they collect will not be consistent. Furthermore, determining how the observation will take place and how each member of the team will contribute observations to form a holistic response to the information learned is a necessary conversation to have prior to observing. Reflecting upon what we learn from a variety of perspectives promotes validity and accuracy of our interpretations and reflections of what is seen and heard and, therefore, results in a more appropriate response.

FREQUENCY VERSUS DURATION

Before examining the types of records in this chapter, there needs to be a discussion about the concepts of frequency and duration. These concepts are totally relevant to understanding what is meant by choosing behaviours for charts, checklists, maps, or rating scales that are easily identifiable, requiring the least amount of interpretation.

frequency

The number of times a specific incident occurs.

Recording frequency, or the number of times something happens, relies on behaviour or factors that are stated in well-defined terms. The preselected behaviour must be a discrete unit and sharply defined to minimize subjective interpretations.

Some examples of behaviours that are easily observed are "throws or kicks ball," "folds paper," "pushes a peer," "draws a circle," and "removes shoes." Each of these samples is a distinct behaviour, and its frequency of occurrence can be recorded with ease. Frequency behaviours are those discrete, self-contained behaviours with a beginning, a middle, and an end. When they are observed, they can be checked off.

duration

The time frame within which an action occurs; how long something lasts.

Duration refers to for how long the behaviour occurred, such as how long it took a child to put away his toys, complete a project, or eat lunch. The purpose of observing and recording duration may be quite different from the purpose of observing. Duration behaviours are complex, occur over a period of time from minutes to hours, and include subsets of behaviours.

Recording duration is effective for the types of behaviours that do not appear to have definite boundaries. These behaviours occur over a varying amount of time and are complex, encompassing other behaviours. For example, while Joseph is painting, he is watching other children, scratching his nose, and wriggling; during small-group time, even though Muriel is sitting, she is talking, tickling her neighbour, and leaning from side to side.

For ease of observing and recording, these examples could be separated into more distinct subsets of targeted behaviours such as those in Exhibit 5.2.

EXHIBIT 5.2   Examples of Subsets of Behaviours

• Wanders around the room at the end of playroom time	• Takes books off shelf and puts them back, pulls toys out of container and walks away, asks what time it is
• Plays cooperatively with peers	• Gets blocks for peers, tells friend the plans for the fort, listens to peers
• Communicates with peers	• Asks questions, listens, smiles, yells, cries, hits, hugs, laughs

Examining the concepts of frequency and duration helps educators in understanding what behaviours they actually want to observe and document. Do you want to document how many times Mattie and Christy argue during the day or how long the behaviour lasts? What is the significance of this behaviour? Reflecting on the focus of your questions or the purpose of your observations is at the heart of appreciative inquiry.

By taking time to reflect and observe, we can be proactive, responsive educators who understand and support each child when they need it. Children's behaviour is a result of an unmet need, and, therefore, it is our role to be curious, responsive, and thoughtful about how we might promote a desired behaviour or assist in decreasing an undesired behaviour. Investigating new methodologies supports our inquiry-based practice and helps to ensure we are being the most effective observers. Observation, inquiry, and reflection form the cycle of observation.

DESIGNING AN OBSERVATIONAL TOOL

Considering the complexity of designing types of records, it is not hard to understand why commercially produced observational tools, such as checklists or rating scales, are popular. Developing an observational tool is a lengthy process involving

- a defined purpose and vision of outcomes,
- effective communication among team members,
- research,
- an educated application of child development knowledge,
- previous knowledge or experience concerning what constitutes quality in early learning environments,
- strategies for monitoring the process, and
- careful reflection of both the process and the outcomes.

This thoughtful process is supported by the cycle of observation depicted in Exhibit 2.19 in Chapter 2. Active reflection occurs throughout the cycle as it systematically engages educators, families, and children in inquiry-based thinking. Observation is supported through reflection and inquiry-based practice, and further observation emerges from those discussions regarding why, who, and how, thus creating the cycle.

Through ongoing dialogue and reflection using an appreciative inquiry approach, educators are able to choose the observational tool most suited to their purpose and most appropriate for their children and families. Each of the records in this chapter will provide opportunities for educators to discover valuable information and respond meaningfully.

CHECKLISTS

Purpose and Unique Feature

checklist

A type of record providing a list of items that, if present, are marked or checked off.

In its most basic form, the checklist is used to record the presence (yes) or absence (no) of what is observed. A checklist is a useful and quick tool in recording distinct, preselected, targeted behaviours or elements of the environment or relationships that influence people. The unique feature of the checklist is that it is formatted to allow for easy recording of achieved outcomes.

Checklists are used routinely to gather information in our professional and everyday lives. Attendance logs, playground checklists, and sanitizing of play materials are some of the required checklists for completion in early childhood settings. Developmental checklists, standardized or informal, are different in that they reflect an assessment component of a target age or population. In fact, developmental checklists are often criticized for their Western-centric bias and oppressive qualities, for many do not appreciate uniqueness of culture-specific skills, traditions, beliefs, or values most important to a particular community. As such, with predefined standardized developmental checklists like those discussed in Chapter 7, children may be unfairly assessed because the tool may not allow for the capturing of their true abilities reflective of the community in which they live. While this may or may not be true for all checklists, this is particularly important to think about as educators, for responsive inclusive values expect that we consider approaches that reflect a true holistic and meaningful view of children.

Format of Checklists

The format of a checklist begins with relevant information such as child's name, date of birth, and age; the name of the observer; and the date of observation. Checklists are not specific to the behaviour of children; they can be used for assessing the environment or as indicators of relationships connecting educators and families. Gathering input from all team members in the design of the checklist can assist in ensuring that the content within is both culturally relevant and respectful of the population being observed, and allows for the capturing of variations in development.

In a checklist, columns of data are listed in a grid: one column lists the behaviours that are to be observed, followed by separate columns for "yes" and "no." The speech and language checklist in Exhibit 5.3 is an example of a simple checklist format to be used with children. In this exhibit, the team of preschool educators began a checklist to ascertain the speech and

EXHIBIT 5.3   Speech and Language Checklist

Child's Name: _____ DOB: _____ Age: _____

Observer(s): _____ Date(s): _____

Item	Yes	No
1. Defines simple words		
2. Follows a two-step direction		
3. Describes similarities and differences in objects		
4. Uses contractions (can't/don't)		
5. Uses plurals other than by adding "s"		

Comments and Examples

_____

_____

language skills of a new child starting in their room. What other skills might you add to this checklist to reflect the preschool age range? An infant age range? How might you ensure the expectations or skills you are looking for are appropriate? How might your checklist be adapted so that it might be used with a group of children? What might be your purpose for gathering this information?

Columns using a check mark indicating the presence or absence of a behaviour can also be organized by using an alternative coding scheme. Educators have used coloured stickers instead of check marks to indicate skills; for example, yellow means "yes," green is "emerging," and red is "not evident." Instead of yes or no, educators may wish to accommodate degrees of skill acquisition by using abbreviations such as in the following examples:

coding scheme

A design or diagram using a specific symbol to represent an idea, for example, colour coding to chart various activities.

NE	Not Evident
Em	Emerging
WO	Working On
Es	Established
NO	No Opportunity
NA	Not Applicable

Why the variations? Some behaviours do not always lend themselves to a yes/no answer. Depending on the circumstances of the day, the environment, the opportunity to observe, the feelings/wellness of the child, or how a child might demonstrate a skill differently, the documentation of certain observed behaviours may not be accurately described as yes/no but, rather, not rated or rated in a way that is reflective of the child. For example, if a child with cerebral palsy had yet to "walk backward for two metres," adding an "NA" would mean that it was not applicable or appropriate to consider this item for that child. What if the child in this circumstance was beginning to walk backward? What abbreviation would be used then?

Further examples that might relate to environmental checklists may use qualifiers such as "Does Not Meet Expectations" to indicate no evidence of inclusive planning that reflects children's interests and development or perhaps poor quality of planning. "Meets or Exceeds Expectations" suggests that there is either evidence of planning that satisfactorily reflects the interests and development of individual children within the group or that creativity and care were taken to develop experiences for the children that reflect a responsive and inclusive approach to planning. These types of abbreviations, plus comments and examples, help educators not only to communicate a child's current abilities or the ability of an environment to stimulate learning for children, but also to explain how the documentation is gathered and factors that affect the outcomes.

When constructing a checklist, decide what the focus will be, what should be included in it, and what the time frame would be, for example, completed during part of the day or every day, and for how long, such as one week or two weeks. Consider also the positive framing of the skills, if the behaviour is readily observable, and if it is able to be demonstrated within a child's natural and familiar setting. Should the checklist require assessment outside of the children's familiar setting, it alerts us to other considerations that will be discussed in Chapter 7. The purpose of the checklist should be clearly reflected in its composition.

Review the checklist examples available online. How is the design of each of those checklists related to their purpose? How might you respond considering the information learned in each?

Developmental Sequence of Skills

A sound knowledge of child development continuums and variations in development is essential when creating specific types of checklists. Choosing the developmental area(s) or behaviours to be included is of critical importance. If gross motor skills are the focus, then the skills reflective of the age group(s) should be listed in sequence. For what age group would a checklist with the following fine motor skills be considered?

- transfer a toy from one hand to another
- use pincer grasp
- play pat-a-cake
- put objects into a container

For the educator in any setting, using a well-constructed checklist provides an understanding of prerequisite skills, which are a precondition or foundation upon which other skills are built. Appreciation for the subsets of skills that form a learned behaviour contributes to an overall awareness of how children grow and develop. For example, an educator of a group of three-year-olds in the cloakroom may not find the term can dress self as accurate as a breakdown of that skill:

- assists in dressing
- puts on front-opening sleeved garment with assistance
- pulls on boots (may be on wrong feet)
- zips front zipper if catch is done up

prerequisite skills

Skills that are required as a prior condition for other skills to develop.

Prerequisite skills can also indicate which skills in a subset have yet to be accomplished, assisting educators with identifying the kinds of planned experiences needed to develop them. For example, if children in a group were able to identify most facial body parts but unable to point to their chin or teeth, then the educator could easily incorporate provocations into any aspect of the day for children to learn new body parts. Educators should consult with standardized checklists to assist in identifying appropriate prerequisite skills, as well as skills and behaviours requiring observation. Educators should also be appreciative of the fact that Westernized views of understanding and supporting prerequisite skills may not be a unified vision. Ask the children and families you work with if the skills being observed are of value to them or their community—perhaps there are other skills of more relevance to watch for and support.

Knowledge of Children within the Group

Experienced educators know that a wide range of skills and abilities exists within any group of young children. These variances can be attributed to but not limited to culture, opportunities, family experiences, linguistic differences, or the unique requirements of a child with special needs. Knowing the children and their families is as critical to developing a checklist as knowledge of child development. Each child demonstrates emerging skills at different times and in different ways. This knowledge can be reflected in the composition of the checklist. How can the understanding of a group of children with unique differences be accommodated without changing the checklist for each child? How might we include and consider the context of the environment in the design of the checklist? If you refer back to Exhibit 5.3, you will note

- a section entitled Comments and Examples and,
- in the list of behaviour items, a number of items that identify receptive language as well as expressive language.

Do these two additions to this checklist allow educators to document the variety of skills and behaviours they observe within the group of children? Yes, they could. How? In the section entitled Comments and Examples, the educator could include comments that illustrate how the child accomplished this skill or cite examples of any variation to a particular item, such as "follows a two-step direction," by stating, "Petra can follow two-step directions when gestures accompany the verbal instruction."

Children tend to understand more than they can communicate, so having items that address a child's receptive as well as expressive language skills gives a more comprehensive look at a child's ability. It also reveals patterns that may not be expressed with a yes/no response.

The comments section gives the observer an opportunity to record important information, such as "Celine has been away for two days and just returned today." That one piece of information speaks volumes. When an educator combines that sentence with knowledge of the individual child and their family, it will give insight into the results of the checklist for the day or week. With the documentation of comments comes further understanding of the child's progress in acquiring a new language if English or French is not the home language. If the child is responding in their own language to questions in English, the comments section is the place to note that; it is an important piece of information.

Knowledge of Children within the Context of Their Environment

Understanding the relationship between the children in a group setting and their environment will be covered in Chapter 8 in more detail, yet here is a good place to remind ourselves that when using methods such as a checklist, we need to keep in mind the group itself and the environment. If toddlers are climbing on

the dramatic play furniture or cupboards, educators will take steps to make changes. If these behaviours occur deep within the winter months, do educators need to bring in the gross motor equipment for more tumble-and-roll experiences? Who is initiating the climbing? Are the other toddlers following the child's lead? What questions could be asked? What would result from those questions or inquiry? Questions help to jog people out of their usual thinking or ways of doing things. Those questions create reflection concerning the relationship between children, the children and the environment, and curriculum. This process is another example of inquiry and the cycle of observation.

Targeting behaviours like the fun of jumping (seen here in the photo) that are likely to be repeated and seen during the day by many children within the environment gives the educator and others many opportunities to observe and document. The educator can adopt a spectator role or a participant role, create openings for communication with parents, or document a group-friendly experience. Take, for example, the arrival-time ritual that children engage in as they enter their early childhood setting. Adopting a spectator role to observe and document how all children transition into your environment would be a great

opportunity to review the role of the educator and the impact of the environment in these types of circumstances. Why is it that Mamta has tears throughout the day and particularly upon arrival?

Devising a checklist or using a commercially prepared checklist that explores self-regulation for children, or one that outlines important roles for the educator or parent to check off as yes/no, might assist in your exploration. Perhaps the checklist could accompany another observational method that provides more context of the situation. Using this information would then aid further inquiry and inform planning for the children, while respecting their interests and abilities.

Prepared/Commercial Checklist Examples

Prepared checklists can be found on the Internet or in published textbooks or trade publications. The key to finding a checklist that is appropriate for a child or group of children is knowing what you are looking for and how to find it. Some commonly used commercial checklists across Canada are the Looksee Checklist by ndds® formerly known as the Nipissing District Developmental Screen [NDDS] and the Ages & Stages Questionnaire.

Each of these commercial checklists is chosen by educators or resource professionals for a variety of reasons. For example, if you look at the Ages & Stages Questionnaires in Chapter 7, you will see that the checklist is quite easy to follow. It asks a number of questions based on identified age ranges, and parents could complete the checklist independently or with an educator or other professional.

Checklist items from the Hawaii Early Learning Profile in Exhibit 5.4 illustrate sign-language skills and wheelchair skills; these are items that are not commonly found in checklists for young children and therefore would be appropriate for those settings where children need assistance with their mobility. If sign language is used as a primary means of communication, then the Hawaii Early Learning Profile would be a good choice to evaluate the child's progress in this area.

Reflecting on the use of checklists prompts us to consider several notions. First, we should keep an open mind about the different ways skills can be demonstrated. Take running, for example. Some children run quickly and with agility, dodging and weaving among their playmates with ease, while others run stiff-legged or stumble often. But all the checklist asks is, "Can the child run? yes/no." Is being satisfied with a check mark good enough? Variations in how children run are important to note. Record that in the comments section.

Recording a "no" on a checklist should not prompt the educator or observer to jump to a conclusion that "this is something a child should do at

EXHIBIT 5.4 — Checklist Items from HELP®

3–9 Wheelchair Skills

Date	Credit	ID#	Age (y.m.)	Skill	Comments
	3.208			Stops wheelchair in any manner	
	3.209			Moves wheelchair forward using 1 push forward and release	
	3.210			Moves wheelchair backward using 1 pull back and release	
	3.211			Turns wheelchair in a circle to the right	
	3.212			Turns wheelchair in a circle to the left	

2–8 Sign Language Skills

Date	Credit	ID#	Age (y.m.)	Skill	Comments
	2.184			Watches face and body of speaker to get clues as to meaning of signed communication	
	2.186			Responds to single signs pertaining to own wants or needs when signed by another	
	2.187			Imitates single signs expressing own wants or needs when signed by another	

Source: Reprinted by permission of the VORT® Corporation from HELP®: 3–6. © 2010. All rights reserved.

this age." Instead, begin with an appreciative inquiry. Ask yourself & your team members questions like, "What other kinds of gross motor skills does this child have?" "Is this an appropriate expectation culturally?" "What have we seen this child do on the playground?" "I wonder why . . . ," or "I wonder if . . ." Wondering is another way of being reflective and being an inquiry-based educator. Finding other means to investigate and gain knowledge of the child in a variety of environments is what's important.

With checklists, it may often be recommended to adapt ones being used, for they are a good opportunity to reflect the social and cultural uniqueness of the centre or community population. Adding items to include or illustrate linguistic and social skills or providing comments is a way to identify or monitor and appropriately value the progress of each child in languages such as Cree, Urdu, Chinese, and Spanish. Children should not be made to fit a checklist; rather, as educators we need to look at how we might adapt one or more checklists to get an authentic and anti-oppressive picture of a child's strengths and abilities. Combining a checklist with other pedagogical documentation such as learning stories or anecdotals, as well as involving the child and adult voice and reflection, may assist in reducing the concerns regarding oppressive and/or Westernized approaches in checklists.

Interpreting and Reflecting upon Information from Checklists

patterns

Observable reoccurring behaviours that become predictable or sequential skill development that follows a particular model or relationship.

Reflection upon information from a basic yes/no checklist would appear to be fundamental. Yet even from a column of "yes/can do," there will be patterns to examine.

These patterns may be an individual child's portfolio or points of educators' discussions with a child's parent. For any observational tool we use, we are in a position as educators to make numerous professional judgments to generate meaning from what we see and hear, thus informing our decision making and responses. Situations where educators take time to interpret and evaluate the outcomes and then reflect upon the information gained tend to inspire inclusive responses and a pedagogical process that supports transformation. This process supports change in many areas of practice, such as examining philosophical approaches, child guidance techniques, and family-centred discussions, or re-examining teaching strategies. Educators could also reflect on whether or not the checklist was, in fact, the most appropriate methodology for their purpose. Did they discover what they had expected, or were the outcomes inconclusive or simplistic for their purpose? Did they find a disproportionate number of "No"s or empty spaces where check marks should have been? In addition to patterning the documentation, further reflections and appreciative inquiry might include the following:

- What have I seen and heard? What have the children or families seen or heard?
- What interpretations or views do other team members, including the family, have of the information gained?

- If pertaining to a child or a group of children, what insights or interpretations were gained regarding development (both their strengths and skills to be developed), their unique abilities, and approaches as a group or as individual children, taking care to preserve the diversity of each child?
- Considering the environmental context, what environmental influences may have had an impact on the information gained?
- What more needs to be known? Why?
- What are the next steps? How will this information be used to inform and change current teaching or educating practices regarding children? The environment? Interactions with families?

Investigate checklist examples online. How would a checklist be used in a child's portfolio? Which ones consider the reflective processes and are used to inform responsive inclusive practice?

To learn more about the advantages and disadvantages of using checklists, please consult the chart in NelsonStudy. Studying the breakdown of advantages and disadvantages for the methods found in this chapter will help you determine which one best suits your purpose for observing.

RATING SCALES

Purpose and Unique Feature

Rating scales are similar to checklists: they record behaviours or other elements of professional practice or learning environments that have been targeted in advance. The rating scale's unique feature is a broader scale against which the behavioural items or those factors relating to an early learning setting are rated. The rating scale is used to judge the degree to which the behaviour occurs along a chosen continuum. The rating scale includes judgments about the behaviour or components being observed; it can tell us the degree to which the targeted behaviour or aspects of professional practice being rated are present.

rating scales

A method of documentation that records behaviours targeted in advance and provides a continuum against which to judge the behaviour by degree or frequency.

continuum

A continuous line of reference

Format of Rating Scales

Items or behaviours for the rating scale are preselected prior to the observations. Essential information is gathered (name of child, date of birth, age, dates of observation, the observer's name) and recorded before observations begin. Rating scales designed with environmental quality indicators would have a different set of essential information, which may include only the date, the name of the observer, and the school room number. What essential information would be needed for an educator performance rating scale?

Rating scales, like checklists, are set up as a grid with the items or behaviour listed, such as the basic rating scale in Exhibit 5.5. This rating scale describes how the children use the books in the book centre. In this example, the educators wanted to get idea of how children use the books.

The skills judged along a continuum provide observers with information such as who in the group was most successful in achieving an outcome and who needs to achieve that skill. The continuum of a rating scale provides us with a scaffolding approach: who might need the most support in their learning and who might require less.

EXHIBIT 5.5 — Rating Scale for Book Centre

Child's Name: _____ DOB: _____ Age: _____

Observer(s): _____ Date(s): _____

	Has Yet to Be Demonstrated	Demonstrates with Prompting or Assistance	Demonstrates Independently
1. Turns book right side up	1	2	3
2. Hands book to adult to read	1	2	3
3. Points to and names pictures	1	2	3
4. Turns pages one at a time	1	2	3

Rating scales can include numerical ratings (1–10) or statements along a continuum ranging from terms such as "strongly agree" to "strongly disagree," or they can be a combination of both. The range of judgment is determined by the descriptors or qualifiers across the top of the scale as in Exhibit 5.5. These descriptors are then given a value on a numerical continuum which can vary from scale to scale.

If a researcher or consultant evaluates these behaviours along the continuum by adding up these and other numbers, they would derive a summative evaluation. A summative evaluation is one that takes place at the end of an observation cycle and yields data that can then be analyzed and critically evaluated.

summative evaluation

A process that concerns final evaluation to determine if the project or program met its goals. It occurs at the end of a learning or instructional experience, such as a class or a program, and may include a variety of activities.

Commercial Examples of Rating Scales

Valid rating scales are complex to construct which is why most educators would use prepared rating scales. This is because their design requires a good deal of research, not only in terms of the components or behaviours to be rated but also in terms of the rating system itself.

The possibilities for judgmental error can exist at several levels:

- the components of what is to be observed
- the order in which these components are listed along the continuum
- how the observer is allowed to rate the behaviour along the continuum
- the possibility of multiple inferences from each descriptor
- the type of scale used
- the appropriateness of the scale in relation to the descriptors being rated
- the weighting of each descriptor
- the appropriateness of the wording of the rating scale

Long as this list is, it represents a limited view of the entire process. The purpose of identifying these variables here is to explain them rather than to dissuade you from developing your own. Rating scales are a major form of evaluation; their value has been proven. We will discuss some of the commercial rating scales in our Chapter 7 discussion on assessment.

Adapting Rating Scales

Early childhood educators rarely design and develop rating scales to evaluate children; rather, they rely on rating scales already on the market and available from educational institutions and publishers. Professionals contributing years of empirical research have developed commercial rating scales for children, and many good examples exist for different populations. These assessment tools can usually be ordered as a package containing a manual, scoring sheets, and other materials. The Childhood Autism Rating Scale (CARS2) is one example of a tool suitable for use by a variety of professionals with children over two years of age; it uses observation as well as parent reports and other information to rate each child. The child is rated along a seven-point continuum, indicating the degree to which the child's behaviour deviates from that of another child of the same age.

See the examples of adapted rating scales available online.

Rating Scale Design Considerations

Adaptations of existing rating scales can be accomplished while still maintaining the reliability and validity of the rating scale by using only sections rather than the scale in its entirety. However, if different rating scales were combined through a cut-and-paste approach, then the validity of the information gathered would be in question, as well as the inferences drawn from such data. The norms from the various tests may not be congruent, which again influences the reliability and validity of the information.

Examples of prepared rating scales can easily be found. The key to selecting a particular rating scale is to inquire about the following:

* Is it appropriate for the purpose?
* Do the language and content reflect the values, beliefs, and philosophies of the children, family, environment, centre, and community appropriately? Are ability, gender, and other areas of diversity considered? What about Indigenous views and traditions?
* What kinds of outcomes are the users hoping to achieve by using a rating scale, for example, to measure literacy?
* Can this information be gathered in ways that are more closely aligned with the practices inherent in the centre philosophy?
* Is the scale consistent with expectations of the licensing and regulatory bodies to ensure its usefulness to inform practice?

Creating your own rating scale modelled on existing rating scales for a particular age group, linguistic needs, or distinct mobility or communication needs leads us back to the issues: are we measuring what we intended to measure, and are the results of our rating scales reliable? Rating scales are complex to construct. The process requires a good deal of time and commitment if the rating scale, and, therefore, the information gathered, is valid and reliable.

Interpretation of Information from Rating Scales

Reflection upon and interpretation of information from rating scales require the same kind of reflective practices outlined in Chapter 4 and in other

reliability

The extent to which a test is consistent in measuring over time what it is designed to measure.

validity

Capable of being justified or supported; the degree to which something measures what it claims to measure.

sections of this chapter. What was discovered? What does it mean for the child or children, the curriculum, the program, the environment, and future decisions? How will this information be communicated to the parent(s)? How will this newly learned information now inform your practice?

When interpreting data from the rating scales, begin by ensuring that you have all the completed pages. Reflect upon the purpose of the observations. Did you obtain the intended information? Are there patterns? What did you uncover that you did not intend to find? If other observers collected the same data, were the findings consistent? Was there inter-rater reliability? Critically analyzing the information, the methods used to gather the information, and other data will lay the foundation for productive discussions with those who observed. What reasons would prompt you to include a rating scale in a child's portfolio? Go online for possibilities.

inter-rater reliability

The degree to which persons who are evaluating a particular behaviour or competency agree that the results are reliable; a method of controlling bias.

It is once again very important to ensure our observations are conducted in a responsive and inclusive way. As we observe, gather information, and progress through the cycle of observation, it is imperative to include the family and the broader team in the discussion of what we know and have learned about the children, the environment, or aspects of our practice. This then aids ongoing inquiry and decision making to continue to promote quality in everything that we do.

To learn more about the advantages and disadvantages of using rating scales, please see the chart in NelsonStudy.

BEHAVIOUR TALLYING AND CHARTING

Purpose and Unique Feature

behaviour tallying

Counting a specific behaviour or monitoring the frequency of a behaviour and adding it up.

Behaviour tallying counts the frequency of behaviours: how many times does it happen? Behaviour tallying works in tandem with other observations as it generates substantial data rather quickly, demonstrating that a behaviour has occurred and how many times. When using this tallying and charting method, the behaviour must be clearly defined so all observers know what to observe and record. Defining what to do helps us do it.

A behaviour tallying chart has typically recorded concerning behaviour such as hitting, biting, or swearing and, rarely, if ever, prosocial behaviour such as hugging, initiating interactions with peers, or smiling. Why is that? we wonder. Perhaps we believe that prosocial behaviours do not need to be monitored or recorded. Instead, we focus on those behaviours we consider inappropriate and those that cause others discomfort or even pain. Biting can be a common issue within a group of young children. We want to know "How many times does Joey bite the other children?" We want to know the frequency with which the behaviour occurs, so we can begin to understand how to respond in a supportive manner for all children. A toddler biting another child once is quite different from a toddler who is using biting to communicate or show frustration.

If we again use our appreciative inquiry approach, documenting and understanding when, how frequently, and what types of prosocial behaviours are evident will assist us in building on what is working well. This type of proactive approach is often forgotten, yet it is an integral component to being responsive to our learners and environment. This natural inquiry also forces us to ask other questions like the following:

1. How might we promote the usage of words among our toddlers so as to reduce this biting?
2. How might we alter our role to prevent some of these behaviours from reoccurring?
3. What is it that we are not doing to decrease these behaviours, and how do we play a role in this?

What questions can you think of?

Behaviour Tallying

Behaviour tallying usually takes on a connecting position in the observation process. Some types of observational tools lay the groundwork for behaviour tallying, which is then followed by further observation. Let's use the behavioural example of hitting to illustrate this process. First, the hitting behaviour may be uncovered by an observational tool, such as an anecdotal record. The behaviour to be tallied or counted is then identified: hitting. When the question is answered (How many times?) by using behaviour tallying to record the frequency, then, based on the data, further decisions can be made. Certain behaviour is significant enough to warrant a closer look. Further observations, such as ABC analysis discussed later in this chapter, could be selected to determine if the educator/observer intervention strategies have been successful in decreasing the number of times the child hits others. To observe and modify behaviour, initial observations are taken, decisions are made, and then a different measurement is used to see the significance of any change.

Format of Behaviour Tallying

The first format is a simple tally of the number of times a child demonstrated a particular behaviour. The numbers can be added on a pre-made chart or grid or recorded on a calendar.

Historically, the behaviours to be observed are defined, the times they occurred are checked off, and then conclusions are drawn on the basis of the completed data. Alternatively, a list of chosen behaviours can be checked off in terms of frequency and then displayed in chart or graph form. The chart or graph will give you a visual picture of a certain set of behaviours over time. From the display, conclusions can be drawn; for example, from Monday to Friday, the number of unacceptable hitting behaviours decreased from ten instances on Monday to five on Friday. What happened? What patterns were seen? Why the decrease in hitting from Monday to Friday? What conclusions can be drawn? From these questions, collaborative discussions can take place and strategies can be generated to support the increase or decrease in behaviour depending on what is being measured. Many different kinds of charts are used within an early childhood environment, and the toileting chart in Exhibit 5.6 is one commonly used with 18-month-olds. In this toilet education chart, we can see how life skills might be tallied or counted to assist educators, families, or any observers in finding patterns of events.

EXHIBIT 5.6   Toileting Chart for Ravi

Child's Name: Ravi   DOB: June 25, 2016   Age: 18 months

Observer(s): Mario, Janice   Date(s): December 19–23rd, 2018

	Monday	Tuesday	Wednesday	Thursday	Friday
8:00–8:30	D	R	W/B	D	D
8:30–9:00 Washroom Break	X	X	R	W/X	W/X
9:00–9:30 Playroom & Snack Time	D	R	D	W/B	X
9:30–10:00 Playroom	D	D	W/B	D	D
10:00–10:30 Washroom Break Before Outdoor Play	X	W/X	P	W	W
10:30–11:00 Outdoor Play	D	D	W/B	D	D
11:00–11:30 Outdoor Play	W/B	W	W	W	W
11:30–12:00 Washroom and Lunch	D	D	D	D	D
12:00–12:30 Lunch	Not taken to the washroom at this time				
12:30–1:00	Sleep time				
1:00–1:30	Sleep time				
1:30–2:00	Sleep time				
2:00–2:30 Washroom Break	W/X	D/P	W/X	W/X	D/P
2:30–3:00 Playroom and Snack Time	R	D/R	D/X	R	D/X
3:00–3:30 Playroom	W/R	W/R	D/P	W/X	W/X
3:30–4:00 Playroom	D/X	D/R	D/X	D/X	D/X

Legend	D = Dry pants	W = Wet pants
	B = Bowel movement–pants	X = On potty–nothing
	P = On potty–urination	R = Refused to try on the toilet
	BP = On potty–bowel movement	
Comments		

This toilet chart is examined in detail in NelsonStudy. Be sure to visit the NelsonStudy exercise to see how this information could be analyzed.

A coding system displayed as a legend provides a quick visual reference in Exhibit 5.6. The toilet education chart includes a legend with a relevant coding system, which has enabled the educators and Ravi's parents to easily see the patterns of when Ravi was wet, when he was willing to try on the toilet, and when he refused to try. The use of symbols or letters to represent a particular concept makes documenting behaviour quick and easy.

Behaviour tallying and charting can also be used to determine a wide range of entry skills in a junior or senior kindergarten class, such as cutting skills. In-class activities often assume that children have mastered the skill of cutting with scissors. Charting the skills of the children within each class will allow you to determine which children have limited experience with scissors and those who can use them with ease. A practical approach to using task analysis is provided online. In this example, children started off cutting simple strips of paper and ended up cutting out specific small objects from magazines without difficulty. The skills were graphed for each child in class. Check out the tallied results of the class after they had been provided many opportunities to use scissors in class.

Using a Conventional Graph

Constructing a conventional graph (see Exhibit 5.7) to display data is easy to do. The standard graph has a vertical axis on which you plot ordinates, or vertical coordinates (the levels of behaviour). The horizontal axis, where you plot the abscissas, or horizontal coordinates, is where you indicate the dimension of time (hours, days, weeks), quality, or another indicator.

Graphs are uncommon to early childhood settings but are worth pointing out briefly if perhaps you are engaged in observational research on the outdoor play preferences of children within your centre or organization, for example, and wish to present your data in visually interesting ways for collaboration and discussion with others. Entering your raw data into a spreadsheet format will allow for conversion of the information into graph form. As you can see in Exhibit 5.7, a graph can display complex data in a less print-dependent way.

ordinates

Plotted on the vertical axis of a graph.

abscissas

Plotted on the horizontal axis of a graph.

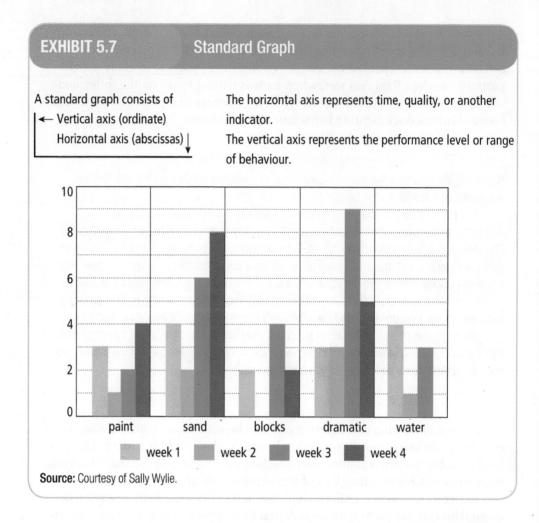

EXHIBIT 5.7 Standard Graph

A standard graph consists of
← Vertical axis (ordinate)
    Horizontal axis (abscissas) ↓

The horizontal axis represents time, quality, or another indicator.

The vertical axis represents the performance level or range of behaviour.

week 1   week 2   week 3   week 4

Source: Courtesy of Sally Wylie.

The curriculum area of sand was most popular in which week? What would be some questions to ask given the data in the graph? In what types of situations might we want to present our information in this way? Other examples of graphs and how to create crafts can be found throughout the Internet and early childhood texts on topics such as child development, use of curriculum, or almost any related topic in early childhood.

Interpreting Behaviours, Charts, and Graphs

Counting how many times a particular behaviour occurs yields different interpretations than those from narrative observations. If your purpose is observing frequency of a behaviour or how many children can accomplish a particular skill, then the interpretation should be straightforward. However, if you want to look for reasons behind the behaviour, to determine if your expectations are appropriate, or reflect on why the frequency of a certain behaviour increased during certain days of the week, then your interpretation will be more reflective. It will include knowledge of other factors such as what you know about family circumstances, development, culture, and so on.

A two-week time span for behaviour tallying is most commonly used in early childhood settings, as that time frame is often adequate for patterns to emerge, and, subsequently, for reflection and conclusions to be formed. However, after two weeks, a pattern may not seem apparent. Perhaps more time is needed for observation? Depending on the child, extenuating circumstances, the context, and the purpose for using this observational tool, a variety of possibilities exist. Another option is to stop documenting, reevaluate the method being used, and analyze the information you have. While there are no easy solutions, keeping open communication and the sharing of information, ideas, and strategies flowing is a key strategy.

For examples, as well as information about the advantages and disadvantages of using behaviour tallying, please see the chart in NelsonStudy.

ABC ANALYSIS

Purpose and Unique Feature

ABC analysis is an open-ended way to record a child's behaviour; coping abilities; and interactions with materials, equipment, and/or setting, as well as educator or adult–child interactions. If educators are unclear about what is causing certain behaviours or how the behaviours affect others in the room, the ABC analysis type of record is a good choice for this purpose.

ABC analysis is recorded as a three-part sequence of related events:

1. What happened prior to a particular behaviour occurring is called the stimulus or antecedent.
2. The behaviour is what the child did.
3. The consequence is what happened as a result of that behaviour.

Because ABC analysis is a cause-and-effect method of observation, the observer is looking for reasons for certain behaviours. What could be causing (antecedent) Kristie to act in such an aggressive manner (behaviour)? Keeping an open mind concerning causality is vital when using ABC analysis. Often a number of factors combined are the catalyst. Teasing out those reasons, uncovering why Kristie behaved as she did, is the strength and power of this method. Here the observer is the detective looking for clues that will help solve the perceived problem or issue.

But that is only the "AB." What about the "C," the consequences? What follows, or consequences, can be just as important as the antecedent in understanding a specific behaviour. If Kristie was acting aggressively (behaviour) and getting what she wanted (consequences), what kind of detective work would be needed to uncover how the consequence was supporting or rewarding the behaviour? The method of ABC analysis is ideal for examining complex behaviours.

ABC Analysis and the Behaviourists

ABC analysis bears a resemblance to the studies of behaviourists such as Pavlov, Skinner, and Watson. These theorists centred on animal learning as an analogue, or model, for human learning and focused on external stimuli in the learning environment rather than on internal states or conditions of

ABC analysis
A type of documentation that records a sequence of related events over time.

antecedent
Occurring before, prior to, preceding.

behaviour
Anything that can be seen, measured, or counted. Additionally, it can be defined as the way one conducts oneself.

consequence
Relation of an effect to its cause; a natural or necessary result.

analogue
Something similar in function or comparable with another; a model.

the learner to explain learning behaviours. The application of their theories is still seen in education settings today. B.F. Skinner's concepts of operant conditioning and reinforcement are commonplace in modern social learning theories, and educators are familiar with the statement that often typifies his theory: "Behaviour that is rewarded is likely to be repeated." The use of rewards, such as stickers for completed work or candy for sitting during educator-directed small-group time, can find its roots in behaviourist theories. Behaviourists tend to maximize the importance of external reinforcers, such as rewards (consequences), and minimize the importance of the internal cognitive states.

Theories that examine antecedents or consequences are looking for explanations for certain actions or behaviours. The behaviourists applied their theories to learning situations that either centred on enhancing the learning process or reduced or redirected unacceptable behaviour or inefficient learning. Using ABC analysis to uncover reasons for certain behaviours or to unravel complicated behaviours reflects a reliance on the scientific principles of these theories of learning. See the further examples of ABC analysis available online.

Often parents ask educators for advice on what to do at home about certain behaviours, such as acting out at mealtime, sibling rivalry, or temper tantrums. Most home-based behaviours that would be considered problematic are highly complex, personal, and certainly not solvable by a quick conversation. What we do know, though, is that behaviour is often the result of an unmet need. It is wise to listen carefully and to engage in appreciative inquiry before giving suggestions. The child's behaviours are usually only one part of the equation. The ABC analysis model can be effective in uncovering the concerns or expectations of the parents. Assisting the parent to see what caused the behaviour and/or identify how the consequences may be adding to the problem is a positive outcome. How the parent feels is also important. Talking through this process may assist the parent in unraveling and, therefore, understanding the complex nature of the situation. A team approach, that is, discussions of information gathered with the parents or educators, is key to changing the response or consequences following the behaviour.

Format of ABC Analysis

The antecedent is the catalyst that triggers a certain behaviour. What the child says and does is obviously the child's behaviour. But we also want to find out what happens because of or as a result of that child's behaviour. What happens to the consequences if the antecedent or the behaviour changes? How do the consequences become the antecedent for future behaviours? Knowing the consequences helps, in turn, to understand how future behaviours may be influenced.

To see how ABC analysis is part of our everyday life in various ways, let us take a look at Exhibit 5.8. Can you think of other examples?

By using ABC analysis, the observer is able to analyze what seemed to cause the behaviour as well as to examine the consequences of that behaviour. The primary reason for using this type of record is to document behaviours that may be unacceptable, unusual, or concerning. These behaviours could be aggressive behaviours such as hitting, pushing, biting, or swearing; bullying

EXHIBIT 5.8   Example of ABC Analysis: A Personal Example

Let's begin with a personal and practical example of a postsecondary student in Example A:

Antecedent	Behaviour	Consequence
Alarm clock rings	Wake up, get out of bed	Make it to school on time
Forgot to set alarm clock	Stay sleeping	Miss exam
Forgot to set alarm clock & Dad wakes you up	Get out of bed	Late for school

Above, the impact of the student's behaviour on what happens next is evident. Let's apply this approach now to an example with a young child.

ABC ANALYSIS: GILLIAN

Child's Name: _Gillian_   DOB: _____   Age:_____

Observer(s): _____   Date: _____   Location/ Time:_____

Time	Antecedent	Behaviour	Consequence
8:45 a.m.	Gillian is sitting with her mom. After sitting together for 10 minutes in the classroom, her mom gets up to leave for work.	Gillian starts crying.	Gillian's educator picks Gillian up and waves goodbye to her mom while telling Gillian that her "Mom will be back after rest time." Gillian stops crying.
9:30 a.m.	Gillian sits on her educator's lap while a morning song is sung and everyone begins walking to the cloakroom.	Gillian cries and clings to the educator.	The educator takes Gillian by the hand to the cloakroom. While walking together, she tells Gillian excitedly, "We are going outside to play, you love the sandbox!" Gillian stops crying.
10:00 a.m.	Gillian sits on the edge of sandbox alone.	Gillian cries with her head down.	Her educator comes over and sits beside her. The educator quietly says, "Let's make a castle together." Gillian stops crying.
10:30 a.m.	Educator rings the bell to come inside for tidy-up time.	Gillian begins to cry.	The educator takes Gillian by the hand and verbally prompts her to "put the toys in the box and line up—we are going to go inside." Gillian stops crying.

(continued)

behaviours; destructive group dynamics; tantrums; or episodes of mild or severe seizures. Observers use ABC analysis to record, unravel, analyze, or explore the relationships between the observed behaviours of a child or group of children and the environment, social dynamics of peers, or influences of educator behaviours.

Embedded in the purpose of using ABC analysis are expectations: expectations of age-appropriate, acceptable behaviour; cultural and familial expectations; or, given our knowledge of a particular child, expectations of what is common behaviour for this child. These expectations can be the underlying reason for the perceived issue or problem. Other examples of ABC Analysis can be found in NelsonStudy.

Adapting ABC Analysis

ABC analysis can be used with a group of children to monitor specific group relationships or to evaluate the environment. This methodology will vary depending on what is being observed. For example, perhaps educators have noticed that the transition time between free play and outdoors seems to result in children pushing, shoving, or crying and the educators having to remind, remove, and reproach. Usually, no one has the luxury of objectively observing this transition because everyone is caught up in it! Yet if educators took time out to observe, they might find the following:

> The transition time from indoor free play to outdoor learning experience begins at 9:30. The educators give warning of the transition by singing songs, reminding children, assisting the children in getting started by tidying up with them, and establishing a presence in the cloakroom. As in most centres, some children run immediately to get dressed to go outside, others dawdle, and still others move their chairs even closer to the tables, sending a clear message that they intend to stay inside.

Anyone who has been in a playroom at a time such as this can predict quite accurately what types of behaviours will occur. Transitions can be difficult for young children; having to stop playing is like asking a theatre full of moviegoers to stop watching the movie, tidy up the area around them, and leave the theatre! Scheduled time is relevant only to older children and adults. Educators are well aware of this fact, but the point of the observation would be to examine the behaviours in the context of the morning transition. The children are telling us something—we need to listen. Reconceptualizing how we do things can happen when we observe and listen. Children exhibit behaviour to communicate that their needs are not being met in some way. It is our role as investigators to determine what that might be. Analyzing and interpreting the observations and looking for patterns may indicate what acts as an antecedent to the behaviours at morning transition time. Perhaps the behaviours of some children are inconsistent, and the only pattern is that there is none. That, too, is always a possibility. However, other interpretations may indicate how the noisy routine evolves or who may be the major players in the complex set of events. Observing and recording behaviour in a meaningful way can and does make a difference. Altering the schedule to allow more playtime, setting the stage for children to lead the day, or putting playtime earlier or later in the day may be some possibilities. Examining strategies that support children in leading the day might also be a possibility. If, after making these observations, the educators conclude that only a few children seem to be having a difficult time during this transition, then they can try to find the best solution for each child. Perhaps the obvious answer is simply to change the amount of time needed in the cloakroom.

Interpretations for this type of methodology will look different from the types of interpretations made for perhaps an anecdotal or learning story. The purpose of this method leads us to look at what is prompting a response in a child or group of children. Therefore, our interpretations may lead us to conclusions that focus on the role and influence of the educator, the response of the adult or child to what is taking place, and the impact of the curriculum, environment, or materials/equipment in the room, as a few examples. What is often discovered is many behaviours and actions communicated by children are a response to the adults' actions, words, and behaviour. Why might this be likely? Would you agree and why? When we take the time to reflect upon what is taking place, we are better equipped to increase or decrease behaviours taking place in the classroom. Take a moment to reflect upon the ABC analysis examples available online. How might that information be patterned and interpreted? What can be learned?

To learn more about the advantages and disadvantages of using ABC analysis, see the chart in NelsonStudy.

PARTICIPATION CHARTS

Purpose and Unique Feature

The participation chart, such as the one in Exhibit 5.9, targets one child's participation at various learning centres and inquiries, and includes examination of a child's documentation time. Participation charts can be organized to record the participation of each child in the group engaging in a particular curriculum area or zone. Participation charts can also be organized to include one or more children participating in all areas available in the playroom or classroom. The unique feature of the participation chart is that it can record

EXHIBIT 5.9	Participation Chart for One Child

Child's Name: _____ DOB: _____ Age: _____

Observer(s): _____ Date(s): _____

Kindergarten Learning Zones	Monday	Tuesday	Wednesday	Thursday	Friday
Sand Play					
Science—Ant Farm Inquiry					
Co-documenting Centre (e.g., clipboards, cameras, tablets, paper, and writing utensils)					
Cozy Book Corner					
Blocks and Construction Centre					
Dramatic Centre					
Calming and Self-Regulation Zone					
Computer and Internet Zone					
Loose Parts and Creative Design Zone					
Writing and Group Project Area					

the participation of one child, a small group, or the entire group of children. This versatility allows observers more possibilities to collect information than some of the other methods. Observers may also vary the depth of information sought. For example, they may collect basic information on all the children (e.g., their participation during outdoor play) but may also choose to focus on one child during this learning experience and include some quality indicators (e.g., what types of play the child is engaged in). If desired, a number of variables can be presented on the chart:

- a column for frequency: how many times the child visited the learning experience
- a column for duration: how long the child stayed at each learning experience
- a comments section: an area to comment on the child's playmates, her interactions, types of play, her questions and inquiries, or specific information relevant to the educators

Extending Learning Opportunities

Using the scenario in NelsonStudy titled "A Peek into Brindy's Kindergarten Day" as well as a copy of the participation chart in Exhibit 5.9, plot Brindy's participation in her kindergarten classroom. Reflect upon the following questions:

- Where did Brindy participate the most? The least? Why might that be?
- What did we learn about her interests, inquiries, questions, and curiosities?
- What curricular responses could be designed by educators and children to extend what was learned from the participation chart?
- How might an educator involve Brindy in developing responses to the information learned?
- How might this chart inform our understanding of the use of pedagogical documentation and engagement of children?

Format of Participation Charts

Organization of the participation chart begins the same way as the checklist and rating scale: the listing of essential information. Just below the information is the grid listing the items based on a child-centred curriculum. The set-up of the participation chart will depend on whom you want to include: all the children, some of the children, or only one child. If the chart is set up for one child, then the initial organization will be similar to that in Exhibit 5.9.

However, if the participation chart is to be organized to include a group or all the children, your set-up will be quite different. For example, if you wanted to observe the group during morning free playtime or class time, you could set up your chart as in Exhibit 5.10. The information provided by this chart is significant. With just a brief look, you can immediately see where children chose to spend their time. Are there any particular learning centres or centres based on children's interests that were used frequently, seldom used, or not used at all? Why? Does this information give you any ideas about the curriculum? Does the chart confirm your hunches about who usually plays with whom?

EXHIBIT 5.10	Participation Chart for More Than One Child

Observer: Heather _____ Date(s): Week of October 10 (Mon.–Fri.) _____

Setting: Indoor learning experiences _____ Time: 9:45–10:30 a.m. _____

Name	Creative	Dramatic	Blocks	Reading Area	Drafting and Paint Easels
Lakesha	✓✓	✓✓		✓	✓✓✓
Devon	✓		✓	✓	✓✓✓✓✓
Tiffany	✓✓✓✓	✓✓			
Ahmed	✓✓	✓✓			✓✓

IS_ImageSource/iStockphoto.com

How can this information further facilitate your planning of new and additional responsive and inclusive learning experiences or inquiries that continue to reflect the interests and developmental abilities of the children? How might you reflect their interests and extend their learning? Considering reflection is a necessary step in pedagogical documentation, how might children and families participate in this documentation? How might they co-plan responsive and inclusive curriculum with the educator?

Participation charts like those in Exhibit 5.10 can be complemented by comments and notes to provide context to the check mark or marking in each section. A check mark in and of itself will not give rationale or information to assist in understanding what took place at that area or why it might have been frequented so much. Adding context to the simple labels in that exhibit could also assist in providing additional insight.

Using a participation chart with a group of children several times over a three-month period presents a rudimentary pattern of group activity. From that information, a variety of educational decisions can be made. You may want to pay particular attention to the group dynamics. Perhaps these charts have indicated a child whose time spent in solitary play inside the large painted "house" boxes within the block area is of concern to you because he wanted to play in them alone. The simplicity or complexity of participation charts provides educators with many possible educational and managerial decisions.

NI QIN/iStockphoto.com

Adapting Participation Charts

If you wanted to focus on social skills or specifically comment on the social skills of the children as they play outdoors in the playground, you could set up a participation chart such as the one in Exhibit 5.11, used by a centre practising an eclectic approach to planning experiences for children.

Adding an open-ended comments section targeting social skills is one way to further adapt a participation chart. Another way to adapt the chart could be by adding other columns or dimensions. Considering children as co-documenters who are not yet able to "read" text, visuals could be used as headings to guide children in where to make their markings. Other examples like including types of play can be found in NelsonStudy.

EXHIBIT 5.11 — Outdoor Participation Chart for Kindergarten Social Skills

Child's Name: _____ DOB: _____ Age: _____

Observer(s): _____ Date(s): _____

Outdoor Experiences	Frequency	Duration	Comments on Social Skills
Swings			
Climber			
Basketball & Net			
Birdfeeder Inquiry/Feeding the Birds			
Puddle Jumping			
Monkey Bars			
Sandbox			
Loose Parts Musical Fence Creations			

Interpreting and Reflecting upon Participation Chart Information

Before you begin writing your interpretations and reflecting upon what was learned, organize the information you collected from your participation charts in rough draft form.

- Use headings that might include but are not limited to frequency, duration, development, environmental considerations, and relationships.
- Lay your charts out and systematically go through them, compiling the behaviour you observed under each appropriate heading. Note any contextual information or other information that might give insight into what was observed.
- Engage the participation of children and families to examine and analyze the results. Children have a lot to offer to the conversation with their thoughts, hypotheses, and opinions regarding how things happen and why they chose to participate in certain areas.
- If you made interpretations in your comments section, make sure to record them using "seems," "appears," "as if," and "perhaps" to indicate your opinions.
- Now reflect and respond. Begin to analyze the information, summarizing it in a meaningful way as the basis for discussions with the team, which includes the parents and children. Some of these aspects could include the curriculum, the environment, the program approach, individual children, or the group as a whole. This information can also be included in the children's portfolios (or in other ways your setting makes learning visible), which will be further explored in Chapter 6.

Frequency of engagement should indicate a number of possible conclusions: the child likes this experience, they demonstrate a number of strengths with a particular learning experience, they like the other children who frequent the learning experience as well, they demonstrate an attention span reflective of their age, or they are attracted to the physical environment of that space. These suggestions are not an exhaustive list but, rather, provide examples of the information that can be generated by one segment of a participation chart. As you engage in your reflection, check your interpretations of the child's behaviour with those of the child, family, and other educators. Did they come to the same conclusions you did?

Similarly, how would you interpret the information in the duration column? What reasons did the child(ren) state for staying/visiting that experience? For a long time? When reflecting upon how long or how little a child's time is spent with another child or in a particular area, consider not only likes and dislikes but also the culture of the child. Is it important that some cultures value silence more than others or that time in other cultures is not meant to be "filled" as it is in North America? A child's upbringing will influence how the child plays and spends her day. Other questions to be asked include the following:

- In what way is the child's behaviour reflective of the age group? Of his own individuality and variations in development?
- What can be said about the interest in the learning areas?
- What can be learned about the child's interests, learning style, or peer relationships?

These are some of the questions that may arise during an appreciative inquiry discussion among educators, children, and families interpreting information from the participation charts. Take time to reflect and gain meaning from what has been seen and heard. In what ways could a participation chart be used in a portfolio?

To learn more about the advantages and disadvantages of using participation charts, please see the chart in NelsonStudy.

PROFILES

Purpose and Unique Feature

profile

A method of communication that focuses on a specific, targeted area of child development, allowing the observer to record behaviours of a child that are typically demonstrated within that development area.

A profile focuses on specific areas of child development, such as fine motor or communication skills, rather than specific behaviours. Targeting a developmental area or domain appears rather broad, yet it does help focus the observer on one area of development at a time. This narrowing of focus typifies the closed methods of conducting and documenting observations. Many say that profiles function as more of an organizational tool rather than an observational methodology and, subsequently, may call them portfolio organizational methodologies. Some feel that this methodology boxes children into a singular lens while others debate its openness allows for documentation of individuality. Let's take a look to see why these views might exist.

The unique feature of the profile is the discoveries that are found when using this type of documentation. Its focus allows the observer to gather specific developmental information that might be demonstrated independently or with support. The observer has the flexibility of gathering positively worded examples of behaviours and skills, as well as the interests of a child that are meaningful in terms of his environment, family, and cultural influences. This contextual or ecological approach offers a broader perspective of a child rather than the narrow confines of preselected skills in standardized checklists or rating scales.

Profiles can be used for a variety of reasons. The purpose for developing a profile will influence what information is gathered and in what ways. For example, if parents ask for feedback about their child's ability to take care of their personal needs, an educator would collect information concerning toileting, dressing and undressing in the cloakroom, and mealtime behaviours. The educator would make point-form notes throughout the day for several days or until a number of representative behaviours were collected. When combined with information from the child and family members on what they see at home, the completed profile would provide the parents with examples of how their child manages their personal needs. An additional benefit perhaps could be the sense of confidence it would give the parents not only in the child's abilities but also in their parenting skills. The behavioural examples would confirm for them that what is being taught at home is being transferred to the early childhood setting. This information may be quite significant for families who have been working on these skills at home or for newcomers who have recently immigrated and wish to gain insight into different methods of learning basic life skills.

ecological approach

An approach for understanding a child's development in terms of the environment, which includes family, neighbourhood, or community.

Format and Adaptability of Profiles

The format for recording profiles can be structured easily by starting with the essential information and then listing the developmental area and allowing space between each area for examples of behaviour and interests displayed by a child to be recorded. Information is documented using a child-centred positive lens, noting and crediting how children demonstrate their knowledge, learning, and skills in their own unique way.

Profiles are more commonly used in the elementary school system, inclusive early childhood settings, by resource professionals supporting understanding of children, and by specialized settings that may be supporting children with special interests or needs. Early childhood settings that use portfolios or e-portfolios as a forum for collecting evidence of children's learning may use this methodology to pull their learning together. Imagine the wonderfully unique behaviours that you would observe in the following environments:

- an infant room
- a drop-in centre in a diverse or multilinguistic community
- an inclusive centre with children with a variety of extra-support needs
- a family grouping in private home child care
- a full-day kindergarten room
- a parent cooperative preschool

Grouping behaviours under a developmental area or domain creates parameters that say, "You can observe and document any behaviours that you would consider to be under this particular domain." For example, if you were

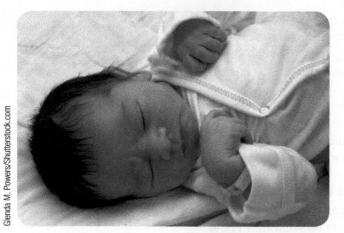
Glenda M. Powers/Shutterstock.com

asked to document examples of gross motor skills within a preschool grouping of young children, do you think you would see jumping, hopping, walking, climbing, rolling? What if there was a child with a walker in the group? Would you record examples of balance, or how the child could let go of their walker to get onto the ground or how they manoeuvred their walker from one place to another? This holistic approach targets the domain of gross motors skills and includes all the well-known ways of locomotion, but also leaves observations open to all kinds of everyday examples.

In early childhood settings, profiles are developed and used in a variety of ways. Take, for example, the infant seen here. In an infant-care setting, this child's parents will want to know how much food their baby ate, how many bowel movements they had, and how long they slept as it supports them in organizing how to care for and support their infant when they get home. A brief list of point-form notes could be given to the parents on "what Christopher did today." Dramatic changes in development occur during infancy weekly, if not daily. One of the authors of this book remembers a student–educator who had her field placement in an infant room. She was struggling at first with this new age group, and we decided that in the back of her binder she would keep a profile on one child. The purpose of the profile was for the student–educator to become acquainted with what infants and emerging toddlers can do (see Exhibit 5.12). When the student–educator told the baby's mother about the observations, the mother was pleased to see the documentation.

EXHIBIT 5.12   Infant Profile

Child's Name: Christina _____   Age: 18 mos. _____

Profile of Areas of Development (Observations, April 27–May 15)

Gross Motor	• climbs onto low mat / in and out of low chair moving hands and legs/feet
	• balances upper torso while sitting and holding onto a pop-up toy
	• squats and maintains balance to pick up objects on the floor
	• walks sideways and forward
Fine Motor	• uses palmar grasp to hold toys and release
	• has eye–hand coordination as she moves objects such as farm animals into the farmhouse, and from one hand to another
	• exhibits pincer grasp as she picks up small objects with her thumb and pointer finger

Self-Help	• uses spoon to scoop food and place in mouth
	• pulls off own shoes independently with both hands
	• holds cup with both hands when drinking
Communication (Receptive)	• listens and responds to greetings and basic one-step directions such as "go get your coat"
	• waves "bye-bye" in response to children saying goodbye to them
Communication (Expressive)	• cries when frustrated (e.g., when she was told she had to wait for her turn)
	• babbles and "la-la"s to himself (sings)
	• knows words such as "mama" and "mommy," "no, all done, cat, cow, eat, look, me," such as "doggie, cat, eat"
	• laughs aloud
	• uses key words to express needs and wants, such as "up," "more"
Socio-emotional	• plays by herself (solitary play)
	• offers hugs to caregivers and peers on her own
	• is interested in exploring and manipulating her environment through mouthing of objects, touching, and looking
	• separates easily from parents upon arrival
Cognitive	• can find object if only a part of the object is in view
	• displays understanding of cause and effect (e.g., presses pop-up top)
	• points to simple objects upon request, such as spoon, coat, and shoes
	• imitates adults and peers, such as patty-cake, and plays social games as in peek-a-boo

Documentation such as this example demonstrates a dedication to understanding the development of Christina. Examine the profiles in each area of development. Based on those examples, an educator could develop an emergent curriculum. Setting up an infant/toddler obstacle course might be part of those further learning opportunities. Imagine how the parent would enjoy seeing pictures or a video of Christina engaged in play. Those examples could prompt dialogue between educator and parent and give the parent some ideas of what they could do at home. When profiles of a child's progress are included in the child's portfolio, they represent the child's growth and development at a particular stage at a certain time. Particularly for this age group, profile examples are invaluable to all of the child's educators.

Having an observational tool with some flexibility to allow for the variety of possible ways to record a child's habits, needs, abilities, interests, and characteristics is important. Children will display their learning and skills in their own unique way—being able to capture this learning within methodologies outlined in Chapters 4 and 5 is important. The profile records behaviours sensitive to the subtle influences of the home culture, diversity, the playroom environment, and even media influences. Profiles can include all developmental areas or only one or two, and the format of the profile may vary. The observer may record periodically throughout a two-week cycle. How do you know what is worth writing down? Some of your notes may reveal significant milestones in the child's life. Others will be more subtle but represent, for example, a shift from one area of interest to another or a deeper understanding of a concept. Go online for more information and examples.

Similar to the many observational tools previously discussed, profiles offer opportunities for communication between educators, children, and families. What we learn from our observations gives rise to questions: an appreciative inquiry. For example, in a toddler room key questions to ask are, How do toddlers communicate? Are they beginning to understand that words are power? What nonverbal ways of communication could be documented? How could pictures and text be combined to show parents and others the toddler's use of communication? Consider revisiting technology-assisted documentation methodologies in Chapter 4 for apps and online forums that would easily accommodate profile-style observations.

To learn more about the advantages and disadvantages of using profiles, please see the chart in NelsonStudy.

PICTORIAL REPRESENTATIONS

pictorial representations

Visual images that are drawn, painted, or photographed, used to represent an idea.

Pictorial representations are, as the term suggests, pictures, images, or graphic drawings that represent persons or objects. Sketches, pictures, or other graphic representations can be useful to illustrate an idea. These images give visual appeal to text-laden publications. But how can they be used to assist in documenting children's learning, interests, and behaviour?

Using prepared pictures with key words, phrases, or sentences is another way educators or others can communicate what they have seen. These prepared pictures can represent a key developmental milestone, such as walking or sitting independently. The pictures could represent a type of grasp, such as palmar grasp or pincer grasp.

Pictorial examples are often accompanied by phrases or sentences depicting the action that is portrayed. The person who observed the child demonstrating these skills can merely circle the picture or copy the description into the child's record e-portfolio or portfolio.

Some educators with seasoned skills in working with children might struggle with writing and find pictorial representation a welcome alternative to print-dependent documentation. Not being able to communicate effectively in writing does not mean that an educator is not a good observer. How unfortunate it would be not to use the skills of a good observer! What are some ways to put those skills to use? Less print-dependent and more visual or graphic ways of recording information provide the means for educators to use their observation skills to full advantage.

Media-assisted observation or graphic representation are methods that can be used with people who are culturally unaccustomed to developing documentation on children yet possess an observant, reflective manner with children. Accommodating their skills within a team approach is a positive and innovative way to use the many methods of documenting children's behaviour. For pictorial examples or graphic representations, please be sure to look at the examples online.

Many early childhood settings use the Boardmaker system to create a daily communication and observation/documentation system for a child. Examples of boardmaker communication systems can also be located online. These visuals would be in pictorial form and would be arranged on a communication sheet for children to circle and self-assess their daily learning experiences for the day. This information would then function as a beneficial document for inquiry for the parent/guardian to prompt the child to communicate, or it may empower a child who otherwise might not yet be able to communicate effectively either verbally or nonverbally to show and point to what she did while at child care or school. Applying this to the cycle of observation, this natural conversation could also prompt provocations to occur at home or at child care as the child debriefs and visually communicates her interests and experiences during the day.

Boardmaker

Picture-based computerized library that is printed and/or used to assist individuals with aspects of their learning, communication, and understanding. Examples include printed schedules, transitions, and pictures for a picture exchange system.

SOCIOGRAMS

A sociogram is a type of social map used to examine the social context of a child. Social maps can be graphic or pictorial representations of how a person interacts within a group.

A common form of a social map is the family tree. Compiling a family tree is popular practice for children in elementary school—drawing a tree and then adding pictures of themselves and their families to the branches. Family trees are a graphic representation of family history and can be represented in several formats, such as the oldest generations at the bottom and the newer generations at the top. Extensive examples of family tree structures and themes can be found on the Internet.

The type of social map that is most useful in documenting social structures of young children is the sociogram. Sociograms are used in the field of early childhood to document and track social acceptance and relationships. For example, in September, children in a group may be relatively new to one another, and an

sociogram

A graphic representation of the social structures and links that a person or group of people have with others.

family tree

A diagram (sometimes in the form of a symbolic tree with branches detailing names of relatives) outlining the ancestry, connections, and relationships between people within multiple generations of a family.

Chapter 5: Observing and Documenting Targeted Behaviours

educator may want to monitor who plays with whom, how often, and for how long. Instead of using pages of written observations, the educator can construct a sociogram. Using this format, shown in Exhibit 5.13, she can indicate by a picture or simple graphic representation children's social connections, using arrows going from and to individual children. A few months later, the educator can, using the same graphic representation, see what new relationships have been formed or see if the same social patterns from September still hold. Sociograms are also known by the new term sociometry.

Sociograms have also been used extensively as a research technique. Sociograms are useful in obtaining information on a particular child, a child within a group, or group dynamics. A sociogram can be created with input from the children; this variation would be used with older children. For the construction of a sociogram of which child in the group is most likely to help others learn, a child would need the understanding and maturity to define the parameters of the educator's questions.

sociometry

The qualitative state of inter-personal relationships in populations.

EXHIBIT 5.13　　　　　*Child–Peer Interactions*

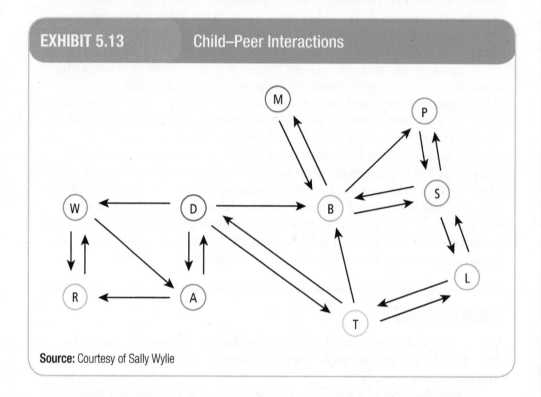

Source: Courtesy of Sally Wylie

Sociogram Variations: Ecomaps

Sociograms can also be created to visually communicate the social influence of others in the life of a child. How many groups of children does a child social-ize with on a regular basis? How can the groupings of family, friends, child care, and other extracurricular events be represented? Examine the social differences between Sarah and Joel in Exhibit 5.14. What is similar? What is different? How would this knowledge of Sarah and Joel assist the educator in developing an awareness and sensitivity to the children's social home culture and the influences in their life?

EXHIBIT 5.14   Ecomaps of Sarah and Joel

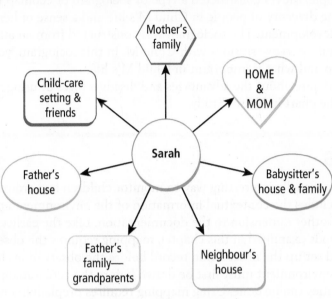

Sociogram/Ecomap of Sarah

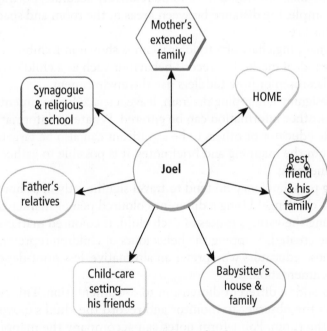

Sociogram/Ecomap of Joel

Source: Courtesy of Sally Wylie

As discussed in other chapters, the family is not the only social influence in a child's life. Discovering the social influences in a child's life is enlightening. Consult with the exhibit online titled Sociogram Variations: Moyra's Examples. In this example, Moyra constructed a type of sociogram or ecomap to get a sense of the diversity of people in Child M's life and a sense of her socio-emotional development. The sociogram was constructed from an audio taping during several interview sessions with Child M. In this sociogram, you can get a sense of who and what is important in Child M's life.

To learn more about the advantages and disadvantages of using sociograms, please see the chart in NelsonStudy.

MAPPING

Mapping is a visually interesting way to monitor children in a group setting. Mapping includes the contextual information of the environment and, therefore, adds another dimension to the documentation. Like the earlier observation methods examined in this chapter, mapping requires the observer to organize and set up the observation record before the observations begin. A map of the environment must first be drawn before the actual mapping of a child's activities can be done. Using mapping requires preplanning with the creation of a diagram of the room with all essential areas and items appropriately indicated, such as the curriculum area, equipment, furniture, supplies, and space. The diagram would have to be relatively accurate, portraying effectively, for example, the distance between areas in the room and spaces between pieces of furniture.

A basic mapping chart of a toddler room is shown in Exhibit 5.15. Mapping is an ideal method to record behaviour such as a child's wandering within the classroom or how toddlers use the environment.

When designing a mapping diagram, leave a space for comments where time spent or other information can be entered. Whatever information is judged by the educator or others to be significant can also be targeted for their attention. From the mapping and brief notes, it is possible to gather inferences and ascribe meaning.

Mapping preschoolers who tend to travel significantly in a short time would pose a challenge! Using a different-coloured pen or marker could be one way of tracking the various routes of each child. If coloured markers are used, a legend can be created. Mapping the behaviours of children represents another option for those educators who prefer an alternative, less print-dependent means of documentation.

Mapping adds a different dimension to documentation. This type of record allows the observer to monitor and record the child's movement throughout the room. Point-form notes can accompany the mapping to detail the significance of the child's activity. Presented with other documentation, mapping is an interesting visual tool to engage children in self-reflection and documentation and reflect upon where they played, whom they played with, where they spent the most time, and so on. As we revisit pedagogical documentation, it is important to think about how each methodology, in this case mapping, can be used with children, families, educators, and the community.

EXHIBIT 5.15   Mapping Chart

Child's Name: Ayla   DOB: October 16   Age: 27 months

Date: June 20   Time: 8:55–9:30

1. Sits on edge of mat watching the children
2. Crawls into and out of the tunnel 2 times
3. Throws balls to educator and other children
4. Stands in the middle of the play equipment and watches
5. Crawls around on the low beams, lies down, and bangs feet on the beam
6. Lines up at the door with peers when her name is called

Source: Adapted from Julia Richmond

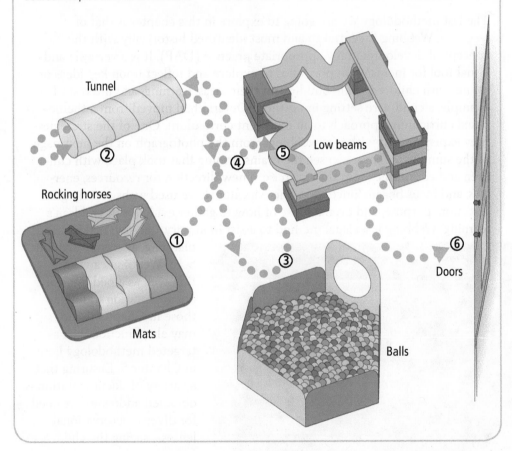

Mapping is also a methodology that could be aided by technology on apps like Educreation or other mind-mapping software. How might you explain mapping to parents and involve them in documentation? What message might you want to convey when offering the mapping as a revealing piece of documentation?

Mapping can also be used to monitor other access considerations such as the mobility of a child with special needs within the playroom. A child with spina bifida who uses a wheelchair for walking may gravitate only to specific areas of the room. Upon examination of the map, in collaboration with the parent or child, the observer recognizes how the set-up of the room is preventing the child from accessing certain learning experiences. As a result of the inquiry, changes can be made to the learning environment allowing the child to move between spaces in the classroom. Monitoring this change over a period of time using mapping can not only show areas of preference over time but also provide a measure for self-confidence.

To learn more about the advantages and disadvantages of using mapping, please see the chart in NelsonStudy.

WEBBING: A MULTIPURPOSE TOOL

webbing

A tool used with an emergent curriculum approach to create a tentative plan where possibilities are explored such as an interest, material, or idea and developed with the input of the children.

The last methodology we are going to explore in this chapter is that of webbing. Webbing is central to and most identified historically with the concept of developmentally appropriate practice (DAP). It is a versatile and visual tool for inclusion in portfolios to explore and reflect upon key ideas or events with children while building on their ideas, learning, and interests. For example, a child-care setting in northern Ontario had moved from a theme-based curriculum approach to an emergent curriculum. One of the strategies they experimented with was webbing. From the photograph on the next page of the summer web, we can see the brainstorming that took place with children and educators. From that exercise, a new direction for resources, energies, and focus began. Since then, the educators have used webs to help give direction, purpose, and even a sense of how to gather evidence of children's learning. Webbing is a visual method to assist in inquiry, decision making, and planning, as seen in Exhibit 5.16. Webbing can function well as a pedagogical documentation tool like those in Chapter 4 and may also function well as a targeted methodology here in Chapter 5. Ensuring that a variety of documentation is obtained addresses the need for diverse observational lenses—seeing the child from many perspectives and acknowledging that what educators may wish to know can be quite different from what families, the children, or indeed the community in which the child lives wishes to know.

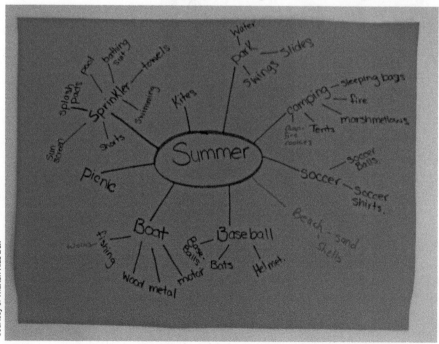

Courtesy of Wiarton Kids Den

EXHIBIT 5.16   Web Showing Types of Documentation

The first web of types of documentation was developed for the staff of the Valeska Hinton Early Childhood Education Center. The purpose was to assist teachers in expanding their concepts of how they might collect evidence of children's learning and to support their developing skills in documentation. seen In the web showing types of documentation, a variety of ways of gathering evidence about children's learning are demonstrated. Radiating out from the web are five clusters: individual portfolios, narratives, observations of progress and performance, child self-reflections, and products (individual or group). Each of these types of documentation can provide a way to view children's work.

Reflecting back upon our discussion of various observational methods in Chapter 4 and this chapter, what other methodologies could we include in this web?

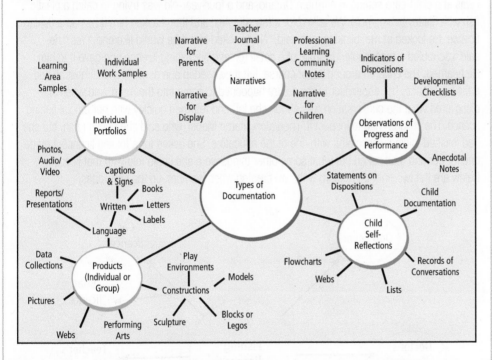

Source: Helm, Judy Harris, Beneke, Sallee, & Steinheimer, Kathy. (2007). *Windows on learning: Documenting young children's work* (2nd ed.). New York: Teachers College Press. Copyright © 2007 by Teachers College Press, Columbia University. All rights reserved. Reprinted by permission of the publisher.

Webbing and Emergent Documentation

Using a web to portray inquiries, questions, various hypotheses, the creation of ideas or concepts, or a framework is a discovery process. The process should include the children as much as possible so that the team is representative of many people in the room. At Wiarton Kids Den, educators brainstormed many ideas and concepts, such as developmental domains, body parts, shadows, water, eye colours, and wind. The topic of fishing licences evolved from a child in the preschool room who was pretending to fish by trying to hook a plastic fish onto a plastic pole. Before long, every child in the room had asked for one, except one girl who received a babysitting licence. This fishing licence web looked something like the one in Exhibit 5.17.

"Thinking and Wondering" in Pedagogical Documentation

How else then, in our understanding of children, families, and community, can we demonstrate that voice through the documentation of children? In what other ways can we show their wonderings and our collective possibilities?

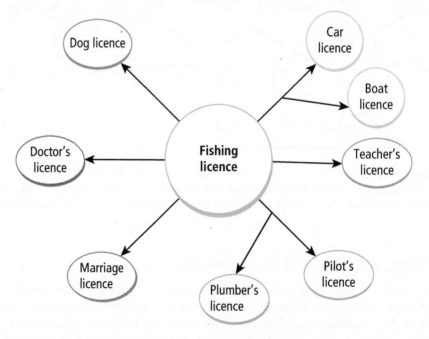

EXHIBIT 5.17   A Fishing Licence

I was at a child-care setting in northern Ontario, and a four-year-old was trying to catch a plastic fish with his toy fishing pole. We talked for a few minutes, and then I asked him if he had a fishing licence. He looked at me, blinking, and said, "No." I asked him if he would like one. "Yes," he said. I scribbled a reasonable facsimile of a small rectangular fishing licence and gave it to him. He beamed. The children around us, of course, felt they needed one as well, until almost all had a fishing licence. The supervisor of the centre happened to come into the room, and when she discovered what the conversation was about, she left and returned quickly with her official fishing licence. The children had to inspect it. Then along came Mabel, who said she doesn't fish, but she had finished folding washcloths with one of the educators. She asked for a folding licence. I made one for her and then asked her what some other things were she could fold with that licence. Below are the two brief curriculum webs we created when we pursued the new ideas.

Emerging Inquiry: Why do some people need a licence to do something? Why does a dog need a licence? What is a licence? How long does it take to get one? Why does a pilot need a licence? How does he or she get one? How much does a licence cost? How long can you have a licence?

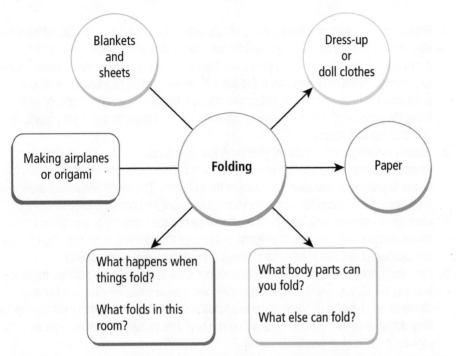

We made several kinds of webs in the preschool room. This one was inspired by Ayla, who apparently loves to fold. Pictures and text would support the investigation of this concept. Take pictures of children folding. Ask them what they are learning and write it down. Include the kinds of things they folded with paper. Create a representation of their learning, which is what emergent curriculum is all about.

Source: Wiarton Kids Den/Sally Wylie

According to Fleet, Patterson and Robertson (2006), pedagogical documentation is also a strategy that allows us to better understand children, to develop meaningful curriculum, to lead an inquiry, and to develop insights into their learning. Using pedagogical documentation of individual and group learning provides opportunities for reflection and reinvention, components essential to professional growth and development. When we document children's learning, we consider and reflect on what the children may be thinking, doing and/or learning and then apply their insights to their unique manner of teaching them. Documentation provides qualitative evidence of the children's current thinking and learning and leads to the development of new possible strategies to assist children in reaching the next learning steps.

Source: Bowne, Cutler, DeBates, et al. "Pedagogical Documentation and Collaborative Dialogue as Tools of Inquiry." *Journal of the Scholarship of Teaching and Learning, 10*(2), 49.

The potential of webbing can be quite significant to the learning, inquiries, and exploration of children within their environment. Be sure to visit examples online for other applications.

1. Each of these closed targeted methods has its own unique features and uses, which allows educators to choose the most appropriate one. These observational tools can be self-designed or commercially made. With input from the learning community (children, educators, family, community), they can stand alone or be adapted (in headers, content, context, or information to be inputted) to reflect the children, families, staff, philosophy, or setting. Know the purpose of each tool; adapt each one to fit the uniqueness and individuality of your children and setting.

2. Chapter 4 pedagogical documentation methodologies focused on the unanticipated and spontaneous narratives and behaviour from young children. Chapter 5 methodologies focus on the targeted and anticipated behaviours from children. The target behaviours are known in advance. Each methodology has an informal structure that can be altered to suit the observer or intended audience. Each methodology has the capability to encompass comments, context, and the voice of children, but require the educator to set the stage for the participation of children in advance (through consultations and co-designing).

3. Each methodology in this chapter can benefit our understanding of the abilities, thinking, learning, and development of children in their own unique ways, for each has her own strengths and benefits. Reviewing the examples and descriptions for each methodology will draw attention to their purpose and will outline how they capture as well as what they can capture in terms of targeted information.

THROUGH THE LENS OF REFLECTIVE, TRANSFORMATIVE PRACTICES

Part 1 of this text started us on our journey with the mantra of a good observer: no matter how much you learn about children, there is always more to learn. Part 1 began by examining the observation process and discussing why observing and documenting the learning, thinking, and inquiries of young children is such a complex and valuable process in the field of early childhood. In Chapter 1, we stated that observation is a practice that is setting-independent, requires the voices of all participants, and is the substance of all pedagogical documentation. Chapter 2 introduced us to the importance of ethics, rights, and confidentiality within the cycle of observation, and Chapter 3 investigated the writing process and introduced the observer to what constitutes observation and interpretations. These chapters also explored the knowledge and skills needed to prepare different pedagogical documentation methods, appreciate and understand the importance of inquiry and asking questions, and understand how these actions guide us through the cycle of observation. Part 2 included two comprehensive chapters detailing the many possible methods of pedagogical documentation, from learning stories and social media approaches to targeted approaches such as ABC analysis. Fortunately, we are not finished—we know that simply engaging in one type of observation will not suffice or give us the information we need to make appropriately informed decisions regarding all areas of our professional practice.

Part 3 is about living in a society that is ever changing, with research and practices that constantly evolve and reframe our thinking. Our profession continues to transform so dramatically that we need to build strong communities of practice as pedagogical leaders in observation in order to support ongoing transformation in this area of practice.

This vibrant process of investigating, learning, and reflecting brings us to the philosophies that are currently evolving and influencing our practice. As Dahlberg, Moss, and Pence (2007) stated, "The greater our awareness of our pedagogical practices, the greater our possibility to change through constructing a new space" (p. 153). That is the purpose of this text. Through appreciative inquiry and the cycle of observation, we invite you to create a new space in your mind where you will see new possibilities that could transform your practice and what you believe.

In Part 3, we continue to explore how our beliefs and practices around observation are reflected in day-to-day interactions, family, community, and the global village. With the immediacy of the social media and the Internet, we are affected by global events, and it is no wonder that we look not only to our own

pedagogical practices

Practices that provide multiple opportunities for students to engage in intellectually challenging and real-world learning experiences; educator practices that are child focused with learning activities that may reflect a particular philosophy.

neighbourhoods but also outward to others for their philosophy and practices regarding children and families. Guided by responsive, inclusive practices, we look to models and principles, goals, and core values to reaffirm, discover, and reflect. Exploring alternative methods that assist us in creating the most useful, meaningful ways of sharing the learning and development of children is part of appreciative inquiry and an attitude of reflection, and is fundamental to developing learning communities.

Acknowledgment and encouragement of parent involvement are equally important if we are to create caring communities. Through dialogue, educators are able to learn about their families, what is important to them, and how they see themselves within the community. Urie Bronfenbrenner's ecological model of human development describes how a child is influenced first by the family and those with whom the child has direct contact, later moving outward from the family to the neighbourhood, to eventually being part of the patterning of environmental events and transitions over the course of life. In this text, we began with the discussion of the observation of children, but through the chapters, we have expanded our discussion to highlight the importance of including not only the voice of the child but also the voices of the family, educators, and community in our observation and documentation practices.

Chapters 6, 7, and 8 assist the educator–observer to understand how observation, inquiry, and documentation change one's professional practice. We examine the environment, how portfolios and e-portfolios are created for children and educators, the steps and processes involved with authentic assessment and early intervention, and the role of the community in our observation and documentation practices. Chapter 8 introduces the transformative role of the educator–observer as leader, researcher, mentor, lifelong learner, and community-capacity builder for observation and pedagogical documentation. Observation and sound pedagogical documentation practices rely on team members who are committed to teamwork, asking questions, inquiry, and participation in the cycle of observation.

Tammy Bryngelson/iStockphoto.com

Ke Yu/iStockphoto.com

INFORMING PEDAGOGICAL PRACTICE
THROUGH THE LENS OF REFLECTION

OVERVIEW

Chapters 1 through 5 have equipped us with the foundational knowledge in which to query how we go about informing and creating curriculum from our observation and pedagogical documentation. We have come to appreciate the intended meaning of the pedagogical documentation we co-prepare; therefore, knowing how this documentation might inform curriculum would be important. What we also know is that there are many considerations we need to integrate into our decisions concerning curriculum including but not limited to philosophy (e.g., emergent, inquiry based, responsive inclusive) and values of a setting, context and the environment, the community of learners (e.g., their inquiries, thinking, wonderings, interest, development), ministry and licensing requirements, established early learning frameworks that guide practice, and so much more. How will we know if the documentation we co-prepare is pedagogically sound, meets ministry and licensing expectations, and satisfies children and parents? How will we know if we're "on the right track" with our curriculum? In response to these questions, the topics in this chapter explore methods of determining strategies and approaches to find or integrate documentation time with our professional practice, fostering collaboration and co-inquiry, and finding a pedagogical framework that works for your community of learners. We have created examples online to illustrate these concepts and support this discussion.

Portfolios in this chapter complete the examination of pedagogical documentation methodologies. It is important to understand that portfolios are part of the cycle of observation and appreciative inquiry processes. A portfolio is developed while co-engaging in and observing children's inquiries, co-collecting their work, and, of course, collaborating with children and their parents. As educators, we do not see the portfolio as an end product but rather as an ongoing process; thus, we would encourage you to think of the portfolio as a visual continuum of a child's interests, "wonders," self-reflection, self-awareness, thinking, development, and learning. Many types of portfolios are outlined in this chapter, from hard-copy file folders (which are not as common) to electronic and digital variations online, on computer hard drives or on relevant apps.

FOCUS QUESTIONS

1. Describe the importance of dialogue, reflection and the preparation of questions within the cycle of observation. How might they support our practice and the inquiries of children?
2. Define strategies for creating time for documentation and reflection.
3. Describe the interrelationship between pedagogical frameworks, documentation and curriculum. How might appreciative inquiry help us to understand their connectedness?
4. In what ways does the cycle of observation support community building?
5. What are the stages and content in portfolio preparation? How might we connect portfolios to pedagogical documentation?
6. In what ways would portfolios support authentic assessment and metacognition, and what are the various types of portfolios?

THE CYCLE OF OBSERVATION: REFLECTIVE AND TRANSFORMATIVE

didactic

Meant to intentionally teach, guide, or instruct.

The cycle of observation is not a structured, didactic, prescriptive formula for educators to direct and demonstrate their observation, planning, and documenting process. If we recall in earlier chapters, the cycle of observation is first an interactive and responsive process involving a team: parents, family, community professionals, educators, and children.

How a cycle of observation is represented, however, varies depending on philosophy and practices, pedagogical frameworks, age groupings, parent involvement, community demographics, and other factors. No longer are educator-directed themes driving the curriculum; research in Ontario, across

Canada and around the world support the need for reflection, inquiry, and sound observational and documentation pedagogy. Pedagogical documentation prompts new perspectives and processes of observing and documenting, and the cycle of observation supports this paradigm shift.

During the cycle of observation, there should be freedom to stop, reflect, question or inquire, revisit, change direction, and/or include others. When including the viewpoints of others, this process can be transformational as people begin to see things in new ways, participate where they had not before, and change practices to reflect those involved. Different perceptions of others are uncovered through close involvement. Discussion based on observation, appreciative inquiry, and documentation is more than something done in a classroom. This community-inclusive process creates a space for dialogue and involvement, as stated in Exhibit 6.1.

For all concerned, this cyclical process invites multiple perspectives so as to provide insight into what is seen and heard. As discussed in Chapter 2 and in Exhibit 6.2, there is no single entry point to this cycle. Observers may begin at any point of the process because observation occurs at any time in any philosophy. Exhibit 6.2 demonstrates active reflection throughout the cycle as it systematically engages educators, families, and children in inquiry-based thinking. A further benefit of engagement within this cycle is that it leads to discoveries that foster self-awareness, the improvement of professional practice, and experiences that promote learning for all. These and other qualities of the cycle of observation such as mutual education and co-inquiry increase its ability to inform aspects of practice such as curriculum, early identification, the environment, and so much more.

Collaboration and Co-Inquiry

The process of appreciative inquiry and the practice of engaging in the cycle of observation with a team—parents, educators, related professionals, and the children—represent a collaborative process that for 21st-century learning makes sense. But is it so new?

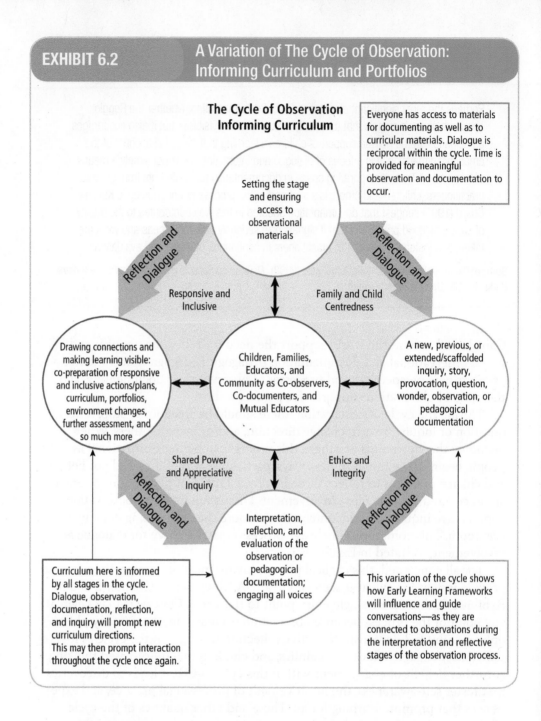

The Cycle of Observation Informing Curriculum

Everyone has access to materials for documenting as well as to curricular materials. Dialogue is reciprocal within the cycle. Time is provided for meaningful observation and documentation to occur.

Setting the stage and ensuring access to observational materials

Reflection and Dialogue

Responsive and Inclusive

Family and Child Centredness

Drawing connections and making learning visible: co-preparation of responsive and inclusive actions/plans, curriculum, portfolios, environment changes, further assessment, and so much more

Children, Families, Educators, and Community as Co-observers, Co-documenters, and Mutual Educators

A new, previous, or extended/scaffolded inquiry, story, provocation, question, wonder, observation, or pedagogical documentation

Shared Power and Appreciative Inquiry

Ethics and Integrity

Reflection and Dialogue

Interpretation, reflection, and evaluation of the observation or pedagogical documentation; engaging all voices

Curriculum here is informed by all stages in the cycle. Dialogue, observation, documentation, reflection, and inquiry will prompt new curriculum directions. This may then prompt interaction throughout the cycle once again.

This variation of the cycle shows how Early Learning Frameworks will influence and guide conversations—as they are connected to observations during the interpretation and reflective stages of the observation process.

The co-inquiry process was originally introduced by John Dewey (1933, 1938) [who] believed that teachers construct knowledge through inquiry with the assistance of colleagues and faculty, who help them refine and clarify their ideas about their learning and teaching experiences in the classroom. [Research into the co-inquiry process shows] a positive correlation between professional development experiences, teacher collaboration, and program quality/child outcomes. (Honig & Hirallal, 1998; Edsource, 2005; Abramson, 2008, p. 4)

The benefits of the co-inquiry process as part of the cycle of observation are that it encourages dialogue and offers opportunities for meaningful parent participation in addition to typical roles such as committee work or supporting a bake sale for example. Being a co-inquirer includes everyone in all steps and stages of the cycle of observation, as well as in the process of dialogue, reflection, the investigation of new ideas, and evaluation to inform a curriculum that encompasses and values the entire community. Instead of "this is what she ate, did, how many hours slept, etc.," parents can be part of "what we did today." Co-inquiry prompts conversation and involvement beyond the maintenance issues of food, sleep, or diapers.

The writings of Dewey, Vygotsky, Malaguzzi, Piaget, and Skinner refer to co-constructing knowledge through inquiry and are summed up well in the article entitled "Skinner Meets Piaget on the Reggio Playground: Practical Synthesis of Applied Behaviour Analysis and Developmentally Appropriate Practice Orientations" by Warash, Curtis, Hursh, and Tucci (2008). Co-inquiry, they say, is an invitation to rethink relationships and communication not only between educators and related professionals but also with parents and families.

In communities across Canada, parent and family literacy teams work cooperatively with families to encourage oral language and parent participation in children's play. Documentation of adult–child play provides families and parents with opportunities to evolve their image of the child to continue to increase understanding and appreciation of the thinking and competencies of children. Rather than just being a spectator of play, providing opportunities for adult and child inquiry through play such as with messy goop or finger painting reminds everyone how exploration leads to new ways of thinking. This playtime also offers an opportune time to document interactions and dialogue, giving another lens from which children and families view themselves.

Mutual Education

Getting to know parents and families right from the first moment we meet them and engage them in the cycle of observation provides opportunities for mutual education and dialogue about questions, queries or wonderings from parents. As children's thinking evolves in complexity, families may communicate or ask about child guidance, safety, relationships, eating or food preferences, communication, napping, and independence versus dependence. It is through these conversations that the uniqueness of each child and family needs to be encouraged, included, and appreciated so that the educator can be responsive within the early childhood setting. In the text *Diversity in Early Care and Education: Honoring Differences*, Janet Gonzalez-Mena (2008) provides revealing examples of cultural misunderstandings and uses those examples to explore how potential differences of opinion can be resolved when families and educators come together in a common place with different perspectives. Among many strong suggestions to creatively problem solve, she offers the concept of "mutual education," as noted in Exhibit 6.3.

The idea of mutual education is fundamental in creating trust and building relationships founded on respect and caring. The "third space" Gonzalez-Mena refers to is a concept that means putting away judgements and assumptions. It suggests views are expressed by one person while the other listens attentively,

Steve Debenport/iStockphoto.com

and then the roles are reversed. From that dialogue and understanding will emerge key ideas or parts of the conversation that they could both agree upon. Perhaps the two people create a totally new perspective dramatically different from either of their previous points of view. This process also illustrates how appreciative inquiry (asking questions in a respectful and kind way) and reflection (considering other's point of view) converge to create an atmosphere of openness to possibilities, creating the third space to which Gonzalez-Mena alluded.

REFLECTIVE EXERCISE 6.1

Examine the questions below. Which questions would be more likely to prompt the development of the "third space" where mutual education, discovery, and new ideas could be generated? Which ones would produce a reciprocal and meaningful discussion? Explain why you chose the questions you did.

❑ 1. A. You mentioned you are worried; can you tell me a little more about Reena's communication and what you have observed? OR

❑   B. Why are you concerned about Reena's communication?

❑ 2. A. Did you enjoy engaging in play with Abraham? OR

❑   B. What wonderings and questions do you have as a result of co-documenting and engaging in play with Abraham?

The concept and practice of mutual education should be extended to children of all ages, not just adults. How many times have you heard educators say that they probably learn more from their children than the children learn from them? That is quite a statement. What does it reveal? It may refer to an educator's modesty or humbleness or to the educator's regard and value for the children's articulation of what, why, and how they have learned. There are many possibilities, and one of them is mutual education. In his article "Reading the Intentionality of Young Children," George Forman (2010) confirms that "just because infants or 1-year-old children cannot tell us what they are trying to do does not mean that they are without plans or expectations. Young children have many intentions that we can read by careful attention to their subtle movements and glances" (p. 1). In this article and six accompanying video clips, he clearly demonstrates not only the social intentions of very young children but also, importantly, the value of careful observation, with the message to us all who work with children to "slow down." When we take the time to observe, not only do we begin to understand and appreciate but also we are rewarded with uncovering the world of children in ways we never thought of before. The photo seen here of infants engaged in inquiry reminds us of our appreciation of children as competent thinkers and collaborators.

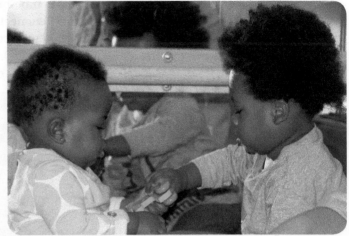
Kristine Fenning

The Reflective Educator: Responding to and Sustaining the Observation Cycle

We've taken a comprehensive look at many integral steps and processes within the cycle of observation in this chapter; it is a complex yet dynamic process that requires educators to be mindful of and reflective upon all aspects of practice. To be able to do this effectively, it is important to now think about how we might begin to prepare pedagogical documentation as part of the cycle.

A Focus on Reflection Time   Seasoned educators have used the term "planning time" so long that even when they are part of an emergent curriculum that no longer focuses on "teacher-directed planning time," the planning term is still used. Realizing the importance of reflection and conversation within the cycle of observation, perhaps what we need is a term like "reflection and dialogue time." Rather than planning a weekly curriculum in advance, educators might replace this time with the daily sharing of observations and reflections, perhaps collaborating with children and other educators and family members to document inquiry and learning taking place. Sharing this role together communicates that collaboration and diverse perspectives matter. Resulting from this collaboration and mutual education might be a variety of documentation artifacts, and, in the case of the Centre A example below, educators experimented with a few documentation methods in their new journey.

Centre A and its educators were new to the documentation process, and in particular the capturing of inquiry demonstrated by the children. Not knowing exactly where to begin, they decided to start this new process with a question: "What is something we can all agree on that we observe in the infant, toddler, and preschool rooms?" Educators listened and watched, and what they agreed on was observing the senses of sight and hearing, as this was an interest consistently demonstrated by the children. What evolved from each room was a curious and interesting mix of questions and responses, which were documented and later posted for all to see. In the toddler room, their documentation was prompted by the interest of one of the toddlers in eye colour. Documentation began with some basic questions posed by the educators, and as time progressed, their documentation methods became increasingly connected to children's actions, words, interests, and inquiry. In this new documentation experience, the educators also related the inquiry to the Ontario Early Learning Framework (OELF), as indicated by one of their entries below.

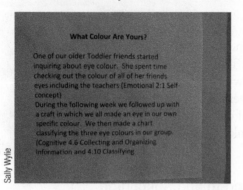

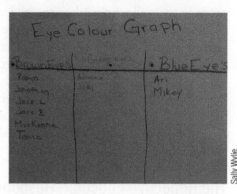

This is a primary example of simply beginning with a question, reflecting upon what it means to look and listen, and taking a leap to try to experiment with new and emerging documentation methods. As knowledge and skills in observation and documentation grow for every setting, so too will the complexity and types of documentation produced. With time, practice, and new learning, educators can also look for opportunities for co-participation from children and their families in the process.

Creating Time for Documentation and Reflection   When creating time for documentation and reflection, the first consideration is to respect the educator. What does that mean? It means that when educators of young children are asked to document during the day, that request needs to consider the age of the children, the number of children in the educator's care, and other factors such as the physical environment, professional responsibilities throughout the day, the need to meet licensing and ministry expectations, scheduling constraints, and other expectations. In our genuine desire and excitement to document the wonderful discoveries of young children, care must be taken to ensure that educators are not pressured by unrealistic expectations of what should be accomplished.

This caveat reminds us of our conversation concerning pedagogical documentation in Chapter 2. No matter our profession, we have to be able to work within the time we have. Being proactive is a good approach toward meeting that challenge. Other possibilities could include

- engaging in conversation with children about what they learned or were interested in;
- revisiting photos that children or others have taken and reflecting upon how that learning could be expanded;

- thinking about your own curiosities and how you might want to provoke additional thinking from children;
- thinking about what you've been documenting with the children and where you might want to lead a discussion today, or how you might support the leadership of children or family members in deciding what kinds of materials would prompt a further investigation of a topic or exploration already visited, for example;
- always engaging in the moment with the children and letting the conversation lead to new discoveries;
- ensuring access and knowledge of use of a variety of materials in the room for documenting, ensuring that the materials are supporting AODA (Accessibility for Ontarians with Disabilities Act) access;
- equipping yourself with "I wonder" questions to provoke inquiry and interest in something. Following are questions that would be helpful to provoke documentation:
  – How will I include some of the reflections from today/yesterday?
  – How might we reflect our learning today and how do we want to make it visible?
  – How might we contribute to our portfolios to reflect our learning? How has or will our learning and new discoveries inform our curriculum today?

AODA (Accessibility for Ontarians with Disabilities Act)

A law requiring the identification and removal of barriers for those diagnosed with special needs or disabilities.

Self-reflection, dialogue, and inquiry will begin the process of inventing possibilities with your colleagues, the children (regardless of their age), the supervisor, and families. Be sure to revisit previous chapters to explore reflective questions posed with different methodologies and aspects of practice.

In conversation with educators in the profession, they have shared questions they've had along their journey with pedagogical documentation. Following are some of these questions:

a. Of all the interests in the classroom, whose ideas or inquiries do we follow/document?

b. What if some children are not interested in pursuing new ideas or inquiries? Is this when I begin a new inquiry?

c. How do I keep an inquiry going or how do I expand it?

d. How do we balance and include all ideas and voices?

e. How might we build group inquiry and additional involvement from family members?

f. What is the best way to capture a new idea or wondering?

g. How do I integrate our pedagogical framework into my documentation?

h. What is the best way to make visible the learning of children for our setting?

i. When do we call what we're doing "curriculum"?

j. Will the documentation we are preparing be acceptable to the ministry or regulatory bodies?

These are all provocative questions requiring a conversation and collaboration from your entire learning community to establish answers that reflect all voices. As we've learned along the way, the educator should not shoulder the sole responsibility for pedagogical documentation. Take a few moments to dialogue with others to seek their perspectives on these questions. What did the children say? What did others say?

REFLECTIVE EXERCISE 6.2

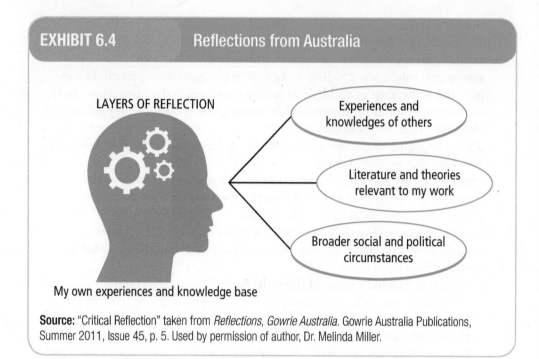

Source: "Critical Reflection" taken from *Reflections, Gowrie Australia.* Gowrie Australia Publications, Summer 2011, Issue 45, p. 5. Used by permission of author, Dr. Melinda Miller.

Mutual education requires us also to respect the rights of children, families, and educators, as well as how we might promote and sustain ethics in our early childhood environments. We also need to be aware of our own biases in order to be positive, responsive, inclusive observers who are open to change, possibilities, and reflection. Be sure to revisit Chapter 2 for a refresher. Appreciation of self and others prompts us to consider all points of view and discourages a superficial, surface-level understanding. As noted in Exhibit 6.4, a commitment to embrace the knowledge and practices of others in early childhood is relevant to an educator's professional practice.

Whether you are a seasoned educator in the profession or a beginning student of early childhood, perhaps some of your reflections include what prompted you to become an educator of young children. Maybe you reflected on people in your past who influenced you to become an educator. As you progress through your studies and career, you will be called upon for your thoughts and feelings about various theories, subjects such as child guidance, or issues like the need for a federal child-care system. As your experience grows, your views will be influenced, changed, or challenged. This is important as it helps you formulate your own philosophy about education and learning.

Early Learning for Every Child Today: A Framework for Ontario Early Childhood Settings (Ontario Ministry of Children and Youth Services, Best Start Expert Panel on Early Learning, 2007), more recently known as the Ontario Early Learning Framework, includes indicators of "taking another person's point of view," listed under the social domain, for the preschool–kindergarten age group (2.5 to 6 years). See Exhibit 6.5 for the domains and skills, indicators of the skill, and interactions for that page.

A brief glance at the interactions in Exhibit 6.5 shows the kinds of questions or comments an educator might make to encourage or reinforce these

Domain and Skills	Indicators of the Skill	Interactions
Taking Another Person's Point of View	• describing their ideas and emotions • recognizing that other people have ideas and emotions • understanding the ideas and emotions of others • beginning to accept that the ideas and emotions of others may be different from their own • adapting behaviour to take other people's points of view into consideration • beginning to respond appropriately to the feelings of others • beginning to take another's point of view • engaging in the exchange of ideas and points of view with others	Create discussion of an experience that was shared by all. "I am wondering about when we were at the fire hall yesterday. I took these photographs. Look at this one, Jed. What do you remember? Becky, Jed remembers. . . . Do you remember that? What do you think?" This gives practice in describing ideas and hearing the ideas of others who had the same experience. In this way, children can recognize the ideas of others and see that they may be different from their own (e.g., theory of mind).

Source: Ontario Ministry of Education. *Early Learning for Every Child Today (ELECT): A Framework for Ontario Early Childhood Settings*, p. 46. © Queen's Printer for Ontario, 2007. Reproduced with permission of the Government of Ontario.

concepts. If we look forward to the example in Exhibit 6.7, what kinds of questions could be generated to re-engage the children in reflecting upon the subject of boats or to co-educate one another? How would those questions and interest encourage this age group to take another person's point of view? What new reflections might be added to the conversation? How would those remembrances contribute to sharing feelings and ideas with others?

There are many theories concerning how, when, and to what degree we reflect upon our professional practice and personal lives. When you observe, interpret, and document what you have seen and heard, you will be reflecting upon many aspects of one event. You may reflect almost immediately as you consider a decision or perhaps pause and think later in the day about the same incident, but in a different way.

Using a ministry document does not preclude educators from using other pedagogical documentation or engaging in appreciative inquiry. They are not exclusive of each other, but rather inclusive practices demonstrating a willingness to create a wide variety of documentation using anecdotal observations, charts, photos, and text—whatever makes visible the daily experiences, learning, and thinking of children.

As we will see later in this chapter, mutual education continues when co-creating a portfolio with colleagues, families, or children, as you will express your views, listen to the perspectives of children, share your reflections on your observations, and invite others to do the same. Making those connections helps you realize your beliefs and values as well as acknowledge those of others. When you develop a portfolio, many questions along the cycle of observation will be asked, such as, "How might we make visible the talents and gifts of this child to others?" or "How has this child's voice been captured?" or "Have I fairly represented the growth and development of this child over the past six months?" These questions are not only a reflection of what you wonder about but are also about you, the educator. These questions are reflections of your professional philosophy. Discussed further in Chapter 8, they illustrate what you have learned about the complex nature of being an educator of young children.

Variations of the Cycle of Observation

Every setting will have their own philosophy and their own approach. Depending on a number of variables within your setting, variations might occur with the cycle of observation. For example, a variation of the cycle of observation could look like the one in Exhibit 6.6. With specific reference to

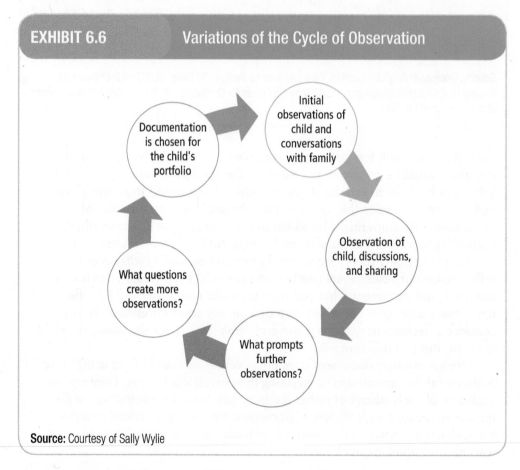

EXHIBIT 6.6   Variations of the Cycle of Observation

- Initial observations of child and conversations with family
- Observation of child, discussions, and sharing
- What prompts further observations?
- What questions create more observations?
- Documentation is chosen for the child's portfolio

Source: Courtesy of Sally Wylie

EXHIBIT 6.7   Does Your Grandpa Have a Boat?

Discussions resulting from children's questions can generate a collaborative interest that can start with a simple question during lunchtime such as, "My grandpa has a boat. Does your grandpa have a boat?" The educator waits and listens for the responses of the children. "My Bompi has a boat." "My grandpa has a really, really big boat!" Just such a conversation was started in Wiarton Kids Den. The discussion of

gvictoria/Shutterstock.com

boats had begun during lunchtime, but when the first opportunity arose, many of the children dashed to paper and markers to draw a boat and continue their interest. Fortunately, they had an educator who fostered that interest, and for the entire week boats became the major interest. The educator arranged for a community visit on Friday to walk down to the marina and see the boats.

When the preschoolers came back, one of the educators interviewed the children individually while the beds were being set up for naptime. After naptime, interviews continued, and the children shouted out, "Chris is asking me what I saw!" "She's writing down what I'm saying!" They were delighted that their individual stories were being recorded. They were happy to be listened to. Then one child asked another child if he could sleep on a boat. Their investigations of boats led to another topic: camping on boats ("What questions create more observations?").

the child, this particular cycle shows relevance and pertinence of observation and documentation to a centre that is perhaps just beginning their journey of observation and documentation, and directing their process to the creation and development of documentation for a child's portfolio.

How is this similar to or different from the cycle of observation presented in Exhibit 2.19 on page 64 or Exhibit 6.2 on page 216? Revisiting the cycle of observation in this chapter with the application of examples will illustrate some concrete strategies of pedagogical documentation. Exhibit 6.7 is an example showing how the questions of children supported by a responsive educator can create an emerging curriculum ("What prompts further observations?"). Observation plays that key role. It brings the educator to a reflective place where she learns and uncovers with the children by paying attention to the artistic desire of a preschooler, the talents of a parent, or the interests of a co-educator in the room.

When interest waned, the educators assembled all the artwork, magazine pictures, photographs, children's narratives, and activities, such as the boats made out of popsicle sticks. They laid it all out and took photographs of it. Now they had electronic copies of their boat investigation for centre records and individual portfolios ("Documentation is chosen for the child's portfolio" in Exhibit 6.6), as well as hard copies to post on their documentation wall. Beginning with one question, the children's interest took their voices into the marina community, caught the interest of the parents, and created the foundation for further exploration. The cycle of observation included their artwork, their stories, pictures, paintings, and new information. It was relevant and meaningful, and it reflected the community in which the children lived. The days of discovery demonstrated a true interest, where educators and children learned together, and extended their conversation into the community while discovering what was meaningful to them.

Another example to show the continuum of the cycle of observation through documentation is the story of Colin and how he found a new identity and purpose at the Family Day events. See Exhibit 6.8 for Colin's story.

These examples demonstrate how appreciative inquiry creates possibilities out of dialogue and how joint collaboration between adults and children creates focus and develops curricula. This process applies to all age groups, not

---

EXHIBIT 6.8 The Family Day Event

Debbie enrolled Colin, aged four, at the Cambridge Springs Child Care Centre in the spring of 2014. When she met with Lorie, the supervisor, she confided that she had just filed for a divorce and needed a secure place of comfort for Colin while she was at work. During the initial interview she said that Colin was quite the soccer player. He was excited that the World Cup would be played in Brazil in the summer ("Initial observations of child and conversations with family" in Exhibit 6.6).

Digital Media pro/Shutterstock.com

Lorie kept in close touch with Debbie and Colin's educators, sharing how he had been settling in, the friends he had, the things he liked to do, and, most importantly, how he was feeling ("Observations of child, discussions, and sharing").

At the end of the day, Lorie asked Debbie if she thought it would be a good idea to put Colin in a leadership role in the upcoming Family Day events. Lorie and others had observed Colin's talents with a soccer ball and wanted him to teach the other children. The childcare centre asked parents to bring in flags, shirts, and other soccer items for the event. Colin was excited and seemed to thrive in his new role ("What prompts further observation?").

In the days leading up to Family Day, the educators took pictures, transcribed the stories of the children, and generally documented the daily process of what it takes to stage a big event. Documentation came from educators, the children, and the families ("Documentation is chosen for the child's portfolio").

Wiarton Kids' Den/Sally Wylie

---

just the children who can articulate their interests, draw elaborate pictures, or challenge accepted meaning. This process includes the age groups of toddlers and infants as well. What may be different are the strategies employed by the educator to draw out the subjects of interest or the complexities of a problem known only to a child in the infant or toddler room. Several examples applying the cycle of observation to professional practice are available online.

More attention to the behaviour, thinking, and actions of the children is necessary, as the younger children do not have the ability to verbally express their understanding in words of what is before them; however, they are able to articulate through sounds and actions their intentions and understanding. It is through behaviour, then, that we can observe, reflect, and learn from them, as perhaps is the case with an older infant outside in the sand who is trying to fit the sand from a large container into a smaller container. Besides puzzlement and problem solving, what is evident is one child's enjoyment of being in the same place with another infant shuffling sand around.

MAKING CONNECTIONS WITHIN THE CYCLE: PEDAGOGICAL FRAMEWORKS, DOCUMENTATION, AND CURRICULUM

We direct our appreciative inquiry now to examine the relationship between early learning pedagogical frameworks, the pedagogical documentation we have learned about, and curriculum. Using the appreciative inquiry approach enables us to do this as we have discussed in previous chapters how this approach enables us as educators and observers to co-discover how they might facilitate problem solving, wondering, and the co-creation of new learning, questions, queries, and curriculum.

That said, by collaborating, listening and appreciating, we can all learn what is relevant, important, and meaningful to others. Sharing ideas and strategies, being supportive, and being respectful of one another are important considerations in the process. Appreciative inquiry prepares educators, children, and families to not only be inquisitive but also conscientious in understanding how various early learning or early childhood frameworks might guide and support their pedagogy, including that of pedagogical documentation practices. Exhibit 6.2 outlines how pedagogical frameworks might fit within the cycle.

Engaging in a systematic and appreciative inquiry approach when observing and documenting considers the children's thinking and learning and how their knowledge might contribute to future curriculum directions. For example, documentation should capture contextual factors that may impact children's thinking and learning, such as relationships, culture, environment, family or diversity, language, gender, philosophy, and values. Consider the winter of 2014 depicted in the photos that follow. This particular winter was one of the coldest in recent records. How might the cold and snow (culture and environment) affect opportunities for expression, documentation, and routines of the day?

REFLECTIVE EXERCISE 6.3

Take a moment to reflect upon the last photo above of the child in the pink jacket and hat sitting in the snow. What appreciative inquiry questions might you ask of this child in this situation to further prompt their curiosity or exploration of the snow outdoors? What questions might prompt and inform new or extended curriculum directions?

Now let's compare your answers from Reflection Exercise 6.3 to Exhibit 6.9. This particular exhibit is a follow-up learning story that was co-created by the child in the photo, her grandmother, and her educator as a result of the child showing her grandmother the photo at the end of the day.

EXHIBIT 6.9   Yulie's Follow-up Learning Story

Snow Fun: Yulie's Chair with "Foot Scratchers"

Co-written by Yulie (3.2 years of age), Lisa (educator), and Isilda (grandmother)

"Lida, you gotta see. Look outside!!"

Yulie ran into the classroom with the mini tablet after the children had spent all morning outdoors in the sun in order to build their "movie theatre" in the snow. Yulie took Lisa by the hand to guide her to a chair to sit down. Yulie proceeded to place the tablet down on the table beside the couch in the reading area, nestled in beside Lisa on the couch, and pulled up the photos she had another peer take of her creation on the tablet.

"My chair have scrakers," said Yulie.

"Scrakers? What might they do, Yulie?" asked Lisa.

"They do this." Yulie proceeded to use her fingernails on both hands to scratch the bottom of both of her feet.

"Oh, I see," said Lisa. "You use the scratchers to itch your feet."

"Yah," replied Yulie. "The scratchers do that when I look at the movie. They take snow off boots too."

"That is quite the invention, Yulie. What made you think of that idea?" asked Lisa.

"So the people in front of me don't get wet. When I'm at the movies, I like to put my feet in the space between the seats in front of me. My mom always tells me to stop doing that and to put my wet feet on the floor so they won't drip snow on the person in front of me," said Yulie with each hand out to each side of her body, palms up, eyebrows raised, and looking straight at Lisa.

"Your hands and your comment make me think that you seem surprised I didn't know that, Yulie," said Lisa.

"Don't you have that rule too?" asked Yulie.

"No, I don't. My legs are too long. If I put them up like you, I think my feet would be in the face of the person in front of me," said Lisa with a giggle.

Yulie also started giggling, putting her one hand in front of her smile, eyes wide open. "OH BOY, YOU'D BETTER NOT DO THAT THEN," Yulie said in a louder voice. "I have another idea too. I think we should use my brush to take snow off of our boots before we come inside," she said.

"What a great idea, Yulie. Let's try it this afternoon."

Yulie's response: "My idea was a good one because Joanne bought us some more brushes to use with our boots. Now we don't have any more puddles on our floor in the classroom. I want to try some other brushes now to see what else I can make." ← [Curriculum suggestion]

Isilda's response: "Yulie, you shared our idea about how to care for other people around us when we are at the movies. This makes me very happy. When you asked me for our car snow brush to take to school, I wondered what you were going to use it for. I see now that you have thought about how to care for your classroom by using car brushes to take snow off everyone's boots and snow pants before they go inside. I think we should do that too before we get into the car." ← [Response and extension of Yulie's idea for further provocation]

Lisa's response: "Yulie, you applied your ideas to problems we were experiencing in our child-care centre and classroom. This really shows how you are thinking about others. I like your idea to experiment with other types of brushes to see what we can do with them in the classroom. In our conversation you mentioned that we could try some different-sized hairbrushes with the paints instead of regular brushes. Let's try that tomorrow to see what creations we can make!" ← [Co-curriculum planning and invitation response]

How might this exhibit apply to your curricular framework?

As we reflect back to the earlier chapters, it is important to think about how we might apply concepts we've learned about. Thinking about questions like, "In what ways can we do this?" and other related questions like, "In what ways does this experience and documentation connect to our early learning framework?" targets the most complex part of the observation: finding a pedagogical framework that reflects the school or centre's philosophy, mission statement, policies and procedures, responsibilities to the provincial/territorial ministries, community, and families. Across Canada, each province will have frameworks that guide early childhood professional practice. Exhibit 6.10 outlines just a few examples.

| EXHIBIT 6.10 | Early Learning Framework Examples |

British Columbia Early Learning Framework	A reflective framework intended to assist early learning practitioners in preparing quality experiences and early learning environments.
How Does Learning Happen?	This is an early years' guide intended to support a variety of early years' programs, and one that prompts reflection upon the foundations for learning and development. This documentation also encompasses and hones on the pedagogical foundations of the *ELECT* (*Early Learning for Every Child Today*) document.
Manitoba's Early Learning and Child Care Curriculum Framework for Infant Programs	This is an early learning framework intended to support diversity and inclusive curriculum as well as further enhance quality in infant child-care programs.

REFLECTIVE EXERCISE 6.4

Examine the documents in Exhibit 6.10. Describe the similarities and differences between the *British Columbia Early Learning Framework*, Ontario's *Early Learning for Every Child Today (ELECT)*, and *How Does Learning Happen?* (HDLH is premised on the *Early Learning Framework* and principles from ELECT), as well as Manitoba's *Early Returns: Manitoba's Early Learning and Child Care Curriculum Framework for Infant Programs*. Which curricular documents resonate with your pedagogical beliefs and practices? Thinking back to Exhibit 6.10, what is the early learning framework that guides your practice, and how does it relate to your pedagogical documentation and curriculum?

Educators would agree that pedagogical documentation like that in Exhibit 6.11 should illustrate and connect to their philosophy and practices, their early learning framework, their views of learning and educating, and, most importantly, their image of a child and their values of childhood. Creating this documentation involves dialogue, respect, reflection, and a willingness to explore and discover ideas.

Finding a systematic process or a pedagogical framework can be especially challenging when no established philosophy or set of practices is adopted. From Vancouver to St. John's, educators have developed documentation to best represent their practices and reflect their values, cultures, and philosophy. A wide spectrum of pedagogical frameworks exist across Canada and illustrate the point that we all hold unique views of children and that there is no one right way to observe and document the daily experiences of young children.

EXHIBIT 6.11   Chairs and Dolls on a Plane

Jacob sauntered into the dramatic centre. He picked up a child-sized rattan chair and looked around. He leaned over the shelf and said to Gilly, "My mom and I rode on a plane, you know. We went to Florida." He plunked the chair down and shoved a doll onto the chair. "Do you want to ride on an airplane with us?" The question invited participation, and soon the two children had all the dolls sitting expectantly in the chairs, the chairs lined up in a row.

The educator who observed the activity and listened to their conversation asked them about their trip. "What did you see in Florida?" She then asked, "What did you pack in your suitcase?" One of the girls ran to the dramatic area for dress-up clothes. The teacher found a box for the suitcase. From that day and for the next two weeks, air travel became the intense subject in the drama centre. Soon the drama centre stretched into the block centre, and eventually into the book area with shelves of books and comfy chairs and a sofa. The educators brought in posters and they collaboratively made a cardboard box cockpit, used a console as the control panel, and set up a table and chairs to take reservations. Props were added: hats, a grass skirt, leis, seashells, bags for luggage, and so on. The travel industry flourished in many forms, all documented by artwork, constructions, photos, text, and stories until the children's interest waned. What educators discovered with the children was a wealth of new vocabulary, understanding of air travel, role playing and relationships, and a glimpse into the experiences of the children in their families.

THE CYCLE OF OBSERVATION AS COMMUNITY BUILDING

In Chapter 1, we talked about the initial exchanges between educators and families and how through daily practices a bond is formed while scaffolding values and expectations. If we could see those educators and families now when discussing the ideas of their shared documentation, we would see how the cycle of observation we have discussed throughout this text becomes a tool of collaboration that extends into the community.

As each adult involved gains insight into the children's thinking and learning and contributes to that process at various stages, a group of learners is formed. Let's apply this to a specific context. It may begin, for example, with the children in a fishing village whose classroom work contained literacy and numeracy examples reflecting life in the village. With interest generated by the children's work, parents may be inclined to comment on the work or perhaps contribute artifacts such as fishing nets to further interest. Parents or grandparents may want to talk about fishing life in class. Would their children contribute new ideas about the stories or add to that of their parents or grandparents? How would a rural community wish to talk about, document, and reflect upon the miles of fence made of rocks pulled from the fields by their grandparents? What would children from rural areas tell us about the old photos of their ancestors, and how would they and the class reflect upon those stories? What would their grandchildren tell us in their learning stories at school?

Stories of the old days mingled with the observations of the young can create a rich documentation of heritage, pride, and sense of belonging like in the photo below. This intergenerational, neighbour-to-neighbour oral history is a valuable social construct for schools and communities. That history creates community memories of events and places such as county fairs, gatherings, and festivals, which are often reflected in school activities for all to see. In some communities it could be the local heritage events, the pumpkin toss, the maple syrup week, or the Royal Winter Fair.

Sally Wylie

In the Arctic, Igloolik celebrates the re-emergence of the sun after weeks of total darkness. Many Inuit consider this celebration more important than New Year's Day. Traditionally, they celebrated the return of the light when they had enough food to last until spring. Today, this festival is a five-day extravaganza filled with igloo building, dog sledding, and talent and fashion shows. Those community ties and events bind families and create a local culture that is echoed across Canada. When children in an early childhood setting are involved, it presents a wonderful opportunity to document that experience, whether the child is 12 years or 12 months. Documentation tied to the community says "we belong" (see Exhibit 6.12).

Joining the Cycle: A Community Response

Inviting organizations within the community can also be part of the cycle of observation. As we reflect back on Exhibit 2.19 in Chapter 2 or Exhibit 6.2 in Chapter 6, we can see opportunities for the voices of community members in our observation and documentation processes. No one works alone anymore. Collaboration is the key with the goal in mind that everyone benefits. For

---

EXHIBIT 6.12   Our Commitment to All Children

We view children as competent, capable of complex thinking, curious and rich in potential. They grow up in families with diverse social, cultural and linguistic perspectives. Every child should feel that he or she belongs, is a valuable contributor to his or her surroundings, and deserves the opportunity to succeed. When we recognize children as capable and curious, we are more likely to deliver programs and services that value and build on their strengths and abilities.

Source: Ontario Ministry of Education. (2013). *Think, Feel, Act: Lessons from Research about Young Children* (p. 7). Retrieved from http://www.edu.gov.on.ca/childcare/document.html.

example, let's say the playground of a schoolyard has not been updated in years, and the supervisor, while outside at recess, has discovered that the concrete is full of holes, raised chunks, and uneven surfaces. The walls near the playground are continually marred by graffiti, and playground equipment has been removed entirely because of vandalism. Some money is available for the playground refurbishment, but not enough. What can be done? Wisely, the supervisor decides that she and the educators will document with photos and text all areas of the playground. Then they take the documentation, including the photos of the graffiti, to the next community consultation meeting. At the meeting, they give a PowerPoint presentation that illustrates what they have recorded. They discuss the issues. This was an effective way of taking clear documentation to an organization to ask for a solution to the problem.

Sharing documentation is a beginning: a way to get others involved. With the appropriate permissions, observations regarding how children play within such an outdoor area could also be included in the documentation. As part of the cycle of observation, some provocative questions could be asked, such as, "What do the children learn to play here? Is this an ideal place for our children to play?" The observation cycle can be used effectively to advocate for the environment. The next stage might be to get professionals from the community to join a discussion and bring their views, ideas, and suggestions as part of a community process. Discussions may point those arrows of the observation cycle in Exhibit 6.2 back to what can be done, who can do it, and other issues, such as examining avenues of funding or raising awareness of the fundamental tenets of outdoor play for children. When gathering the perspectives of others, the load is shared as well as the responsibility. The inclusion of others promotes a holistic approach for the community, which ultimately builds community capacity.

THE CYCLE OF OBSERVATION: INFORMING PORTFOLIOS

Earlier sections of this chapter have introduced us to the importance of understanding the steps and processes within the cycle of observation. Let's turn our attention now to portfolios, an important part of the cycle and a necessary part of being a responsive educator.

Educators might ask, "So what now? What do I do with this new knowledge? In making children's learning visible, what else can we do with our observations, pedagogical documentation, and interpretations?" Portfolios are one way in which educators, children, and families can collect and present information about a child.

What Is a Portfolio and What Is Its Purpose?

Although the definition varies, there seems to be general consensus that the portfolio is a malleable collection of work that conveys relevant information about a child. A portfolio profiles often in a chronological collection the evolution of children's thinking, learning, understanding and development, and how a child changes over time. The concept of portfolio development involves a philosophy, teamwork including families, and practices that support this ongoing process.

A portfolio is a work in progress—a dynamic process that reflects the individuality of the child. A portfolio should reveal what is important to the

portfolio

A purposeful collection of work, such as artwork, photographs, and text, that reflects the individuality of the child.

children, educators, and families. More specifically, "If the main purpose of the portfolio is to tell the child's story of learning and discovery, then it follows that the children themselves should play a major role in deciding its contents (Moore, 2006). Children, parents, peers and staff can make reflections on artifacts. It is by adding these reflections that artifacts become evidence" (Walters, 2006, p. 9).

However begun, a portfolio offers opportunities for reflecting upon the image of each child and their thinking, as well as opportunities for interpreting and building upon their knowledge and development. They allow for revisiting and recalling of moments, feelings, experiences, or learning events to perhaps create new knowledge, inquiries, and learning opportunities in one's curriculum. A portfolio can be assembled in a number of ways and therefore could

- reflect the many languages of children—a child's communication, projects, and artwork;
- be open-ended so that the collection process represents a child's interests, skills, participation, health, growth, and development;
- outline a child's learning over time;
- demonstrate a child's involvement and interactions with a group of children; and
- reflect the child's culture and family and may include input from involved professionals.

Trends and changes in observation and documentation methods and expectations within the early childhood profession have prompted change in both the format and usage of portfolios for children. While the value of the traditional paper portfolio has not changed, it is less common in relation to digital portfolios with the infusion of technology, apps, and digital media that provide digital access to portfolio forums for conversation and reflection (by peers or by educators and families), sharing, and accessibility.

authentic assessment

As assessment that is connected to practical, pragmatic, real-world skills to demonstrate performance and understanding.

standardized assessment

An assessment that has reliability and validity and that specifies how the assessment is administered, which materials are used, and how it is scored/evaluated.

Kristine Fenning

▲ Here we see a boy in kindergarten building his own portfolio of experiences from the previous day. His class had gone to see bees making honey, and he was inspired to make his learning visible from that trip.

What Constitutes an Artifact? Deciding what to put into a portfolio isn't easy, as it requires reflection and understanding of the intent of the artifact. A child's portfolio will reflect the centre's philosophy, practices, and culture; the child's family culture; and other considerations. Once you know what type of portfolio is being created, the artifacts can then be selected.

Portfolios are a multipurpose, systematic form of authentic assessment and a forum in which to present a child's progress over time. Portfolios are not scrapbooks of information. Portfolios are strengths based and inquiry driven, and they reflect each child's interests, abilities, individuality, and diversity within his or her natural learning environment. Rather than a series of checklists or a prescribed standardized assessment, portfolios are meant to contain a variety of informal observational methods and information. Portfolios are malleable, for they constantly change as each child grows and develops. Portfolios are a holistic way for educators, families, and children to document each child's learning journey, developmental and meaningful life experiences, as well as their thoughts and feelings, all within the context of the child's family and world.

Portfolios for many years have traditionally been based on a developmental perspective, with artifact submissions often tied to developmental milestones or skills demonstrated. This is still important, as understanding where children are developmentally, what skills they have yet to achieve, and what skills they are working on enables educators to respond in ways to extend children's learning. However, if we challenge this single-lens paradigm and invite a socio-cultural lens to the portfolio process such as the artifact in Exhibit 6.13, a more holistic lens of understanding about a child is attained, as the portfolio

---

EXHIBIT 6.13　　　　Owen's Portfolio Example

Owen's Traffic Jam

By Owen, aged 3.6 years　　　　　　　　Date: September 14, 2018

Courtesy of University of Toronto Child Care on Charles Street

Transcription of Dialogue with Owen

Question posed to Owen: Thanks for asking, Owen. You seem excited to talk about your handling of the traffic jam today with the vehicles (trikes). Owen, can you tell me more about your experience?

Owen's response: I tow-ded Child A with my tow truck. I used skipping rope to pull him. The rope stick-ded in the wheels. It didn't come off. I 'turd' my truck over to pull at the rope but it was too hard. Child A moved his car closer and we used our muscles to pull the rope off the wheel. It came off!! Then we used the rope on the handles instead cause Child A's motor was broken. I tow-ded him to the shed to fix his motor.

The Educator then read the words to Owen to ensure they had documented his thoughts correctly. Owen, does this capture your adventure that you shared with me just now?

Owen's reflection: Yeah, his motor was really broken! I fixed the problem just like a real driver. I think I need tools next time though cause it was hard with my hands. I need a wrench and some screwdrivers.

(continued)

Educator reflection: Owen—you really had to think through possible options in order to solve the issue of the tangled-up skipping rope around the wheels of the two vehicles (tricycles). It was evident that you were persistent and thought of a few ideas to work through your problem; your first idea was to try to pull the vehicles apart which was not successful. You tried again by pulling the rope off by yourself which seemed to frustrate you as you walked away saying, 'This is a big problem,' and sat looking at the rope. Your sitting down to think was an excellent decision as you came back at the problem with a new solution which was to flip the vehicles on their sides which loosened the rope, allowing you to pull it off the wheels. You seemed to have a number of theories you were proposing today, which led to your best decision and solution. Your idea of adding tools is a good one—let's look at what you think we need to add to our outdoor environment to allow you to continue to solve vehicle problems such as these!

then contains information, interpretations, and evidence from a variety of sources and people. Children in this case would have equal power and influence on what would go into the portfolio.

Portfolios are a rich resource of information to inform inclusive responses to children's interests, hypotheses, and queries and the co-creation of new curriculum and learning opportunities that reflect the voices and perspectives of each child within the learning environment. They are an important part of the observation cycle, as they create opportunities for appreciative inquiry and reflection. It is through team discussion of this information learned that relationships are built and quality environments are created.

Meaningful evidence or artifacts collected by the team might include but are not limited to the following:

- anecdotals
- photo narratives
- blogs, social media feeds
- art samples
- math samples
- sociograms
- movies
- photos of 2D/3D projects
- word clouds and poetry
- music
- peer assessments
- log books
- certificates of achievement
- language or writing samples
- audio files reflecting language use or social conversations between children
- videos of inquiries, conversations, experiences, or learning made by the child
- self-assessment scripts or pieces of writing
- group projects or inquiries (names of other children must be withheld if inserting into a child's portfolio)
- running records

- ABC analysis
- learning stories
- documentation panels
- charts or profiles of information whereby artifacts are combined to inform more holistic and comprehensive interpretations
- sticky notes or information collected at a glance
- events or moments in time / learning experiences that hold meaning for the child, family, or educator
- goals and objectives

Think about the setting you work in or have placement in. What other examples can you think of that children could possibly place in their portfolio? What have you or others placed into a portfolio? For your convenience, examples of portfolios and portfolio entries are available online.

REFLECTIVE EXERCISE 6.5

Portfolio Preparation, Stages, and Content

Reflection and dialogue is once again at the heart of the portfolio process, as artifacts gain their meaning through this process. To engage in reflection, we again begin by formulating questions to prompt inquiry. As McCoy-Wozniak (2012) puts it,

> Inquiry is a continuous cycle of learning that involves questioning, investigating, analyzing, communicating, and reflecting on the knowledge gained. Reflecting on the evidence and conclusion produces more questions and the cycle of learning and discovery continues. Reflection connects the components of the inquiry cycle and serves as the catalyst to move to the next level of learning and discovery. (pp. 220–221)

Let's reflect, then, on the various types of questions we need to consider when embarking upon this portfolio process. Taking the time to reflect upon how the questions below might be answered supports appreciative inquiry and responsive practice. Questions that an early childhood team, including the educators, families, and children, might reflect upon include the following:

- What type of portfolio is best for the setting? For children and families? Who is your audience?
- How will the identity of the child be respected and preserved? If in electronic or e-form, it is important to think about password protection. Families have the right to choose how their child's information is conveyed, portrayed, viewed, and accessed. If hard-copy portfolios are preferred, it is important to consider the same question. Only families and authorized users should be able to access the child's file. Educators also need to consult with their licensing or ministry expectations regarding storage and confidentiality requirements for information on children, with the ethical standards for their profession and organization regarding observation and documentation, and with families and other educators

concerning setting preferences. Be sure to consult with Chapter 2 regarding bias and ethics considerations.

- Where and how will the portfolio be stored?
- How will the information be organized?
- How will each child's story be told?
- How will each child be introduced?
- What will the headings be?
- Will they be sorted by connections to learning, development, or curriculum standards, by profile entries or dates throughout the year, by interests and strengths, or in some other way? Organization of a portfolio will depend on a number of variables and should reflect the voices and preferences of children, families, and educators collectively. Exhibit 6.14 presents two ways in which two different settings organized and linked their portfolio artifacts to frameworks or standards that guide professional practice.

Other final questions we might reflect upon in the portfolio process include the following:

- Who will determine what is submitted and how often? Where and how can children, families, or educators write, document, and reflect?
- How will it be ensured that a variety of artifacts are submitted?
- How will the voices of the child, family, and educator be reflected?
- How will we know what is permitted to be placed in the portfolio?
- When and how might the portfolio be used to support and extend children's learning/inform practice?
- How might educators increase accessibility and use of the portfolio by children and families to encourage shared and collaborative observation, documentation, interpretation, reflection, and application of knowledge gained?

By considering these and other important questions, educators follow the cycle of observation while supporting the integrity of the information being collected, selected, and reflected upon. This process also helps users to steer clear of using portfolios as a scrapbook. While scrapbooks are a great tool for capturing special memories and life events, the intent of portfolios is different in that they are meant to prompt reflection, discussion, demonstration of learning and the voices of children, evaluation, responsive planning, and new inquiries. Understanding the difference between the two is important. What other questions might you consider for this to be a meaningful process?

Further examples of portfolio entries and artifacts are available online.

Roles of the Educator, Child, and Family   Educators continue to assume the primary role of ensuring that each child within their program has a portfolio, and they usually are responsible for ensuring that specific types of documentation are present. This role is often largely due to a centre's or setting's philosophy, or it may be due to licensing or legislative requirements. During this process of preparing portfolios for each child, the educator may experience a variety of roles including but not limited

EXHIBIT 6.14   Portfolio Organization: Two Settings Compared

Kristine Fenning

Jada and her baby
September 1, 2015 – Written by Asima

Observation: Jada was observed spending approximately 30 minutes today at the dolly centre. From the very moment Jada entered this area, her curiosity was evident and her actions were purposeful. Attempting to grab a baby from a peer, Jada stated "mine" and held the baby tight to her chest. When Asima introduced a different baby to Jada, she quickly accepted the baby and gave the other baby back to her friend. Holding the baby by its arms, Jada walked over to the easel and selected a piece of chalk. She began to draw straight lines on the belly of the baby while whispering "dere, dere you go baby." "Oh oh, your baby is all dirty." Asima began to wash a different baby and then asked Jada to wash her baby too. Jada immediately said "no." Asima then said "the baby needs a bath." Jada replied "yah, baby all dirty" and with a cloth she began washing off the chalk from the baby's belly.

Reflections and Interpretations
Educator: Jada seemed to be very interested in cause and effect as she would colour the baby and then wash the baby several times. Jada appeared to be able to participate in parallel play with her peers as she engaged in her own imaginary play scenario.

Parent: Jada is always very curious, wanting to do different things with materials she uses. At home she is fascinated with her easel chalk board as she is able to wipe her markings clean.

Jada: "That's my baby. I bathed baby."

New Inquiry Possibilities/Extension of Learning: Jada and her teacher will put out some baby bathtubs with washing materials to build on Jada's interests in cleaning her baby and to further her participation in pretend play (2.1.)

OELF Toddlers :Social/ Emotional	OELF: Indicators
1.1 Social Interest	☐ observing and imitating peers ☐ beginning to play "follow the peer games" ☑ observing and playing briefly with peers – may turn into struggle for possession ☐ offering toys ☐ engaging in short group activities
1.2 Perspective Taking	☑ In simple situations beginning to take the point of view of others
1.3 Parallel Play	☑ playing in proximity of peers with similar playthings without an exchange of ideas or things
2.1 Expression of Feelings	☐ expressing aggressive feelings and behaviour ☐ beginning to show self-conscious emotions (shame, embarrassment, guilt, pride) ☑ expressing feelings in language and pretend play

(continued)

Observer: Cassandra Time: 8:30 a.m. Date: May 12, 2015	OELF Domain /Skill/Indicators	Centre Principle
Observation: As Oliver sat and watched the bubbles come out from the bubble machine, he imitated a peer who had previously said "pop" and repeatedly said "pop, pop, pop" as he broke the bubbles on the floor. Oliver was also heard saying "bub" as the educators in the room said "look at the bubbles!". He watched and listened to his educator quietly.	Provocation was based on the following domain(s): 3.3 Expressive Language 5.3 Visual Exploration and Discrimination	This experience and suggested extensions of play reflect: #1Healthy development is built on relationships #3 Experiences should reflect the voice, interest, and development of each child within the group.
Interpretation: Oliver seemed to use two new words today "pop," and "bub" for bubble. He was also able to use his pointer finger to pop the bubbles as he smiled. Parent reflection: "Oliver is attempting to repeat a lot of words lately. Tonight we will add bubbles to his bath to build on the words he was using today."	Indicators demonstrated in experience: 3.3 – using one word to communicate 4.4 Spatial Exploration – tracking moving objects with eyes 4.7 (Imitation) of adult actions and words	
Extension of Oliver's Play: In addition to home suggestions, we can build on Oliver's curiosity with bubbles by providing a sensory bin with water, bubbles, and floating animals for him to stand to pop the bubbles in the bin, express and label materials in the bin, engage in cause and effect, and interact with peers and educators.	Linked to: 4.7 Symbolic Thought, Representation and Root Skills of Literacy 4.3 Cause and Effect Exploration	

Kristine Fenning

Bubble Bubble Pop!

In the first example, the observer has linked the overall learning to the Ontario Early Learning Framework by checking off what has been demonstrated. In the second learning story example, we see a centre linking the experience, what has been learned from the experience, and extensions to the play experience to the Ontario Early Learning Framework. This centre also links this learning to the centre's mission principles.

Source: Domains and indicators retrieved from Ontario Ministry of Children and Youth Services, Best Start Expert Panel on Early Learning (2007, January). *Early Learning for Every Child Today: A Framework for Early Childhood Settings*. Retrieved from http://www.cfcollaborative.ca/wp-content/uploads/2010/10/ELECT.pdf

to the creator/co-creator, gatherer of information, editor, communicator, questioner, inquirer, provocateur, monitor, and decision maker. By sharing these roles with children and families, the potential for a more holistic view of a child is gained. Everyone should have a voice and a role in creating, evolving, and discussing which artifacts represent most meaningfully a child's experiences, special or aha moments, learning, proud moments, a milestone or achievement, or something of interest. Sound pedagogical practice emphasizes the importance of portfolio creation as a collaborative process. The educator continues to collect and organize the material with the cooperation of children, parents, and colleagues right from the time in which they begin in a setting. Collaboration in the beginning stages and throughout prompts collective reflection upon and interpretation of artifacts for submission and their meaning. Helping children to notice and name their learning assists the children in setting their own learning goals. It might also prompt reflection upon opportunities experienced and how learning took place, areas for further growth, strengths and interests, environmental variables that support growth and development, and ways that a child's learning might be extended.

Using the pedagogical documentation from Exhibit 6.14, if you were an educator in Nunavut, would your connections look different from your early learning framework? What about if you were from Newfoundland? What connections might be made there?

Ultimately, eliciting all perspectives assists in reducing bias and misperceptions, therefore leading to a more accurate and comprehensive understanding of a child. Take a look at Exhibit 6.15, for example. Without the accompanying descriptive story of Chelsea sharing her experience with her stepdad, one might think the photo is simply of a child having fun, making a silly face into the camera. This was not the case. Chelsea's review of the narrative in Exhibit 6.15 spawned a whole reflection by Chelsea of her experience in the situation and how she might prepare for future teeth to fall out.

EXHIBIT 6.15   I SPY: LOST TOOTH

Chelsea, the photo you had your friend take today captures your tooth news in a very exciting way! Today you had shared with everyone that you had predicted that your tooth would fall out by this evening, and that the predictions of your dad and stepdad were that it wouldn't fall out for a few more days. You were very aware of when your tooth wanted to come out. It seems that your theories of bending it and wiggling it with your tongue were effective to helping it come out. What made you think of these helpful ideas?

Anastasia Tveretinovae/Shutterstock.com

You had a plan to have your friends stand and join beside you as you talked with your stepdad about the photo. This made it into a fun I SPY game. Your friends reported you saying, "Dad, DAD, DAAAAAADDD! Take a look! I have to show you something re-e-e-al-l-l-y important." This must have caught the curiosity of your stepdad right away.

You also shared and reflected upon your experiences earlier in the day as you brought your stepdad to the digital frames on the wall to watch the photos of the day. Your decision to make it an "I SPY" game with your stepdad was an interesting one as you exclaimed: "Dad, I SPY with my eye something that is different on my head. When you see my picture, I want you to look at me and then at my friends. You have to guess what is different, okay?" Your stepdad willingly responded with an "All right".

You waited so patiently for your stepdad to look at the photo. You even gave him a hint when you had everyone smile at the same time. He did not see the difference right away. It seemed that your final hint of "Quick, look again! Do you see anything different?" was helpful.

We wonder if you knew that your stepdad was smiling when he said, "Okay, Chelsea. I don't see anything different," and you replied back with an

"Ugh, I lost my first tooth!"

Everyone soon learned that you were joking with one another. We learned this when you and your stepdad both said, "I'm joking!" Your research with your friends at lunch about soft foods seemed to help you determine what you thought would help your mouth when you got home. Ice cream, Jello, and soup were your suggestions for dinner— it sounds like you have a solution!

(continued)

Days later, you placed your photos in the digital Dropbox for your family to share in your ideas and experiences. This prompted many new ideas by you in your portfolio!

Chelsea's Reflection:

Refer to NelsonStudy for her response.

Chelsea's Stepdad's Reflection:

Refer to NelsonStudy for his response.

Educator Reflection:

Refer to NelsonStudy for the educator response.

Future inquiries:

Refer to NelsonStudy for future inquiries.

Take a moment to review these reflections online. There you will find various portfolio examples in addition to Chelsea's reflection and subsequent interpretations by her educators, dad, and stepdad. Chelsea's experience prompted the creation of "lost tooth" stories for the bookshelves in the room.

What does Exhibit 6.15 tell us? It portrays the unique and important perspective of the child, and the excitement children have to share their learning and experiences. Having the opportunity to share this learning is what makes these moments special. Take the time to sit and reflect with children on an event in their lives; you'll be surprised by what you hear and learn when you truly listen. Meeting regularly with families and children to review and discuss a portfolio, whether it is daily, spontaneously, or at designated times throughout the year, is a necessary step in the pedagogical documentation process and is an important role of the responsive educator.

REFLECTIVE EXERCISE 6.7

Using Exhibit 6.15 and the reflections on NelsonStudy for Chelsea, prepare your own reflection in response to this pedagogical documentation. Then think about the learning that has taken place from Chelsea and her peers and create a curriculum response to Chelsea's exciting news. Think from a co-constructive perspective, including the questions you might ask to extend the children's thinking, as well as strategies for implementation for your ideas.

According to Copple & Bredekamp (2009), "Involving families in this process enables them to share their expertise about their children and creates an exchange of information between families and teachers that supports children as their strengths and needs change. . . . Moreover, children thrive when they are part of a community in which families and teachers understand children's strengths and areas of need and then individualize teaching to match the children's capabilities" (as cited in Caspe, Seltzer, Lorenzo Kennedy, Cappio, and DeLorenzo, 2013, p. 9).

Being a responsive educator means using this information in way that supports the preparation of co-created and inclusive curriculum for both individual and groups of children in the same setting.

Roles of the Supervisor, Director, or Principal   All early childhood settings have an administration department or office, for it is the role of the administrator to ensure that the staff and educators are fulfilling their responsibilities as per their licensing, ministry, legislative, or board of directors requirements. An important role of the administrator is supporting the educator to create opportunities for portfolio creation and entries for each child. This support could come in the form of

- assisting educators to introduce the portfolio process to families and children when they first start the program;
- supporting educators, families, and children to attain materials and the room necessary for ongoing access to documentation to promote joint ownership of observing and documenting how learning happens for children;
- scheduling reflection time for educators to meet with children and families to co-select representative artifacts for insertion. This would include time for preparing documentation that would invite reflections and interpretations from children, families, and educators. This time would also include discussion of a child's thinking and inquiries that day, their learning and growth over time, as well as providing time for a child to reflect upon and discuss meaningful moments in their learning. These discussions are great opportunities for revisiting how children learn through play as educators and families listen to children recalling events that took place. Often we are consumed by whether or not a child knows thier numbers, shapes, or colours, and we lose track of how a child might be building friendships, resolving conflicts or handling changes in their life or day, forming hypotheses and taking risks, or exploring various aspects (or not) of the learning environment. These are just some of the inquiries we might have in building our understanding of a child. What else might be important to a parent? A child? An educator?;

- scheduling time for co-writing, rewriting, and editing documentation, or for preparing documents in hard copy for a portfolio or in digital form for an e-portfolio. This process includes making connections between the documentation collected and what can be learned or gained by reflecting upon what has been gathered. This step might include co-preparing curriculum that scaffolds upon the child's learning and interests; or
- providing time for planning for individual supports if identified through discussion that a child is struggling with an aspect of her or his development, an Individual Educational Plan is necessary, or referrals for outside support are needed. For more information on Individual Education Plans and early intervention, please go to Chapter 7.

Understanding how to build a sustainable portfolio system for every child in a room requires a commitment from all participants in a setting. When everyone understands what the process is and what is required, the value of portfolios as a means to inform practice is increased.

Portfolios and Authentic Assessment: Types and Forms

The authentic assessment context of the portfolio allows it to be associated with a variety of curriculum approaches, philosophies, and settings. With the evolvement of pedagogical documentation and observational/assessment methods that reflect the individuality of children within familiar environments, it is important to understand that there are various types of portfolios and many forms they can take as a means for documenting and making visible the thinking and learning of a child. Portfolios as a means for documenting the continuous professional learning of educators is a topic that will be further explored in Chapter 8.

Portfolios for children can be prepared in either paper or digital format; it is a philosophical choice of a setting. When in traditional paper form, portfolios may be prepared in a file folder format with tabs, in a binder with sleeve protectors, or in an accordion file, for example. A number of variables might influence the format of the portfolio, including philosophy, storage capacity, stage of portfolio development, skills and knowledge of those contributing to the portfolio, and number and type of artifacts submitted. Paper means are less common, as apps and websites facilitate the building of portfolios quite easily.

Understanding the purpose of using a portfolio and who the audience might be can assist in determining the type of portfolio most appropriate for a child, family, or setting. While the organization of a portfolio will vary with the setting, hard-copy portfolios are traditionally presented in three different ways depending on the purpose and intention of the documentation being collected. The most common and traditional categories of portfolios are display or showcase portfolios, working or developmental portfolios, and assessment portfolios. Let's examine each below.

display or showcase portfolio

A digital or hard-copy portfolio that showcases end-of-year/semester accomplishments/interests (according to an educator) or children's/student's perspectives of their best or most important work.

Display or Showcase Portfolios   The intention and purpose of a display or showcase portfolio is exactly as it sounds. Ranges of artifact submissions from informal to formal are appropriate for insertion in this approach. Selected artifacts demonstrating a child's "best" work are presented for review and reflection. The educator with this type of portfolio is often charged with the task of selecting a child's best work or traits so as to show connections to curriculum frameworks, professional standards, or skills and knowledge as outlined in standardized assessments. Children and families might also have the opportunity to perform this task; however, they tend not to provide authentic artifact evidence that shows other elements of a child's experiences and interests, or moments in time that are of significance to the child.

Take, for example, Exhibit 6.16. Ms. Smith, the educator, had been selecting writing samples she felt represented Rachel's growth and development and her "best work." Take a look in this exhibit at Ms. Smith's rationale for not only including the artifact she had collected but also placing Rachel's choice and her rationale beside hers. What do you notice about these two artifacts? Why might it be important to keep both?

This portfolio may house formal and standardized assessment information; however, it is imperative that the educator check with their licensing body to determine if this information should be in a more separate and secure location.

Working/Developmental Portfolios   A working/developmental portfolio is sometimes seen as a temporary home for information because it evolves and changes as the individual grows and changes. Others will argue that it is not temporary but rather a portfolio system that is continually building and changing so as to reflect the learning journey of a child. "It includes selected but typical work samples along with educator documentation to show the child's progress as well as the educator's observations. It is on these Portfolios that curriculum is based and future actions planned for the child, with input from the child, the family, and other professionals if needed" (Nilsen, 2014, p. 9). This particular type of portfolio resonates with appreciative inquiry and pedagogical documentation principles, as artifacts are more often culturally, developmentally, and authentically relevant, capturing the diversity of the child within the learning environment. Any artifact that holds meaning for the child, family, or educator can be included in this portfolio. Standardized checklists

working/developmental portfolio

A growing and changing hard-copy or digital portfolio representing a child's growth and development aimed to house information, observations, and a variety of artifacts prepared by a family, child, or educator.

EXHIBIT 6.16	A Comparison of "Best Work"

Artifact submitted by Rachel, age 10.1

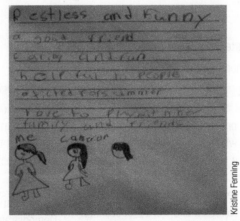

Kristine Fenning

Grade Four Portfolio Artifact

Name of Child: Rachel **CA:** 10.1 yrs. **Date:** September 8, 2012

Submitted by: Rachel

Type of Artifact	Rationale for Entry	Reflections on Artifact
Poem	"I think this is a good poem because I wrote it with my friend Cam and she is my best friend. This poem has words in it that we both like, and it is my favourite. We used some really good adjectives that show how I feel about Cam, like restless and funny and helpful."	Ms. Smith: "Rachel, you have really put your thoughts into some great words that describe your friend. She is lucky to have you as a friend." Curriculum strand: Writing—reflects understanding and organization of ideas to communicate with an intended audience

Notes: Share at parent–teacher conference

Source: Kristine Fenning

(continued)

Draft journal reflection artifact submitted by the teacher

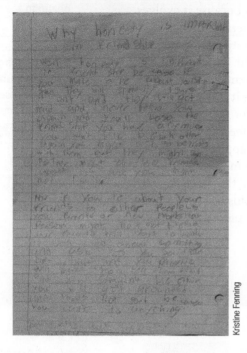
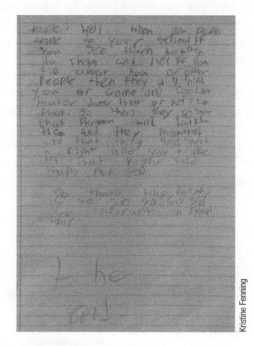

Kristine Fenning

Grade Four Portfolio Artifact

Name of Child: Rachel **CA:** 10.1 yrs. **Date:** September 8, 2012

Submitted by: Ms. Smith, Grade 4 teacher

Type of Artifact	Rationale for Entry	Reflections on Artifact
Draft writing sample	This draft was prepared as a reflection on a guest speaker who came in to speak about bullying and the importance of friendships with everyone. It demonstrates Rachel's connection to the concepts presented by the speaker. Rachel was to then proofread it and word process it for display in the classroom.	**Parent comment(s):** We didn't realize she was thinking at this level about the ways in which she needs to act to maintain friendships. This is great to see. **Curriculum strand:** Demonstrates processing skills, forming opinions, forming some connections to concepts

Note: Was reviewed by Rachel and her parents in the parent–teacher conference and compared to her final revised version on display—final grade was level 3+

Source: Kristine Fenning

assessment portfolio

A collection of documentation demonstrating a child's growth or change over time; assists in the process of self-evaluation and goal setting, identifying areas of focus, or tracking development of one domain or more.

and information should be stored separately from this type of portfolio in a secure location.

Assessment Portfolios   The assessment portfolio is most commonly associated with the demonstration of knowledge and skills related to curriculum outcomes. This does not necessarily mean that only a child's best work is entered to reflect mastery or attainment of an outcome; instead, artifacts are submitted that provide opportunity for assessment of the level of achievement for a particular standard or grade. The child or the educator may create artifact submissions, which are open for discussion in a parent–educator meeting.

E-Portfolios/Digital Portfolios   It is an increasing expectation that children will use technology as an information source for new learning and exploration. In education today, children are expected to be self-driven with technology and to access the knowledge needed for just-in-time learning. E-portfolios provide opportunities for children to practise these skills, while furthering self-awareness of their strengths, their aha moments, and areas for growth and development. Common e-portfolio sites such as Weebly, Mahara, Notability, Desire2Learn, Three Ring, Kidblog, Easy Portfolio, ePortfolio Mashup, Google Docs, and Dreamweaver are set up to allow different types of users to populate the e-portfolios with artifacts and text in various ways. It is strongly suggested that educators research these and other e-portfolio sites to find the best fit for them.

Robert Kneschke/Shutterstock.com

e-portfolio

An electronic portfolio that contains a purposefully selected collection of documentation over time; similar to a traditional portfolio but presented electronically.

E-portfolios are conducive to capturing the individuality of children's learning and thinking, thus promoting, recognizing, and valuing learning that happens in different ways for different children. As students collect, digitize, and publish their digital portfolios, the process of forming responses and meaningful reflections upon their past and current learning becomes natural (Rees, 2015). Also important to note is that "research shows how the use of digital portfolios can produce an improvement of learning through the stimulation of students' motivation. According to Multisilta, Suominen, and Östman (2012), the idea of motivation is also tied to the use of "technology-enriched learning tools and spaces with mobile technology, Web 2.0 applications, social media, and all existing digital resources providing powerful arenas for learning, both in formal and informal education settings" (p. 68). Students continue to be engaged by different social media tools such as blogs, forums, and platforms eliciting contact and friendship with others. This connected online learning environment provides a motivating arena for digital portfolio construction" (Ito, Baumer, Bittanti, Boyd, Herr-Stephenson, Horst, Lange, Mahendran, Martinez, Pascoe, Perkep, Robinson, Sims & Tripp, 2010; Rees, 2015, p. 21).

E-portfolios, then, are not restricted to specific types of artifacts; in fact, artifact possibilities are endless. Possessing the ability to select and choose artifacts provides ongoing opportunity for reflection, interpretation, conversation, and connection to new learning. Revisiting blogs in Chapter 4, we realize that these digital forums provide great opportunity for self-assessment and evaluation of pedagogical documentation produced by children, their educators, and families. Being creative and open with our strategies for portfolio creation prompts enthusiasm for making one's own learning visible.

In many circumstances, families also benefit from e-portfolio use. According to the research by Bates (2014), family engagement is enhanced when participating in the e-portfolio process.

Digital portfolios can give families a glimpse into their child's day because one of the advantages is the capability to share a child's work.

To ensure privacy, teachers control who has access to the portfolio. When sharing it, different levels of permission are available, including the view and modify options. The view option lets families see the contents of the portfolio, and the modify option lets them contribute by uploading images and recordings from home. This approach supports family engagement and provides a more complete picture of children's development. (Bates, C.C. *Digital Portfolios: Using Technology to Involve Families*, National Association for the Education of Young Children [NAEYC], Sept. 2014, p. 56)

Let's take a look at the excerpt of a parent who added to an artifact in her child's portfolio in Exhibit 6.17.

More information on the NAEYC e-portfolio suggestions and examples of e-portfolios are available online and in NelsonStudy.

Portfolios and Accessibility

The hard-copy portfolio typically remains at the early childhood setting for viewing until the child leaves a setting or the portfolio has reached its capacity and a new one is created. The e-portfolio has the capacity to be accessed at any time by any authorized user with computer and Internet access no matter where they are. With the introduction of web-based and app-based portfolios, hard-copy portfolios can be transformed into digital formats by simply scanning, taking a photo, and then loading the information onto a computer. As the child changes, the portfolio can be personalized with the simple click of a button to add, remove, or alter information.

Electronic portfolios have a number of capabilities that hard-copy portfolios do not. Audio and visual capabilities of the e-portfolio enable the revisiting of a moment in time so as to allow those viewing the information to experience the situation as it occurs. For example, video vignettes or audio files provide opportunity to dialogue and reflect upon a learning moment together. This gives authentic insights into what took place, thus increasing the accuracy of knowing what has been seen, heard, and understood.

Portability of the electronic portfolio is often an asset. However, the early childhood setting needs to consider whether those who wish to contribute to the electronic portfolio have the necessary electronic skills and abilities to prepare, modify, view, post, or even access technology. Time is a valuable asset for early childhood settings, and, thus, it is important that educators not be bogged down with trying to figure out systems rather than spending time with the children. Technology also may or may not increase a family's access to their child's information, as some families may not have a computer at home or access to the Internet. This is something to consider when planning for accessibility.

Digital portfolios also allow a large volume of historical information to be retained over long periods of time, whether it is password protected in a web or e-based portfolio site, on a USB or DVD, or on a computer mainframe. Finding opportunities to allow a child to compare their learning to previous learning is a great opportunity for them to engage in

EXHIBIT 6.17   A Parent's Artifact Entry to a Digital Portfolio

Ammentorp Photography/ Shutterstock.com

Name of Child: Alexander **Date:** February 19, 2015 **CA:** 3.3 years

Name of Observer: Mary (Alexander's mother)

Digital Artifact Rationale

I took this photo of Alexander at the table doing some artwork as it demonstrates Alexander's imagination and love for superheroes and explosions. He is always so excited about them, and he kept talking about this particular picture for quite some time while I was washing the dishes. When I asked him about this artwork, he said, "The bad guy's car went boom like that when he crashed." I feel this demonstrates his ability to make lots of different movements with his crayons, including large circles, squiggles, and swirly lines—these were things I had never seen him do before because he usually just wants to colour in a colouring book. He tends to get frustrated trying to make pictures of his own.

Reflections

Alexander (written by his mom, Mary): Yeah, the bad guy's gone now. The fire in his car is out 'cause of the water.

Educator A: (to his mom): Thanks for sharing this interesting picture and information with me. Alexander has creatively used his imagination here by showing us what superheroes look like and that they can create some very big explosions.

Educator A (to Alexander): I can see with your dark blue that you were showing how large the explosion was. *Alexander—your ability to draw diagonal and zigzag lines independently allowed you to form closed circles and designs to create your superheroes. Your very detailed explanation (6- to 11-word sentence) helped me to understand your story as you recalled what was happening in your picture. Perhaps we should provide larger paper here at school for you to further explore other superhero ideas. I'd like you to select different drawing materials and paper with me tomorrow so that other children can create their ideas on paper too.

Note: This experience supports "engagement" (How Does Learning Happen?) in our program as this discussion utilized perspectives of the child and family as we learned together about Alexander's creations.

*OELF (Ontario Early Learning Framework)
3.5: Using Descriptive Language to Explain, Explore, and Extend
3.9 Retelling Stories
4.8 Communicating Findings

self-assessment. This poses a number of benefits for the child, including recognition of their individual learning and developmental journey, increased self-awareness, and a supportive dialogue regarding their progress and the setting of new goals and personal objectives of interest or relevance to them.

E-Portfolios and Voice-to-Text Programs   Voice-to-text programs open up a whole new world for e-portfolios and use by children. With popular voice-to-text programs like Dragon Dictation, Evernote, Voice Texting Pro, Voice Assistant for social media users, and other apps specific to different educational subjects, users can translate their speech into text that then can be used for an e-portfolio or printed for hard-copy viewing. These programs enable children to be less dependent on adults in navigating and populating their portfolios, thus enhancing literacy and increasing opportunities for the child's voice to be a part of the reflection and dialogue process in parent–educator–child meetings. These programs are also a viable option for educators and families who are constrained for time to write reflections or interpretations during or following an observation or who may struggle with the writing process. These types of apps do change frequently, as technology changes happen daily and new apps come out while others become obsolete. Every app also has its own strengths and limitations, such as specific devices required, price, and usability.

Individual Education Plans (IEPs) or standardized assessments may be a part of a child's files but are often stored separately from a child's portfolio for confidentiality reasons. Again, it is important to check with your licensing or governmental regulations to determine how confidential information is to be stored and viewed. More information on standardized assessments can be found in Chapter 7.

Exhibit 6.18 demonstrates the uniqueness of entries in children's portfolios. Based on the entry that follows, what types of entries might we see in an infant portfolio? The portfolio of a child in full-day kindergarten? Be sure to see the examples available online.

As we explore assessment tools in Chapter 7, it would be interesting to apply our learning from portfolio entries like that in Exhibit 6.18 to a screening tool to determine how we might continue to support a child in his language development if it was identified by the team (educators, child, parent(s)) that there were concerns requiring more investigation. If we were to apply this portfolio example further to the Ontario Early Learning Framework and the Ontario Ministry of Education *How Does Learning Happen?* document, what else might we learn? What new questions or inquiries might we have?

Portfolios: Supporting Children's Metacognition

Portfolios provide a lens to capture the voice of the child. Reflecting, thinking about, interpreting, and communicating about one's learning and progress is a complex and important skill to practise and master. Portfolios provide the platform necessary for this self-reflection to take place. Velez Laski (2013) describes metacognition as

EXHIBIT 6.18   Short Language Sample

This language sample has been voice-to-text transcribed from the Voice Memo App on Santos's digital portfolio dated January 4, 2015.

Name of Child: Santos   **DOB:** February 14, 2013   **CA:** 25 months

Date: April 24, 2015

Documenter: Erik (student–educator)

Location: Book centre—Santos is sitting with his legs crossed on the floor beside a student–educator with a social story book created for Santos called My New Baby Sister.

> **Student–Educator:** Santos, what are you reading?
>
> **Santos:** Dis, my book.
>
> **Student–Educator:** Who is in your book, Santos?
>
> **Santos:** Bith. Bith cying. Stinky dipa.
>
> **Student–Educator:** Oh dear, a stinky diaper. What do we do with a stinky diaper?
>
> **Santos:** Wipe bum. Put garbage dere. (He points to the garbage can in the bathroom for diapers.)
>
> **Student–Educator:** What do you like to do with Elizabeth?
>
> **Santos:** I hoded Bith.
>
> **Student–Educator:** I bet you held her very carefully, Santos. Did you feed her a bottle?
>
> **Santos:** No, Mum feed er.

Interpretations

It seems that Santos is able to use approximated and intelligible full words in two- to three-word sentences to communicate, and he appears to be able to answer the questions of his educator with information in context, such as identifying who is in his book and what he does with his sister. It seems he uses past and present tense (hoded, cying).

Reflections/New Inquiries

Educators to offer baby supplies, blankets, dolls, and beds in the dramatic centre to build on Santos's interest in his new baby sister. Building on this book with things he does with his sister might be an option to explore to further build on his expressive language and his interest in babies. This extension would then further promote well-being and a sense of belonging as outlined in How Does Learning Happen?

Parent Reflection

"It is great to see Santos so interested in his new baby sister. We were worried about how he would adjust to this new situation. We would like to prepare a book for him on why he is such a great big brother, as we think this will help him to be more gentle with his sister.

"thinking about thinking" such as knowing what we know or do not know, monitoring the outcomes of our work, setting goals, and planning ahead. . . . Essentially, children with good metacognitive skills are self-directed learners who are able to self-evaluate and select new strategies when appropriate rather than rely on someone else to guide them. (Bransford, Brown, & Cocking, 2000, p. 38)

When children are provided the materials necessary to self-document and reflect, and ongoing opportunities for conversation and reflection are available, they develop awareness of their strengths and skills requiring development. During these opportunities, children are able to recall proud, exciting, or challenging moments in their learning; revisit old and develop new hypotheses; and develop a passion for literacy as they authentically review their developmental progress and perhaps set goals of their own for future learning. Children of all abilities are able to view their portfolios and communicate through imagery, pictures, and artifacts selected to share with others what they know and understand.

Elementary school teachers with older school-age children at a school in the United States were asked to think about why they wanted system-wide e-portfolios for children in their classes. Reflecting upon the reasons provided in Exhibit 6.19, we can see that their reasons centred on children's learning and the development of metacognition.

Portfolios and Professional Standards, Frameworks, and Documents

In the process of preparing and creating portfolios for children, making connections between selected artifacts to defined professional standards, curriculum frameworks, environmental design, ministry documents, or developmental continuums is a common role and expectation for educators around the world. When meaningful artifacts are collected, selected, and reflected upon, the process of applying and connecting the new knowledge gained to developmental continuums, to professional standards of practice, or to standards held by a particular setting becomes more defined. Exhibit 6.20 connects a

---

EXHIBIT 6.19	School-Wide E-Portfolios

The following "are several important reasons driving us toward school-wide e-portfolios." Central among these reasons:

- students learn to think beyond the grade;
- students increase their self-awareness;
- students develop the essential dispositions for lifelong learning—self-motivation, self-discipline, self-scheduling, responsibility, and organization;
- students understand, set, and discuss their learning goals and strategies for getting there;
- teachers individualize the student learning experience; and
- teachers, students, and parents become partners in the student's learning experience"

Source: Shriver, Chris. (2014, Winter). "E-Portfolio: A 21st-Century Tool for 21st-Century Learning." *Independent Schools*, 72. Used by permission of the author.

EXHIBIT 6.20 Making the Connection

Kristine Fenning

Lauren, age 4.2 years. Date of artwork: July 22, 2015

"The Pumpkin Patch"

Lauren made lots of pictures using orange today. This one she proudly shared with everyone in the room. Lauren said, "This pumpkin is growing so big, even bigger than the other plants in the field cause of the sun and the rain. We brought this pumpkin home and we are going to make lots of pies."

Parent Post-it:

We weighed it and it was 15 pounds! Lauren has been scooping out the seeds and so far she has counted 50! She wants to show her friends.

Educator Post-it:

Lauren's family are bringing in the pumpkin for the group to explore. We are going to compare our pumpkins from the centre garden to this one to provoke new inquiries.

If we link this artifact, experience, and accompanying reflections to the *How Does Learning Happen?* document (Ontario Ministry of Education, 2014), we can see its pertinence to the goal of engagement as the educators and Lauren connect her family experience to the inquiries of the children in the room who are already interested in the growing pumpkins in their centre garden. Inviting the participation of the family is responsive to Lauren's interests, it prompts inquiry through play and exploration of the natural world, and it presents a number of provocations and new questions for the children as they explore this large pumpkin. In what other ways can you connect this experience and Lauren's learning to the Ontario Early Learning Framework?

Source: Kristine Fenning

documentation artifact to the *How Does Learning Happen? Ontario's Pedagogy for the Early Years* document prepared by the Ontario Ministry of Education (2014). What do you notice about this documentation? How might you structure your documentation to link to frameworks or guidelines that inform your practice? Remember that all the documentation methods we have discussed can be formatted in digital or hard-copy form and can be configured in ways that align with your centre, agency, or school requirements.

<table>
<tr><td>**REFLECTIVE EXERCISE 6.8**</td><td>What questions might the children have when the pumpkin is brought in? How might these connections and this information now inform curriculum? How might families, children, and educators use this information collaboratively to extend learning? How might it inform additions or changes to the environment? What would you suggest as a response to the question in Exhibit 6.20?</td></tr>
</table>

Other provincial documents also remind us to be mindful of the needs and desires of newcomer children and families and, when documenting the activity of children from other cultures who speak languages other than English or French, to do so with awareness and respect.

In Ontario, documents such as *Many Roots, Many Voices: Supporting English Language Learners in Every Classroom* (Ontario Ministry of Education, 2005) are inclusive and supportive of newcomers to Canada:

> Newcomers from all backgrounds have a wide variety of interests and skills and often can contribute a great deal to a school's co-curricular activities. Some may have highly developed skills in a sport that does not have a long history at the school. Others may want to form a language club. Many newcomers will have talents and stories to contribute. . . . All of these activities provide opportunities for English language learners to participate in school life. (p. 41)

Alberta's document *Working with Young Children Who Are Learning English as a New Language* (2009) advises,

> Research shows that when young children are developing two languages at the same time, the two developing languages build on each other rather than take away from each other. The stronger the first (or home) language proficiency is, the stronger the second language proficiency will be, particularly with academic literacy. Maintaining the home language is key to a child's success in school. . . .
>
> Family, community members and the children themselves are great resources as you seek to establish a learning environment where cultural and linguistic diversity is valued. As you get to know families, you will want to be responsive to what you see, hear and observe. (pp. 5, 7)

Both of these provincial documents speak to responsive, inclusive practice respecting the cultures of families of Canada.

1. Dialogue, reflection, and asking questions are foundational components of the cycle of observation. Each of these approaches promote authentic interactions, pedagogical documentation, and capacity building within early childhood settings. Considering our image of children as mutual educators who are competent, confident, and equal partners in the pedagogical documentation processes, it is clear the role they must play in the co-creation of and co-responding to dialogue, reflection, and questions. Be sure to examine the cycle of observation closely to understand the reciprocal and fluid nature of the cycle.

2. There are a number of different strategies that can support the creation of pedagogical documentation and time for reflection and inquiry. It is important to remind ourselves that pedagogical documentation infers that ALL members of a team participate in observing, documenting, reflecting, and informing curriculum/changes in practice. Educators are not alone in making visible the learning and thinking of children. Examine the strategies provided in this chapter for this leads the reader into looking at ways to make the cycle of observation a natural part of one's day.

3. Understanding the pedagogical frameworks that guide and support our observation and documentation practices are important, for they help us to look at how they align with and inform curriculum and all aspects of our practice. Examples of frameworks that exist in Canada are provided within this chapter. Readers are encouraged to research frameworks within their own province or territory to determine how they support learning, quality, and pedagogy in early childhood settings. Inquiry approaches will help us to form the necessary questions that will guide us in our examination of this interrelationship.

4. The cycle of observation functions as a tool in which inquiry, dialogue, and reflection prompt collaboration, which in turn informs holistic and authentic pedagogical documentation and responses that value and build on community strengths.

5. The possibilities for portfolio preparation are endless as settings and teams can determine what portfolios might look like or what form they might take. Whether they are hard copy, digital form (through an e-portfolio app or website), or via a blog forum, portfolios embrace reflection, dialogue, and the participation of the child, two principles that support pedagogical documentation. To prepare and engage in the portfolio process requires the participant to reflect on a number of elements, all of which are outlined in this chapter.

6. There are three types of portfolios that would support authentic assessment and metacognition including display or showcase portfolios, working/developmental portfolios, and assessment portfolios, all of which can be in digital or hard-copy form and prepared in ways that are reflective of the setting and its learners. Knowing the purpose and intent of developing a portfolio will lead to the type of portfolio that would be used. The purpose of portfolios is to document the continuous learning and thinking of learners and to support learners in developing a reflective lens. Artifacts include authentic representations of children's learning, and enable children to think about their thinking. For more information, please consult with this chapter.

Courtesy of Scotia Plaza Child Care Centre

CHAPTER 7

INFORMING PRACTICE THROUGH THE LENS OF EARLY IDENTIFICATION

OVERVIEW

In Chapter 6, we discussed how reflection, dialogue, and the cycle of observation informs curriculum, community awareness, portfolios, and other aspects of practice. This process inevitably requires us to step outside the box to look back in, and to assess ourselves as a community of learners and as partners with families, and to ensure that we co-create optimal environments for all children to thrive in the community.

A core focus of this chapter will be on practical insights into working with children and families with special needs as well as on changing trends and perspectives regarding assessment, family-centred practice, early identification, and early intervention in the early childhood profession. Included will be the importance of considering the whole child in the early intervention / early identification process to ensure that the child's needs are being addressed within the context of their family and community.

As perspectives of the child, of observation, and of assessment evolve with our profession, it is important to look with a fresh lens toward what is needed by and provided to all children and families who have special needs and/or who might require special supports and/or services. We will discuss a little later in this chapter the importance of reflecting on traditional Westernized approaches to assessment to rethink and approach assessment in a more holistic way so as to be responsive to all families and communities. As has been often said, it takes a village to raise a child; therefore, our focus in this chapter is not only on the child and family but also on responsive inclusive services, resources, and relationships in the community.

FOCUS QUESTIONS

1. Describe the relationship between the cycle of observation and early intervention. How might one inform the other?
2. Describe the early intervention process and what it might look like as a system. What might be some of the possible outcomes? What role might observation play in the early identification of children with special needs?
3. Whom might educators collaborate with in the early intervention process and what might some of their roles be?
4. What are the components of family-centred services or practices?
5. What is the difference between authentic and standardized assessment? Describe how assessment might look within environments or settings utilizing an inquiry approach.
6. What is an individualized plan and how might these plans support making children's learning visible?
7. In what ways might observation and assessment inform a child's well-being? What is the role of the educator in this process?

THE CYCLE OF OBSERVATION AND EARLY INTERVENTION

Reflecting on content from other chapters, we are reminded that appreciative inquiry is a strengths-based approach to change, focusing on an openness to see new possibilities from a collective knowledge. Also, remember that the cycle of observation is a reflective process that is transforming, allowing participants the flexibility of thought and action to observe, discuss, reflect, monitor, and plan. The cycle of observation expands in this chapter to reflect further the family-centred and team approach through the unique process of early intervention: initial observations, assessment, an individual plan, strategies with adaptations and supports, implementation, monitoring, and evaluation. This process, as you can see from Exhibit 7.1, is part of the cycle yet uniquely on its own.

To illustrate the process of appreciative inquiry and the cycle of observation as it relates to responsive practices in the classroom, let us consider Jazz. This is a true story about the role of careful observation, inquiry, and the importance of relationships. Imagine a half-day community program that has a professional support network and, therefore, is able to have within its

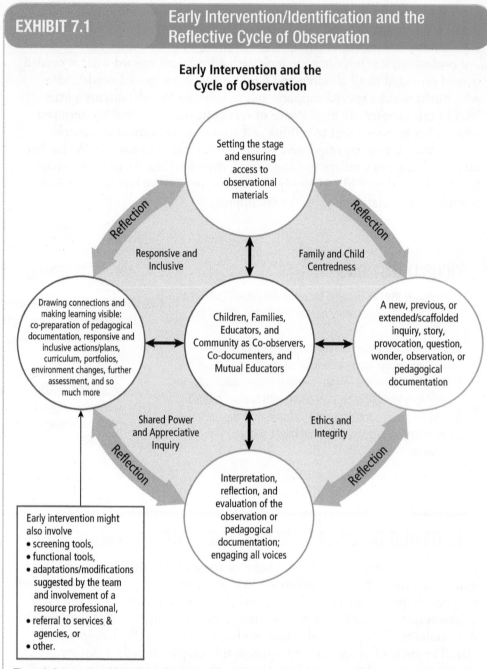

Early Intervention and the Cycle of Observation

Setting the stage and ensuring access to observational materials

Reflection

Reflection

Responsive and Inclusive

Family and Child Centredness

Drawing connections and making learning visible: co-preparation of pedagogical documentation, responsive and inclusive actions/plans, curriculum, portfolios, environment changes, further assessment, and so much more

Children, Families, Educators, and Community as Co-observers, Co-documenters, and Mutual Educators

A new, previous, or extended/scaffolded inquiry, story, provocation, question, wonder, observation, or pedagogical documentation

Shared Power and Appreciative Inquiry

Ethics and Integrity

Reflection

Reflection

Interpretation, reflection, and evaluation of the observation or pedagogical documentation; engaging all voices

Early intervention might also involve
- screening tools,
- functional tools,
- adaptations/modifications suggested by the team and involvement of a resource professional,
- referral to services & agencies, or
- other.

There is interaction throughout the cycle. Through application of appreciative inquiry, observers can begin at any point and can move fluidly through the process. Examples demonstrating the application of this cycle to early identification and intervention are available online.

Source: Kristine Fenning

enrolment a number of children who have been referred from the community for additional support. The child in Exhibit 7.2 is described by an educator.

In what ways does the situation in Exhibit 7.2 provoke our thinking? What wonders and questions led to this discovery by the educator and how does it challenge us to see beyond what we consider to be obvious? The educator

EXHIBIT 7.2	Appreciating and Listening to Understand the Whole Child

Jazz is a three-year-old child with Down syndrome who was referred from the community hub to our program for "behavioural issues" identified by her family. Initially, Jazz lived up to her referral with outbursts of temper, refusal to cooperate, and, more importantly, almost constantly pushing and shoving other children around her. Jazz wore glasses, which I discovered she had been wearing only for the past six months. I observed her over a number of days, and one observation in particular was highly interesting.

Jazz was sitting at a table trying to construct a six-piece single-inset puzzle. This was the first time I had seen her attempt a puzzle. As I watched, she fumbled with the pieces, bringing each one up to her face and leaning over the puzzle before she wiggled each one into position. As I sat down beside to support her problem solving, she brought another piece close to her eyes rotating it around in her hands for examination. To provoke a conversation and to engage with Jazz, I stated, "Oh, I see, Jazz, that you are looking closely at the photos to place the pieces in the right spots," to which she replied, "Uh huh, I need to see them." When her mother arrived to take Jazz home, I asked her about Jazz's vision. "Oh, she can see fine," she said, "now that she has her glasses." Several days passed. As I completed more observations, I began to suspect that she might not actually be seeing all that clearly; perhaps her glasses were not helping her see as well as they could. After much inquiry, co-learning with and listening to Jazz, as well as discussion with her mother, my supervisor, and colleagues, we decided it might be worth investigating further into her vision and glasses. Jazz's mother was able to get an appointment with an ophthalmologist to have her eyes tested again. This time, she was diagnosed with strabismus in one eye and was immediately scheduled for an operation to correct her field of vision. When she returned from her operation with new glasses, it was not long before we saw a changed child; she seemed happier and more confident and was less aggressive with her peers. Her mother noticed a change at home as well.

Jazz's referral to us from a different program as a perceived "unruly" child was based on her behaviour. Staff had labelled her without uncovering the cause of her behaviour. Jazz pushed and shoved because she could not see. Perhaps she pushed and shoved because she felt anxious and vulnerable, and that frustration poured out into almost all aspects of her social encounters. She could not see, but because she had glasses, the assumption was that she could see. Jazz did not really understand that her vision was challenged; she just tried to cope with life around her.

who proceeded to inquire about this child's outward expression of frustration prompted them to engage in additional observation and inquiry with questions such as the following:

What situations and times of the day is the pushing, shoving, and frustrations of the child occurring? (This led to further observations and use of other methodologies to gather information.)

How might I connect with this child to assist them in communicating verbally? (This led to engagement with the child in different experiences in order to listen.)

How might I use the learning stories about this child such as their puzzle exploration and other observations to inform understanding of their thinking?

(This led to dialogue with Jazz, her mother, and other educators to discuss a holistic view of her learning and understanding.)

How might I involve the voice of this child in helping them to resolve their frustrations? (Ongoing engagement and dialogue/listening with Jazz led to her voice being heard—that she wasn't seeing as clearly as she could.)

This inquiry and these questions are reminders that there is no substitute for appreciative inquiry, listening, and reflection within the cycle of observation. The sustainability of learning, rather than a "Band-Aid" approach to learning that is short lived and often superficial, is key to understanding and appreciating children. Observation gets to the core to uncover the root of children's actions and thinking. Children communicate through what they say and do that something is "not right" or that a need is not being met. It is our role as responsive educators to listen, learn, observe, document, and reflect alongside children and families to understand, support, and respond.

It takes a community to build collective knowledge and a paradigm of possibilities for children, their families, and the community. This is especially true for children with special needs, children who are vulnerable, and children who need extra supports or services. How well we co-construct a plan for observing and documenting, co-develop a model for early intervention that is culturally and individually safe and respectful for everyone, implement our required ministry policies, or prepare and follow policies and procedures in our early childhood settings hinges on our discussion of our collective beliefs and commitment, our services and resources, and our vision of what can be. How creatively do we problem solve perceived barriers or challenges? How do we scaffold new knowledge by rethinking our perspectives to see things in different ways? Asking questions like these helps us create quality inclusive and responsive practices and environments. If we can engage in appreciative inquiry and mutual education, we will make a significant difference in our approach to the welfare of our children and families.

Iakov Filimonov/Shutterstock.com

What Are Early Intervention and Early Identification?

Early intervention and identification no longer have the connotations of being both a system and a group of services exclusively designed to support only children with diagnosed special needs and their families. A significant change in the field has been an attitudinal one, looking at special needs as something experienced by all people. As societal attitudes and the needs of children and families change, so, too, do the terms of reference, legislation, and policies that guide the delivery and availability of services and early learning spaces for children. While services may change regularly, what we do know is that all children are entitled to have access to quality early childhood settings, opportunities, and early intervention and identification services.

The terms *early intervention* and *early identification*, while complex in terms of systems and processes, are actually simple in their intentions. At the heart of early intervention and identification is the process of supporting and nurturing the individual variations in growth, development, and thinking demonstrated by every child, and providing the necessary supports, materials, resources, and services to enable them to flourish and thrive. We can do this by establishing assessment processes that are holistic and meaningful, anti-oppressive in their approach, and, ultimately, family- and child-centric. Let's explore this further . . .

Early Intervention and Identification: Process and Outcomes

The early intervention and identification process starts the moment any child and family begins a program. It begins the building of a relationship that embraces conversation about the relevance and importance of observation and pedagogical documentation. It also includes how family priorities, beliefs, and values are carefully integrated into an observational plan so as to lead to the understanding of how to support a child's inquiry, learning, and development. Observation as an everyday practice and dialogue requires every participant within an early childhood setting to co-participate in establishing an observational and pedagogical documentation plan that is sustainable and realistic.

When time is taken to explain what early identification and early intervention mean to the child's overall success and to the responsibilities of educators to support children's learning to be the best they can be, then a shared value and understanding of why it is necessary to observe, inquire, dialogue, reflect, and respond is established. This open-ended communication-based strategy creates a proactive rather than a reactive approach to this process, enabling the building of reciprocal trust between the educator, parent(s), and child and to the promotion of teamwork and collaboration.

Collaboration means many different things to different people and professionals within the early childhood profession. At its core, it is a relationship between a group of people, agencies, or organizations who share a common vision while fulfilling related or different roles to achieve an agreed-upon outcome. It is a process, an action, a value, a skill, and an attitude, and it can exist at any level (program, municipally, provincially, nationally, or internationally). While it is not without complexity, it is an important aspect of practice not to be underestimated. It is recommended that family and child priorities and needs direct the collaboration, the process, and the direction of the intervention. Building open communication and appreciative inquiry into this process helps to promote an anti-oppressive approach keeping the flexibility and reciprocity needed for an inclusive response.

It is through this collaboration that decisions can be made by the team. These decisions might include or inform curriculum changes for individuals or groups of children based on their strengths, opportunities for growth, and interests. They might also inform changes to teaching approaches, environmental design, the need for more observation, or perhaps the introduction of assessment and early intervention for children with special needs. How does your early childhood setting implement observation as part of everyday practice? Within your setting, do you have an early identification plan based upon a strong observational foundation? How might your plan be connected to an appreciative inquiry approach? How are families and children involved in that plan? The inquiry process will generate these and other important questions, which will focus and guide the cycle of observation and observational plan. Exhibit 7.3 highlights the responsibilities of registered early childhood

Standard II: Curriculum and Pedagogy

A. Principle

Registered early childhood educators (RECEs) co-construct knowledge with children, families and colleagues. They draw from their professional knowledge of child development, learning theories and pedagogical and curriculum approaches to plan, implement, document and assess child-centered, inquiry and play-based learning experiences for children.

B. Knowledge
RECEs:

1. Are knowledgeable about child development theories and understand that children's development is integrated across multiple domains and within a variety of contexts and environments.
2. Are knowledgeable about current learning theories and pedagogical and curriculum approaches that are based on inclusion and inquiry and play-based learning.
3. Are knowledgeable about methods in observation, pedagogical documentation, planning, implementation and assessment in order to support children's individual and group learning experiences.
4. Understand that children are capable and enthusiastic learners with unique personalities, skills, and interests.

C. Practice
RECEs:

1. Observe children to identify individual and group needs and interests.
2. Collaborate with children to co-plan and implement a child-centred and play-based curriculum.
3. Use a variety of materials to intentionally create or adapt indoor and outdoor learning environments that support children's exploration and learning.
4. Respond to the uniqueness of individuals and groups of children. They identify appropriate strategies, access the necessary resources and design curriculum to ensure full participation of all children, taking into account ability, cultural and linguistic diversity and Indigenous identity. They provide all children with opportunities for engagement, exploration and expression.
5. Use technology and assistive technological tools as appropriate to support children's learning and development.
6. Document children's learning experiences in order to reflect upon and assess children's growth and the curriculum. They use documentation and critical reflection to enhance the program and consider new ideas and approaches.
7. Use appropriate and effective communication methods and strategies to share information with families regarding the development and learning of children.
8. Design the daily program to allow for appropriate amounts of uninterrupted inquiry and play-based learning in indoor and outdoor environments.
9. Work collaboratively with families and colleagues to plan meaningful learning experiences and support problem solving and decision making (pp. 10–11).

Source: College of Early Childhood Educators. (2017). *Code of Ethics and Standards of Practice*. Retrieved from https://www.collegeece.ca/en/Documents/Code_and_Standards_2017.pdf

educators in Ontario regarding observation, pedagogical documentation, and assessment. Take a moment to reflect upon each of these responsibilities to determine how you plan to fulfill them as educators in the profession. Be sure to check with Chapter 2 as it explores standards of practice in other provinces. More information on the Ontario Ministry of Education observation and documentation expectations, as well as examples of how observation and documentation inform aspects of our practice, including early intervention, is available online.

In addition to curriculum, other outcomes of this ongoing process of learning about each child within the group might involve the use of screening or functional assessments, or further pursuit of diagnostic assessment (either done simultaneously or in conjunction with ongoing observation). Each of these terms will be discussed later in this chapter. In any context or situation relating to observation, assessment, or early intervention and identification, parents and their child(ren) are seen as key contributors and decision makers. Their involvement is accorded deep respect for their expertise, knowledge, and perspectives. In addition to authentic observational methods (such as those discussed in Chapters 4 and 5) capturing the inquiry, interests, and abilities of each child, many early childhood settings may choose to conduct screenings on each child with permission and participation from their family (and the child). Consideration of participatory rights of children as per Chapter 2 is a necessary step in this process. This process further considers such things as prerequisite skills evident or requiring further development, how to better break down a task for a child, what materials and resources might support a child the best, and so on. In many circumstances involving assessment, outside paraprofessionals will be involved.

paraprofessional

A trained person who works under the guidance of a more qualified professional in that field.

Note that in Exhibit 7.4, every family's experience with early intervention and identification is unique and, therefore prompts constant movement and exchange within the entire early intervention system and process, as indicated by the arrows. A family or child's progress may be guided and influenced by new variables introduced or if a specific step is skipped, not achieved, or achieved simultaneously with another goal. If, for example, recommended adaptations to the environment were not made, then failure to follow through would prompt discussion between those involved. If a child continued to struggle within an environment despite a number of accommodations that had been made to support them, (e.g., interesting materials added to extend the child's learning based on observations made, adapted grips for paintbrushes and colouring materials), the family may wish to inquire how further assessment might be obtained to better understand how to support their child. What should be apparent is the flexible nature of this process and how it is guided by observation, vigilant monitoring of the child's progress and interactive relationships, ongoing team discussions, and the provision/creation of a responsive, inclusive curriculum and environment.

Take a moment to reflect upon Exhibit 7.4. How is your early intervention and identification system similar or different from the one shown there? Why? Take a moment to adapt and/or discuss the example in Exhibit 7.4.

REFLECTIVE EXERCISE 7.1

EXHIBIT 7.4   An Early Identification/Intervention Sample

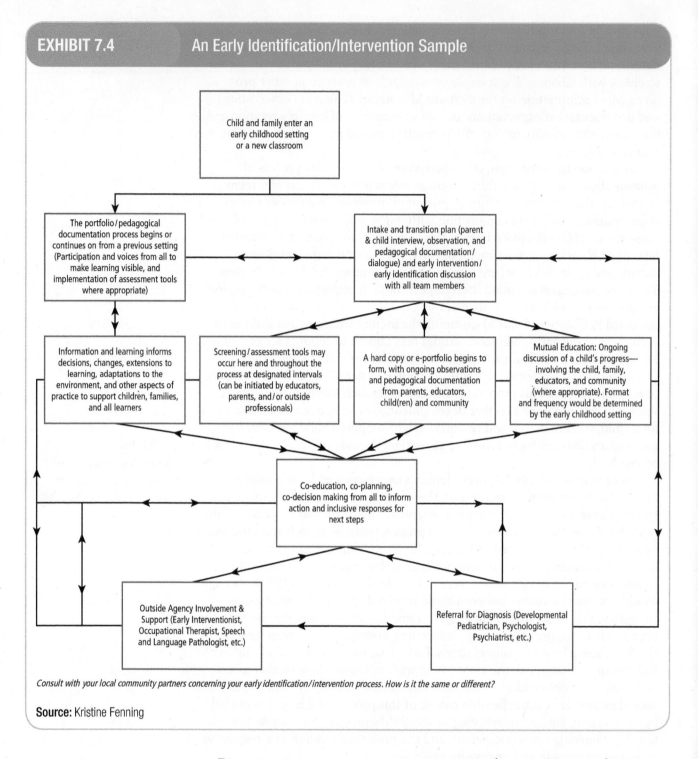

Child and family enter an early childhood setting or a new classroom

The portfolio/pedagogical documentation process begins or continues on from a previous setting (Participation and voices from all to make learning visible, and implementation of assessment tools where appropriate)

Intake and transition plan (parent & child interview, observation, and pedagogical documentation/dialogue) and early intervention/early identification discussion with all team members

Information and learning informs decisions, changes, extensions to learning, adaptations to the environment, and other aspects of practice to support children, families, and all learners

Screening/assessment tools may occur here and throughout the process at designated intervals (can be initiated by educators, parents, and/or outside professionals)

A hard copy or e-portfolio begins to form, with ongoing observations and pedagogical documentation from parents, educators, child(ren) and community

Mutual Education: Ongoing discussion of a child's progress—involving the child, family, educators, and community (where appropriate). Format and frequency would be determined by the early childhood setting

Co-education, co-planning, co-decision making from all to inform action and inclusive responses for next steps

Outside Agency Involvement & Support (Early Interventionist, Occupational Therapist, Speech and Language Pathologist, etc.)

Referral for Diagnosis (Developmental Pediatrician, Psychologist, Psychiatrist, etc.)

Consult with your local community partners concerning your early identification/intervention process. How is it the same or different?

Source: Kristine Fenning

Demonstrating an appreciative inquiry approach, a responsive, inclusive mindset and dedication to the process should lay the foundation for positive relationships, minimizing delays in process or miscommunication. Working collaboratively with paraprofessionals or resource professionals and families is key. With collaboration and interprofessional education, much good can be achieved. More information on paraprofessionals can be found online and in this chapter.

Understanding Early Intervention as a System

Early intervention is a multilayered and multifaceted system providing services to children and families. The types of agencies and professionals providing services may vary depending on how services are offered within different communities. Within each layer, there is a multitude of services, perhaps from different professions or systems that interrelate with one another. Some examples of who or what might compose that aspect are provided in Exhibit 7.5.

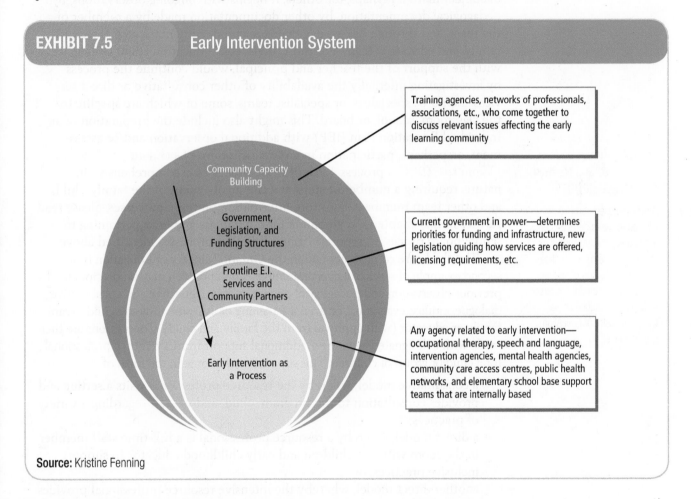

EXHIBIT 7.5   Early Intervention System

Training agencies, networks of professionals, associations, etc., who come together to discuss relevant issues affecting the early learning community

Community Capacity Building

Government, Legislation, and Funding Structures

Frontline E.I. Services and Community Partners

Early Intervention as a Process

Current government in power—determines priorities for funding and infrastructure, new legislation guiding how services are offered, licensing requirements, etc.

Any agency related to early intervention— occupational therapy, speech and language, intervention agencies, mental health agencies, community care access centres, public health networks, and elementary school base support teams that are internally based

Source: Kristine Fenning

Using Exhibit 7.5 to guide our examination of the many components of early intervention as a system and a concept, we can see that the dynamics of each layer within the early intervention system can change at any time, which then has an impact on other aspects of the system and, most inevitably, the process and delivery of services. Variables such as changes in the government and ministry, service delivery model, funding streams, the organizational mandate, and the service catchment area are common influences. Let's take a look at a couple of examples of early intervention processes.

Our first example is the Ontario Ministry of Education. Here, support services are varied depending upon whether the child is enrolled in an elementary classroom, an early childhood setting, or, perhaps, a kindergarten, for example. Common to Ontario elementary settings, when a child has self-identified or either a parent or an educator identifies the child as requiring extra supports in the classroom, a complex process begins. For some, the process might begin with a conversation with the local school principal or school support team to discuss the transition of a child to school. For others, it might begin at the parent–teacher interview or reporting period where the child or another member of the team identifies that the child is struggling with a particular skill or subject matter. Perhaps, for others, it begins with ongoing observations, by pedagogical documentation, by other documentation made by a member of the team, and through day-to-day dialogue and documentation by the child, family, and education team. For most, the special education resource teacher, with the support of the teacher and principal, would continue the process by investigating internally the availability of other consultative or direct services, supports, specialists, or specialist teams, some of which are specific to the classroom, school, or board. This might also include the preparation of an Individual Education Plan (IEP) with additional observation and/or assessment, or, perhaps, participation in an Identification, Placement, and Review Committee (IPRC) process. Each of these processes is comprehensive in nature, requiring a number of steps and the involvement of the family, child, and other team members. For more information on these processes, please read further in this chapter and go online for documents and links pertaining to school board processes, report writing, and other processes identified above.

The child-care community within the Ontario Ministry of Education is our second example of service delivery variations. This approach may be precipitated by previous observation and pedagogical documentation, reflective and collaborative dialogue, inquiry, evaluation, or even a screening or assessment by the child's team, family or educator (with approval from the family and child). Connections are then made with a designated agency for additional support from a resource professional for a child or group of children. This support might come in the form of

- a consultative model, whereby the resource professional visits a setting and provides consultation to the program, child, and/or staff regarding a variety of practices;
- a direct model, whereby a resource professional is a full-time staff member in the room with the children and early childhood educator to support inclusive practices; or
- another direct model, whereby the intensive resource professional provides contracted one-on-one support for a defined and limited length of time to set in process goals and objectives for the child and/or program.

Identification, Placement, and Review Committee (IPRC)

A school-based committee created to make decisions and allocate support/resources for children concerning identification (categorization of special need) and placement (classroom setting best suitable) as per Ontario Ministry of Education requirements.

REFLECTIVE EXERCISE 7.2

The above text discusses common processes experienced by children and families in Ontario. Processes can vary within the province, and are likely to vary outside of the province. Take a moment to research and document the early identification and intervention processes within your child care, school community, or province. How are they similar or different?

The Role of the Resource Professional

The resource educator / early interventionist / resource professional (among other titles) is often involved with a child, family, and early childhood team when further supports and services are being sought. This professional's role has expanded significantly. Take a look at Exhibit 7.6 to see the vast knowledge and skills required by current resource professionals to do their role effectively with children and families. Educators collaborate with these resource professionals, parents, and children closely to support a best practices and responsive, inclusive approach for their own setting. It can be very overwhelming for a family if a multitude of professionals are working with a child at the same or at different times; therefore, a coordinated team approach is crucial. Understanding the complexities of the resource role is important and requires individuals with unique skill sets. For every child and family, the process is unique and individualized, which may have benefits as well as challenges, depending on the individuals, circumstances, and settings.

At the heart of the diagram in Exhibit 7.6 are common processes by which we conduct our practice and the steps we follow when engaged in early intervention and identification, when ensuring quality environments are being maintained,

resource educator / early interventionist / resource professional

Professionals who provide services, materials, equipment, facilities, or personnel to meet the needs of children, families, and the communities they serve.

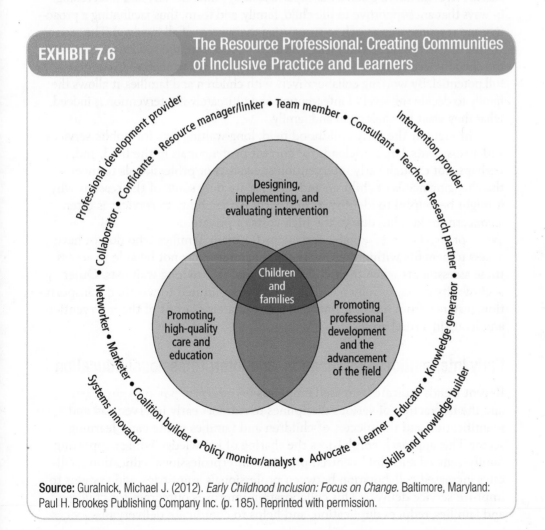

EXHIBIT 7.6 — The Resource Professional: Creating Communities of Inclusive Practice and Learners

Source: Guralnick, Michael J. (2012). *Early Childhood Inclusion: Focus on Change*. Baltimore, Maryland: Paul H. Brookes Publishing Company Inc. (p. 185). Reprinted with permission.

and specifically when working with a resource professional to support a child. As a process, early intervention and identification can be defined as when a team documents, observes, and uncovers a child's strengths, thinking, and interests, all within the context of the child's natural learning and home environments. Together with the resource professional, the team will have conversations to debrief observations, screenings, and/or assessment outcomes, and the influences, reasons, or causes that may have had an impact on those outcomes. The team may generate collaborative reports, family support plans, possible referrals, and individual education plans that could involve the preparation of goals and objectives, curriculum changes, environmental design changes, accommodations, and teaching strategy changes. While this process is typically very developmentally focused, it is recommended that teams explore a holistic view of the child through the use of a variety of anti-oppressive pedagogical documentation approaches like those discussed in Chapters 4 and 5. For example, a child's achievement of a skill may be affected by external factors such as lack of exposure to practise the skill, cultural variations (some of which include background, abilities, spirituality, family values and priorities, community practices and beliefs, and language), and the child's interests. Each of these reasons could facilitate a different approach or plan. The process also involves identifying concerns experienced by children early and intervening in ways that are supportive to the child, family, and team, thus facilitating a proactive and responsive approach to supporting the success of all involved. The sooner we are able to provide a child with services and supports, the sooner we can assist the child in developing the skills and knowledge needed to achieve his or her full potential. By working collaboratively with children and families, it allows the family to decide the level of intervention and ultimately if intervention is indeed what they want for their child and family.

Throughout the early childhood field, long waiting lists for public services and assessments, large caseloads for current professionals in the field, and, perhaps, not enough early intervention specialists or professionals to meet the changing needs of children and families are only some of the reasons why it might be helpful to identify a child early. Accessibility to services is often a concern for families due to the high costs of private developmental assessments or psychoeducational assessments for many families who do not have access to benefits within their workplace. Families may not be able to access these assessments when their child is in school due to long wait lists. Other accessibility concerns may be attributed but not limited to weather, transportation, distance from services, finances, appropriateness of fit of the intervention, and living in a rural area.

Early Intervention, Identification, and Interprofessional Education

Recent trends indicate increased emphasis on interprofessional education and the interaction of various disciplines to support early intervention and identification and the success of children and families in the early learning sector. This approach emphasizes the sharing of knowledge while supporting family-centred and child-centred practices. Interprofessional education facilitates increased collaboration between professionals, ministries, and systems to improve service delivery. This collaboration improves outcomes for children and families, reduces duplication, and helps to coordinate delivery of services.

In the early learning profession, many have recognized the need for inter-professional interactions and have invited the participation of community organizations that assist in supporting children and families. With the dynamics of children and families continuing to change, we are sometimes presented with complex situations that are beyond our resources or expertise. Extending invitations for community members (beyond the early learning profession) to provide other discipline expertise or services is advantageous. The rise of mental health- and trauma-informed care questions and concerns in our community are current examples. Perceived often in the narrow context as demonstrating attention-getting behaviour (e.g., aggression, swearing), school-age children with mental health needs are often overlooked because educators may miss observing the "whole" child and the multitude of influences upon children. Rather, it is helpful to reframe our lens to look at behaviour that is communicated as a result of an unmet need as a more responsive inclusive approach to mental wellness. By enlisting knowledge and expertise from children, their families, and professionals in other disciplines (e.g., physiotherapists, social workers, psychotherapists, public health workers, pediatricians), we are better equipped to support the children and families in our programs. Understanding each of the professional's roles and how they might work together to support a child and family is equally as important. Reaching out to the community for their expertise builds capacity in any organization, which in turn provides better services to families. This collaboration also increases our knowledge of community services, empowering us to become even better at assisting future families in our care.

Early Intervention and Identification: The Family-Centred Approach

Chapter 1 introduced us to the multifaceted family-centred approach and philosophy; it is a concept, a process, and, at its very core, an attitude and a very specific way of being. It is also a personal choice. What do we mean? The choice is one that you have as an educator to either continue your practice in ways that you see fit or to evolve your practice, putting families, children, and community at the heart of everything that you do.

> Family-centred service recognizes that each family is unique; that the family is the constant in the child's life; and that they are the experts on the child's abilities and needs. The family works with service providers to make informed decisions about the services and supports the child and family receives. In family-centred service, the strengths and needs of all family members are considered. (Law et al., 2003a, p. 2)

Ongoing discussions within the team between parents and educators concerning this approach may have or will need to have taken place in numerous aspects of practice, some of which might include the following:

- how to build relationships with each family member as well as support, collaborate with, and communicate with families (for example, determining roles, behaviour);
- how families want to be involved and make decisions, and how their strengths are utilized in the program;
- how resources and new knowledge will be shared and created;

- how current observation and assessment methodologies recognize or value family diversity and input. Discussions can also consider how families and children can be involved in deciding how the documentation is to be used; and
- how transitions for children and families can be supported from one room, program, or service to another.

Families and children have different strengths, needs, desires, and values, resulting in the creation of unique strategies and processes being used to support their success in various aspects of the program. To support your work with families as well as your efforts to reflect upon and improve your own practice, the CanChild Centre for Disability Research at McMaster University developed some very useful reflective checklists for families, service providers, and organizations to use in this regard. One of these checklists is provided in Exhibit 7.7. Each question in the exhibit prompts you to think about your own strengths and needs regarding family-centred services and practices. Each question could easily be transformed into goals for further development, reflection, and improvement.

Sharing personal or sensitive information with parents about their child can be an emotional experience for both the educator and the parents; it can make everyone involved feel very vulnerable. It is never easy for a parent to hear that their child is having difficulties or is struggling in some way. Sharing the information can be just as uneasy for educators as they attempt to anticipate and empathize with how the parent might feel or how they might react to the information about to be shared. Have you ever experienced hearing information that made you feel uncomfortable? What did you do to make yourself feel more comfortable?

Building relationships is fundamental to strong network building in the field of early childhood. When working with families and children with special needs, the consistency, trust, and sustainability of people, agencies, and expectations are very important. Trust is key in establishing relationships, and that is never more important than for a family or child who is vulnerable. Families need to know that when they attend meetings or arrive at the school, they will meet someone familiar. Families thrive on the knowledge that they and their child are cared for personally as well as professionally. A common outcome of trusting relationships is families who demonstrate strong psychological and emotional well-being or health, increased confidence and self-advocacy capability, and the knowledge or resourcefulness needed to locate important supports for their children. What strategies do you use to build trust?

self-advocacy

The process of taking action for oneself to share one's views.

Family-Centred Conversations: Finding the Right Time When in your early childhood setting, take some time to observe the current conversations taking place with families about their children. What are you hearing? Where are these conversations taking place? Is it convenient for the parent, or is the parent in a rush to get out the door? Most conversations with families are currently taking place at pick-up

EXHIBIT 7.7   Family-Centred Service: A Checklist for Service Providers

Do you . . .	For more information, refer to FCS sheet	
. . . know how to work with families in a family-centred way?	#1	What is family-centred service?
. . . talk to your colleagues and the families you work with about what family-centred service means to them?	#2	Myths about family-centred service
. . . understand the research on family-centred service and use this evidence to advocate for the use of family-centred approaches?	#3	How does family-centred service make a difference?
. . . discuss family-centred service with your colleagues and support each other in being family-centred?	#4	Becoming more family-centred
. . . offer families a choice of location and time to meet and schedule appointments that work best for them?	#5	10 things you can do to be family-centred
. . . ask parents about their strengths and resources, including the people they find supportive and their own skills?	#6	Identifying and building on parent and family strengths and resources
. . . ask families if they would like to connect with another family and provide resources to do so?	#7	Parent-to-parent support
. . . listen to what families tell you, believe them, and trust in them?	#8	Effective communication in family-centred service
. . . describe families in the same respectful way, whether or not they are recent?	#9	Using respectful behaviours and language
. . . ask parents how involved they want to be in the planning and delivery of their child's services? Do you respect their decision?	#10	Working together: from providing information to working in partnership
. . . negotiate solutions with families when there is a difference of opinion?	#11	Negotiation: dealing effectively with differences
. . . present and explain all options to the family to allow them to make decisions?	#12	Making decisions together: how to decide what is best
. . . collaborate in goal setting with the child, the family, and others (such as preschool or school personnel)?	#13	Setting goals together
. . . help parents identify and navigate through the "systems" when they are advocating for their child?	#14	Advocacy: how to get the best for your child
. . . develop an action plan that outlines what tasks need to be done, who will do them, and timelines?	#15	Getting the most from appointments and meetings
. . . communicate openly and frequently with parents about things that are happening at school?	#16	Fostering family-centred service in the school
. . . help families prepare for the first formal appointment or assessment by giving them a list of questions to consider?	#17	Family-centred strategies for waiting lists

Source: Law, M., Rosenbaum, P., King, G., King, S., Burke-Gaffney, J., Moning-Szkut, T., Kertoy, M., Pollock, N., Viscardis, L., & Teplicky, R. (2003). *Fact Sheet #18: Are We Really Family-Centred? Checklists for Families, Service Providers, and Organizations.* Hamilton, ON: CanChild Centre for Childhood Disability Research (www.canchild.ca), McMaster University.

or drop-off time right near the entranceway to the room. As parents are coming to sign their children in or out, many educators are seeing this as a prime time to "catch" the parent to share some important information. Considering that inquiry and pedagogical documentation are to be reciprocal and meaningful experiences full of rich dialogue, is "catching" the parent our intention? Not likely.

If we are wanting to engage with families and children in meaningful ways to discuss thinking, inquiries, learning, or even concerns, we need to be thoughtful in our approach. Parent and child voices are just as important as educator voices; we co-learn together when we have co-planned for these team conversations to take place. If we look back to Chapter 3, it is more likely for families and children to partake in meaningful conversations when they understand the ways in which they can contribute, how they too can make visible their learning, and the meaning and details of the cycle of observation (and its processes). When families are involved in all aspects of the cycle of observation, the early intervention and identification process and experience becomes less scary and frustrating. Private information should be discussed in a private location.

Knowing that the early intervention and identification process may involve sensitive information from time to time, it is important to think about how we will communicate the information and where we might have these very personal conversations. As we learned earlier in this chapter, we start first by beginning the observation or early intervention and identification dialogue with families as part of their intake process when they enter a new centre. Parents can then begin to develop a "language of learning" that enables them to see these conversations within the context of observation, pedagogical documentation, and early identification as beneficial to the overall holistic success of their child.

As we continue on our teaching and learning journey with families, there are a number of things we can do to keep our language respectful, positive, culturally appropriate, and meaningful. Let us think back to what we discussed in earlier chapters regarding writing and communicating information on paper for the intended audience. Previously, we discussed the importance of seeing children as children and documenting our observations of their actions, thinking, and behaviours in a respectful way.

Communicating verbally with parents is no different; they deserve the same level of respect and thoughtfulness when we are discussing information about their child and their family. Take care not to label and judge, be open-minded and culturally sensitive, and actively listen to what they are sharing. Other things to keep in mind when conversing with families about early identification and early intervention include the following:

- maintaining an emotionally and culturally safe environment—taking the time to build rapport and trust
- using culturally appropriate communication—ask for feedback from the family on your communication style. Do they feel comfortable with what you are saying?
- assuming ownership for the information you share and respecting the differences in opinion that parents may have when sharing what they see, perceive, and understand
- using "I" messages, taking care to actively listen and pay attention to your verbal and nonverbal cues—do they match?

- always maintaining confidentiality, never sharing information about other children or a child with someone else (without their permission)
- posing thoughtful questions that encourage inquiry and sharing by parents and enabling them to share their values, priorities, and wishes for their child. Let them lead!
- ensuring that the setting is appropriate for a conversation—find somewhere where there is privacy. Bring in some water and snacks if at the end of a day.
- ensuring that timing is agreed upon and that a meeting time has been scheduled for their convenience
- asking parents in advance if there are things they would like to talk about
- ensuring that any observations or documentation has been shared ahead of time so that the parents have time to reflect on it as well
- sharing knowledge and educating one another
- letting parents know that you are appreciative of their time

Can you think of other considerations? Be sure to see the further research and resources on communication available online.

Always remember that parents are our partners in the process of early identification and intervention. Taking care of other members of our team is an integral part of collaboration. Give families the opportunity to be participating partners.

Understanding Special Rights and Needs

In early childhood education in Canada, the term *special needs* is generally understood to refer to a child who has been diagnosed with an exceptionality. Depending on the province or territory, the definition of what constitutes a "special need" varies. How special needs are defined is determined by a number of factors, some of which include treatment eligibility, services, developmental functioning, funding, community infrastructure, the degree of need, and the number of developmental domains affected. Having special needs means that a child could be born with a medical condition such as a visual impairment or a loss of hearing or have sustained a severe injury that has permanently affected the child's growth and development. A special need could also be emotional or behavioural concerns, a history of abuse or neglect, or a risk factor such as fetal alcohol syndrome. The definition of special needs is not exclusive to diagnosed special needs; it also includes children without identified or diagnosed needs. A special need could refer to those whose English is a second language; those who require extra supports, such as equipment, visuals, or orthotics; children with mental health challenges; and those who may benefit from specialized services or careful monitoring. Special needs may also be short term in nature (perhaps a child with a broken leg who needs assistance with mobility) or lifelong (e.g., a child diagnosed with autism). Depending on where you practise, the term may have a very broad definition or a direct focus. If the focus is direct with a narrow definition,

autism

A lifelong neurological and developmental disorder that may affect one's ability to develop relationships, communicate with others, and function intellectually.

often it may be due to ministry funding requirements stating that for eligibility purposes, a child must have a need with a specific diagnosis.

Directing our focus on special rights within the Reggio Emilia philosophy,

> We have also learned that if we pay attention to the differences among children and, in particular, children with special rights, we can see that each child has a different way of being a child. It is important to let the children show us their approach to life. From their approach, we learn how to be with them. The children's approach to life is a kind of research to try to understand the world around them—a very human way to try to know. Our experiences with children with special rights have given quality to our work because we have become better observers. (Edwards, C., Gandini, L., and Forman, G., eds. [2012]. *The Hundred Languages of Children: The Reggio Emilia Experience in Transformation*, 3e. Santa Barbara, California: Praeger)

Special Rights values the differences of everyone.

Teams: Collaborating and Creating

In the field of early childhood, the concept of teams and team building has to be more than words. In working with families and children, particularly children who have special needs, rights, or extra-support needs, teams internal to a school or centre are augmented by those external to it. This collaborative approach is an important part of the efforts made by all on behalf of children and families. Coordination of these efforts is facilitated by team members who know the family, supports and services required, and appropriate professionals in the community. Organization and communication within the teams at a school or centre as well as with and between other disciplines and professional teams is of vital importance to get things right—to reflect the needs and desires of the family. If a child has complex special needs, it is possible to have as few as one or as many as ten or more different professionals or agencies involved. There may be different types of team structures, and each team may present with different challenges (further information on team structures and paraprofessionals is available online). Depending on these factors, specifically the familiarity and collaboration of the professionals with each other and

their organizations, successful progress can be made to assist the child and the family. Educators will be expected to work with a number of paraprofessionals; be sure to visit NelsonStudy to explore who they might be.

What does it mean to work within an effective team? It means building a team vision or mission and determining people's philosophies, developing relationships and shared understandings of meanings, and understanding the purpose of gathering or meeting together. When provided with the opportunity to engage in the process as collaborative partners, parents are further empowered as the primary decision makers for their children and are seen as key partners in the early intervention process and during the process of individualized instruction. Parents and families who have a stronger role in early learning teams build advocacy skills that can be transferred to future advocacy scenarios requiring their leadership and support of their children. These advocacy skills can also be applied to efforts to attain higher-quality care and services for all children and families. Team building within a school or early childhood setting should represent a conscientious approach to include all the involved members, to provide opportunities for appreciative inquiry, and to investigate and learn together. Including parents and families adds to a community voice, motivates participation, and promotes collaboration.

Logue (2006) wrote of the action research carried out by a team of educators working together as researchers to investigate multi-age groupings. The educators demonstrated their understanding of the importance of observation in research. They raised questions concerning the hypothesis that age-segregated groups may be negatively contributing to social issues. The key point of this article was not only their action research but also their work as a team. This teamwork is a good example of what happens when early childhood professionals, schools, agencies, or child-care organizations empower themselves and make use of each member's skills and knowledge, thus increasing the potential of any one of the team members alone. When working as a team, the workload is shared, ideas are exchanged concerning what is possible, or a new space is created, thus building capacity within the team and community.

action research

A collaborative and reflective inquiry process assumed by a community or team of individuals who actively research, plan, and implement solutions to solve real problems and/or improve practice.

Who comprises your team in your environment? What paraprofessionals are considered part of your team and what are their roles?

REFLECTIVE EXERCISE 7.3

EARLY IDENTIFICATION AND INTERVENTION: ASSESSMENT

Assessment is a word used to describe appraisal, judgment, review, measurement, and evaluation. The word has been used interchangeably with observation as a catchword for all types of assessment, such as authentic, screening, functional, and diagnostic assessment; as another word for monitoring; and as an appraisal strategy employed by any educator who may be grading or evaluating work of some kind according to a particular curriculum outcome or standard. According to the Ontario Ministry of Education, it is important that assessment, evaluation, and reporting

- are fair, transparent, and equitable for all students;
- support all students, including those with special education needs, those who are learning the language of instruction (English or French), and those who are First Nation, Métis, or Inuit;
- are carefully planned to relate to the curriculum expectations and learning goals and, as much as possible, to the interests, learning styles and preferences, needs, and experiences of all students;
- are communicated clearly to students and parents at the beginning of the school year or course and at other appropriate points throughout the school year or course;

- are ongoing, varied in nature, and administered over a period of time to provide multiple opportunities for students to demonstrate the full range of their learning;
- provide ongoing descriptive feedback that is clear, specific, meaningful, and timely to support improved learning and achievement;
- develop students' self-assessment skills to enable them to assess their own learning, set specific goals, and plan next steps for their learning. (Ontario Ministry of Education. [2010]. "The Seven Fundamental Principles," *Growing Success: Assessment, Evaluation, and Reporting in Ontario Schools*, p. 6. Queen's Printer for Ontario. Used with permission.)

Ultimately, the intent of observation as part of the assessment for learning process is to uncover the realm of children's everyday experiences, learning, and development through authentic means such as pedagogical documentation. Observation asks the questions, "What will I discover today? What will it mean?" Evaluation on the other hand asks questions such as, "What did I/the children learn?" and "Was it meaningful? How does what I have learned inform my practice? How does evaluation support learning?" Each have particular relevance to the cycle of observation.

Interestingly, the terms evaluation and assessment are used interchangeably depending on which province, region, or country is using them. Expanding upon evaluation, formative evaluation refers to an evaluation that is ongoing. This type of evaluation is informal, is used at any point starting soon after a child is admitted into the program, and includes reference to families, educators, and other professionals; the collaborative efforts of the team to compile information for individualized instruction; and implementation. Different from formative evaluation, summative evaluation is perceived as being a more formal type of evaluation. A summative evaluation takes place at the end of a timeline, when the process has come full circle. Throughout this process, monitoring occurs. "Monitoring early learning through documentation is based on the gathering of layers of information to provide rich and rigorous evidence about children's early learning and development. It is not the measurement of discrete skills, out of context with the children's daily lived lives. Young children show their understanding by doing, showing, representing and telling" (Pascal, n.d., p. 23). Within the cycle of observation, monitoring could refer to the tracking of a child's contributions to a documentation panel, the questions we might ask when engaged with a child during play, when we are co-documenting with a child or family, a child's progress during the implementation of an IEP, the daily monitoring of a child's emotional health, or monitoring the transition of a family from one agency to another.

Traditionally, assessment and evaluation can provide the knowledge and insight needed to lead toward the development of goals, objectives, interventions, supports, and a number of other outcomes for children based on their interests, thinking, and abilities. In this section of the chapter, we will approach assessment in a multitude of ways, exploring traditional methods of assessment still used in practice today as well the discourse that exists in balancing assessment and pedagogical documentation alongside pedagogical frameworks, inclusive of ministry, licensing, and curriculum expectations within early childhood settings.

Exhibit 7.8 begins our inquiry as it provokes significant reflection in the presentation of three theoretical perspectives with which to view assessment.

formative evaluation

Evaluation that can be done at any point for reasons identified by any members of the team. Through discussion and reflection, the team can make changes as the process evolves.

monitoring

Periodic assessment of a person or event to inform the state of compliance with an expectation, objective, or outcome.

According to MacAlpine (2017, pp. 35–36),

> From a constructivist perspective, assessment is often times associated with meeting predetermined objectives, with teacher practices "focus[ed] on judging individual achievement in relation to pre-set goals and outcomes" (Lenz Taguchi, 2010, p. 9). The purpose of assessment places proof of, or product of, learning at the forefront (Dahlberg & Moss, 2005, p. 95).

This is more of a standardized and normative approach to learning whereby the child is more passive in the process.

> The social constructivist perspective, on the other hand, looks at the learning process and infers that "rather than 'proof of learning', the focus shifts to the process of learning and the use of documentation, or, more aptly, pedagogical documentation, to reflect on and inform an educator's pedagogical practice." (Pence & Pacini-Ketchabaw, 2008; Wien, 2013; Wien, Guyevsky, & Berdoussis, 2011).

> Lastly, MacAlpine states that assessment is perceived by the post-humanist perspective as something that

> > blurs knowing and being, there is a call for a complete shift in thinking, from "judging individual achievement in relation to pre-set goals and outcomes" to "engage[ing] in collaborative knowledge-production with children that challenge their and our own possibilities and potentialities beyond what we already think we know" (Lenz Taguchi, 2010, p. 9).

Source: MacAlpine, K. (2017). "Through The Looking Glass: Interpreting Growing Success, the Kindergarten Addendum, Ontario's Assessment, Evaluation, and Reporting Policy Document." *Journal of Childhood Studies, 42*(2), pp. 34–41.

REFLECTIVE EXERCISE 7.4

Take a moment to reflect upon how your setting views assessment. Does your setting and team align with one of the theories in Exhibit 7.8, perhaps a combination of the theories, or perhaps another theory not depicted in that exhibit? How does your particular view of assessment inform and guide your practices in your setting?

In this text, we have come to be familiar with a number of authentic assessment methodologies within Chapters 4 and 5 that align with pedagogical principles and that fall within the socio-cultural approach. Authentic assessment falls into the non-standardized versions of assessment because it is culturally sensitive and respectful of the rights of children as it envelopes their voices and perspectives.

Navarrette believes that

> if children are to be regarded as capable participants in the learning process, they must be listened to and invited to participate in democratic dialogue and decision-making (Dahlberg et al., 2007), as well as given the opportunity to become self-assessors of their own learning (Fleer & Richardson, 2004). According to Dunphy (2008), regarding children as agents is considered of vital importance in developing their identity and self-esteem, taking into account their active role in the process of assessment. The involvement

non-standardized

An informal method not based on validity or reliability measures. This type of assessment is intended to capture the thinking and learning of the person being observed in an authentic way.

of children in the assessment of their own learning and encouraging a reflective attitude presents opportunities not only for the children, but for educators as well. (Navarrete, A. [2015]. *Assessment in the Early Years: The Perspectives and Practices of Early Childhood Educators*. Master's Dissertation, Dublin Institute of Technology, 2015)

Let's apply this learning of authentic assessment toward two philosophical approaches to assessment: one from the Ontario Ministry of Education's *Kindergarten Program* (2016; premised on the 2007 *Early Learning for Every Child Today, The Ontario Early Years Policy Framework* [2013] and *How Does Learning Happen? Ontario's Pedagogy for the Early Years* [2014]) and the other from New Zealand's *Te Whāriki: He Whāriki Mātauranga MōNgā Mokopuna O Aotearoa Early Childhood Curriculum* approach. We begin with the *Kindergarten Program*. This program, using a play-based and child-centred approach to learning, is premised on four frames as in Exhibit 7.9.

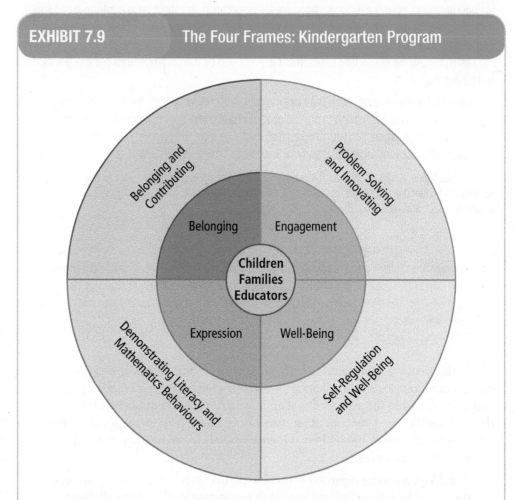

EXHIBIT 7.9 The Four Frames: Kindergarten Program

Each quadrant of this figure represents the foundations necessary within an early learning environment for children to thrive, grow, and learn.

Source: Ontario Ministry of Education. (2016). "The Four Frames of Kindergarten." *The Kindergarten Program*, p. 14. Queen's Printer for Ontario. Used with permission.

We would be remiss if we didn't indicate that the four frames in Exhibit 7.9 are rooted in inquiry and pedagogical documentation. The approach to authentic assessment in the Kindergarten Program document illustrates very clearly how inquiry makes visible the thinking of children as in Exhibit 7.10.

EXHIBIT 7.10	The Inquiry Process in the Kindergarten Classroom	
Elements of the child's inquiry process	**When children are engaged in the inquiry process, they:**	**When educators are modelling or supporting the inquiry process, they:**
Initial engagement noticing, wondering, playing	• raise questions about objects and events around them	• observe and listen
Exploration exploring, observing, questioning	• explore objects and events around them and observe the results of their explorations • make observations using all of their senses, and generate questions	• act as co-learners with the children, posing thoughtful, open-ended questions. • encourage children to observe and talk among themselves and to the educators
Investigation planning, using observations, reflecting	• gather, compare, sort, classify, order, interpret, describe observable characteristics and properties, notice patterns, and draw conclusions, using a variety of simple tools and materials	• provide a rich variety of materials and resources, and strategically question and observe children to discover, clarify, and expand on the children's thinking • model how to plan, observe, and reflect
Communication sharing findings, discussing ideas	• work individually and with others, share and discuss ideas, and listen to ideas	• listen to the children to help them make connections between their prior knowledge and new discoveries

Source: Ontario Ministry of Education. (2016). "The Inquiry Process in the Kindergarten Classroom." *The Kindergarten Program*, p. 23. Queen's Printer for Ontario. Used with permission.

Turning our attention now to New Zealand, their philosophy is situated in the exemplar of "empowerment, holistic development, family and community, and relationships" (Te Whāriki, 2017). The Te Whāriki principles and method reflect a socio-cultural approach to learning as in Exhibit 7.11.

Exhibits 7.10 and 7.11 present socio-cultural approaches to authentic assessment which support children in holistic ways based upon their foundational frameworks. Each framework uses pedagogical documentation such as learning stories and other methodologies to make visible children's thinking and learning rather than standardized approaches. This is not to say that standardized

EXHIBIT 7.11   Te Whāriki

▲▲▲

MINISTRY OF EDUCATION
TE TĀHUHU O TE MĀTAURANGA

TE WHĀ...

PRINCIPLES |

EMPOWERMENT	WHAKAMANA	HOLISTIC DEVELOPMENT	KOTAHITANGA
Early childhood curriculum empowers the child to learn and grow.	Early childhood curriculum reflects the holistic way childr... learn and grow.
Mā te whāriki e whakatō te kaha ki roto i te mokopuna, ki te ako, kia pakari ai tana tipu.	Mā te whāriki e whakaata te kotahitanga o ngā whakahaere... mō te ako a te mokopuna, mō te tipu o te mokopuna.

STRANDS, GOALS AND LEARNIN...

WELLBEING	MANA ATUA		BELONGING	MANA WHENUA		CONTR...
The health and wellbeing of the child are protected and nurtured.		Children and their families feel a sense of belonging.		Opportun... and each...
Ko tēnei te whakatipuranga o te tamaiti i roto i tōna oranga nui, i runga hoki i tōna mana motuhake, mana atuatanga.		Ko te whakatipuranga tēnei o te mana ki te whenua, te mana tūrangawaewae, me te mana toi whenua o te tangata.		Ko te whakatipe... i te mokopu... ki t...
GOALS Children experience an environment where:	**LEARNING OUTCOMES** Over time and with guidance and encouragement, children become increasingly capable of:	**GOALS** Children and their families experience an environment where:	**LEARNING OUTCOMES** Over time and with guidance and encouragement, children become increasingly capable of:	**GOALS** Children experience an environment where:
Their health is promoted	Keeping themselves healthy and caring for themselves	te oranga nui	Connecting links with the family and the wider world are affirmed and extended	Making connections between people, places and things in their world	te waihanga hononga	There are equitable opportunities for learning, irrespective of gender, ability, age... ethnicity or backgrou...
Their emotional wellbeing is nurtured	Managing themselves and expressing their feelings and needs	te whakahua whakaaro	They know that they have a place	Taking part in caring for this place	te manaaki i te taiao	They are affirmed as individuals
They are kept safe from harm	Keeping themselves and others safe from harm	te noho haumaru	They feel comfortable with the routines, customs and regular events	Understanding how things work here and adapting to change	te mārama ki te āhua o ngā whakahaere me te mōhio ki te panoni	They are encouraged... learn with and alongs... others
		They know the limits and boundaries of acceptable behaviour	Showing respect for kaupapa, rules and the rights of others	te mahi whakaute	

PATHWAYS

EXAMPLES OF LINKS TO THE THE NEW ZEALAND CURRICULUM	EXAMPLES OF LINKS TO THE TE MARAUTANGA O AOTEAROA	EXAMPLES OF LINKS TO THE THE NEW ZEALAND CURRICULUM	EXAMPLES OF LINKS TO THE TE MARAUTANGA O AOTEAROA	EXAMPLES OF LINKS TO... THE NEW ZEALAND CUR...
Key competency: Managing self For example, students have a 'can do' attitude and see themselves as capable learners. They are enterprising, reliable and resilient, set personal goals and have strategies for meeting challenges. Learning area: Health and physical education Students learn about their own wellbeing, and that of others and society, in health-related movement contexts.	Values Individual learners develop values and attitudes that help them to identify and understand their own personal values and beliefs. Learning area: Hauora (waiora strand) Students will explore and learn about food and nutrition that sustain the physical body, and explore the notion of sustenance that contributes to the wellbeing of mind and spirit.	Key competency: Participating and contributing For example, students are actively involved in communities, including those based on a common interest or culture for purposes such as learning, work, celebration or recreation. Learning area: The arts Students explore, refine and communicate ideas as they connect thinking, imagination, senses and feelings to create works and respond to the works of others.	Values The learner understands the values of their whānau, hapū and iwi, enabling access to the Māori world. They also know their identity and origins. Learning area: Ngā toi Students investigate, use, develop knowledge of and explain how physical movement and the voice are used and applied in a wide range of dramatic contexts.	Key competency: Relating ... For example, students inter... with a diverse range of peo... of contexts. They learn to l... recognise different points e... negotiate and share ideas. Learning area: Social scien... Students explore how socie... and how they can participa... take action as critical, infor... responsible citizens.

THE WEAVING | Local curriculum design involves a complex weaving of principles and strands (Te Whāriki), values, key compe...

1. 'Oral language' encompasses any method of communication the child uses as a first language; this includes New Zealand Sign Language and, for children who are non-verbal, alternative and augmentative communication (AAC).
2. For children who are deaf or hard of hearing, 'hearing' includes watching.

Te Whāriki is a comprehensive socio-cultural curriculum reflective of its community and culture. Listening to and demonstrating respect for the voices, feelings, cultural roots, and capabilities of children are just some of the many held values within this curriculum. Reciprocity in relationship... with children as well as active engagement of children's knowledge, theories, and competencies

HE WHĀRIKI MĀTAURANGA
MŌ NGĀ MOKOPUNA O AOTEAROA
EARLY CHILDHOOD CURRICULUM

WHAKAHAERE

FAMILY AND COMMUNITY	WHĀNAU TANGATA	RELATIONSHIPS	NGĀ HONONGA
wider world of family and community is an integral part of early childhood curriculum.	Children learn through responsive and reciprocal relationships with people, places and things.
Me whiri mai te whānau, te hapū, te iwi, me tauiwi, me ō rātou wāhi nohonga, ki roto i te whāriki, hei āwhina, tautoko i te akoranga, i te whakatipuranga o te mokopuna.	*Mā roto i ngā piringa, i ngā whakahaere i waenganui o te mokopuna me te katoa, e whakatō te kaha ki roto i te mokopuna ki te ako.*

S | TAUMATA WHAKAHIRAHIRA

ANGATA	COMMUNICATION	MANA REO		EXPLORATION	MANA AOTŪROA	
equitable, is valued.	The languages and symbols of children's own and other cultures are promoted and protected.		The child learns through active exploration of the environment.	
au tangata i roto te manaaki, e ao.	*Ko te whakatipuranga tēnei o te reo. Mā roto i tēnei ka tipu te mana tangata me te oranga nui.*		*Ko te whakatipuranga tēnei o te mana rangahau, me ngā mātauranga katoa e pā ana ki te aotūroa me te taiao.*	

COMES	GOALS	LEARNING OUTCOMES	GOALS	LEARNING OUTCOMES
ance and encouragement, singly capable of:	Children experience an environment where:	Over time and with guidance and encouragement, children become increasingly capable of:	Children experience an environment where:	Over time and with guidance and encouragement, children become increasingly capable of:
y and including them makuru	They develop non-verbal communication skills for a range of purposes	Using gesture and movement to express themselves | he kōrero ā-tinana	Their play is valued as meaningful learning and the importance of spontaneous play is recognised	Playing, imagining, inventing and experimenting | te whakaaro me te tūhurahura i te pūtaiao
ppreciating their own rangatiratanga	They develop verbal communication skills for a range of purposes	Understanding oral language[1] and using it for a range of purposes | he kōrero ā-waha	They gain confidence in and control of their bodies	Moving confidently and challenging themselves physically | te wero ā-tinana
ategies and skills to others	They experience the stories and symbols of their own and other cultures	Enjoying hearing[2] stories and retelling and creating them | he kōrero paki	They learn strategies for active exploration, thinking and reasoning	Using a range of strategies for reasoning and problem solving | te hīraurau hopanga
		Recognising print symbols and concepts and using them with enjoyment, meaning and purpose | he kōrero tuhituhi	They develop working theories for making sense of the natural, social, physical and material worlds	Making sense of their worlds by generating and refining working theories | te rangahau me te mātauranga
		Recognising mathematical symbols and concepts and using them with enjoyment, meaning and purpose | he kōrero pāngarau		
	They discover different ways to be creative and expressive	Expressing their feelings and ideas using a wide range of materials and modes | he kōrero auaha		

AND KURA

OF LINKS TO THE ...ANGA O AOTEAROA	EXAMPLES OF LINKS TO THE *THE NEW ZEALAND CURRICULUM*	EXAMPLES OF LINKS TO THE *TE MARAUTANGA O AOTEAROA*	EXAMPLES OF LINKS TO THE *THE NEW ZEALAND CURRICULUM*	EXAMPLES OF LINKS TO THE *TE MARAUTANGA O AOTEAROA*
...rners develop values and ...mpathy and regard for ...ir the school whānau. ...orks cooperatively with ...groups. ...a: Tikanga ā-iwi ...elop their knowledge and ...g of peoples' interactions ...d environments and how ...n the environment.	Key competency: Using language, symbols and texts For example, students work with and make meaning of the codes in which knowledge is expressed. They learn that languages and symbols are systems for representing and communicating information, experiences and ideas. Learning area: Mathematics and statistics Students explore relationships in quantities, space and data and learn to express these relationships in ways that help them to make sense of the world around them.	Values Individual learners develop values and attitudes which lead to a desire to participate in all school learning activities, whether by contributing ideas, reading or listening. Learning area: Pāngarau Students explore the use of the patterns and relationships seen in aspects of quantity, sets of data, and space and time.	Key competency: Thinking Students use creative, critical and metacognitive processes to make sense of information, experiences and ideas. Intellectual curiosity is at the heart of this competency. Learning area: Science Students explore how both the natural and physical world and science itself work so that they can participate as critical, informed and responsible citizens in a society in which science plays a significant role.	Values Individual learners develop values and attitudes of understanding, awareness and aptitude in all learning as a guide into the contemporary world. The learner understands the values of their whānau, hapū and iwi, enabling access to the Māori world. Learning area: Pūtaiao The student will gain competence in the skills of research, experimentation, investigation and problem solving. The student will develop scientific literacy as well as physical, ethical and cognitive competence.

...eas (*The New Zealand Curriculum* and *Te Marautanga o Aotearoa*) as children and young people engage in learning experiences.

ISBN 978-0-478-16975-1

...re also evident.

For a more comprehensive comparison of this curriculum to the Full Day Kindergarten document, ...ease visit https://tewhariki.tki.org.nz/en/early-childhood-curriculum-document/.

approaches are wrong but, rather, they present a perspective that there are other ways to appreciate and understand how children learn, think, and grow. Let's explore standardized assessment to further build upon our knowledge in this area.

Standardized Assessments: Terms, Tools, and Perspectives

We introduced earlier in this chapter the three general stages of assessment: screening, functional, and diagnostic. Screening and functional assessments are discussed later in this chapter as several types of these assessments are used in early childhood settings throughout Canada, while diagnostic assessment tools are beyond the scope of this text.

Before proceeding further, it is necessary to establish a basic acquaintance with the complex world of standardized assessment. What are some of the terms or jargon associated with the topic of assessment tools? First, the kinds of assessments conducted in early childhood settings tend to be those that are criterion referenced. What does that mean? Criterion-referenced assessment tools are those assessment tools that measure a child's progress against a fixed standard rather than comparing them with the skills or knowledge of others. A fixed standard is an item or competency that is typical for children of that age group to perform, such as tying shoelaces, running without falling, or following a two-step, related direction. If a child can accomplish these skills independently, that competency or fixed standard is checked off as being achieved. If the child is unable to achieve that task, then a different kind of scoring is noted to indicate that the child has yet to accomplish that competency. The educator or resource professional, in collaboration with the parent, records the observations in the assessment tool: "Yes, the child has achieved that skill" or "Sometimes the child demonstrates this skill" or "No, the child has yet to achieve that skill." If the person using the screening tool like the ASQ-3™ (*Ages & Stages Questionnaires®*; see Exhibit 7.12) or the *Looksee Checklist* by ndds® (formerly known as the *Nipissing District Developmental Screen* [NDDS]; see Exhibit 7.13) records many "no" responses in an area, then it may require further conversation with the family and team to determine whether a skill has simply not been attained, a skill is not reflective of the child's culture or community (and subsequently would not have been practiced or developed), or further probing of the child's abilities may be necessary with further assessment (e.g., diagnostic assessment from a qualified doctor or professional).

criterion-referenced assessment tools

Fixed standards used to evaluate an individual's performance; points of reference used when an individual is assessed against himself or herself rather than compared to the performance of others.

fixed standard

A rule, principle, or measure established by an authority that is accepted without deviation.

REFLECTIVE EXERCISE 7.4

Using the ASQ-3™ and/or the Looksee checklists in Exhibits 7.12 and 7.13, explore some videos in NelsonStudy or online of 6-month-old and 12-month-old children to gauge your understanding of the screening process. Have a peer complete the same exercise and compare your observations. What was the same or different in your scores? Or, dialogue with a colleague in your field practicum or other setting in which you work to discuss their experiences with screening tools. What was their experience like completing them with families?

As can be seen by Exhibit 7.12 and Exhibit 7.13, every assessment tool has its own terminology; each one contains terms that are specific to that particular assessment. For example, one assessment tool may refer to areas of child development as domains or sectors. Each assessment tool contains different terms to describe

EXHIBIT 7.12   Ages & Stages Questionnaires®: 6 Month and 12 Month Examples

ASQ·3   **6** Month Questionnaire   5 months 0 days through 6 months 30 days

On the following pages are questions about activities babies may do. Your baby may have already done some of the activities described here, and there may be some your baby has not begun doing yet. For each item, please fill in the circle that indicates whether your baby is doing the activity regularly, sometimes, or not yet.

Important Points to Remember: **Notes:**

☑ Try each activity with your baby before marking a response.   _____

☑ Make completing this questionnaire a game that is fun for you and your baby.   _____

☑ Make sure your baby is rested and fed.   _____

☑ Please return this questionnaire by _____.   _____

GROSS MOTOR

		YES	SOMETIMES	NOT YET	
1.	While your baby is on his back, does your baby lift his legs high enough to see his feet?	○	○	○	___
2.	When your baby is on her tummy, does she straighten both arms and push her whole chest off the bed or floor?	○	○	○	___
3.	Does your baby roll from his back to his tummy, getting both arms out from under him?	○	○	○	___
4.	When you put your baby on the floor, does she lean on her hands while sitting? (If she already sits up straight without leaning on her hands, mark "yes" for this item.)	○	○	○	___

page 2 of 6

E101060200

ASQ·3   **12** Month Questionnaire   11 months 0 days through 12 months 30 days

On the following pages are questions about activities babies may do. Your baby may have already done some of the activities described here, and there may be some your baby has not begun doing yet. For each item, please fill in the circle that indicates whether your baby is doing the activity regularly, sometimes, or not yet.

Important Points to Remember: **Notes:**

☑ Try each activity with your baby before marking a response.   _____

☑ Make completing this questionnaire a game that is fun for you and your baby.   _____

☑ Make sure your baby is rested and fed.   _____

☑ Please return this questionnaire by _____.   _____

COMMUNICATION

		YES	SOMETIMES	NOT YET	
1.	Does your baby make two similar sounds, such as "ba-ba," "da-da," or "ga-ga"? (The sounds do not need to mean anything.)	○	○	○	___
2.	If you ask your baby to, does he play at least one nursery game even if you don't show him the activity yourself (such as "bye-bye," "Peeka-boo," "clap your hands," "So Big")?	○	○	○	___
3.	Does your baby follow one simple command, such as "Come here," "Give it to me," or "Put it back," without your using gestures?	○	○	○	___
4.	Does your baby say three words, such as "Mama," "Dada," and "Baba"? (A "word" is a sound or sounds your baby says consistently to mean someone or something.)	○	○	○	___
5.	When you ask, "Where is the ball (hat, shoe, etc.)?" does your baby look at the object? (Make sure the object is present. Mark "yes" if she knows one object.)	○	○	○	___
6.	When your baby wants something, does he tell you by pointing to it?	○	○	○	___

COMMUNICATION TOTAL ___

By eighteen months of age, does your child:

Y N

O O 1 Identify pictures in a book? *"show me the baby"*

O O 2 Use a variety of familiar gestures?
waving, pushing, giving, reaching up

O O 3 Follow directions using "on" and "under"?
"put the cup on the table"

O O 4 Make at least four different consonant sounds? *b, n, d, h, g, w*

O O 5 Point to at least three different body parts when asked?
"where is your nose?"

O O 6 Say 20 or more words? *words do not have to be clear*

O O 7 Hold a cup to drink?*

O O 8 Pick up and eat finger food?

O O 9 Help with dressing by putting out arms and legs?*

O O 10 Walk up a few stairs holding your hand?

O O 11 Walk alone?

O O 12 Squat to pick up a toy and stand back up without falling?

O O 13 Push and pull toys or other objects while walking forward?

O O 14 Stack three or more blocks?

O O 15 Show affection towards people, pets, or toys?

O O 16 Point to show you something?

O O 17 Look at you when you are talking or playing together?

* Examples are only suggestions.
Use similar examples from your family experience.
** Item may not be common to all cultures

Child's Name: _____

Birthdate: _____

Today's Date: _____

Try these tips to help your child grow:

I feel safe and secure when I know what is expected of me. You can help me with this by following routines and setting limits. Praise my good behaviour.

I like toys that I can pull apart and put back together—large building blocks, containers with lids, or plastic links. Talk to me about what I am doing using words like "push" and "pull".

I'm not too little to play with large crayons. Let's scribble and talk about our art work.

Don't be afraid to let me see what I can do with my body. I need to practise climbing, swinging, jumping, running, going up and down stairs, and going down slides. Stay close to me so I don't get hurt.

Play some of my favourite music. Encourage me to move to the music by swaying my arms, moving slowly, marching to the music, hopping, clapping my hands, tapping my legs. Let's have fun doing actions while listening to the music.

Let me play with balls of different sizes. Take some of the air out of a beach ball. Watch me kick, throw, and try to catch it.

I want to do things just like you. Let me have toys so I can pretend to have tea parties, dress up, and play mommy or daddy.

I like new toys, so find the local toy lending library or play groups in our community.

I am learning new words every day. Put pictures of people or objects in a bag and say "1, 2, 3, what do we see?" and pull a picture from the bag.

Pretend to talk to me on the phone or encourage me to call someone.

I like simple puzzles with two to four pieces and shape-sorters with simple shapes. Encourage me to match the pieces by taking turns with me.

Help me to notice familiar sounds such as birds chirping, car or truck motors, airplanes, dogs barking, sirens, or splashing water. Imitate the noise you hear and see if I will imitate you. Encourage me by smiling and clapping.

I enjoy exploring the world, but I need to know that you are close by. I may cry when you leave me with others, so give me a hug and tell me you will be back.

I may get ear infections. Talk to my doctor about signs and symptoms.

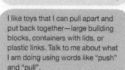

the areas of child development; these areas are represented in very distinct ways with terms such as belonging, receptive language, fine motor adaptive, and auditory attention. Terms used for scoring items within assessment tools also vary.

It is important to understand that strategies and skills used for assessments do not always provide the context necessary to understand a child's culture, values, family beliefs, or accessibility to materials and things. For some populations, the children may not even have a word in their language for the picture they are asked to identify. This could be a particularly anxiety-provoking moment from the perspective of a child who is being asked to do or say something but isn't able to, possibly because their culture does not place importance or value on what is being asked. Then, educators need to reflect upon the appropriateness of the methodologies they are using to ensure they are reflective and respectful of the persons they are being used with. Educators also

According to Ball and Janyst (2009, pp. 1–2),

> Many Aboriginal parents and early childhood practitioners believe that formal tools and approaches to support non-Aboriginal children and families are not either culturally appropriate or the most helpful for Aboriginal children (Royal Commission on Aboriginal Peoples, 1996). Many find the very concept of "testing" and scoring or comparing the developmental levels of children, as is often done in developmental assessment, offensive (Stairs & Bernhard, 2002). Some see assessment as conflicting with cultural values that affirm the "gifts" of each child, with accepting children's differences, or with the wisdom of waiting until children are older before making categorical attributions about them (Greenwood, n.d.).
>
> Aboriginal leaders and agencies across Canada have argued that culturally inappropriate assessment and intervention practices, as well as lack of services, frequently result in serious negative consequences for Aboriginal children (Assembly of First Nations, 1988; B.C. Aboriginal Network for Disabilities Society, 1996; Canadian Centre for Justice, 2001). Negative consequences of inappropriate assessment and intervention practices include

- over- and under-recognition of children with developmental challenges,
- interpretations focusing on challenges in the child rather than in the environment,
- services directed at a misinterpretation of the primary problem,
- services introduced too late,
- undermining Indigenous language and cultural goals for development through an over-valuing of the dominant culture (European heritage) and language (English),
- cultural alienation, and
- high rates of placement in non-Aboriginal foster care.

Source: Ball, J., & Janyst, P. (2007). *Screening and Assessment of Indigenous Children: Community–University Partnered Research Findings.* Early Childhood Development Intercultural Partnerships.

need to look at how to integrate pedagogical documentation and assessment so that the co-constructive nature of children's play, thinking, and learning becomes evident. To premise and provoke reflection on this subject matter, let's take a look at the perspective of Indigenous peoples toward assessment and early intervention.

Cultural safety, preservation of identity, and the 94 Calls to Action from the Truth and Reconciliation Commission of Canada come to mind when reflecting upon the impactful perspectives shared in Exhibit 7.14. According to Williams (1999), cultural safety can be defined as "an environment that is spiritually, socially and emotionally safe, as well as physically safe for people; where there is no assault challenge or denial of their identity, of who they are and what they need" (p. 213). Understanding what others bring to the environment, demonstrating respect for their knowledge, ways of being, spirituality and one's community is a necessary part of relationship building, leading to the building of trust within the observation and early intervention team. We hold an important lifelong responsibility in learning how to address and incorporate cultural safety within our observation, pedagogical documentation, assessment,

cultural safety

An environment in which people feel spiritually, socially, emotionally, and physically safe, and are able to express their identity

and early intervention practices as part of our commitment to the Truth and Reconciliation Commission Canada: Calls to Action.

REFLECTIVE EXERCISE 7.5

Reflecting upon Exhibit 7.14, how might we go about supporting, embracing, and respecting important views like these? How do we go about learning about these feelings and vulnerabilities? And, lastly, considering our learning about observation, pedagogical documentation, assessment, and early intervention thus far, how do we determine the best approaches for our community of learners? Spend some time within your own community to talk about these issues as dialogue is definitely the first step!

As can be seen through the elaborate discussions and exhibits thus far about assessment and early intervention, there is significant interplay and debate between authentic/non-standardized (inclusive of pedagogical documentation) and non-authentic/standardized (such as screening, functional, and diagnostic tools) methods by observers within the early childhood profession.

Even after all we know about children has been studied and researched and become public domain, tests, assessments, and evaluations are still being used to the disadvantage of some children. "Via survey research, psychologists reported that 42.96% of the more than 7000 children they assessed would be considered 'untestable' if they had to solely rely on traditional assessment instruments to determine eligibility. This is particularly concerning because more than 90% of the children considered 'untestable' were determined eligible once authentic and curriculum-based methods were applied" (Keilty et al., 2009, p. 245). This illustrates that not every child fits every assessment tool, or vice versa, and not every tool will be appropriate for children and families with whom you work. The implications of this statement and of these types of normative Eurocentric assessments are that we need to think carefully about a number of things relating to the assessment process, some of which include the strengths and weaknesses of the assessment tools we choose to evaluate young children, how we plan to use them, and whether using more than one tool might capture a child in a more holistic way. Equally as important to reflect upon are how one's cultural beliefs, community, personal values, accessibility, and exposure to experiences influence a professional's beliefs about assessment.

Assessment is a term that, when used loosely or understood poorly, contributes to misinformation and misunderstanding. When faced with, for example, "Melissa's assessment" or "We've assessed your child," ask for clarification. Some valid questions might be, "Can you tell me more about what assessment tool was used? Under what conditions did the assessment take place? Who made the decision to assess? How was that decision made and why? Were the parents involved in the assessment process? Did they understand what permissions meant and why the assessments were planned? Was the child able to demonstrate knowledge and skills in different ways and other skills more appropriate to their family and culture? Did the child understand what they were participating in?" As observers, we hold a very big responsibility in this area of practice!

Screening Tools

The primary purpose of a screening tool like those identified in Exhibits 7.13 & 7.14 is to supplement other observations and pedagogical documentation, and guide the team (educators, family, child) in discussing a child's abilities, areas for growth, or knowledge and skills requiring more attention. Stemming from this dialogue may be new curriculum approaches that would stimulate and extend the child's thinking and abilities, or possibly a referral for further assessment. It is important to note that screening tools are often not designed for children to be co-documenters or co-assessors in the process; it is up to the educator and the parent to ensure that each child's voice and perspectives are captured holistically and thoroughly. Rethinking our paradigms of practice regarding how we might implement these tools is necessary.

Another reason for using a screening tool is to target what services, supports, or people are required to meet the needs of the referred children. For example, if a particular area has a prevalence and incidence of fetal alcohol spectrum disorder in babies, then health services would be most in demand. Depending on geography, accessibility could be a problematic issue within a large urban or small rural city. Problematic issues could include not enough diagnostic services or support personnel to meet the demands of the population; an inadequate tax base to support the hiring of professionals, doctors, or supports needed for a population; or a rapidly growing community without the funding and recognition as an area requiring services or supports.

Screening tools are used in familiar settings and are typically completed informally through observation during daily experiences. Generally speaking, learning experiences are not set up or contrived to achieve a specific skill but, rather, are observed during the regular course of the day. The screening tool chosen should be appropriate for use with the child, the family, and those administering the screen.

A screening tool does not diagnose, nor does it provide a clear overview of all the necessary skills in all developmental areas. The results from screening tools should not be the sole source used for planning an individualized program for a child with special needs.

prevalence

The quality or condition of being prevalent; superior strength, force, or influence, such as the prevalence of a virtue, a fashion, or a disease.

incidence

The frequency, rate, or number of times something happens or occurs.

Commonly Used Screening Tools in Canada   Two commonly used Canadian screening tools are the *Ages & Stages Questionnaires*® (ASQ-3™) from the United States and the *Looksee Checklist* by ndds, which was compiled in North Bay, Ontario (see Exhibits 7.13 and 7.14 as well as NelsonStudy/online for more information on both). The *Looksee Checklist* is an example of a criterion-referenced tool where groupings of age-related behaviours can be checked by the parent and educator. The *Ages & Stages Questionnaires*® come in the form of two different screening measures, one of which targets the socio-emotional behaviours of young children using different rating criteria.

These and the following screening tools and reference guides are discussed further online:

- *The Brigance Infant and Toddler Screen* (Brigance & Page Glascoe, 2002)
- *Rourke Baby Record* (Rourke, Rourke, & Leduc, 2009).
- The Battelle Developmental Inventory, 2nd edition (Newborg, 2004)
- Infant Toddler Sensory Profile (Dunn, 1999)

The Ontario Best Start On Track Guide (www.beststart.org/OnTrack_English/
8-screeningtools.html) is not a screening tool but offers professionals a
comprehensive description of a variety of recommended assessment tools, as
well as a practical guide to assist in understanding the process of screening
and assessment. What assessments have been used in your province
or community?

"It is important to thoughtfully examine tools," such as those mentioned
earlier, "in order to choose ones that are most appropriate for the purpose
for which they are being used, as well as for the individual needs of the children and families served by programs. For example, many norm-referenced
assessment tools have not included in their norming population children who
are culturally and linguistically diverse" (Yates et al., 2008, p. 6). Be sure to
also search the Internet for other screening tools relevant to your practice
and community.

Functional Assessment Tools: How Are They Initiated?

Functional assessment tools are often initiated by the resource professional,
who, with the parents and educators, uses pedagogical documentation from the
child's portfolio, their own anecdotal observations, as well as new information
from the developmental assessment tool they've used in collaboration with the
team in order to understand the "whole" child. These tools may be introduced
after a screening process has highlighted areas of concern warranting further
investigation of specific domains of a child's development. In some circumstances, informal observations and pedagogical documentation will have led to
the developmental assessment process, bypassing the screening process alto-
gether. Each level of assessment has its own merits; it is up to the parents, the
educators, and the resource professional(s) to determine the best way to collect
information on each child. Educators are also encouraged to consult with the
child in the process with parent and child permission.

During the process of collection, the types of methods and procedures
may vary; therefore, it is important to look at which one will best represent
the child. Some developmental tools do not permit flexibility in administration, which can influence the results gained from a child; in fact, these tools
may paint a picture of a child with more "skills yet to be developed" than what
would have been gathered if the child had been observed in his or her own
natural and familiar learning environments.

Go online to learn more about the many tools available to the early intervention and early childhood community.

The Role of the Educator in the Assessment Process

The role of the early childhood professional in the screening and functional
assessment process is a very important one. Ongoing observations, pedagogical
documentation, co-completing screening tools, providing input, and dialogue/
feedback from the educator, parent, resource professional, and other members
of the team can inform and produce a multitude of outcomes and information.
Each perspective provides insights needed to respond to a child's strengths,
needs, and interests, and to parent priorities and concerns arising from the

process. Communicating adjustments to any aspects of practice, such as positive child guidance, the curriculum, the environment, or the team, is part of the process. A collective knowledge of the child that can support appropriate referrals to other agencies and perhaps a diagnostic assessment (which would be done only by a psychologist, psychiatrist, or developmental pediatrician) is also created through this process. Clearly, assessment refers to all aspects of this practice rather than just a specific assessment tool or practice.

Family-centred practice reminds us that parents have the sole decision "in consultation with their child" on how to act upon the information they have gained from the process. In conjunction with the resource professionals we are working with, it is our role as educators to provide the family with the necessary tools to make informed decisions; we are not expected to, nor should we, decide the directions we should take with a child. The sooner parents are informed as to the benefits of this process, the sooner they are able to receive the supports they need.

What Is an Individualized Plan?

One of the many outcomes of the assessment process, formal or informal, will be the creation or preparation of a plan of action for the child and their family. Developmental and/or holistic in nature, this plan can be simplistic or complex in its approach and will be an outcome of the collaborative efforts of the child (where possible), the professionals and team members involved (interprofessional and/or educators specific to the early learning setting), and the family. IEPs (Individual Education Plans), IPPs (Individual Program Plans), ISPs (Individual Support Plans), and ITPs (Individual Training/Teaching Plans) are some of the more common acronyms that represent the names of specific yet related plans of action for the child. It is important to note that, depending on the setting, one or more of these acronyms may be interchanged to infer the same meaning, while for other settings or school boards, they may very well have different purposes and meanings. We will discuss them here as broad plans that may incorporate a number of similar components.

Let's discuss some variances; for example, according to the Ontario Ministry of Education, IEPs detail the strengths and needs of a child related to the curriculum aspects of the specified grade level as well as those identified accommodations and modifications necessary to support children in their learning. If you are an educator in Ontario's full-day kindergarten, it is important to understand what an IEP is and is not as well as to understand the terms accommodation and modification. Accommodation involves the provision of adaptations that support children in attaining the grade level they are in, whereas modifications infer changes made to curriculum when a child is not at the same level or attaining the same grade level as their peers.

These plans could also include prioritized goals and objectives, implementation considerations and task analysis, the roles and responsibilities of those involved in the implementation, a documentation process to measure progress, and, of course, an evaluation component. Guided by observations and input from the family, child, educators, resource professionals, and other team members, these plans also involve a combination of skills to be further developed as well as a description of the child's current strengths and interests. A child's strengths and interests are used to respond with an appropriate learning experience that would further extend a

psychologist

An individual holding a doctoral degree in psychology who is qualified to support the mental health of others through the provision of research, therapy, and diagnosis.

psychiatrist

A physician with additional medical training and experience in the diagnosis, prevention, and treatment of mental disorder.

developmental pediatrician

A physician with the credentials to diagnose special needs or attend to special needs or extra-support concerns for children.

IEPs (Individual Education Plans), IPPs (Individual Program Plans), ISPs (Individual Support Plans), and ITPs (Individual Training/ Teaching Plans)

Plans co-created by the team that could include, for example, a child's strengths, interests, skills to be developed (needs), goals, adaptations, and/or accommodations or resources supporting their success.

accommodations

Resources or adaptations that can support a child or individual to fully participate and attain the same grade level as his or her peers.

modifications

Alterations to student work that change the level of academic performance and achievement expected from a student, resulting in the student not attaining the same grade level or prescribed curriculum as their peers.

goals

Generalized statements of intended change in direction, ability, knowledge, or outcomes. They are usually composed of a number of objectives that support movement toward and attainment of the intended goals.

objectives

Goals that can be reasonably achieved within an expected time frame and with available resources.

task analysis

A step-by-step breakdown of a targeted task or skill; defining all knowledge, skills, materials, sequencing, steps, resources, safety issues, related procedures, and training for that task or skill.

Individual Family Support Plan (IFSP)

A setting-dependent plan outlining the strengths of a child and family, their goals/priorities, services/supports being received or required, roles assumed by each member, service directions, as well as expected outcomes and timelines.

child's thinking or support a child's development in a particular area. These plans also assist in the creation and development of adaptations that are responsive to the child. For example, if a child loved robots, an educator, based on that interest, would co-create experiences involving robots with that child. This would then enable additional opportunities to be created as a result of that collaboration and planning, further promoting and engaging the voice and knowledge of the child while simultaneously working on areas requiring additional support. Whatever the focus, the learning experiences for the child should not differ from others but should complement whatever is set up in the environment for the other children, and implemented in the child's natural settings (home and/or the early childhood setting). If implemented appropriately, the learning that takes place should be fun and enjoyable for the child and peers.

A final component that might fall within this individualized process is a plan for the family because the child cannot be looked at in isolation. Directed by the family, and with assistance from a resource professional or educator if requested, an appropriate Individual Family Support Plan (IFSP) can be created. These plans would revolve around the family and would contain an evaluation timeline, breakdowns of roles and responsibilities established with input from other community and/or centre team members, service timelines for all involved, and next steps for service. Incorporating both the home and early learning environments, the IFSP might also outline a child's current strengths and skills to be developed but would go beyond supports for the child to include the supports necessary for the entire family. The collection of authentic input, pedagogical documentation, and assessment data for these IFSPs requires time; therefore, the evaluation timeline for these plans is typically every six months or upon request by the family or member of the team. "Participants also identified time as necessary to build a trusting relationship with a family and to acquire, through experience, proficiency in child development and authentic assessment methods" (Keilty et al., 2009, p. 254).

For additional learning in this aspect of practice, think about consulting with your setting or community regarding individualized plans and terminology associated with the planning process.

Observation and Assessment: Informing Adaptations

As educators, we are fortunate to have the opportunity every day to learn from, learn with, and educate young children—this is a privilege that we cannot take lightly. We have an important responsibility: educating a very vulnerable population. As educators, we can have a profound effect on young children in a multitude of ways.

Throughout this text, we have learned the importance of collaborating with colleagues and professionals, with children and families, and with our community so that we might plan the most optimal learning communities possible. We realize now that observation is important for many reasons: it provides us with information and the tools we need to be responsive and inclusive educators. More specifically, it provides insight into a child's strengths, needs, or skills to be developed; the child's interests; the child's learning styles and preferences; the family; and the socio-cultural context in which they live. All of this can inform our next steps: selecting materials and equipment reflective of the children in our classroom; implementing universal design for learning; identifying the best place for

Jaren Jai Wicklund/Shutterstock.com

materials; and, perhaps, determining teaching strategies and adaptations that will be most effective to assist a variety of children.

Adaptations may be made for an individual child to enable her or him to achieve skills with assistance or independently. The adaptations we create, however, can be beneficial to many children. Take a look at the examples of creative adaptations online. Many of those adaptations were informed by full participation in the cycle of observation and appreciative inquiry process, and were the result of collaboration among the child, educators, and family.

All the information we have discussed in this and other chapters—observations, pedagogical documentation, portfolios, IPPs, IEPs, and various forms of assessment—can inform the adaptations we design for all children. Adaptations are one way we can respond to children to include them within the classroom through the adjustments we make in our interactions, in the physical environment, and in the materials and experiences provided for children in the classroom. Adaptations can be defined as changes or alterations we make to increase the success of a child in achieving skills in a task independently or with assistance. Increasing the accessibility, responsiveness, inclusivity, and universality of all elements within our professional practice to increase the success of children and their families is our ultimate goal.

ASSESSMENT: INFORMING CHILDREN'S HEALTH AND WELL-BEING

We've learned a lot about assessment and evaluation for the purposes of children's growth and development, and to make their learning visible. Another purpose of assessment is for educators to evaluate the well-being of children

Age fotostock

by observing the physical health and disposition by a health and wellness check when each child arrives in the morning. According to Ontario provincial legislation, a daily log must be kept of the health, safety, and well-being of all enrolled children in a program.

Educators are active observers. They are attuned to the growth and development of each child in their care. For example, observations relating to a child's health (e.g., ear infection, contagious disease) and welfare (e.g., bumps, bruises, changes in behaviour) are noted and communicated to the supervisor immediately. The morning health check is part of a centre's policies and procedures, and includes the process for reporting child abuse.

Reporting Child Abuse

As part of the early identification and intervention process, if educators suspect child abuse or neglect, they must legally bound to report these findings to the Children's Aid Society (CAS) immediately. According to Ontario's Child and Family Services Act, the responsibility to act is in keeping with the best interest, protection, and well-being of children (see Exhibit 7.15).

EXHIBIT 7.15	Child Abuse and the Duty to Report

Under the Child and Family Services Act,

Professionals and officials have the same duty as the rest of the public to report their suspicion that a child is or may be in need of protection. However, the Act recognizes that people working closely with children have a special awareness of the signs of child abuse and neglect, and a particular responsibility to report their suspicions. As per http://www.children.gov.on.ca/htdocs/English/childrensaid/reportingabuse/abuseandneglect.aspx. Any professional or official who fails to report a suspicion is liable on conviction to a fine of up to $5,000. And the CFSA has been replaced with the CCYFSA.

This would include but would not be limited to the following professionals:

- health care professionals, including physicians, nurses, dentists, pharmacists and psychologists
- teachers and school principals
- social workers and family counsellors
- religious leaders, including priests, rabbis and members of the clergy
- operators or employees of child care programs or centres
- youth and recreation workers (not volunteers)
- peace officers and coroners
- child and youth service providers and employees of these service providers
- any other person who performs professional or official duties with respect to a child (p. 5)

Source: Ministry of Children, Community and Social Services. *Reporting Child Abuse and Neglect: It's Your Duty.* Copyright Queen's Printer for Ontario (2018). Used with permission.

The format used to report abuse or neglect is not important; the main point is that the suspected abuse or neglect is documented as objectively as possible, separating feelings, interpretations, judgments, and conclusions from the actual description of the perceived abuse or neglect. When documenting, remember that your description or observation must be accompanied by the following:

- date and time
- location
- your name and position
- your actions: what you said and did
- your description, documentation, and comments written in pen or typed on a computer
- your signature and the date of your report

As this may become a document used in a court of law, remember not to make any changes to the original paper document, such as strikeovers, pen marks made on top of pencil marks, or whiteouts. No changes, deletions, or additions to the original can be made when reporting electronically. Early childhood professionals play an important role in the early identification of possible cases of abuse or neglect. In their *Professional Advisory: Duty to Report* document (2015), the College of Early Childhood Educators in Ontario further solidifies this responsibility in their statement: "RECE's work with a vulnerable population and it is among their responsibilities to build positive, trusting relationships with families and children. As such, they are in a unique position to recognize possible signs of child abuse, neglect and family violence. It is important that RECEs are aware of, and prepared to act on, their legislated duty to report suspicions of harm or misconduct towards children" (p. 1).

Examine either the occupational standards, child protective laws, or the code of ethics documents within each province and territory for their protocols regarding the reporting of child abuse. What do they say? Are the protocols and responsibilities similar? What are the observation and documentation responsibilities?

REFLECTIVE EXERCISE 7.6

Refer to the school or centre's policies and procedures for child abuse, and make yourself aware of your responsibility to children under the appropriate provincial ministry and the Department of Justice Canada. The Department of Justice website (n.d.) lists the types of abuse and neglect as well as the most current initiatives being undertaken on behalf of Canada's children.

No matter where you practise in the world, be informed about your role and the processes involved in reporting suspected abuse. This process can be intimidating for a variety of factors too lengthy to cover in this chapter, but the fact remains that it is incumbent on the person who suspects abuse to act upon it. Search the Internet for further information about reporting child abuse as it relates to your province or territory.

CHAPTER REFLECTIONS

1. Through appreciative inquiry and reflection, observers are able to consider ways in which to assist children who may require extra support: listening, questioning, and engaging the voices and perspectives of children and the team help to uncover the thinking, learning, and struggles of children. Due to the cycle of observation being cyclical and interactive, each component of the cycle informs the other in order to be responsive and inclusive.

2. When families and their children begin at an early childhood setting, the early intervention process begins. Composed of observation, pedagogical documentation, and, sometimes, standardized assessment methodologies, the early intervention process is highly collaborative and intended to support the overall success of children. Families are at the centre of early intervention and, along with their children, have decision-making rights in directing the service direction. Observations, documentation, dialogue, and inquiry inform collective decisions which may result in curriculum changes, infusion of adaptations to materials and equipment to support individual success, environment changes, further assessments or referrals, and many other outcomes. Observations give us the information we need to be responsive and inclusive with our early intervention processes.

3. Educators will work directly with families and many other paraprofessionals in the early intervention process. Who the paraprofessionals might be are reflective of the child's and family's needs and abilities. Resource professionals are one of many paraprofessionals who can support children and families in obtaining the supports and services they need. Interprofessional teams might include physiotherapists, social workers, psychotherapists, speech and language pathologists, pediatricians, and many others.

4. Building relationships with families are an important and primary responsibility for every educator. This allows all observers/educators to learn about each family's strengths, needs, desires, and values. The Family-Centred Service Checklist outlines a number of reflective questions that can guide service providers through the values, components, and considerations of family-centred practices.

5. Authentic assessments regarding children are holistic in nature and include methodologies covered in Chapters 4 and 5. Each in their own way is sensitive and reflective of the voices, inquiries, rights, thinking, and abilities of those being documented or observed. These assessments and inquiries make visible the learning and thinking of children, and inform many aspects of practice for settings utilizing an inquiry approach. In some circumstances, authentic assessments may inform decisions by families to pursue standardized assessments of some kind. Standardized assessments are not individualized; they are intended to measure a child's progress and compare to a fixed standard, and typically inform the development of individual education plans, goals, objectives, interventions, supports, next steps regarding referrals, and many other purposes. There are several different types of assessments outlined in this chapter.

6. Individualized plans are plans of action for children and/or families, and may come in many different forms depending on the purpose and setting. These plans are intended to be responsive to children and inclusive of their knowledge, skills, and natural environments familiar to them to further promote positive growth and development.

7. Observing and documenting about children's health and well-being is an important role for all educators. In order for children to thrive, they need environments that are safe, healthy, and responsive to their abilities and needs. Observation, documentation, listening, and dialogue provide educators with the information they need to protect young children. Legislation across Canada requires educators to be attuned to the health and well-being of children. Should educators suspect that neglect or abuse is occurring, they must report their findings to the authorities immediately. Further details can be located within the chapter regarding one's duty to report.

Hero Images/Getty Images

CHAPTER

8

REFLECTIVE AND TRANSFORMATIVE: OBSERVER AS LEADER

OVERVIEW

We have come full circle, exploring the many facets of observation and pedagogical documentation, including the exploration of numerous methodologies and the important role educators play in making children's learning visible. That said, we also emphasize the importance of observing and documenting to understand and appreciate the child within the context of his or her environment. Viewing the environment as co-educator, we can begin to understand, assess, and appreciate what contributes to healthy and responsive interactions as well as delineate what is necessary to prepare quality inclusive and universally designed environments reflective of the diversity of its learners. Analyzing and assessing the many facets of the environment is an important focus for this chapter.

We also acknowledge the changing landscape of early childhood education and the role of the educator in early childhood. We realize that "through pedagogical documentation, the roles in education are shifting; what it means to be a learner and an educator are being transformed. Students and teachers alike are demonstrating ownership of and engaging in teaching and learning. Consequently, pedagogical documentation is a vehicle for learning that bridges understanding of children and adults" (Ontario Ministry of Education, 2012, p. 4). Educators must then look to new ways of doing things and to new roles to further support this transition.

Some of these roles include the observer as pedagogical leader, mentor, and researcher. "There is argument that we cannot expect educators to create a community of learners among children if they do not have a comparable community to nourish their own growth" (Grossman, Wineburg, & Woolworth, 2001; Brown & Inglis, 2013, p. 14). Educators have an important role to play in research and action research, whether through involvement in research specific to a setting or community or involvement in longitudinal research over time. It is through research that capacity within early childhood settings, observation, and new ways of documenting can flourish. Staying ahead of and in tune with observational trends, particularly those that promote access and engagement from all members of an observational team, is key to understanding how we might continue to collaborate with children, families, and communities. We finish this chapter with a look into educator development and portfolio preparation. The profession expects and children deserve knowledgeable educators who are committed to lifelong learning, and excellence in observation and pedagogical documentation.

longitudinal research

Observational studies consisting of research over extended periods of time.

FOCUS QUESTIONS

1. Why is it important to observe the learning environment? Describe the various elements of the environment as they relate to universal design for learning (UDL).
2. What are environmental assessments, and what are their purpose?
3. Why are observation and appreciative inquiry so important to pedagogical leadership and mentorship?
4. How might action research improve our professional practice regarding observation and pedagogical documentation?
5. Continuous professional learning and e-portfolios for educators have become an expectation of the profession. Why? What impact do they have on our observational practices?

THE ENVIRONMENT DEFINED

Throughout this text, we've taken many opportunities to introduce aspects of the learning environment in order to prepare for this in-depth examination of the dimensions that compose a quality learning environment for children. When we take a moment to pause, reflect, and observe, what appears more clearly to us is the intimate relationship occurring between the children and their surroundings. We envision this relationship with the environment moving beyond the traditional views of just the physical space, for it also encompasses the ambiance, the "feeling," and the overall atmosphere of the environment. We use observation, pedagogical documentation, and assessment to assist us in understanding and appreciating this subtle but complex relationship between a child and the environment because these tools provide insight into how the environment might influence the functioning and interactions of children and others within their learning space. We present the environment as a reciprocal co-educator and co-play partner in the early childhood setting, for it holds a significant role in the co-education process. Preparing environments for children to be fully engaged in play and with others (like the children in Reflective Exercise 8.1) is a very important responsibility.

REFLECTIVE EXERCISE 8.1

Narrative 1

Portia and Binqing were actively setting up an ice cream stand in preparation for what they called "their family night." Portia was eager to make sure the ice cream flavours could stack upon one another as she communicated her thinking: "We are gunna get more money for the bigger ice cream cones." She was seen hypothesizing which colours together made a rainbow. Binqing was happy to support Portia with her problem solving and she was giggling when the pieces would fall on the floor. Binqing could be overheard telling Portia that they needed to make sure the tables were high enough for her chair to fit under so that she "could be the cashier so that it was fair." Portia responded by saying, "Whadda we gunna do so that you can scoop ice cream out of the freezer (while pointing to the sensory bin)? You can't reach like this." Portia leaned her body forward into the bin arching her arms over to the bowls to the

opposite side of the sensory bin. For the next several minutes, Portia assisted Binqing in trying different theories about "fit and size" as they raised different pieces of equipment using blocks from the block centre. After several attempts, Portia and Binqing had raised the sensory bin high enough for Binqing's legs and wheels to fit under it.

Educator Reflection:

"Portia and Binqing—you were discussing and planning for well-being and belonging in your interactions here. Portia, you responded to Binqing's request and need to adapt the table for her full inclusion in the experience you were creating together. That is what friends do for one another. Each of your theories resulted in trying different-sized materials as well as examining how balance works with a long rectangular bin."

Your Reflection: What other reflections might we come up with here? What other learning is being made evident here?

Informing Curriculum and the Environment

Later that same morning, two questions were posed to Portia and Binqing to understand and make visible their thinking in this experience. The first questions were, "How did you come up with your solutions to the problem?" and "How might we extend this experience into other areas of our room?" This sparked a documentation panel that had the class exploring different heights of equipment and materials to ensure the inclusiveness of their peers. Informal measurements using hands, feet, and blocks were the top materials selected for estimating, predicting, and documenting. The result was a list made of drawings created by the children in the room of measurements they needed to change the height of things in the classroom.

Narrative 2

Caris had come over to the toddler room to be a "big helper" as her younger sister Adelaide was scared to go down the slide. The educator Luke was trying to coach Adelaide to go down the slide while holding her hand but Adelaide declined. Adelaide shook her head rapidly from side to side shouting "noooooooooooo." She was holding onto the climber wall with her one hand very tightly, while other children were moving in behind her wanting to go down the slide. Seeing that it was her sister at the climber, Caris sauntered over grabbing two construction helmets along the way. "Hey, Adelaide! I got two helmets for us to wear while you go down the slide." Wiping her tears from her face, Adelaide slowly raised her cheeks to smile. She put the helmet Caris had brought onto her head and reached her two hands outward to her sister. Adelaide squatted down in front of the slide asserting, "I've got you, Caris." Without thinking and appearing not to realize she wasn't holding on anymore, Caris slid down the slide.

omgimages/iStockphoto.com

Caris's Reflection:

"I did it. I went down. No more cry."

Adelaide's Reflection:

"Caris has been scared before to go down slides because she doesn't do it very often. My mom has told me before to direct her attention to something else when she gets upset. I remembered to do that when I came to see her and it worked. I think my sister trusts me and that makes me feel good. You did it, Caris!"

Educator Reflection:

For this reflective exercise, finish this example with an educator reflection. How might you support the reflections already stated yet make Caris's learning visible in a positive way from the experience she had? Once completed, prepare a curricular and environmental response. How could Caris's thinking be extended? How might the environment be designed to support her capabilities? How might you involve Caris in the preparation of curriculum?

Observation and pedagogical documentation as part of the cycle of observation enable us to understand the interplay between children and the learning environment. When combined with the other elements of the cycle such as appreciative inquiry and reflection, we acquire the holistic and authentic information needed to co-create quality inclusive and responsive environments for all learners that incorporate socio-emotional/psychological, temporal, and physical considerations. The Universal Design for Learning approach prompts us to look at each of these environmental considerations using the following principles:

- Choice of how to best understand information: Multiple Means of Representation (the "what" of learning)—present content in different ways.
- Choice of how to express what they know: Multiple Means of Action and Expression (the "how" of learning)—give learners different ways to show what they know.
- Choice of how to reinforce and motivate: Multiple Means of Engagement (the "why" of learning)—use multiple ways to motivate learners (Mistret, 2017, p. 1)

Let's take a look at each of the environments through the lens of the cycle of observation and the Universal Design for Learning (UDL) principles stated above.

The Socio-emotional/Psychological Tone of an Environment: The Cycle of Observation and Universal Design for Learning

We know that care and learning are inextricably linked—one cannot function without the other. In his *Hierarchy of Physical, Emotional, and Intellectual Needs*, Abraham Maslow theorized that people are involved in an ongoing process of self-actualization. Universal Design for Learning prompts observers to ensure they are available emotionally and physically to children in order to build trust, which in turn equips them with the confidence to take risks, to try new things, and to immerse themselves as secure, attached participants in a learning community.

Deep, caring, enduring relationships between children and educators provide predictability and secure attachment in children's lives. Forming warm and responsive relationships with children typically means respecting their emotional rhythms, listening carefully to their conversations, taking their suggestions for problem solving seriously, and following their lead in curriculum planning. Flexible educators respond to children's interests, passions, and strengths; engage children in multiple

Universal Design for Learning (UDL)

Making learning environments, buildings, materials, and equipment accessible to all and barrier free without the need for adaptation or specialized design.

self-actualization

Motivation to realize one's maximum potential. In Maslow's hierarchy of needs, self-actualization is the final level that can be achieved when all other basic needs are met.

▶ Here we see an educator responding to an infant communicating through different facial expressions. The infant seen here was making sounds with her tongue and extending it outward. This educator imitated the child's sounds to extend and reciprocate the interaction.

Kristine Fenning

forms of communication, creativity, and expression; and encourage joint endeavours where children and adults learn and play together. (Early Childhood Research and Development Team, 2008, p. 11)

For families and practitioners alike, creating a child-centred environment that is inspiring and inclusive of the variations in abilities, learning approaches, and diversity of individual children within a group is important. Brain development, self-regulation, and resiliency are examples of children's socio-emotional health that can be affected by the psychological and emotional tone of their surroundings. A relationship-based environment influences early brain development, builds trust and the security needed to take risks, enhances the ability of children to self-regulate, and supports the adjustment to a group experience. How we design environments for learning can have lifelong consequences upon a child's quality of life and learning.

Children new to an early learning environment are a good example. They stand by the entrance door having just been dropped off by their parent/guardian, tears streaming down their face, lacking the security or trust in an unfamiliar environment or educators to feel that their needs will be met. It is integral, then, for educators to observe and respond to situations like this in order for children to adjust and develop the connections and attachments necessary for their health and well-being. Curriculum responses or environmental changes in this case might include involving the new child in adding items of interest to various areas of the room, looking at ways to document and make visible the connections the child is making to others and to their environment, creating a safe and comfortable space with pillows, soothing fabrics, and soft seating, and/or perhaps co-designing an "all about me" book to put on the bookshelf for viewing by all.

Jean Clinton, in her publication within the *Think, Feel, Act* series entitled *The Power of Positive Adult–Child Relationships: Connection Is the Key* (2013), states that

children learn best in an environment that acknowledges this interconnectivity and thus focuses on both emotional and cognitive development. There is now an explosion of knowledge that tells us that healthy development cannot happen without good relationships between children and the important people in their lives, both within the family and outside of it. (pp. 5–6)

Observers must use observation, inquiry, and pedagogical documentation to prepare environments that encompass a positive socio-emotional and psychological tone. In doing this, observers are prompted to reflect upon what they believe and value, as well as their feelings and the feelings of others toward different aspects of the early learning environment. What might you be curious about? What are the learners (child, family, educator, students, etc.) in your classroom curious about? It is necessary to understand how we affect our interactions with others, as well as how what we believe and feel influences the design and creation of learning communities for children and their families. Exhibit 8.1 explores some of the many reflective questions and universal design considerations we may formulate to inform and complement our observations and pedagogical documentation, and subsequently aid our co-creation of this type of environment.

Any one of the questions in Exhibit 8.1 will lead observers (children, educators, families) to design and co-create positive changes in the environment and new curricular directions.

child-centred environment

An environment adapted to meet the interests, strengths, and needs of children.

self-regulation

The ability to control or adapt one's own behaviour and/or emotions according to the context, goals, or expectations of a situation or person.

resiliency

The positive capacity of people to cope with stress and adversity. This coping may result in the individual "bouncing back" to a previous state of normal functioning.

Reflective Questions

- What is our current environment communicating about the four foundations (Well-being, Belonging, Engagement, and Expression) of *How Does Learning Happen? Ontario's Pedagogy for the Early Years* (Ontario Ministry of Education, p. 8). Are they valued?
- How do we create nurturing and caring relationships with others and with the environment? In what ways are we approachable, calm, and welcoming to all learners within each aspect of the environment? (UDL—Multiple Means of Engagement)
- How does the environment reflect our image of the child and family? Are photos and documentation made visible in the environment that capture home languages and authenticity of family interactions?
- How are children able to make decisions and choices with materials and design of the environment? In what ways are they involved in co-designing the environment? (UDL—Multiple Means of Action & Expression, Multiple Means of Engagement)
- In what ways do our indoor/outdoor environment and relationships promote shared and individual values?
- What are our shared values (or do we have shared values?) concerning relationships and socio-emotional and psychological well-being? If shared values are not evident, how might we create them?
- In what ways is respect for the individuality and emotional needs of each learner represented in our relationships and the environment? For example, how do we use experiences and materials within the environment to support the expression of feelings (verbal and nonverbal) and the development of pro–social skills? (UDL—Multiple Means of Representation)
- Examining our spaces in the environment, how do they support self-regulation? What materials and elements of the environment promote engagement and acceptance?
- In what ways do our interactions and the environment as the third educator promote reciprocity, collaboration and co-inquiry, confidence, and the co-construction of new knowledge?

▶ Tia and Ella are demonstrating their excitement as their classes were combined to go on a field trip together. Together they discuss what they think they are going to see in the forest.

Juanmonino/iStockphoto.com

Tia and Ella in the photo seen here affirm that social inclusion is an important aspect of this approach because all children want to feel respected and included alongside their peers in an environment that enables them to develop and expand their identity, whether it be gender, ability, culture, or other aspects of their being. Reflecting on your childhood, was feeling included also an important part of your self-identity and your ability to self-regulate and be resilient?

We must not take our role and influence upon young children lightly. Documenting children's actions and behaviours and observing our environment can give us significant insight into how we might support their building of self-regulation and resilience. How we act and respond, what we prepare, and how we design our environments or learning communities for children require us to be diligent in our observation and reflective processes! More information regarding resiliency and emotional well-being can be found online.

REFLECTIVE EXERCISE 8.2

Considering your learning environment and the learners within it, reflect upon the questions in Exhibit 8.1. Discuss with your colleagues or peers your answers to those questions. What other questions or considerations might you make/create to address the principles of UDL and the socio-emotional/psychological tone of the environment?

The Physical Environment: The Cycle of Observation and Universal Design for Learning

The physical design of an environment both indoors and outdoors is an important consideration in the preparation of quality learning experiences. We can achieve further understanding of the impact of the physicality of a space by engaging in each step within the cycle of observation and reflecting upon our observations and pedagogical documentation that has been prepared by all learners.

Universal design elements promote children having the right to learning spaces and experiences that expand all areas of their thinking and development. Space allotment for children may vary according to where the early childhood setting is located or it may be influenced by licensing or ministry requirements; however, we know that there must be adequate space to accommodate individual variations in development and to allow children to demonstrate their learning in different ways (Multiple Means of Representation, Actions, & Expression). This would be reflective of all children, and would be inclusive of children with special needs who might use specialized equipment to support their learning (e.g., wheelchairs, standers, orthotics). Observing how equipment and furniture are positioned can inform our understanding of accessibility issues. Exhibit 8.2 presents some of the many pieces of legislation/acts/regulations/frameworks guiding accessibility practices in different provinces and territories within Canada.

Accessibility laws like some of the above outline expectations of individuals and organizations (including early childhood and school settings) to improve accessibility and reduce barriers for all people. This list is not exhaustive as there are a number of other important government documents associated with each province concerning accessibility. Educators are encouraged to explore their expectations of practice regarding accessibility and the early childhood environment online.

standers

Assistive devices aimed to support an individual physically to be able to stand. This metal and Velcro-strapped piece of equipment might also have a table attached to it.

orthotics

Braces, pads, and/or splints designed and created specifically to provide support and strength for parts of the body, particularly the foot and ankle.

EXHIBIT 8.2	Acts/Legislation/Frameworks Supporting Accessibility across Canada
Province	**Act/Legislation/Framework Referencing Physical Designs of Environments or Relating to Accessibility**
Ontario	*Ontario Human Rights Code* *Accessibility for Ontarians with Disabilities Act (AODA)* *The Ontario Building Code* *The Education Act*
Manitoba	*The Accessibility for Manitobans Act (AMA)*
Saskatchewan	*Saskatchewan Human Rights Code*
Alberta	*Alberta Human Rights Act* *Alberta Building Code* *The Barrier-Free Design Guide* *Standards for Special Education* *Safety Codes Act*
British Columbia	*BC Human Rights Code* *Children and Youth with Special Needs Framework for Action: Making It Work*
Nunavut	*Nunavut Human Rights Act*
Northwest Territories	*Equity, Accessibility, Inclusion and Participation Framework* from the Department of Health and Social Services (a framework to guide practices, not law)
Yukon	*Yukon Human Rights Act*
Quebec	*An Act to Secure Handicapped Persons in the Exercise of Their Rights with a View to Achieving Social, School and Workplace Integration* *Quebec Charter of Human Rights and Freedoms*
Nova Scotia	*Nova Scotia Human Rights Act Building Code Regulations*
Newfoundland and Labrador	*The Buildings Accessibility Act*
New Brunswick	*The New Brunswick Human Rights Act* *New Brunswick Building Code Act*
Prince Edward Island	*Access to Public Buildings Act* *Barrier Free Design Regulations PEI* *Child Care Facilities Act*
Canada	*Canadian Human Rights Act* *Accessible Canada: Creating New Federal Accessibility Legislation*

xefstock/iStockphoto.com

REFLECTIVE EXERCISE 8.3

Considering the list in Exhibit 8.2, take some time to prepare appreciative inquiry–based/reflective questions that can prompt educators, children, and families to examine the physical learning environment. A list of reflective questions has been provided below to provoke your thinking. What new questions can you add about the physical environment?

There are a number of other universal design for learning considerations in the physical space requiring observation and reflection such as those below.

Design considerations include but are not limited to the following:

- Entranceway design—is it inviting and welcoming? Do children and families see themselves in the space?
- Are the colours in the room calming rather than over-/under-stimulating?

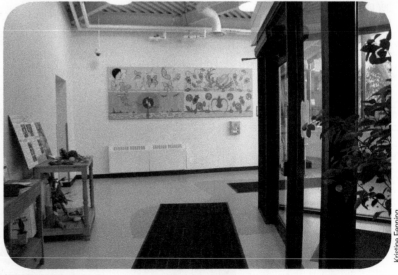
Kristine Fenning

- Are there a variety of natural play materials, blocks, and sensory opportunities (variety of textures) that promote exploration?
- Is there a balance of loud and quiet areas of the room to support children to focus and sustain their attention at experiences in the room?
- Are there spaces for quiet relaxation and self-regulation?
- What traffic flow considerations have been made?
- Is there a flow between zones or areas of the room to allow children to explore in their own way?
- Are materials reflective of the children within the environment? Are they open ended, do they incorporate loose parts, and are there enough materials? (Multiple Means of Representation, Action, & Expression)
- Are there different flooring variations for children?

The aesthetic use of space as it relates to the children and your community

- Is the use of artwork and pedagogical documentation created by the children in the room considered? How this artwork and documentation is displayed infers the importance of children's work and thinking. Too much on the wall can be distracting and overstimulating—engaging the voices of children in this and other decisions is necessary.
- Are there opportunities for different types of art for freedom of expression? (Multiple Means of Engagement)
- Are photos and materials at eye level?
- Are spaces inviting with natural light and greenery?
- Are storage containers for materials organized and labelled?
- Is the furniture in the room geared to children (i.e., sturdy, comfortable, inviting, and child-sized)? Are all areas of the room accessible?
- Are there opportunities for individual and groups of children to allow for choice making? (Multiple Means of Engagement)
- Are rooms including the diapering and sleep areas clean and organized?

▶ Here we see a junior kindergarten child providing her perspective on experiences she took part in that day. Her thinking is evident as she details her learning in her explanations to her peers and educators and in her subsequent documentation in their Google classroom.

Kristine Fenning

As we revisit the concept of pedagogical documentation, eliciting feedback from children and families regarding the questions above is just as integral to this evaluation and reflection process. When children and families are involved in the selection of materials and experiences in the room, as well as in the layout and design of their classroom and wall spaces, children are more apt to become engaged, extend their own learning and understanding of self-assessment, and perhaps become more confident in taking risks and trying new things. Furthermore, when children see their contributions to their environment, there is a sense of pride and a feeling of community because they are able to evolve their identity and see themselves and their families in the environment (e.g., through photos and artwork at children's level).

The physical environment also requires us to look at the quality of the outdoor learning environment.

> Ask any adult to recall their best play memories. These were almost always outside—often in natural surroundings—with friends; exciting, social, creative experiences often high in anticipation. Ask the same adults if their children can play in the same way today and silence falls. (Shackell et al., 2008, p. 13)

Sacha Cabezas/Sally Wylie

With increased exposure to video games, computers, the Internet, and numerous other stresses facing parents who are raising children in today's society, the time spent by children outdoors is becoming less and less. Merge these factors with the statistics and research highlighting the increase in obesity in young children around the world and there is reason for concern. Focusing our attention and observations on creating natural outdoor play environments that encompass responsive and inclusive elements is therefore extremely necessary. The health and well-being of children in our community and in our care requires us to take action.

Providing a healthy and safe outdoor play space that will attract and engage children in active and sensory-based play experiences is an important investment we need to make. One such approach is the introduction of natural design and loose parts elements into the indoor and outdoor learning environments. Take a look at Exhibit 8.3, which portrays a number of natural elements and loose parts made available to children. What do you think might occur if these materials were provided as a provocation to three- to four-year-old children in your early childhood setting?

natural design

Environmental design that incorporates natural materials and natural elements in an indoor and outdoor play space.

loose parts

Open-ended natural or manufactured materials (e.g., stones, sticks, logs, cones) used creatively for "possibility thinking" and play opportunities.

Chapter 8: Reflective and Transformative: Observer as Leader

EXHIBIT 8.3   Natural Materials and Loose Parts

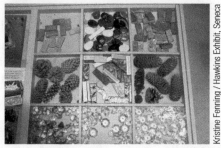

Above we find a number of loose parts, natural and manufactured, prepared for young children to use in ways of their choosing. Below we see educators and teachers engaged in a professional development day preparing a creation with some of the loose parts offered to them for exploration. Why might it be important for educators to play and experiment?

If you offered these materials to children in your setting, what do you think they would do with them?

Source: Kristine Fenning, with thanks to the Hawkins Exhibit and the Reggio-inspired Summer Intensive.

The Temporal Environment: The Cycle of Observation and Universal Design for Learning

The cycle of observation once again guides us through examination of yet another component of the learning environment; the temporal environment. When provided time, routines, and consistency in their environment, children are able to manage their engagement (Multiple Means of Engagement), perhaps choose to extend their time in specific experiences as well as successfully query, observe, and navigate transitions and different components of their schedule to anticipate what comes next. Exhibit 8.4 is a universal design for learning checklist that explores a number of environmental considerations for this area of the learning environment.

The checklist in Exhibit 8.4 is from an American source; therefore, it is important to note that items may be different depending on checklist in Exhibit 8.4 design for learning considerations in your community. In addition to the above, stable and predictable schedules like those in the Ontario Ministry of Education Kindergarten Program known as the "flow of the day" (2016, p. 95) are important for children. In child-care settings, the flow of the day is also known as visual schedules. Visual schedules can be developed using various visual schedule apps, such as Choiceworks, or by interacting with a program known as Boardmaker. Routines and daily experiences that can be supported through the use of social stories and visual schedules will assist children in building trust and security. The Kindergarten Program with the Ontario Ministry of Education also encourages "large uninterrupted blocks of time . . . devoted to play- and inquiry-based learning in indoor and outdoor settings" . . . so that . . . "the children and educators negotiate and co-construct the learning that happens during these

visual schedules

Photographs, pictures, and accompanying written words that help children understand and manage parts of the day, which assists in clarifying expectations for the child.

EXHIBIT 8.4	Temporal Environment Universal Design for Learning Considerations

Temporal Environment UDL Items	Reflections and Applications
• Daily schedules and changes to the schedule are in photo/picture format • Choice boards for selecting learning centers • Charts + signups help to manage numbers in popular centers • A mix of individual, dyad, small and large group activities are planned and flexible; children may engage more in smaller groups (Multiple Means of Representation) • Active and quiet activities are balanced and sequenced • Pacing of activities is appropriate and flexible • Visual/auditory activity sequences are available to support independence (Multiple Means of Engagement) • Verbal and non-verbal transition cues (lights, music, sounds 5-minute warning) are present; visual cues for line up activities. Graphic timers are available. • Time is allowed within the schedule for children to revisit things that need further attention or are not finished.	• What other aspects of the Temporal Environment could be added? • How might the other considerations here be aligned with the principles of UDL?

Source: Mistrett, S.G. (2017). *Universal Design for Learning: A Checklist for Early Childhood Environments.* Center on Technology and Disability. Retrieved from https://www.ctdinstitute.org/sites/default/files/file_attachments/UDL-Checklist-EC.pdf

---

blocks of time. Transitions are kept to a minimum—for example, consideration should be given to how many times during the day the children are asked to 'stop and tidy up'" (2016, p. 95). As co-educators in the environment, we always want to consider ways in which children can design their day. Several examples of social stories and visual schedules can be found online.

It appears that Exhibit 8.5 demonstrates the value of collaboration and authentic assessment. It was through observation, pedagogical documentation, and listening that Yaa and Nathan were able to incorporate some universal design for learning ideas. What were they? Why did they make an impact?

EXHIBIT 8.5 — Transitional Support

Nathan and Yaa are two new senior toddler educators at Natural and Inquiring Minds Child Care Centre. The ten senior toddlers in their program are all new; over the last six weeks, each child began with a staggered intake to ensure that their adjustment to their new group setting was a positive one. Each child has now settled in their room and appears to be exploring all aspects of the environment. Nathan and Yaa have been collaborating with the children to begin photo narratives on the bulletin boards. Each child now has a portfolio consisting of entries from children, the educators, and, on occasion, family members, and the educators have recently acquired some pedagogical documentation materials for the children to use on their own.

Recently, the inquiries of children have led them to materials that sink and float and to different ways they can construct pretend play houses (e.g., blankets over tables, placing chairs together along with a broom and blanket to make a triangle for tents). Things have become so exciting that several children are now avoiding the need for washroom breaks (resulting in some accidents), and they often choose not to transition to snack times for fear of missing out on something.

Out of concern for the children, Yaa and Nathan on their own tried a number of strategies with the children that didn't work. They soon realized that they did not consult with the children nor did they listen to their ideas on how to solve this issue. Realizing this error, Yaa and Nathan began observing and documenting with the children, conducting team discussions in the tents they so wonderfully created. What came of this?

The listening and observing led to children deciding that peers would hold their "spot" in their play experience while the others went to the washroom and had snack. The children also decided that they needed to take photos of themselves and have them laminated on cards so that they could place their card in the area where they were playing to indicate to others they were coming right back. Before too long, the children themselves were directing one another when they needed to use the washroom and eat.

Kristine Fenning

For further information regarding the socio-emotional/psychological, physical, and temporal elements of an early childhood environment, please consult with online examples within NelsonStudy. It is also recommended to examine further the universal design for learning principles within indoor and outdoor environments online.

Let's turn our attention now to environmental assessments that further assist us in preparing quality inclusive and responsive environments for children, educators, families, and the community.

EARLY CHILDHOOD FRAMEWORKS AND ENVIRONMENTAL ASSESSMENTS

Caregivers and educators use early childhood frameworks in addition to a multitude of methods to gather information on the status of responsiveness and inclusiveness in their relationships and early childhood environments. Observation methods like those mentioned in earlier chapters, including learning stories, narratives, and anecdotals, are just some of the many ways information can be gathered as a team to reflect upon and implement action or change in holistic and authentic ways. Environmental assessment measures and community early childhood frameworks of practice can add additional knowledge and learning to our professional practice, and subsequently support the creation of quality learning environments.

We have learned in this chapter and in all other chapters of this text that the act of inquiry through questions and dialogue is a sound pedagogical approach used in many early childhood frameworks around the world. These frameworks, on their own or in conjunction with observations and assessment tools, give us significant insights into and understanding of how we might continue to provide quality early childhood environments.

The observation and pedagogical documentation approaches we've discussed throughout the book are important to the environmental assessment process for they provide an authentic look and lens into an early learning environment from the perspectives of the learners within it. Let's take a look.

Environmental Assessment Tools and Measures

There is no one universal tool that is available to professionals to observe and assess all the environmental components that contribute to a meaningful "learning community" for children. Instead, a number of informal and formal tools are available to educators to aid their analysis of their learning community's strengths and needs. As you continue your research exploring these and other environmental assessment tools, be sure to consider pedagogical principles and inclusive values so that your measure meets the needs of your learners.

A number of formal assessment tools have been developed by stakeholders and agencies in different cities, provinces, and states which reflect the geographical and cultural aspects of their community. Assessment

stakeholders

People, groups, or organizations that have a direct or indirect stake in an organization because they can affect or be affected by the organization's actions, objectives, and policies.

measures like the ones below may be necessary to pattern and gain insights into the context of an environment, so as to assess its strengths and areas for improvement. Most of the checklists noted here are rating scales or checklists allowing for easy completion. Some may require multiple assessors to ensure reliability and validity in the scoring. Some of these environmental assessments include

- *SpeciaLink Child Care Inclusion Practices Profile and Principles Scale* (Lero, 2004);
- *SpeciaLink Early Childhood Inclusion Quality Scale* (Hope Irwin, 2009);
- *Infant Toddler Early Childhood Environment Rating Scale*, Third Edition (Harms, Cryer, & Clifford, 2017), the *Early Childhood Environment Rating Scale*, Third Edition (Harms, Clifford, & Cryer, 2014), and the *School Age Care Environment Rating Scale* (Harms, Jacobs, & White, 2013);
- *Family Child Care Environment Rating Scale* (Harms, Cryer, & Clifford, 2007);
- *Early Learning and Care Assessment for Quality Improvement*, available for infant, toddler, preschool, playground, nutrition, and school age (Toronto Children's Services, 2014);
- *NAEYC Accreditation Criteria for Physical Environments: Standard 9* (NAEYC, 2005);
- *Classroom Assessment Scoring System for Infants* (Hamre, Laporo, Pianta, & Locasale-Crouch, 2014), the *Classroom Assessment Scoring System for Toddlers* (Hamre, Laporo, Pianta, & Locasale-Crouch, 2012), the *Classroom Assessment Scoring System for Pre-K* (Hamre, Laporo, Pianta, & Locasale-Crouch, 2008b), and the *Classroom Assessment Scoring System for K–3* (Hamre, Laporo, Pianta, & Locasale-Crouch, 2008a). Each of these assessments measures the quality of interactions between the educator and the child, and is not philosophy-specific.
- *Rating Observation Scale for Inspiring Environments* (ROSIE) measuring the aesthetics of an early childhood environment (Deviney, Duncan, Harris, Rody, & Rosenberry, 2010);
- *Arnett Caregiver Interaction Scale* (Arnett, 1989). This scale measures the quality of interactions between the educator and the child; and
- *Australia's National Quality Standard Assessment and Rating Instrument* (Australian Government, Department of Education, Employment and Workplace Relations, 2018). This instrument is intended to assess settings against the quality standards evident in this document.

This list is not exhaustive; it is only a short list of the many comprehensive tools out there. Note that some of the measurements identified above are standardized, while others are not. Each environmental assessment will have a different focus. It is the responsibility of the educator to use, create, and/or combine assessment tools with other frameworks and authentic documentation to obtain a holistic understanding of their environment. Some are specific to certain age ranges (e.g., toddler/preschool environment) while others may focus on specific dimensions of an early learning environment.

Observers are encouraged to engage in inquiry to research some of the environmental tools listed. Note their similarities and differences. What assessment tool reflects pedagogical principles and approaches? Are there tools that invite reflection and voice from children, families, educators, and the community? Are some more culturally relevant and sensitive than others? What quality assurance or licensing assessment mechanism is used in your community to license or guide the creation of your early childhood setting? What aspects of each tool resonate with your setting's philosophy? What other tools have you come across in your research that also look at the aspect of environmental design? Web links and further information on environmental assessments are available online and on NelsonStudy.

Environmental Assessment: Stakeholder Contributions

Throughout our examination of the environment, we discussed repeatedly the importance of including the voices of children, families, and educators in the observation and documentation processes. We now turn our attention to the importance of including the community in our environmental scan or assessment.

We begin this examination on a broader scale with the following questions:

- Who could potentially be a stakeholder and thus have opportunity for observation of, influence on, and input into the creation of these environments? How can they influence what takes place?
- What environmental elements or designs would we request their perspectives on? Where do we start? What aspects of quality and environmental design might we obtain their support with?
- How do we know what is "right" for our own early childhood settings?

These questions are important to many people; their relevance moves beyond the boundaries of an early childhood setting, its staff, children, and families.

In Exhibit 8.6, we can see the various players who may at times influence or provide input into the design or environmental elements that make up a learning community. We see that governmental regulations and policy-makers (province or territory wide) as well as local or municipal licensing bodies require us to develop, implement, and/or evaluate specific environmental elements or standards mandatory for settings within their jurisdiction. For example, in a 2017 announcement, the federal government of Canada announced their plan for a new "fully inclusive child-care system" premised on universality and meeting the needs of families (Cossette, 2017).

If you were to ask families in your community if they look for quality in learning environments and surroundings for their children, 100 percent of families would say yes. Keep in mind that quality is determined by a number of factors and may vary from province to province and region to region. Each province may have their own quality assurance or environmental criteria they use to promote quality early learning and care.

One example illustrating the design and creation of a quality assessment measure that reflects collaboration with external stakeholders is the *Early Learning and Care Assessment for Quality Improvement* measure prepared by Toronto Children's Services. Developed as separate measures for infant,

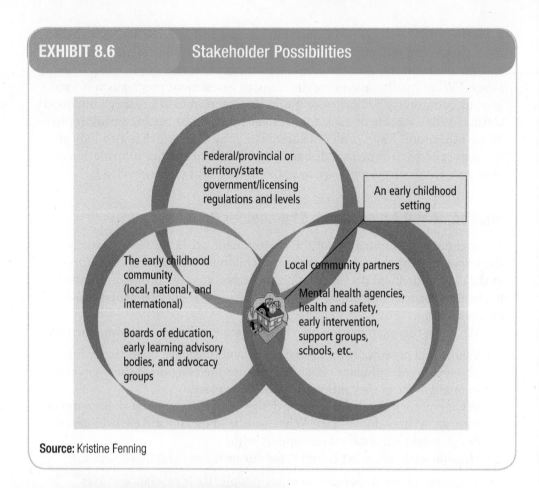

EXHIBIT 8.6   Stakeholder Possibilities

Federal/provincial or territory/state government/licensing regulations and levels

An early childhood setting

The early childhood community (local, national, and international)

Boards of education, early learning advisory bodies, and advocacy groups

Local community partners

Mental health agencies, health and safety, early intervention, support groups, schools, etc.

Source: Kristine Fenning

toddler, preschool, and school-age programs, the measures within the *Early Learning and Care Assessment for Quality Improvement* identify the environmental components being evaluated for an infant program. Measures and environmental assessment tools like this have been developed for good reason, and it is the responsibility of educators to know about, understand, and access a variety of these tools, perspectives, materials, and research to inform the best approach for their setting and the children and families within it. What licensing measures for the environment are used in your geographical area?

What do you notice about the assessment? It is designed like a rating scale, and it requires educators to reflect upon their observation and pedagogical documentation skills to ensure that children's learning and thinking have been

EXHIBIT 8.7

Early Learning and Care Assessment for Quality Improvement: Learning Experiences for Infants

Assessment: Infant	Does Not Meet Expectations ❶ or ❷	Meets Expectations ❸	Exceeds Expectations ❹ or ❺	Score
Learning experiences	❑ Learning experiences offered are not developmentally appropriate ❑ Learning experiences do not promote choice for children ❑ There is no current documentation which demonstrates that observations of children are used in the development of learning experiences	❑ Evidence of opportunities to discuss developmental progress with families ❑ Standardized Developmental Screening tool is completed for all children	❑ Photo documentation of learning experiences available ❑ Enrichment program, in addition to regular program, is included monthly ❑ Activity resources accessible for families ❑ Portfolios regarding each child's development are accessible to families	1 2 3 4 5

Source: Toronto Children's Services. (2014). *Early Learning and Care Assessment for Quality Improvement*, p. 4. Used with permission.

documented in specific ways. What environmental assessment tools do you use with your early childhood setting?

The College of Early Childhood Educators in Ontario is a regulatory body that requires educators to prepare learning environments for children that are responsive and inclusive to all learners. For example, in Standard III of the *Code of Ethics and Standards of Practice* document, the college expects licensed educators to provide "Safety, Health and Well-Being in the Learning Environment" (2017, p. 12). Exhibit 8.8 outlines the knowledge and practice skills required to demonstrate this.

It is easy to detect the "value-added" benefits when other stakeholder groups and community partners collaborate with early childhood professionals, families, and children in creating learning communities and assessment measurements that "fit" and reflect community participants. According to Martha Friendly and Jane Beach (2005), the benefit of collaboration is that

> it makes it possible to involve community members, parents and children in the issues of program delivery that are most important for them—staffing, facility design and programming—to ensure responsive programming. Above the level of the individual program, community

Chapter 8: Reflective and Transformative: Observer as Leader

A. Principle

Registered early childhood educators (RECEs) intentionally create and maintain environments that support children's play and learning as well as contribute to a sense of belonging and overall well-being. They ensure that the environment is safe and accessible for all children and families. They also ensure that the environment reflects the values and diversity of the community.

B. Knowledge

RECEs:

- Are knowledgeable about the research and theories related to the role and impact of the indoor and outdoor learning environments in curriculum design and pedagogy.
- Are familiar with a variety of strategies to promote and support children's well-being and safety in the learning environment including, but not limited to, nutrition and physical, mental and emotional health.
- Are knowledgeable about a variety of methods to monitor and evaluate the quality of learning environments.
- Know and understand safety, health and accessibility legislation.

C. Practice

RECEs:

- Work in partnership with children, families and colleagues to create a safe, healthy and inviting environment that promotes a sense of belonging, well-being and inclusion.
- Take appropriate steps to ensure that the environment complies with safety, health and accessibility legislation. They observe and monitor the learning environment and take responsibility to avoid exposing children to harmful or unsafe situations.
- Obtain and familiarize themselves with available information concerning children's relevant medical conditions, special needs, disabilities, allergies, medication requirements and emergency contact information. This information is obtained when a child comes under the RECE's professional supervision or as soon after that time as the information becomes available and is reviewed on an ongoing basis.
- Access the necessary resources and design the environment to ensure safety and inclusion for all children in the environment. They work with colleagues to embed early intervention strategies into the program and environment.
- Provide safe and appropriate supervision of children based on age, development and environment.
- Design or modify indoor and outdoor learning environments to support children's self-regulation, independence, reasonable risk-taking, meaningful exploration and positive interactions.
- Promote physical and mental health and well-being by encouraging good nutrition, physical activity and providing daily opportunities for children to connect and interact with the natural world and the outdoors.
- Consider how the environments affect children through daily care routines and transitions including meal times and snacks, personal care, sleep or rest time. They implement strategies to ensure sufficient time for safe and supportive transitions while maintaining supervision at all times.
- Use current evidence-informed methods to monitor, evaluate and improve the quality of the learning environment

Source: College of Early Childhood Educators. (2017). *The Code of Ethics and Standards of Practice: For Registered Early Childhood Educators in Ontario*, pp. 12–13.

members and parents can be involved with setting priorities, planning and quality assurance for a locally managed system. (p. 2)

One example worth noting is the Bernard Van Leer Foundation; they have provoked their readership to think larger scale regarding physical spaces in cities for children. In the November 2014 article entitled "Small Children, Big Cities," Lisa Karsten was interviewed saying she has observed that "children used to be seen as resilient, whereas today they are primarily seen as vulnerable" (Cary, 2014, p. 5). This statement speaks volumes about the need for stakeholders to think about the physical design of community natural outdoor space in order to challenge children to take risks and explore their environments independently without constraints, allowing them to build resiliency. Lisa Karsten also states that it is important to observe and document the changing landscape of childhood within the context of family life and lifestyles so that cities can improve physical environments to prompt more children to connect to the outdoors. The cycle of observation supports this level of examination by educators, families, children, and stakeholders to create the best possible experiences for children within their natural environments.

Environmental Assessment, Pedagogy, and Context: Voices of Children and Adults

We've learned the importance of beginning an inquiry with a question, for it leads us to many new discoveries about our practice. We also understand that use of any of the assessment tools mentioned earlier yields valuable information about environmental design, use, materials, interactions, and other areas. We finish this environmental component by bringing you back to the voices of children and adults. No matter what approach is taken to collect information about an early childhood environment, nothing is more important than ensuring that all voices, observations, and pedagogical documentation collected and shared by all members within an early childhood environment are heard and respected. In doing this, quality is enhanced in our curriculum, our materials, our interactions, and our environment.

THE OBSERVER AS PEDAGOGICAL LEADER: BUILDING SUSTAINABILITY IN OBSERVATION AND PEDAGOGICAL DOCUMENTATION

Appreciative inquiry is a concept and practice that has guided us in our learning throughout this text. We therefore begin with a question and new inquiry: why are we talking about pedagogical leadership in a book about observation and pedagogical documentation? Pedagogical leadership has its own unique set of questions beginning with the most fundamental inquiry: what does it mean? In the online article "Pedagogical Leadership," authors Coughlin and Baird (2013) define pedagogical leadership by simply stating,

IS_ImageSource/iStockphoto.com

Pedagogy can be defined as the understanding of how learning takes place and the philosophy and practice that supports that understanding of learning. Essentially it is the study of the teaching and learning process. Leadership is often defined as the act of leading or guiding individuals or groups. If we are to combine these two we are offered the notion of pedagogical leadership as leading or guiding the study of the teaching and learning process. (p. 1)

As shown in Exhibit 8.9, central to leadership is developing relationships and trust with people involved while learning everything possible about a project, situation, or endeavour. In the photo, led by Dr. Diane Kashin and Louise Jupp, educators and teachers are engaged in dialogue about their teaching and learning experiences regarding the development of learning stories and portfolios for children within their classrooms. In this dialogue educators question, problem solve, and share the way in which these pieces are created, how they involve the families, and how they fit pedagogical documentation into everyday practice considering the multifaceted roles they must fulfill during the course of the day.

Leadership evolves and influences over time. Every province in Canada had those early pioneers who developed standards of practice and worked with great perseverance to establish early childhood as a profession. Their work

| EXHIBIT 8.9 | Leadership in Teaching and Learning: Sharing Portfolio Strategies |

Reggio Summer Intensive, Acorn School / Kristine Fenning

Evidenced by this photo, central to leadership is the development of relationships and trust with others while learning everything possible about a project, situation, or endeavour.

continues through this generation of educators and will continue to influence future early childhood professionals.

Can leadership be demonstrated without the benefit of institutions, agencies, or schools? Educators, parents, resource professionals, and many other members of an early learning community hold the potential to lead and guide others. Leadership does not have to stem from the "top"; leadership can come from within oneself because it is not restricted by gender, culture, language, ability, or any other aspect of a person. Many of us likely know several educators and parents who started out simply with a passion for advocating for a child with special needs and, through their experiences and struggles, took a leadership role in advocating for all children and their families, not just their own child. Such is the example of Georgina Rayner, who is a parent advocate. She is on several boards of directors of agencies such as Aspergers Ontario and the Centre for ADHD Awareness, Canada (CADDAC).

Pedagogical leadership within the early childhood profession can be demonstrated in a number of ways. Pedagogical leadership as it relates to observation has prompted trends in pedagogical documentation resulting in a number of new trends in observation, as discussed in earlier chapters. Dr. Diane Kashin and Louise Jupp (2013) capture some of these trends as they describe the changing definition of a pedagogical leader:

> Now a pedagogical leader can disseminate information through social media platforms like Facebook, Twitter, and Pinterest. Kagan and Bowman (1997) also suggest that pedagogical leadership is linked to:
>
> • How you believe children learn best
> • Your program philosophy, goals and everyday practices
>
> Being a pedagogical leader is value laden. How you lead reflects your underlying philosophy. If you believe as we do that children learn best in a social construct that is collaborative, reciprocal and respectful then you too will recognize teachers learn best that way as well! ("What Is a Pedagogical Leader?" para. 2)

Observer as Mentor: The Important Role of Mentorship

Mentoring is one of many leadership approaches aimed at capacity building in early childhood education with regards to observation and pedagogical documentation, quality in early childhood settings, and overall professional practice. According to Wong and Waniganayake (2013), "Mentoring is a facilitated process involving two or more individuals that have a shared interest in professional learning and development. . . . It has been shown to boost teachers' professional confidence, identity and their willingness to participate in professional learning" (p. 163). Mentorship also builds social capital, for it builds a social network of teams and professionals that ultimately benefits the learning community.

Traditional and historical approaches to mentoring typically involved persons in higher authority such as supervisors or directors mentoring and guiding their staff. While it is still important for supervisors and directors to provide this leadership role, mentoring can occur between any two people for any

capacity building

Refers to all stakeholders within a community network who are working collaboratively to provide support, resources, services, and opportunities to strengthen all members and promote their success within their community.

particular purpose. Viewing mentoring from an appreciative lens, its intention is to lend a voice and feedback mechanism to two or more people desiring to build knowledge and skill, share in teaching and learning with and from one another, and co-construct new knowledge together. Each participant (child, educator, family) in the mentoring relationship may hold knowledge and expertise (in this case, regarding observation and pedagogical documentation) they wish to share with the other. Long term or short term in nature, this proactive, educational, and reflective approach assists those who participate to build capacity for positive change in professional practice. It requires a number of skills to be present in the person who desires to mentor someone else, including having the ability to self-reflect, collaborate with others as a team member, take risks, appreciate and respect the perspectives of others, and be open to change.

"Often success is forged in the workplace by the existence of a local mentor or pedagogical leader who has a vision for the capacity building of staff, and willingness to support the growth and the implementation of ideas (Carter & Curtis, 2010). The mentor acts as someone to encourage, to exchange ideas with, to assist in deciphering and contextualizing information and to 'risk take' alongside (Peterson, 2000, p. 13)."

Source: Brown, A., & Inglis, S. (March, 2013). "So What Happens after the Event? Exploring the Realization of Professional Development with Early Childhood Educators." *Australasian Journal of Early Childhood, 38*(1), 11–15.

Association of Early Childhood Educators of Ontario (AECEO)

A non-profit professional organization committed to advocating, supporting, and promoting the early childhood profession. This is demonstrated through the provision of professional development, research, and actions that support capacity building in the community.

continuous professional learning

Continually developing, planning for, and improving one's skills and knowledge in order to promote quality and maintain competence throughout one's career.

Whether you are a preservice educator about to embark upon your first position or a seasoned educator in the profession, it is important to engage in mentoring practices that support observation, reflection, and pedagogical documentation. It is through this supportive team approach that innovative ideas and approaches are generated, the voices of everyone are reflected, and quality environments are created.

Observer as Lifelong Learner: The Importance of Continuous Professional Learning

Over the last five to ten years, significant changes have occurred in the early childhood profession, one of which has been increased emphasis on having well-trained, knowledgeable, responsive, and inclusive educators working in early childhood settings. The College of Early Childhood Educators (CECE), the Association of Early Childhood Educators of Ontario (AECEO), and changes to the *Early Childhood Educators Act* all place value and emphasis on continuous professional learning for educators. The Child Care and Early Years Act, 2014 indicates that registered educators in Ontario are expected to engage in a continuous professional learning program in order to maintain their registration with the College of Early Childhood Educators (CECE, 2014b). "Continuous professional learning refers to the systematic and intentional maintenance and expansion of the knowledge, skills, and ethical values and behaviours necessary to ensure ongoing quality professional practice throughout an early childhood educator's career" (CECE, 2017, p. 4). As you reflect upon Ontario expectations, what are the expectations in your community for continuous professional learning?

It is a professional and ethical responsibility of registered early childhood educators to engage in continuous professional learning, particularly in the areas of observation and pedagogical documentation. Children and families deserve to have educators who are competent, reflective leaders committed to co-creating the best possible pedagogical documentation possible.

Reflecting back on previous chapters, we are reminded of the importance of questioning, inquiry, and evaluation of our own professional practice, including reflection upon ourselves as professional educators so that we might meet the needs of our children, families, and communities. In addition to engaging in continuous professional learning, learning can also be achieved by providing training to others, sharing your knowledge, and co-constructing new knowledge together. The following photo illustrates educators coming together for professional development purposes, engaging in conversation to examine how they might document children's learning. It is through this process that they begin to inquire and question the environment, materials, and space through a child's perspective. In the photo, Helen, a kindergarten teacher and lifelong learner, documents her exploration of light through photo narratives on her cellphone while tweeting her learning through social media and text to colleagues who are part of an online community of educators interested in pedagogical documentation with young children. This social media connection allows her to engage her families and children in co-creating, co-documenting, co-leading, and co-learning together in real time. Be sure to visit some of the suggested blogs and Twitter feeds provided online demonstrating the leadership of teachers and educators like Helen.

Reggio Summer Intensive, Acorn School / Kristine Fenning

EXHIBIT 8.10   Reflective Practitioners

Reflective practitioners integrate theoretical frameworks, research findings and their own daily experiences to guide their interactions with young children and their families. Reflective practitioners figure out how the children in their program think, learn, and make sense of the world. They know what the children are currently capable of doing and what next steps are possible. Responsive adults help to focus children's observations, use language that describes events and ask questions that provoke children's thinking. Thus, curriculum is meaningful when there are clear matches between a child's current knowledge and interests and the opportunities provided. (p. 19)

Ontario Ministry of Children, Community, and Youth Services, Best Start Expert Panel on Early Learning. (2007, January). *Early Learning for Every Child Today: A Framework for Ontario Early Childhood Settings*, p. 19. Copyright Queen's Printer for Ontario, (2007). Used with permission.

EXHIBIT 8.11   Co-constructing Learning

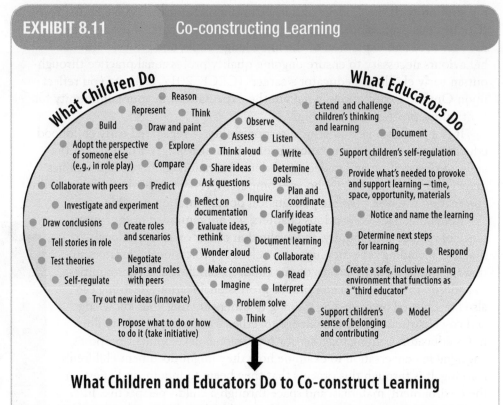

What Children and Educators Do to Co-construct Learning

Ontario Ministry of Education. (2016). "What Children and Educators Do To Co-Construct Learning." *The Kindergarten Program*, p. 25. Copyright the Queen's Printer for Ontario. Reproduced with permission.

Continuous Professional Learning, Action Research, and Pedagogical Documentation   As educators, we have the privilege of having ongoing daily interactions with observation and pedagogical documentation. Combined with our ongoing engagement in the cycle of observation, we become open to transformation in all elements of our professional practice. Collaboration with children, families, and the community as part of the cycle also enables us to develop new ways of thinking and doing in our observation and pedagogical documentation practices. If we examine Exhibit 8.11, we can easily view the plethora of ways in which we might co-construct new learning in our practice every day.

Essentially we are continually in a cycle of "think-do-think" (MacNaughton & Hughes, 2008, p.1), a cycle associated with continuous professional learning and action research. This form of research prompts us to think about our observation and pedagogical documentation practices in a variety of ways.

> Action researchers improve their practice (what they do) both by changing their practice and by finding new ways to think about it. Each of us tries to make sense of our world by studying it in order to decide how to act in it. We observe our surroundings, think about our observations, act accordingly and then observe whether and to what extent our actions had the effect we wanted. (MacNaughton & Hughes, 2008, pp. 8–10)

If we were to start with a question to prompt the thinking of new ideas or ways of doing, we might think about

- how we might move our observational practices beyond the Westernized lens; how we might want to observe, listen, and document more about our learnings with the Truth and Reconciliation Commission of Canada and about the power of storytelling and spiritual narratives from Indigenous elders;
- how to promote children's voice and perspectives in our program; and
- how to follow children's inquiries, and how to transform them into pedagogical documentation.

There are many possibilities to reflect upon. Exhibit 8.12 provides us with a reflection in action template to assist educators in looking at aspects of their environment. Examining what is working, what isn't working, and where we need to change our paradigms of practice are necessary as observation and pedagogical documentation expect observers to be reflective at heart and inquisitive in nature.

Be sure to visit NelsonStudy for exercises that explore action research as it relates to observation and pedagogical documentation.

EXHIBIT 8.12	Reflecting upon Professional Practice and the Learning Environment	
Reflection and Next Steps		
	What am/are I/we thinking or wondering about, as a result of this learning?	**How might I/we act on my/our wonderings?**
Repeating These practices have proven successful and are supported by current research.		
Re-thinking These practices have had some measure of success but may need some modifying to enhance their effectiveness.		
Removing These practices have had little measure of success and are not supported by current research.		
Replacing These practices are based on current research and have proven successful for others.		

Adapted from Ontario Ministry of Education. (2016). *Assessing Learning in the Four Frames Learning Module.* Copyright the Queen's Printer for Ontario. Reproduced with permission.

Using the template in Exhibit 8.12, and combining it with an active research and appreciative inquiry approach, think about your current observation and pedagogical documentation practices. Considering all that you have learned about observing children and the environment, which aspects of your practice do you wish to repeat (continue doing), rethink (that there could be a better way of doing something), remove (do not use it anymore—perhaps it is irrelevant or lacks currency), or replace (with something new).

Share with your colleagues or peers: What was similar or different? What might you prioritize?

PEDAGOGICAL DOCUMENTATION AND EDUCATOR E-PORTFOLIOS

Chapter 6 introduced us to the use of e-portfolios in early childhood education as a way in which to document children's learning in a digital way. We can apply that discussion directly to our new discussion here on educator e-portfolios. The use of e-portfolios for educator development provides an excellent forum for reflection and self-evaluation of one's growth and development, goal setting, and demonstration of learning. Educators like Helen mentioned previously in earlier pages, can incorporate their continuous professional learning opportunities into the professional practice and e-portfolios to reflect their development over time. This allows them to store, discuss, and share their teaching and learning journey with their superiors, families, or other educators.

> Early childhood teachers believe in constructing knowledge and experiential learning. One major advantage of creating an e-portfolio is that . . . you are learning to construct your portfolio by putting into practice skills and abilities using technology and the Internet. You are also learning the technological skills that the profession now agrees are important to teaching. Many of the skills that you acquire can be passed on to children. You can teach them to gather information, research topics, access data, and create reports using today's tools: the computer and the Internet. (Lowe Friedman, 2012, p. 114)

E-Portfolio Design and Considerations

If embarking upon e-portfolio creation for the first time, be assured that any one of the e-portfolio websites mentioned in Chapter 6 possesses tutorials that will walk you through the set-up of a site. Many will say to consult with children when embarking on this process, as they often possess the computer literacy skills required to navigate different toolbars and computer language. They have much to teach us!

Most postsecondary institutions that have an early childhood program prepare preservice educators with e-portfolios that outline their acquired knowledge, skills, and attitudes relating to the profession for future use in interviews with employers. If you are a seasoned educator about to embark on this journey, we recommend that you consult with various preservice educator

Rebecca Martin
E.C.A.S., Hons B.A.

in ✉

Home

Self Assessment

Professional Goals

Resourcing Philosophy

Professional
Development

Course Summaries

Academic Recognition

Certifications

Resume, Cover Letter
& Professional
References

Reference Page

As a June 2014 Graduate from Humber College's Early Childhood Advanced Studies in Special Needs Program, Rebecca is passionate, professional, and dedicated to helping children and families with special needs.

LinkedIn Profile: http://www.linkedin.com/pub/rebecca-martin/85/a96/a27

Kristine Fenning

portfolio websites to assist you in determining your presentation design, how to organize your artifacts, and how best to feature key knowledge you wish to profile. An advantage of the electronic nature of this portfolio is that educators can populate their site with videos of their professional practice, including their work with children, interactions and classroom design, curriculum examples aligned with the *Ontario Early Learning Framework*, and much more! Once begun, educators will be amazed by what they have accomplished over time to evolve their skills. Like children's e-portfolios, consideration of confidentiality and ethics is a necessary step in e-portfolio creation. Examples of sites that feature educator e-portfolios are provided online.

Observer as Researcher: Longitudinal Studies and Ethnographic Research

The early childhood profession is changing at a rapid pace; this means a core responsibility of current and future educators is to stay abreast of requirements and changing expectations in the profession, as well as to look at ways to lead the profession. To do this well, it is important for educators to also think about engaging in observational research opportunities to further inform their practice, as well as to contribute their own publications back to the profession.

In Chapter 1, we introduced you to the role of the educator with ethnographic research and its relevance to longitudinal studies. There may be opportunities in your career path to work inter-professionally or within the profession on research relating to early childhood education. Longitudinal studies, research conducted over an extended period of time, are used to confirm the relevance of a particular practice, explore the merits of government policy, or examine issues such as childhood obesity, low infant birth rates, or the impact of funding on certain early childhood programs.

Decades of research go into the investigation of theories and policies before human resources capital is dedicated. Policymakers, economists, government officials, and early childhood professionals must consider multiple variables and factors during a specific time frame to put forward their case.

To illustrate the complexity of this kind of research, check out the three most referenced longitudinal studies on the impact of preschool education on children from disadvantaged backgrounds:

> Ypsilanti's Perry Preschool [initiated in 1962], the Abecedarian study in North Carolina [1972] and the Chicago Child-Parent Centers [1967] have tracked their original cohorts for up to four decades. Each study was unique, but all provided a group program emphasizing parent involvement and the development of children's literacy skills. (McCuaig, 2013, p. 1)

See McCuaig (2013) for a thorough discussion of these longitudinal studies.

CHAPTER REFLECTIONS

1. There is significant interplay and relationship that occurs between children and their learning environment(s). Depending upon how environments are designed, they can either make a child feel included and that they belong, or they can demotivate and disengage children due to not being responsive or reflecting things they are interested in. As educators it is important to observe how children interact with different spaces, and how they respond to others, the ambiance, and different components of their day. The environment is more than just the physical space—it also encompasses the socio-emotional/psychological ambiance and temporal components. There are a number of considerations within each area that can be made to promote accessibility and reduce barriers (UDL) for all children to ensure a positive learning experience. These three components are expansive in nature; consult with this chapter for more information.

2. The intention of environmental assessments is to assist educators to create quality learning environments for children and families. Most are rating scale or checklist based, requiring one or more assessors (primarily educators) to rate specific components within the learning environment. Many environmental tools are standardized requiring a specific process to follow in their implementation. Each environmental tool is geared toward specific age groups as different learning environments require different types of materials for their learners. Licensing and quality assurance typically require the assessment of the environment for children as a measure of quality child care.

3. It is through observation and appreciative inquiry that educators/observers are able to gain new knowledge, insights, and skills to apply to their professional practice. This informs how to co-design and co-prepare learning environments that are responsive and inclusive for all children. Leadership and mentorship are integral to the sustainability of observation, appreciative inquiry, and pedagogical documentation. When we take the time to mentor others, we build communities of practice that support new and exciting ways to document and make visible the learning of children, families, and educators.

4. Action research involves a process of "think-do-think" (MacNaughton & Hughes, 2008, p. 1) and is intended to provoke educators and other members of the team to think about their practice (in this case, observation and pedagogical documentation) in new and different ways. Observation teams may reflect upon, "What do we want to change, why we need to make the change, and how we might plan to make that change?" This aligns with

the cycle of observation in that reflection and observation help inform next steps in how we might respond. Centres who may need support in changing their observation practices are encouraged to engage in this action research cycle to support positive changes in their approach.

5. Continuous professional learning and e-portfolios for educators have become an expectation of the profession. Why? What impact do they have on our observational practices? The early childhood profession is not stagnant but, rather, an exciting profession in constant change. Expectations of the profession, specifically licensing and standards of practice, include educators honing their observation and pedagogical documentation skills to document not only children's thinking but also their own thinking and development. Ongoing development contributes to quality in our abilities to support children and families in the early childhood setting. Children and families deserve to have well-informed educators supporting them.

Chapter 8: Reflective and Transformative: Observer as Leader

Glossary

ABC analysis (p. 187)
A type of documentation that records a sequence of related events over time.

abscissas (p. 185)
Plotted on the horizontal axis of a graph.

accommodate (p. 109)
To bring into agreement; for example, adapt new information to previous knowledge.

accommodations (p. 289)
Resources or adaptations that can support a child or individual to fully participate and/or attain the same grade level as his or her peers.

action research (pp. 21 & 275)
Involves selecting an aspect of professional practice that one wishes to change or improve as well as formulating questions and making a plan for change; a collaborative and reflective inquiry process assumed by a community or team of individuals who actively research, plan, and implement solutions to solve real problems and/or improve practice.

advocate (p. 29)
Someone who amplifies a client's voice, gives support, and pursues objectives according to instruction while empowering the client to self-advocacy.

agentic (p. 8)
Introduced by Albert Bandura whereby the child is seen as a contributing being and shares equal power with the adult. Power is seen to be balanced and shared between the adult and the child.

analogue (p. 187)
Something similar in function or comparable with another; a model.

anecdotal record (p. 119)
A narrative form of observation, a word picture, a description so clearly written that when read, the image of what is seen and heard immediately comes to mind. Anecdotal records capture spontaneous behaviour as it occurs.

antecedent (p. 187)
Occurring before; prior to; preceding.

anti-oppressive approach (p. 21)
Intended to reduce the potential for oppression and abuse of power between adult and child, and views children as capable and competent members of an early childhood community.

AODA (Accessibility for Ontarians with Disabilities Act) (p. 221)
A law requiring the identification and removal of barriers for those diagnosed with special needs or disabilities.

appreciative inquiry (p. 6)
Relating to the cycle of observation, appreciative inquiry prompts observers to query their practice and engage in processes that will assist them in achieving positive change.

artifacts (p. 138)
Objects that are representative of a culture and are made by a human being, typically an item of cultural or historical interest.

assessment portfolio (p. 246)
A collection of documentation in hard copy or digital form that show a child's growth or change over time; it may help in the hard copy process of self-evaluation and goal setting, identify areas of focus, or track development of one domain or more.

Association of Early Childhood Educators of Ontario (AECEO) (p. 320)
A nonprofit professional organization committed to advocating, supporting, and promoting the early childhood profession. This is demonstrated through the provision of professional development, research, and actions that support capacity building in the community.

audio recording (p. 150)
A way of recording sound waves, such as spoken voice, singing, instrumental music, or sound effects.

aural (p. 150)
Referring to hearing or concerning the ear.

authentic assessment (p. 234)
An assessment that is connected to practical, pragmatic, real-world skills to demonstrate performance and understanding.

autism (p. 273)
A lifelong neurological and developmental disorder that may affect one's ability to develop relationships, communicate with others, and function intellectually.

behaviour (p. 187)
Anything that can be seen, measured, or counted. Additionally, it can be defined as the way one conducts oneself.

behaviour tallying (p. 182)
Counting a specific behaviour or monitoring the frequency of a behaviour and adding it up.

best practices (p. 29)
Based on or originating from evidence-based research and outcomes, these are ideal practices suggested by the early learning and care profession or other agencies or licensing bodies.

biases (p. 44)
Preconceived ideas or attitudes (personal or philosophical) that affect objectivity; prejudice.

Boardmaker (p. 201)
A picture-based electronic library used to create a variety of communication or print visuals to individuals with aspects of their learning, communication, and understanding. Examples include schedules, transitions, and pictures for a picture exchange system.

capacity building (p. 319)
Refers to all stakeholders within a community network who are working collaboratively to provide support, resources, services, and opportunities to strengthen all members and promote their success within their community.

caveat (p. 107)
A warning or specification of conditions that must be considered before taking action.

central tendency error (p. 112)
A judgment error that evaluates all children the same way, regardless of their individual characteristics.

checklist (p. 172)
A type of record providing a list of items that, if present, are marked or checked off.

child-centred environment (p. 301)
An environment adapted to meet the interests, strengths, and needs of children.

child-sensitive (p. 24)
Attitudes, awareness, and practices that demonstrate care and sensitivity to the uniqueness of each child and his or her family and culture in a group setting.

closed methods (p. 168)
Records or methods used for targeted behaviours.

code of ethics (p. 35)
Guidelines for responsible behaviour; principles and practices that guide the moral and ethical conduct of professionals in a field or discipline.

coding scheme (p. 173)
A design or diagram using a specific symbol to represent an idea; for example, colour coding to chart various activities.

consequence (p. 187)
Relation of an effect to its cause; a natural or necessary result.

contextual information (p. 121)
Relevant information from the environment that directly or indirectly influences the behaviour of a child; information that helps explain or give meaning to a child's behaviour.

continuous professional learning (p. 320)
Continually developing, planning for, and improving one's skills and knowledge in order to promote quality and maintain competence throughout one's career.

continuum (p. 179)
A continuous line of reference.

contrived observation (p. 124)
Observation that is prearranged for a specific purpose in a formal or informal setting.

criterion-referenced assessment tools (p. 282)
Fixed standards used to evaluate an individual's performance; points of reference used when an individual is assessed against himself or herself rather than compared to the performance of others.

cultural bias (p. 113)
The action of interpreting what one sees by the values, beliefs, and principles attributed to one's own culture.

cultural safety (p. 285)
An environment in which people feel spiritually, socially, emotionally, and physically safe, and are able to express their identity.

culturally responsive (p. 113)
The act of being respectful toward others and using and incorporating knowledge of another's culture, beliefs, values, and approaches to learning to be both responsive and inclusive.

cycle of observation (p. 33)
This cycle, grounded in ethics, integrity, anti-oppression, family- and child-centredness, and responsive and inclusive values, outlines the many interactive and appreciative components of the observation process.

descriptors (p. 85)
Words or phrases that characterize an idea or item; the adjectives used to rate the items of a rating scale continuum.

developmental assessment (p. 268)
Diagnostic or informal assessment meant to ascertain an individual's current level of functioning in all domains of development.

developmental pediatrician (p. 289)
A physician with the credentials to diagnose special needs or attend to special needs or extra-support concerns for individuals.

dexterity (p. 106)
Skilled physical movement or ease of use, typically relating to the hands.

didactic (p. 214)
Meant to intentionally teach, guide, or instruct.

direct quotations (p. 84)
When exact words have been used in another source and are supported with quotation marks to indicate the exact phrasing selected.

display or showcase portfolio (p. 244)
A digital or hard copy portfolio that showcases end-of-year/semester accomplishments (according to an educator) or children's/students' perspectives of their best or most important work; also a means to communicate a child's current interests, skills, and inquiries.

diversity (p. 13)
A reference to a range of categories, such as those of culture, religion, ethnicity, abilities, or beliefs.

documentation panels (p. 137)
Panels that display the ideas and feelings of a child or group of children through artwork, photographs, and text.

domains (p. 106)
Spheres of activity or function; psychology; areas (of development); for example, cognitive, gross motor.

duration (p. 170)
The time frame within which an action occurs; how long something lasts.

Duty to Report (p. 22)
Professionals who are concerned with children's safety, and who have reasonable grounds to feel a child requires protection, must report all suspicions and necessary information to a Children's Aid Society.

early intervention/early identification (p. 257)
A system or set of social and educational services and supports aimed to provide referrals, supports, and resources for children with extra-support or special needs and their families.

eclectic approach (p. 30)
A method of selecting what seem to be the best practices from various philosophies or programs.

ecological approach (p. 197)
An approach for understanding a child's development in terms of the environment, which includes family, neighbourhood, or community.

emergent curriculum (p. 10)
A form of curriculum development where educators follow the children's leads by observing their interests, skills, areas for improvement, and family and community cultures, and then reflect, document, and plan accordingly.

emotional intelligence (p. 30)
Often associated with highly sociable, self-reflective, emotionally focused, communicative, and motivated individuals who are able to manage relationships well, and who can easily identify with the needs and desires of others.

e-portfolio (p. 247)
An electronic portfolio that contains a purposefully selected collection of documentation over time; similar to a traditional portfolio but presented electronically.

ethics (p. 33)
A set of beliefs or guiding principles one uses to understand the difference between right and wrong, and demonstrating these principles in our actions, words, and attitudes.

expanded observation (p. 123)
Multiple observations of one child from different settings, during different times, or with other educators and, as a result, will include multiple examples of behaviour.

expectancy or logical error (p. 112)
An assumption made about two seemingly related behaviours, without a base from direct observation.

family support plan (p. 268)
A written plan created in collaboration with a family outlining resources, services, goals and objectives, and roles assumed by family and/or professionals. This plan varies according to the agency in terms of content and format.

family tree (p. 201)
A diagram (sometimes in the form of a symbolic tree with branches detailing names of relatives) outlining the ancestry, connections, and relationships between people within multiple generations of a family.

fixed standard (p. 282)
A rule, principle, or measure established by an authority that is accepted without deviation.

formative assessment (p. 138)
Evaluation that can be done at any point for reasons identified by the team. Through discussion and reflection, the team can make changes as the process evolves.

formative evaluation (p. 276)
Evaluation that can be done at any point for reasons identified by any members of the team. Through discussion and reflection, the team can make changes as the process evolves.

Four Directions (p. 20)
In the medicine wheel are the mental, emotional, physical, and spiritual aspects of humanness; the four primary elements of earth, air, fire, and water; and the four stages of human life.

frequency (p. 170)
The number of times a specific incident occurs.

Gender Schema and Developmental Intergroup Theory (p. 90)
Theories proposing that as children acquire their gender identity, they are also subject to developing knowledge, bias, and stereotypes about gender roles and behaviours from observing and interacting with their social environment(s) (e.g. culture, society, peers, family).

generic (p. 29)
Relating to or descriptive of an entire group or class; universal.

goals (p. 290)
Generalized statements of intended change in direction, ability, knowledge, or outcomes. They are usually composed of a number of objectives that support movement toward and attainment of the intended goals.

guide (p. 106)
To direct the way with the implication being that those following will benefit.

High Scope (p. 30)
A curriculum model based on a constructivist approach originating from David Weikart. Through hands-on experiences, children engage in a plan-do-review cycle to direct and scaffold their own learning. Adults and children are partners in learning.

Identification, Placement, and Review Committee (IPRC) (p. 266)
A school committee created to support children with diagnosed special needs and their families. They make decisions regarding identification (categorization of special needs) and placement for children as per the Ontario Ministry of Education requirements.

incidence (p. 287)
The frequency, rate, or number of times something happens or occurs.

inclusion (p. 5)
An attitude, a process, and a concept that accepts, respects, and embraces equal opportunity and individuality of people, regardless of ability, race, class, gender, language, ethnicity, age, sexual orientation, family, beliefs, or values.

Individual Education Plan (IEP) (p. 289)
A document outlining a child's strengths, interests, and skills to be developed (needs) in each developmental domain; may include other aspects such as goals, adaptations and/or accommodations required, an evaluation date, and who is responsible for implementation.

Individual Family Support Plan (IFSP) (p. 290)
A family-centred written plan of action outlining their strengths, their goals and priorities, services and supports currently being received or required, directions of service, timelines, and what roles are being assumed by each member.

Individual Program Plan (IPP) (p. 289)
Captures the strengths, developing skills, and interests of an individual. It is collaboratively developed by those who work directly with the individual (e.g., parent, educator, outside professionals) and changes as the individual changes and evolves.

Individual Training/Teaching Plan (ITP) (p. 289)
An alternative name for an action plan for a child, outlining items as specified in an IEP.

inference (p. 99)
An opinion based on given data or assumptions; judgment.

integrity (p. 33)
Demonstrating the values of honesty, trust, fairness, respect, responsibility, and courage in our observation and documentation practices.

interpretations (p. 109)
Subjective responses to what is observed; personal or professional judgments or beliefs.

interprofessional education (p. 268)
Professionals from different and same disciplines working within their scope of practice to collaborate, educate, and learn about the roles of other members of the team for the betterment of a client.

inter-rater reliability (p. 182)
The degree to which persons who are evaluating a particular behaviour or competency agree that the results are reliable; a method of controlling bias.

interview (p. 204)
A face-to-face meeting, usually within a formal context for a specific purpose.

key feature (p. 119)
An integral or central part or component of something.

labelling (p. 102)
To attach a term or phrase to a person or thing that classifies or characterizes him, her, or it.

learning stories (p. 142)
A narrative approach incorporating the feelings, actions, strengths, needs, and interests of a child or group of children.

leniency bias (p. 112)
A common judgmental bias that occurs when the observer is overly generous when rating children.

Livescribe pen (p. 152)
This is a ballpoint smart pen housing an embedded computer and digital audio recorder. While the individual writes, it records audio for digital uploading to a computer for transcription.

longitudinal research (p. 297)
Observational studies consisting of research over extended periods of time.

loose parts (p. 307)
Open-ended natural or manufactured materials (e.g., stones, sticks, logs, cones) used creatively for "possibility thinking" and play opportunities.

mapping (p. 204)
A graphic representation (map or visual drawing) detailing the context of the environment and movements of a child/group of children.

meta-learning/meta-cognition (p. 9)
Self-discovery and learning about how one learns.

microcosm (p. 26)
A small representational system with the characteristics of a larger system; a little world.

mindfulness (p. 42)
The ability to be in the moment in a non-judgmental way, while being aware of context, feelings, thoughts, and actions.

modifications (p. 289)
Different from accommodations and specific to education, modifications involve changing the level of academic performance expected, resulting in the student attaining learning outcomes not within the same grade level or prescribed curriculum as their peers.

monitor (p. 21)
To check or test a process in a systematic fashion.

monitoring (p. 276)
Periodic assessment of a person or event to inform the state of compliance with an expectation, objective, or outcome.

Montessori school (p. 30)
A program employing the principles and teachings of Maria Montessori, known as the first female physician in Italy. Children learn at their own pace through discovery, using all five senses to understand their world.

narrative (p. 77)
The describing or telling of an event involving characters and setting; a story.

natural design (p. 307)
Environmental design that incorporates natural materials and natural elements in an indoor or outdoor play space.

natural observation (p. 124)
Observation that is recorded as it happens within a familiar environment.

non-standardized (p. 277)
An informal method not based on validity or reliability measures. This type of assessment is intended to capture the thinking and learning of the person being observed in an authentic way.

objectify (p. 4)
Seeing only the development of children and their ability to achieve/not achieve knowledge and skills (as per an assessment process). Children are not seen holistically, and are often not viewed as competent and capable beings.

objectives (p. 290)
Goals that can be reasonably achieved within an expected time frame and with available resources.

observation cycle
See *cycle of observation*.

observational drift (p. 112)
A common error made by teachers when observing a targeted behaviour with an ambiguous definition; for example, sharing.

occupational standards (p. 22)
Standards in Canada that have been developed to define acceptable professional behaviour and the knowledge required for a particular occupation.

open method (p. 117)
Records or methods used for unanticipated behaviours and thinking.

operant conditioning (p. 188)
Associated with B.F. Skinner and Ivan Pavlov, it is a form of behaviour modification using positive or negative reinforcement to increase or decrease a behaviour under the same conditions or circumstances.

ordinates (p. 185)
Plotted on the vertical axis of a graph.

orthotics (p. 303)
Braces, pads, and/or splints designed and created specifically to provide assistance, support, and strength for parts of the body, particularly the foot and ankle.

palmar grasp (p. 106)
A grasp whereby the tool or utensil lies across the palm of the hand with fingers curled around it, and the arm, rather than the wrist, moves the tool.

paradigm shift (p. 144)
To have a sudden change in perception, a change in a point of view, of how you see a set of assumptions, concepts, values, and practices that constitutes a way of viewing reality.

paraphrasing (p. 84)
To say the same thing but in other words; a restatement; to give meaning in another form.

paraprofessional (p. 263)
A trained person who works under the guidance of a more qualified professional in that field.

participation chart (p. 168)
A method in chart form of recording the participation of one or more children engaged in the environment, noting the areas where they play, their playmates, duration of time, and any other pertinent information.

participatory mode (p. 84)
Observing simultaneously while engaged or interacting with children or within the environment.

patterning (p. 122)
Determining the repetition or recurrence of behaviour. Common behaviours of individuals can be easily patterned through the integration of information gathered from various observation tools, looking for common or similar actions or skills.

patterns (p. 178)
Observable reoccurring behaviours that become predictable or sequential skill development that follows a particular model or relationship.

pedagogical documentation (p. 2)
A shared documentation and pedagogical process intended to make visible the thinking, inquiries, and theories of children and others. It involves listening, observing, reflection, and analysis to prompt new and more complex learning and thinking.

pedagogical practices (p. 211)
Practices that provide multiple opportunities for students to engage in intellectually challenging and real-world learning experiences; educator practices that are child focused with learning activities that may reflect a particular philosophy.

pedagogy (p. 18)
The art or practice of a profession of teaching or instruction.

peer-reviewed research (p. 163)
Articles/research that are reviewed by experts in the field for authenticity in the subject matter.

perceived surveillance (p. 47)
Being aware or thinking that one is being watched and documented in a variety of ways (e.g., photo, video, hard copy documentation) all the time; lacking privacy.

perception (p. 124)
An intuitive judgment often implying subtle personal bias; insight.

pincer grasp (p. 106)
A grasp whereby small objects are picked up using the thumb and forefinger.

pictorial representations (p. 200)
Visual images that are drawn, painted, or photographed, used to represent an idea.

play-based curriculum (p. 10)
A form of curriculum and learning based on the child's play interests and competencies, with its methodology reflected in journaling, documentation, and an educator's reflective practices.

play therapist (p. 124)
A therapist or consultant who specializes in working with children in a play-based environment to assist with their social, emotional, or communicative development.

Pledge of Confidentiality (p. 54)
A written declaration indicating that information shared within an early childhood setting will not be discussed, revealed, or transmitted outside the setting in any way without the expressed consent of those involved.

pluralistic (p. 30)
The idea that there is more than one method, philosophy, or pedagogy.

portfolio (p. 233)
A purposeful collection of work that conveys relevant information about a child; a collection and a dynamic process that reflects the individuality of the child through artwork, photographs, and text.

pragmatics (p. 91)
Dealing with events sensibly and realistically in a way that is based on practical rather than theoretical considerations; practical.

predisposition (p. 66)
The act of predisposing or the state of being predisposed; previous inclination, tendency, or propensity; predilection, such as a predisposition to anger.

prerequisite skills (p. 174)
Skills that are required as a prior condition for other skills to develop.

prevalence (p. 287)
The quality or condition of being prevalent; superior strength, force, or influence, such as the prevalence of a virtue, a fashion, or a disease.

profile (p. 196)
A method of documentation that focuses on a specific, targeted area of child development, allowing the observer to record behaviours of a child that are typically demonstrated within that developmental area.

provocations (p. 4)
Inspired by Reggio Emilia, provocations are materials or experiences that educators set out to provoke children's thinking.

psychiatrist (p. 289)
A physician with additional medical training and experience in the diagnosis, prevention, and treatment of mental disorders.

psychoeducational assessment (p. 268)
This assessment involves a psychologist gathering background and educational history from an individual's teachers and/or parent(s), conducting educational and psychological diagnostic assessment tests, and preparing a report involving a diagnosis or recommendation component.

psychologist (p. 289)
An individual holding a doctoral degree in psychology who is qualified to support the mental health of others through the provision of research, therapy, and diagnosis.

rating scales (p. 179)
A method of documentation that records behaviours targeted in advance and provides a continuum against which to judge the behaviour by degree or frequency.

reciprocal (p. 12)
Mutual; corresponding to each other as being equivalent or complementary.

referral (p. 268)
To send or direct someone to a treatment/program or service.

reflective journal entry (p. 10)
The act of reflecting and documenting one's thoughts, theories, and ideas concerning critical learning experiences or events in a journal, book, or medium of choice. The intention is to promote deep critical thinking.

Reggio Emilia (p. 12)
Started by Loris Malaguzzi and the parents in villages around Reggio Emilia, it is a child-centred approach emphasizing children's symbolic representations, documentation of children's experiences in projects, and extensive involvement of parents and community.

reinforcement (p. 188)
Consequences that increase the likelihood that a certain behaviour will occur again; in behavioural theory, any response that follows a behaviour that encourages repetition of that behaviour.

reliability (p. 181)
The extent to which a test is consistent in measuring over time what it is designed to measure.

report (p. 268)
Report purposes will vary and may include but are not limited to research, observations and conclusions made, appropriate services/resources/referrals for a family/child, program planning, and licensing requirements, to name a few.

resiliency (p. 301)
The positive capacity of people to cope with stress and adversity. This coping may result in the individual "bouncing back" to a previous state of normal functioning.

resource educator/early interventionist/resource professionals (p. 267)
Professionals who provide services, materials, equipment, facilities, or personnel to meet the needs of children, families, and the communities they serve.

responsive (p. 4)
The act of responding with respect and intention to another's requests, needs, or situations; a pedagogy grounded in educators displaying sensitivity and responsiveness to others.

running record (p. 128)
A series of chronological observations represented in minutes, hours, days, or weeks. A running record generally focuses on a child throughout the day, recording samples of behaviour from morning until the child leaves the centre.

scaffolding (p. 65)
Developed by Lev Vygotsky (involving the zone of proximal development), who stated that an adult will scaffold, or put in place some assistance, whereby a child gradually develops the ability to do tasks without help.

self-actualization (p. 300)
The motivation to realize one's own maximum potential and possibilities. In Maslow's hierarchy of needs, self-actualization is the final level of psychological development that can be achieved when all other basic needs are met.

self-advocacy (p. 270)
The process of taking action for oneself to share one's views.

self-rectifying (p. 64)
To set right; to correct by calculation or adjustment.

self-regulation (p. 301)
The ability to control or adapt one's own behaviour and/or emotions according to the context, goals, or expectations of a situation or person.

semantics (p. 91)
The study of the meaning of language; the relationship between words (symbols) and what they refer to, and how these meanings influence behaviour and attitudes.

severity bias (p. 112)
The strict or severe treatment of a child by a teacher who is predisposed by a sometimes inexplicable dislike for that child.

social media (p. 49)
Social networking digital mediums (e.g., websites, apps, blogs) that allow users to communicate and share information in various forms (e.g., photos, videos, music, private messages/texts, opinions, affirmations, events).

social story (p. 157)
A simple description of an everyday social situation written from a child's perspective. The stories can help a child prepare for upcoming changes in routine or learn appropriate social interactions.

socio-cultural theory (p. 12)
Many may refer to Vygotsky for this perspective. This is a theory implying that society, interactions between people, and culture contribute to and influence individual development.

sociogram (p. 201)
A graphic representation of the social structures and links that a person or group of people have with others.

sociometry (p. 202)
The qualitative state of interpersonal relationships in populations.

spectator approach (p. 82)
Observing from a distance; not involved with the children.

stakeholders (p. 311)
People, groups, or organizations that have a direct or indirect stake in an organization because they can affect or be affected by the organization's actions, objectives, and policies.

standardized assessment (p. 234)
An assessment that has reliability and validity and that specifies how the assessment is administered, which materials are used, and how it is scored/evaluated.

standers (p. 303)
Assistive devices aimed to support an individual physically to be able to stand. This metal and Velcro-strapped piece of equipment might also have a table attached to it.

summary report (p. 91)
A report that presents the substance or general idea in brief form; summarizing; condensed; the compilation of the pertinent factors of an educator's notes that is shared with the child's family.

summative evaluation (p. 180)
A process that concerns final evaluation to ask if the project or program met its goals. It occurs at the end of a learning or instructional experience, such as a class or a program, and may include a variety of activities.

targeted behaviours (p. 168)
Behaviours that are preselected by the observer.

task analysis (p. 290)
A systematic breakdown of knowledge and skills required for a particular task whereby all elements of the task are defined, including knowledge requirements, skills, materials, sequencing, steps, resources, safety issues, related procedures, and training.

tenets (p. 40)
Principles, beliefs, or doctrines generally held to be true by a person or, especially, by members of an organization, movement, or profession.

total communication (p. 136)
An approach using as many kinds of communication as necessary for a child to understand an idea or concept; for example, sign language, hearing aids, pictures.

tourist curriculum (p. 44)
An approach marked by trivializing diversity, such as by organizing activities only around holidays or food. This curriculum disconnects cultural diversity from daily classroom life by bringing it up only on special occasions.

transformation (p. 27)

A process of profound and radical change that orients a person or organization in a new direction; a basic change in character or structure that bears little resemblance to the past configuration.

Truth and Reconciliation Commission of Canada: Calls to Action (p. 1)

A report by the Truth and Reconciliation Commission of Canada identifying *94 Calls to Action* that promote reconciliatory action in order to right the unjust treatment of Indigenous peoples and the legacy of residential schools.

Universal Design for Learning (UDL) (p. 300)

Making learning environments, buildings, materials, and equipment accessible to all and barrier free without the need for adaptation or specialized design.

unobtrusive (p. 82)

Blending with the environment so as not to stand out; inconspicuous.

validity (p. 181)

Capable of being justified or supported; the degree to which something measures what it claims to measure.

video recording (p. 153)

An electronic capture of both the audio and visual aspects of what is seen and heard.

visual schedules (p. 309)

Pictures communicating steps of a specific activity. It is meant to help children manage the daily events in their lives by using photographs, pictures, written words, or physical objects that clarify expectations for the child.

webbing (pp. 145 & 206)

A tool used with an emergent curriculum approach to create a tentative plan where possibilities are explored—such as an interest, material, or idea—and developed with the input of the children.

wonder board (p. 147)

A board (whiteboard/wall) used to document the wonderings of children and to prompt new inquiries and foster creative thinking.

working/developmental portfolio (p. 245)

A growing and changing hard copy or digital portfolio prepared by a family, child, or educator aimed to house information, observations, and a variety of artifacts representing a child's growth and development.

References

Abramson, S. (2008). *Voices of practitioners: Co-inquiry meetings for facilitated professional interchange.* Washington, DC: National Association for the Education of Young Children. Retrieved from http://www.naeyc.org/files/naeyc/file/vop/Voices_Abramson_Co-Inquiry.pdf

Agbenyega, J. (2009). The Australian Early Development Index, who does it measure: Piaget or Vygotsky's child? *Australasian Journal of Early Childhood, 34*(2), 31–38.

Alberta Children and Youth Initiative, Government of Alberta. (2006, March). *Guidelines for supporting successful transitions for children and youth. Children and youth in transition: An Alberta children and youth initiative.* Retrieved from http://www.assembly.ab.ca/lao/library/egovdocs/2006/alac/158807.pdf

Alberta Education. (2006). *Standards for the provision of early childhood special education.* Edmonton, AB: Alberta Education. Retrieved from https://education.alberta.ca/media/452316/ecs_specialedstds2006.pdf

Alberta Education, Early Learning Branch. (2009). *Working with young children who are learning English as a new language.* Edmonton, AB: Government of Alberta. Retrieved from http://education.alberta.ca/media/1093791/earlylearning.pdf

Alcock, S. (2000). *Pedagogical documentation: Beyond observations.* Occasional Paper No. 7. Wellington, New Zealand: Institute for Early Childhood Studies. Retrieved from https://core.ac.ukdownload/pdf/41336239.pdf

Andracjil. H., et al. (2014, June). Forest and nature school in Canada: A head, heart, hands approach to outdoor learning. *Forest and Nature School in Canada,* 0–62. Retrieved from http://childnature.ca/wp-content/uploads/2016/05/FSC-Guide_web.pdf

Andrews, K. (2008, May). *Family centred practices in children's services.* Retrieved from http://www.gowrie-melbourne.com.au

Ashton, J., Woodrow, C., Johnston, C., Wangmann, J., Singh, L., & James, T. (2008). Partnerships in learning: Linking early childhood services, families and schools for optimal development. *Australian Journal of Early Childhood, 33*(2), 10–16.

Atkinson, K. (2012). Pedagogical narration: What's it all about? *The Early Childhood Educator,* 3–7.

Austin, S. (2005). Community-building principles: Implications for professional development. *Child Welfare, 84*(2), 106–122.

Australian Government, Department of Education, Employment and Workplace Relations. (2010, November). *Draft assessment and rating instrument: National quality standard for early childhood education and care and school age care.* Retrieved from http://apollo.hutchins.tas.edu.au/community/asc/Resources%20for%20Parents/National%20Quality%20Standards/Assessment%20and%20Rating%20Instrument.pdf

Australian Government, Department of Education, Employment and Workplace Relations for the Council of Australian Governments. (2009). *Belonging, being, and becoming: The early years learning framework for Australia.* Retrieved from https://docs.education.gov.au/system/files/doc/other/belonging_being_and_becoming_the_early_years_learning_framework_for_australia.pdf

Bailey, M. (2007). *Digital learning stories: Empowering students' representations and reflections.* Retrieved from http://education.ed.pacificu.edu/bailey/resources/papers/Lstories/whatare.html

Ball, J. (2006). *Cultural safety in practice with children, families and communities.* School of Child and Youth Care, University of Victoria. Retrieved from http://www.ecdip.org/docs/pdf/Cultural%20Safety%20Poster.pdf

Ball, J., & Janyst, P. (2009). *Screening and assessment of Indigenous children: Community–university partnered research findings.* Retrieved from http://www.ecdip.org/docs/pdf/ECDIP%20Screening%20&%20Assmt%205%20PAGE.pdf

Bankovic, I. (2014). Constructions of childhood and the concepts of children as beings and becomings. *Practice and Theory in Systems of Education, 9*(2), 129–135.

Barrett, H. C. (2010, September). Electronic portfolios—a chapter in *Educational Technology*; an encyclopedia to be published by ABC-CLIO, 2001. Retrieved from http://electronicportfolios.com/portfolios/encyclopediaentry.htm

Bates, C. C. (2014, September). Digital portfolios: Using technology to involve families. *Young Children, 69*(4), 56–57.

BC Aboriginal ChildCare Society. (2014). *BC First Nations early childhood education occupational standards.* Retrieved from http://www.acc-society.bc.ca/files_2/documents/BCFirstNationsOccupationalStandards_BCACCS.pdf

Beard, B. K. (2013). *Ethical standards—Anishinaabe art posters.* Ontario College of Teachers. Retrieved from https:/www.oct.ca/resources/categories/ethical-standards-anishnaabe-art

Beaty, J. (2006). *Observing development of the young child.* Upper Saddle River, NJ: Prentice Hall.

Bentzen, W. R. (2009). *Seeing young children: A guide to observing and recording behaviour* (6th ed.). Belmont, CA: Delmar.

Bertrand, J. (2008). *Understanding, managing, and leading: Early childhood programs in Canada.* Toronto, ON: Thomson Nelson.

Bigler, R. S., & Liben, L. S. (2007). Developmental intergroup theory: Explaining and reducing children's social stereotyping and prejudice. *Current Directions in Psychological Science, 16*(3), 162–166.

Billman, A. C., & Sherman, J. (2003). *Observation and participation in early child settings: A practicum guide* (2nd ed.). Boston, MA: Allyn & Bacon.

Boardman, M. (2007). I know how much this child has learned. I have proof! *Australian Journal of Early Childhood*, *32*(3), 59–66.

Bøe, M., Hognestad, K., & Waniganayake, M. (2016). Qualitative shadowing as a research methodology for exploring early childhood leadership in practice. *Educational Management Administration & Leadership*, *45*(4), 605–620.

Boise, P. (2010). *Go Green Rating Scale for early childhood settings*. St. Paul, MN: Redleaf Press.

Bone, J. (2008). Creating relational spaces: Everyday spirituality in early childhood settings. *European Early Childhood Education Research Journal*, *16*(3), 343–356. doi:10.1080/13502930802292122

Bouvier, R. (2010). Good community schools are sites of educational activism. *Our Schools/Our Selves*, *19*(4), 169–184.

Bowers, F. B. (2008). Developing a child assessment plan: An integral part of program quality. *Exchange: The Early Childhood Leaders Magazine*, *184*, 51–57.

Bowne, M., Cutler, K., DeBates, D., Gilkerson, D., & Stremmel, A. (2010, June). Pedagogical documentation and collaborative dialogue as tools of inquiry for pre-service teachers in early childhood education: An exploratory narrative. *Journal of the Scholarship of Teaching and Learning*, *10*(2), 48–59.

Boynton, H. M. (2011). Children's spirituality: Epistemology and theory from various helping professions. *International Journal of Children's Spirituality*, *16*(2), 109–127. doi:10.1080/1364436X.2011.580727

Bradley, J., & Kibera, P. (2006). Culture and the promotion of inclusion in child care. *Young Children*, *61*(1), 34–38.

Briody, J., & McGarry, K. (2005). Using social stories to ease children's transitions. *Young Children*, *60*(5), 38–42.

British Columbia Ministry of Education. (2009). *Understanding the British Columbia early learning framework: From theory to practice*. Retrieved from http://www.bced.gov.bc.ca/early_learning/pdfs/from_theory_to_practice.pdf

British Columbia Ministry of Education. (2017). *Supporting the self-assessment and reporting of core competencies*. Retrieved from https://curriculum.gov.bc.ca/sites/curriculum.gov.bc.ca/files/pdf/supporting-self-assessment.pdf

Broadhead, P. (2006). Developing an understanding of young children's learning through play: The place of observation, interaction and reflection. *British Educational Research Journal*, *32*(2), 191–207.

Broderick, J. T., & Hong, S. B. (2011). Introducing the cycle of inquiry system: A reflective inquiry practice for early childhood teacher development. *Early Childhood and Parenting Collaborative*. Retrieved from http://www.ecrp.uiuc.edu/

Brotherson, M. J., Summers, J. A., Naig, L. A., Kyzar, K., Friend, A., Epley, P., Gotto, G. S., IV, & Turnbull, A. P. (2010). Partnership patterns: Addressing emotional needs in early intervention. *Topics in Early Childhood Special Education*, *30*(1), 32–45.

Brown, A., & Inglis, S. (2013, March). So what happens after the event? Exploring the realisation of professional development with early childhood educators. *Australasian Journal of Early Childhood*, *38*(1), 11–15.

Brown, W. H., Odom, S. L., & Halcombe, A. (1996). Observational assessment of young children's social behaviour with peers. *Early Childhood Research Quarterly*, *11*(1), 19–40.

Browne, K. W., & Gordon, A. M. (2009). *To teach well: An early childhood practicum guide*. Upper Saddle River, NJ: Pearson Education.

Buldu, M. (2010). Making learning visible in kindergarten classrooms: Pedagogical documentation as a formative assessment technique. *Teaching and Teacher Education*, *26*(7), 1439–1449.

Bullard, J. (2010). *Creating environments for learning: Birth to age eight*. Upper Saddle River, NJ: Pearson Education.

Burke, A. (2012, Fall). Empowering children's voices through the narrative of drawings. *Morning Watch: Educational and Social Analysis*, *40*(1–2). Retrieved from http://www.mun.ca/educ/faculty/mwatch/mwatch_sped13/Burke.pdf

Buysse, V., & Wesley, P. (2004). *Consultation in early childhood settings*. Baltimore, MD: Paul H. Brookes.

Buysse, V., Welsey, P., & Skinner, D. (1999). Community development approaches for early intervention. *Topics in Early Childhood Special Education*, *19*(4), 236–243.

Bzock, K. R., League, R., & Brown, V. L. (2003). *Receptive-Expressive Emergent Language Test (REEL-3)*. Austin, TX: PRO-ED.

Cameron, C., & Macdonald, L. (2015, Fall). The challenges of cultural competence: Exploring the impacts of race, culture and identity on early childhood educator practice. *Interaction*, 22–26.

Canadian Child Care Federation. (2000). *A self-assessment checklist based on National Statement of Quality Early Learning and Child Care*. Retrieved from http://www.cccf-fcsge.ca/practice/assessment/self-reflection.pdf

Canadian Child Care Federation. (2006). The child's right to be heard. *Interaction* 20(3). Retrieved from http://www.cccf-fcsge.ca/pdf/Interaction-focus.pdf

Canadian Child Care Federation. (2010, November). *Supporting and encouraging children's right to be heard* (Resource Sheet No. 8). Retrieved from http://www.cccf-fcsge.ca/pdf/81_en.pdf

Canadian Child Care Federation. (2012). *About CCCF*. Retrieved from http://www.cccf-fcsge.ca/about/

Canadian Coalition for the Rights of Children. (2009). *Promoting children's rights in Canada*. Retrieved from http://rightsofchildren.ca/

Canadian Council on Learning. (2010). *State of learning in Canada: A year in review*. Ottawa, ON: Author. Retrieved from http://www.ccl-cca.ca/pdfs/SOLR/2010/SOLR-2010-Report-FINAL-E.pdf

Canadian Heritage. (2009, March). *Rights of children*. Retrieved from http://www.pch.gc.ca/pgm/pdp-hrp/canada/enfnt-eng.cfm

Canadian Partnership for Children's Health and Environment. (2010). *Advancing environmental health in child care settings: A checklist for child care practitioners and public health inspectors*. Toronto, ON: Author. Retrieved from http://www.healthyenvironmentforkids

Carl, B. (2007, December). *Child Caregiver Interaction Scale* (Doctoral dissertation). Retrieved from http://www.dspace.lib.iup.edu:8080/dspace/bitstream/2069/53/1/Barbara

Carr, M., & Lee, W. (2012). *Learning stories: Constructing learner identities in early education*. Thousand Oaks, CA: Sage.

Carrasco, J. (2018). *Rough notes: Spanish and English*. Toronto, ON: Humber College.

Carlucci, M. (2018). *Child E's Water Play*. Toronto, ON: Humber College.

Carter, M. (2010, November/December). Using "learning stories" to strengthen teachers' relationships with children. *Exchange*. Retrieved from http://www.ecetrainers.com/sites/default/files/Using%20Learning%20Stories%20to%20Strengthen%20Teacher%20Relationships.pdf

Cartwright, C. A., & Cartwright, P. G. (1984). *Developing observation skills*. New York, NY: McGraw-Hill.

Cary, J. (2014, November). Small children, big cities. *Early Childhood Matters, 123*. The Hague, The Netherlands: Bernard van Leer Foundation. Retrieved from http://www.bernardvanleer.org/English/Home/Publications/Browse_by_topic.html?ps_page=1&getTopic=104#.VITskNyTTy8

Caspe, M., Seltzer, A., Lorenzo Kennedy, J., Cappio, M., & DeLorenzo, C. (2013, July). Engaging families in the child assessment process. *Young Children, 4*(7), 8–14.

Catapano, S. (2005). Teacher professional development through children's project work. *Early Childhood Education Journal, 32*(4), 261–267.

Centre for Adult English Language Acquisition. (2001). *Helping adult English language learners transition into other educational programs*. Retrieved from http://www.cal.org/caela/esl_resources/

Centre for Canadian Language Benchmarks. (2010, March). *Canadian language benchmark test*. Retrieved from http://www.language.ca

Chandler, K. (2008). *Families and practitioners: Collaborating to support cultural identity in young children* (Canadian Child Care Federation Resource Sheet No. 9). Retrieved from http://www.cccf-fcsge.ca/wp-content/uploads/RS_91-e.pdf

Chen, D. W., Nimmo, J., & Fraser, R. (2009). Becoming a culturally responsive educator: A tool to support reflection by teachers embarking on the anti-bias journey. *Multicultural Perspectives, 11*(2), 101–106.

Cheung, K. H., Yip, K. Y., Townsend, J. P., & Scotch, M. (2008). Health care and life sciences data mashup using Web 2.0/3.0. *Journal of Biomedical Informatics. 41*, 694–705.

Child and Family Services Act, R.S.O. 1990, c. C. 11.

Child Care Human Resources Sector Council. (2010, March). *Occupational standards for early childhood educators*. Retrieved from http://www.ccsc-cssge.ca/sites/default/files/uploads/ECE-Post-Secondary-docs/OSECE_2010_EN.pdf

Child Rights Information Network. (2011). *Convention on the rights of the child*. Retrieved from http://www.crin.org/themes/ViewTheme.asp?id=2

Chorney, D. W. (2006). Teacher development and the role of reflection. *Physical and Health Education Journal, 72*(3), 22–25.

Clark, A. (2005). Ways of seeing: Using the mosaic approach to listen to young children's perspectives. In A. Clark, A. T. Kjørholt, & P. Moss (Eds.), *Beyond listening: Children's perspectives on early childhood services* (pp. 29–49).

Claxton, G., & Carr, C. (2004). A framework for teaching learning: The dynamics of disposition. *Early Years, 24*(1), 87–97.

Clinton, J. (2013). *The power of positive adult–child relationships: Connection is the key*. Toronto: ON: Queen's Printer for Ontario. Retrieved from http://www.edu.gov.on.ca/childcare/clinton.pdf

Cohen, N. J., Kiefer, H., & Pape, B. (2004). *Handle with care: Strategies for promoting the mental health of young children in community-based child care*. Retrieved from http://www.cmha.ca/data/1/rec_docs/156_handle_with_care

Coleman, D. (1995). *The nature of emotional intelligence*. New York, NY: Bantam Books.

College of Early Childhood Educators. (2014a, September). *Reflective practice and self-directed learning*. Retrieved from http://www.college-ece.ca/en/Members/Documents/Reflective%20Practice%20and%20Self-Directed%20Learning%20Booklet%20September%201%202014.pdf

College of Early Childhood Educators. (2014b, December 9). *Child Care Modernization Act, 2014*. Retrieved from http://www.college-ece.ca/en/Public/News/Pages/Child-Care-Modernization-Act,-2014-(Bill-10)-.aspx

College of Early Childhood Educators. (2015). *Professional advisory: Duty to report*. Retrieved from https://www.college-ece.ca/en/Documents/Professional%20Advisory%20Duty%20to%20Report%202015.pdf

College of Early Childhood Educators. (2017a). *Code of ethics and standards of practice. College of Early Childhood Educators*. Retrieved from https://www.college-ece.ca/en/Documents/Code_and_Standards_2017.pdf

College of Early Childhood Educators. (2017b). *The code of ethics and standards of practice: For registered early childhood educators in Ontario* (Poster). College of Early Childhood Educators. Retrieved from https://www.college-ece.ca/en/Documents/Code_and_Standards_2017.pdf

College of Early Childhood Educators. (2017c). *Continuous professional learning portfolio cycle*. Retrieved from https://www.college-ece.ca/en/Documents/CPL_Portfolio_Handbook_EN.pdf

Cooperrider, D. L., Whitney, D., & Stavros, J. M. (2008). *Appreciative inquiry handbook: For leaders of change* (2nd ed.). San Francisco, CA: Berrett-Koehler.

Corks, I. (2004, Summer). The case for family-centred service: A best-practice approach for special needs children. *Paediatrics: Rehab & Community Care Medicine*. Retrieved from http://www.canchild.ca/en/ourresearch/resources/RCCM_Smr04_CanChild.pdf

Cossette, M. (2017). *Ottawa and provinces sign deal to create "fully inclusive" child care system*. CBC News. Retrieved from http://www.cbc.ca/news/politics/liberal-government-unveils-child-care-framework-1.4156348

Coughlin, A. M., & Baird, L. (2013). *Pedagogical leadership*. Retrieved from http://www.edu.gov.on.ca/childcare/Baird_Coughlin.pdf

Cox-Suárez, S. (2010). Show me again what I can do: Documentation and self-determination for students with social challenges. *Theory Into Practice, 49*, 21–28.

Craft, A., & Paige-Smith, A. (2007, December). *Developing reflective practice in the early years*. Berkshire, UK: Open University Press, McGraw-Hill Education EMEA.

Crowther, I. (2006). *Inclusion in early childhood settings: Children with special needs in Canada*. Toronto, ON: Pearson Education Canada.

Cryer, D. (2003). Defining program quality. In D. Cryer & R. Clifford (Eds.), *Early childhood education and care in the U.S.A.* (pp. 31–46). Baltimore, MD: Paul H. Brookes.

Curtis, D. (2006). No ordinary moments: Using observations with toddlers to invite further engagement. *Child Care Exchange, 3*(6), 36–40.

Curtis, D. (2008). Seeing children. *Child Care Exchange, 307*(6), 38–42.

Dahlberg, G., Moss, P., & Pence, A. (2007). *Beyond quality in early childhood education and care: Language of evaluation* (2nd ed.). London, England: Routledge.

Dalton, E. M.., & Brand, S. T. (2012). The assessment of young children through the lens of universal design for learning (UDL). *Forum on Public Policy: A Journal of the Oxford Round Table*, 1–18.

Damjanovic, V., Quinn, S., & Branson, S. (2017). The use of pedagogical documentation techniques to create focal points in a school–university partnership in early childhood education: Technologies that create a "third space". *School University Partnerships, 10*(3), 30–50.

Darragh, J. (2007). Universal design for early childhood education: Ensuring access and equity for all. *Early Childhood Education Journal, 35*(2), 167–171.

Davies, A . (2013). *Appreciating learning: Children using appreciative inquiry as an approach to helping them to understand their learning*. (Thesis, master of social sciences (MSocSc)). Retrieved from http://hdl/handle.net/10289/8464

Davis, E. L., Levine, L. J., Lench, H. C., & Quas, J. A. (2010). Metacognitive emotion regulation: Children's awareness that changing thoughts and goals can alleviate negative emotions. *Emotion, 10*(4), 498–510.

Department of Justice Canada. (n.d.). *Child abuse: A fact sheet from the Department of Justice Canada*. Retrieved from http://www.justice.gc.ca/eng/pi/fv-vf/facts-info/child-enf.html

Derman-Sparks, L., & Edwards, J. O. (2010). *Anti-bias education for young children and ourselves*. Washington, DC: National Association for the Education of Young Children.

Devereux Early Childhood Assessment Program. (n.d.). *Enhancing social emotional development*. Retrieved from http://www.kaplanco.com/media/DECA_Manual.pdf

Devereux Early Childhood Initiative. (2007). *The Devereux early childhood sssessment for infants and toddlers (DECA-I/T)*. Retrieved from http://www.devereux.org/site/PageServer?pagename=deci_index

Devereaux Early Childhood Initiative. (2009). *Devereux early childhood assessment for infants and toddlers. Reflective checklist for connecting with families.* Retrieved from http://www.centerforresilientchildren.org/wp-content/uploads/DECA-IT-ReproduciblePlanningForms.pdf

Dickinson, P., Lothian, S., & Jonz, M. B. (2007, March). Sharing responsibility for our children: How one community is making its vision for children a reality. *Young Children, 62*(3) 49–55.

Dietze, B., Penner, A., Ashley, S., Gillis, K., Moses, H., & Goodine, B. (2014). Listening to faculty: Developing a research strategy in early childhood education. *Transformative Dialogues: Teaching & Learning Journal, 7*(1), 1–15.

Division for Early Childhood and National Association for the Education of Young Children. (2009). *Early childhood inclusion: A summary.* Chapel Hill, NC: University of North Carolina, FPG Child Development Institute. Retrieved from http://www.naeyc.org/files/naeyc/file/positions/DEC_NAEYC_ECSummary_A.pdf

Dixon, M., & Halfon, S. (2015). *College of Early Childhood Educators of Ontario: The evolution of professional learning for RECEs in Ontario.* Retrieved from https://d3n8a8pro7vhmx.cloudfront.net/aeceo/pages/772/attachments/original/1436205963/The_Evolution_of_Professional_Learning_for_RECES_in_Ontario.pdf?1436205963

Dockett, S., Einarsdottir, J., & Perry, B. (2009). Researching with children: Ethical tensions. *Journal of Early Childhood Research, 7*(3), 283–298.

Dodge, E. P., Dulik, B. N., & Kulhanek, J. A. (n.d.). *Clouds come from New Hampshire: Confronting the challenge of philosophical change in early childhood programs.* Retrieved from http://ceep.crc.uiuc.edu/pubs/katzsym/dulik.pdf

Dunn, W. (1999). *Sensory Profile Caregiver Questionnaire-SPCQ.* San Antonio, TX: Psychological Corporation.

Earl, L. (2003). *Assessment as learning: Using classroom assessment to maximize student learning.* Thousand Oaks, CA: Corwin Press.

Early Childhood Educators of British Columbia. (2008). *Early Childhood Educators of British Columbia: Code of ethics*. Retrieved from http://www.ecebc.ca/resources/pdf/ecebc_codeofethics_web.pdf

Early Childhood Development Association of PEI. (2017). *Code of ethics.* Retrieved from http://www.ecdaofpei.ca/about/ethics.php

Early Childhood Research and Development Team, Early Childhood Centre, University of New Brunswick. (2007). *Early learning and child care: English curriculum framework for New Brunswick, 2007.* Fredericton, NB: Family and Community Services. Retrieved from http://eyeonkids.ca/docs/files/nb_early_learning_framework%5B1%5D.pdf

Early Childhood Research and Development Team, Early Childhood Centre, University of New Brunswick. (2008, March 31). *New Brunswick curriculum framework for early learning and child care.* Fredericton, NB: Department of Social Development. Retrieved from http://www.gnb.ca/0000/ECHDPE/curriculum-e.asp

Edwards, C., Gandini, L., and Forman, G., eds. (2012). *The hundred languages of children: The Reggio Emilia experience in transformation* (3rd ed.). Santa Barbara, California: Praeger.

Feeney, S., & Freeman, N. K. (2015). Smartphones and social media: Ethical implications for educators. *YC Young Children, 70*(1), 98–101. Retrieved from https://www.naeyc.org/system/files/YC0315_Focus_on_Ethics.pdf

Ferns, C., & Friendly, M. (2014). *The state of early childhood education and care in Canada 2012*. Toronto, ON: Moving Childcare Forward Project. Retrieved from http://childcarecanada.org/sites/default/files/StateofECEC2012.pdf

Finlay, L. (2008). *Reflecting on reflective practice.* The Open University. Retrieved from http://www.open.ac.uk/opencetl/sites/www.open.ac.uk.opencetl/files/files/ecms/web-content/Finlay-(2008)-Reflecting-on-reflective-practice-PBPL-paper-52.pdf

First Nations Health Authority. (2013). *Parents as first teachers: A resource booklet about how children learn for First Nations and Metis parents in BC.* National Collaborating Centre for Aboriginal Health. Retrieved from http://www.fnha.ca/Documents/par

Flanagan, K. (2011). *PEI early learning framework: Relationships, environments, experiences.* The Curriculum Framework of the Preschool Excellence Initiative. Retrieved from: http://www.gov.pe.ca/eecd/eecd_EYFrWrk_Full.pdf

Fleet, A., et al. (2011). *What's pedagogy anyway? Using pedagogical documentation to engage with the early years learning framework.* Marrickville, New South Wales: Children's Services Central.

Foley, J., & Green, J. (2015). Supporting children's reflection with phones and tablets. for the preschool professional. *NAEYC, 8*(5), 21–23. Retrieved from https://www.naeyc.org/resources/pubs/tyc/jun2015/supporting-childrens-reflection

Ford, D. Y. (2010). Culturally responsive classrooms: Affirming culturally different gifted students. *Multicultural Issues, 33*(1), 50–54.

Forman, G. (1999). Instant video revisiting: The video camera as a "tool of the mind" for young children. *Early Childhood Research and Practice, 1*(2), 1–6. Retrieved from http://ecrp.uiuc.edu/v1n2/forman.html

Forman, G. (2010). Documentation and accountability: The shift from numbers to indexed narratives. *Theory into Practice, 49*, 29–35.

Forman, G., & Hall, E. (2005). Wondering with children: The importance of observation in early education. *Early Childhood Research and Practice, 7*(2). Retrieved from http://ecrp.uiuc.edu/v7n2/index.html

Forman, G. E. (2010). Reading the intentionality of young children. *Early Childhood Research & Practice, 12*(1). Retrieved from http://ecrp.uiuc.edu/v12n1/forman.html

Fraser, S. (2012). *Authentic childhood: Experiencing Reggio Emilia in the classroom* (3rd ed.). Toronto, ON: Nelson Education.

Free Play Network. (n.d.). *PLACES for PLAY: Exhibition.* Retrieved from http://www.freeplaynetwork.org.uk/playlink/exhibition/index.html

Friedman, D. L. (2004). When teachers participate, reflect, and choose change. *Young Children, 5*(6), 64–70.

Friendly, M., & Beach, J. (2005). *Elements of a high quality early learning and child care system* (Quality by Design Working Document). Toronto, ON: Childcare Resource and Research Unit, University of Toronto. Retrieved from http://www.childcarequality.ca/wdocs/QbD_Elements.pdf

Friendly, M., Grady, B., Macdonald, L., and Forer, B. (2015). *Early childhood education and care in Canada 2014.* Toronto: Childcare Resource and Research Unit. Retrieved from http://childcarecanada.org/sites/default/files/ECEC-2014-full-document-revised-10-03-16.pdf

Friendly, M., & Prabhu, N. (2010, January). *Can early childhood education and care help keep Canada's promise of respect for diversity?* (Occasional Paper No. 23). Toronto, ON: Childcare Resource and Research Unit, University of Toronto. Retrieved from http://www.childcarecanada.org/sites/default/files/crru_op23_diversity.pdf

Gans, K. (2017). *A practical guide for forest school leaders (or anyone, really!) to facilitating reflection in the outdoors.* Retrieved from http://docs.wixstatic.com/ugd/8dd281_d349c30264684c9f99940d7a8e754812.pdf

Gee, J. P. (2008). A sociocultural perspective on opportunity to learn. In P. A. Moss, D. C. Pullin, P. Gee, E. H. Haertel, & L. Jones Young (Eds.), *Assessment, equity, and opportunity to learn* (pp. 76–108). New York, NY: Cambridge University Press.

Gerlach, A. J. (2015*). Early intervention with Indigenous families and children in British Columbia: A critical inquiry.* (Thesis, University of British Columbia). Retrieved from https://open.library.ubc.ca/clRcle/collections/ubctheses/24/items/1.0165832

Gestwicki, C. (2011). *Developmentally appropriate practice* (4th ed.). Delmar, NY: Thomson.

Gestwicki, C., & Bertrand. J. (2008). *The essentials of early childhood education* (3rd Canadian ed.). Toronto, ON: Thomson Nelson.

Gilman, S. (2009). "Social stories": Pathways to inclusion. *English Quarterly, 39*(2), 33–45.

Gjems, L. (2001, December). What explanations matter: A study of co-construction of explanations between teachers and children in everyday conversations in kindergarten. *European Early Childhood Education Research Journal, 19*(4), 501–513.

Goeson, R. (2014, June). Finding our voices through narrative inquiry: Exploring a conflict of cultures. *Voices of Practitioners, 9*(1), 2–22.

Gonzalez-Mena, J. (2008). *Diversity in early care and education: Honoring differences* (5th ed.). New York, NY: McGraw-Hill.

Good, L. (2005–2006). Snap it up: Using digital photography in early childhood education. *Childhood Education: Infancy through Early Adolescence, 82*(2), 79–85.

Goode, T. D. (2009). *The self-assessment checklist for personnel providing services and supports in early intervention and early childhood settings.* Washington, DC: National Center for Cultural Competence, Georgetown

University Center for Child and Human Development, University Center for Excellence in Developmental Disabilities Education, Research & Service. Retrieved from http://www11.georgetown.edu/research/gucchd/nccc/documents/Checklist.CSHN.doc.pdf

Gordon, A. M., & Williams Browne, K. (2007). *Beginning essentials in early childhood education*. Clifton Park, NY: Thomson Nelson.

Government of British Columbia. (2007). *British Columbia early learning framework*. Victoria, BC: Ministry of Education; Ministry of Health; Ministry of Children and Family Development, Queen's Printer for British Columbia. Retrieved from http://www2.gov.bc.ca/gov/DownloadAsset?assetId=245C9B82FFF94171BB61818A53F0674A&filename=early_learning_framework.pdf

Government of British Columbia. (2015). *Aboriginal policy and practice framework in British Columbia*. Retrieved from https://www2.gov.bc.ca/assets/gov/family-and-social-supports/child-care/aboriginal/abframework.pdf

Government of Canada. (2004). A message for Senator Landon Pearson. A Canada fit for children: Canada's plan of action in response to the May 2002 United Nations Special Session on Children.

Government of Saskatchewan, Early Learning and Child Care Branch, Ministry of Education. (2009, May). *Creating early learning environments*. Retrieved from http://www.education.gov.sk.ca/Default.aspx?DN=4de38060-953f-4922-9b9b-1d3bec94400d

Government of Saskatchewan. (2015). *Essential learning experiences: For three, four, and five-year-olds*. Retrieved from https://www.edonline.sk.ca/bbcswebdav/library/Curriculum%20Website/Kindergarten/Resources/Additional/Essential_Learning_Experiences.pdf

Gowrie Australia. (2011, Summer). Reflections. *Gowrie Australia Publications*, 45. Retrieved from http://gowrieqld.com.au/wp-content/uploads/2014/11/reflections_summer.issue45.pdf

Greenwood, M. (2013). Being Indigenous: Commentary on Chandler. *Human Development*, 56, 98–105. Retrieved from https://www.researchgate.net/publication/274057825_Being_Indigenous_Commentary_on_Chandler

Greenwood, M., Fowler, A., Graham, K., Boulton, P., & Hall, E. (2016, March/April). A beginning: Images of rights: Children's perspectives project. *Exchange*, 38, 18–21.

Guralnick, M. J. (2012). *Early childhood inclusion: Focus on change*. Baltimore, Maryland: Paul H Brookes Publishing Company Inc.

Hall, E., & Maher, A. (2012, May/June). A conversation about children's rights. *Exchange*. Retrieved from https://www.childcareexchange.com/article/a-conversation-about-childrens-rights/5020524/

Hall, E., & Rudkin, J. K. (2011). *Seen & heard: Children's rights in early childhood education*. New York, New York: Teacher's College Press.

Hall, N. S., & Rhomberg, V. (1995). *The affective curriculum: Teaching the anti-bias approach to young children*. Scarborough, ON: Nelson Canada.

Hallam, R., Fouts, H., Bargreen, K., & Caudle, L. (2009). Quality from a toddler's perspective: A bottom-up examination of classroom experiences. *Early Childhood Research & Practice*, 11(2), 1–16.

Hamilton Wentworth District School Board. (2016). *Media consent form*. Retrieved from http://www.hwdsb.on.ca/waterdown/files/2017/01/Media-Consent-Sept2016.pdf

Hamlin, M., & Wisneski, D. B. (2012, May). Supporting the scientific thinking and inquiry of toddlers and preschoolers through play. *NAEYC*, 2(3), 82–88.

Harcourt, D., & Jones, L. (2016). Rethinking professional development: Positioning educational documentation as everyday professional learning. *Early Childhood Australia*, 41(4), 81–85.

Harcourt, D., & Sargeant, J. (2011, September). The challenges of conducting ethical research with children. *Education Inquiry*, 2(3), 421–436.

Harms, T., Clifford, R. M., & Cryer, D. (2014). *Early childhood environment rating scale* (3rd ed.). New York, NY: Teachers College Press.

Harms, T., Cryer, D., & Clifford, R. M. (2007). *The family child care environment rating scale*. New York, NY: Teachers College Press.

Harms, T., Cryer, D., & Clifford, R. M. (2017). *The infant toddler early childhood environment rating scale* (3rd ed.). New York, NY: Teachers College Press.

Harms, T., Vineberg Jacobs, E., & Romano White, D. (2013). *The school age early childhood rating scale*. New York, NY: Teachers College Press.

Haugen, K. (2005, January/February). Learning materials for children of all abilities: Begin with universal design. *Child Care Exchange*, 161, 45–48.

Healthy Kids Toronto. (n.d.). *Keeping track: Child developmental support record*. Retrieved from http://www.healthykidstoronto.ca/pdf/ChildDevelopmentalRecord_Jan2017.pdf

Helling, G. (n.d). *Trust, listening and the role of the principal: Building a community of learners with principals, teachers, students and parents at St Sebastian School, Toronto*. Retrieved from http://www.yrdsb.ca/Programs/PLT/Quest/Documents/2015HellingArticle.pdf

Helm, J. H., Beneke, S., & Steinheimer, K. (2007). *Windows on learning: Documenting young children's work* (2nd ed.). New York, NY: Teachers College Press.

Hope Irwin, S. (2009). *The SpeciaLink Early Childhood Inclusion Quality Scale*. Sydney, NS: Breton Books. Retrieved from http://www.specialinkcanada.org/about/rating%20scales.html

Hope Southcott, L. (2015). Learning stories: Connecting parents, celebrating success, and valuing children's theories. *Voices of Practitioners*, 10(1), pp. 33–50. Retrieved from http://citeseerx.ist.psu.edu/viewdoc/download;jsessionid=7DE36B51A188C1C84548BAB19360BC40?doi=10.1.1.731.3259&rep=rep1&type=pdf

Houston, L., Worthington, R., & Harrop, P. (2006, March). *Design guidance for play spaces*. Retrieved from http://www.forestry.gov.uk/pdf/fce-design-guidance-for-play-spaces.pdf/$FILE/fce-design-guidance-for-play-spaces.pdf

Hughes, E. (2005). Linking past to present to create an image of the child. *Theory into Practice, 46*(1), 48–56.

Human Resources and Skill Development Canada. (n.d.). *Writing tip sheet*. Retrieved from http://www.nald.ca/library/learning/hrsdc/essential_skills/writing_tip_sheet/writing_tip_sheet.pdf

Humber, J., Caine, V., Huber, M., & Steeves, P. (2013). Narrative inquiry as pedagogy in Education: The extraordinary potential of living, telling, retelling, and reliving stories of experience. *Review of Research in Education, 37,* 212–242.

Hunt, A., Nason, P. N., & Whitty, P. (2000). Documentation as a forum and showcase in an education faculty. In *Issues in early childhood education: Curriculum, teacher education, and dissemination of information*. Proceedings of the Lilian Katz Symposium. Champaign, IL, November 5–7, 2000. Retrieved from http://ceep.crc.uiuc.edu/pubs/katzsym/hunt.pdf

Hurt, A. C., & Callahan, J. L. (2013). A fractured fable: The Three Little Pigs and using multiple paradigms. *New Horizons in Adult Education & Human Resource Development, 25*(3), 27–40. doi:10.1002/nha3.20029

Hyland, N. E. (2010). Social justice in early childhood classrooms: What the research tells us. *Young Children, 65*(1), 82–90.

Ineese-Nash, N., Bomberry, Y., Underwood, K., & Hache, A. (2018). Raising a child with early childhood dis-ability supports Shakonehya:ra's ne shakoyen'okon:'a G'chi-gshkewesiwad. *Indigenous Policy Journal, XXVII* (3), 1–14. Retrieved from http://www.indigenouspolicy.org/index.php/ipj/article/view/454/521

Janus, M., Kopechanski, L., Cameron, R., & Hughes, D. (2008). In transition: Experiences of parents of children with special needs at school entry. *Early Childhood Education Journal, 35,* 479–485.

Janus, M., Lefort, J., Cameron, R., & Kopechanski, L. (2007). Starting kindergarten: Transition issues for children with special needs. *Canadian Journal of Education, 30*(3), 628–648. Retrieved from http://asq.org/education/why-quality/overview.html

Johanson, S., & Kuh, L. (2013, November). Critical friends groups in an early childhood setting: Building a culture of collaboration. *Voices of Practitioners, 8*(2), 1–16. Retrieved from https://www.naeyc.org/files/naeyc/file/Voices/Voices_Johanson_v8n2.pdf

Kashin, D. (2013, April 11). *Leading the Reggio way: A profile of a pedagogical leader* [Blog post]. Retrieved from Technology Rich Inquiry Based Research blog: https://tecribresearch.wordpress.com/2013/04/11/leading-the-reggio-way-a-profile-of-a-pedagogical-leader/

Kashin, D., & Jupp, L. (2013). *Documentation and assessment: The power of a learning story* [Blog post]. Retrieved from Technology Rich Inquiry Based Research blog: https://tecribresearch.wordpress.com/2013/04/24/documentation-and-assessment-the-power-of-a-learning-story-10/

Keilty, B., LaRocco, D. J., & Bankler Cassell, F. (2009). Early interventionists' reports of authentic assessment methods through focus group research. *Topics in Early Childhood Special Education, 28*(4), 244–256.

Kennedy, A., & Stonehouse, A. (2012). *Victorian early years learning and development framework: Practice principle guide*. Melbourne, Australia: State of Victoria (Department of Education and Early Childhood Development). Retrieved from http://www.education.vic.gov.au/Documents/childhood/providers/edcare/pracfamily.pdf

Keyes, C. R. (2000). Parent-teacher partnerships: A theoretical approach for teachers. In *Issues in early childhood education: Curriculum, teacher education, and dissemination of information*. Proceedings of the Lilian Katz Symposium. Champaign, IL, November 5–7, 2000. Retrieved from http://ceep.crc.uiuc.edu/pubs/katzsym/keyes.pdf

King, G., King, S., Law, M., Kertoy, M., Rosenbaum, P., & Hurley, P. (2002). *Family-centred service in Ontario: A "bestpractice" approach for children with disabilities and their families*. Retrieved from http://www.canchild.ca/en/canchildresources/resources/FCSinbriefNov2002.pdf

Kirmani, M. H., & Kirmani, S. (2009). Recognition of seven spiritual identities and its implications on children. *International Journal of Children's Spirituality, 14*(4), 369–383. doi:10.1080/13644360903293630

Kline, L.S. (2007). Documentation panel: The "making learning visible" project. *Journal of Early Childhood Teacher Education, 29,* 70–80.

Kurtz, K. (2009). Twittering about learning: Using Twitter in an elementary school classroom. *Horace, 25*(1), 1–4. Retrieved from https://files.eric.ed.gov/fulltext/EJ859276.pdf

Lansdown, G. (2005). *Can you hear me? The right of young children to participate in decisions affecting them*. Working Paper #36. Bernard Van Leer Foundation. The Hague, Netherlands. Retrieved from http://www.bibalex.org/Search4Dev/Files/282624/114976.Pdf

Lansdown, G. (2011). *Every child's right to be heard: A resource guide on the UN Committee on the Rights of the Child*. General Comment no. 12. London, England: Save the Children UK. Retrieved from http://www.unicef.org/french/adolescence/files/Every_Childs_Right_to_be_Heard.pdf

Larsen, E. R. (2010). *Making the team: Teams, teamwork, and teambuilding*. Retrieved from http://findarticles.com/p/articles/mi_qa5350/is_201006/ai_n54366116/pg_/

Laverick, D. M. (2008). Starting school: Welcoming young children and families into early school experiences. *Early Childhood Education Journal, 35,* 321–326.

Law, M., Rosenbaum, P., King, G. S., Burke-Gaffney, J., MoningSzkut, T., Kertoy, M., … Teplicky, R. (2003a). *What is family-centred service?* (Fact Sheet No. 1). Hamilton, ON: CanChild Centre for Disability Research, McMaster University.

Law, M., Rosenbaum, P., King, G. S., Burke-Gaffney, J., MoningSzkut, T., Kertoy, M., … Teplicky, R. (2003b). *Are we really family-centred? Checklists for families, service providers, and organizations* (Fact Sheet No. 18). Hamilton, ON: CanChild Centre for Disability Research, McMaster University.

Lero, D. (2004). *The SpecialLink Child Care Inclusion Practices Profile and Principles Scale*. Sydney, NS: Breton Books. Retrieved from http://www.specialinkcanada.org/about/rating%20scales.html

Lero, D. S. (2010, February). *Assessing inclusion quality in early learning and child care in Canada with the SpecialLink Child Care Inclusion Practices Profile and Principles Scale*. A report prepared for the Canadian Council on Learning. Retrieved from http://www.specialinkcanada.org

Lewin-Benham, A. (2006). One teacher, 20 preschoolers, and a goldfish: Environmental awareness, emergent curriculum, and documentation. *Young Children, 61*(2), 28–34.

Liebovich, B. J. (2000). Children's self-assessment. In *Issues in early childhood education: Curriculum, teacher education, and dissemination of information*. Proceedings of the Lilian Katz Symposium. Champaign, IL, November 5–7, 2000. Retrieved from http://ceep.crc.uiuc.edu/pubs/katzsym/liebovich.pdf

Lindgren, A. -L. (2012, November). Ethical issues in pedagogical documentation: Representations of children through digital technology. *International Journal of Early Childhood, 44*(3), 327–340.

Lirenman, K. (2018). *Peeking into Division 17 Blog*. Retrieved from http://mslirenmansroom.blogspot.ca

Logue, M. E. (2006). Teachers observe to learn: Differences in social behavior of toddlers and preschoolers in same-age and multiage groupings. *Young Children, 61*(3), 70–76.

Loppie, S., Reading, C., & de Leeuw, S. (2014). *Aboriginal experiences with racism and its impacts*. National Collaborating Centre for Aboriginal Health. Retrieved from http://epub.sub.uni-hamburg.de/epub/volltexte/2015/39325/pdf/2014_07_09_FS_2426_RacismPart2_ExperiencesImpacts_EN_Web.pdf

Lowe Friedman, D. (2012). *Creating and presenting an early childhood education portfolio: A reflective approach*. Belmont, CA: Wadsworth Cengage Learning.

Luckenbill, J. (2012, March). Getting the picture: Using the digital camera as a tool to support reflective practice and responsive care. *Young Children, 67*(2), 28–36.

MacAlpine, K. (2017). Through THE looking glass: Interpreting growing success, the kindergarten addendum. Ontario's assessment, evaluation, and reporting policy document. *Journal of Childhood Studies, 42*(2), 34–41.

MacDonald, B. (2006, November/December). Observation—the path to documentation. *Exchange, 172*, 45–49.

MacDonald, M. (2007). Toward formative assessment: The use of pedagogical documentation in early elementary classrooms. *Early Childhood Research Quarterly, 22*, 232–242.

Maclean, D. C. (2006). Learning to see … seeing to learn: The role of observation in early childhood development. *Child Care Exchange, 3*(6), 42.

Mac Naughton, G. M., & Hughes, P. (2008a). *Doing action research in early childhood studies*. Berkshire, England: Open University Press.

Mac Naughton, G., Hughes, P., & Smith, K. (2008b). Young children as active citizens: Principles, policies and pedagogies. Newcastle, UK: Cambridge Scholars Publishing.

Maione, L., & Mirenda, P. (2006). Effects of video modeling and video feedback on peer-directed social language skills of a child with autism. *Journal of Positive Behaviour Interventions, 8*(2), 106–118.

Makovichuk, L., Hewes, J., Lirette, P., & Thomas, N. (2014). *Play, participation, and possibilities: An early learning and child care curriculum framework for Alberta*. Retrieved from www.childcareframework.com

Maloch, B., & Horsey, M. (2013). Living inquiry. *The Reading Teacher, 66*(6), 475–485.

Manitoba Child Care Association. (2011a). *Manitoba code of ethics: Early childhood educators*. Retrieved from http://mccahouse.org/wp-content/uploads/2014/12/CodeofEthicsforEarlyChildhoodEducators2011.pdf

Manitoba Child Care Association. (2011b). *MCAA code of ethics*. Retrieved from http://mccahouse.org/code-of-ethics/

Marich, H. (2016). Twitter in the elementary classroom: A teacher's journey. *Language Arts, 94*(1), 67–70. Retrieved from http://www.ncte.org/library/NCTEFiles/Resources/Journals/LA/0941-sept2016/LA0941POP.pdf

Marshall, H. (2001). Cultural influences on the development of self-concept: Updating our thinking. *Young Children, 56*(6), 19–25.

Mathers, S., Linskey, F., Seddon, J., & Sylva, K. (2007). Using quality rating scales for professional development: Experiences from the UK. *International Journal of Early Years Education, 15*(3), 261–274.

McArthur Butterfield, P., Martin, C. A., & Pratt Prairie, A. (2004). *Emotional connections: How relationships guide early learning*. Washington, DC: National Centre for Infants, Toddlers and Families.

McCain, N. M., Mustard, J. F., & McCuaig, K. (2011). *Early years study 3: Making decisions, taking action*. Toronto, ON: Margaret & Wallace McCain Family Foundation. Retrieved from http://eys3.ca/media/uploads/report-pdfs-en/i_xii_eys3_fm_2nd_ed.pdf

McCoy-Wozniak, N. (2012). Enhancing inquiry, evidence-based reflection, and integrative learning with the lifelong eportfolio process: The implementation of integrative eportfolios at Stony Brook University. *Journal of Educational Technology Systems, 41*(3), 209–230. doi:10.2190/ET.41.3.b

McFadden, A., & Thomas, K. (2016). Parent perspectives on the implementation of a digital documentation portal in an early learning centre. *Australasian Journal of Early Childhood, 41*(4), 86–94.

McFarland, L., Saunders, R., & Allen, S. (2009). Reflective practice and self evaluation in learning positive guidance: Experiences of early childhood practicum students. *Early Childhood Education Journal, 26*, 505–511.

McKeough, A., et al. (2008). Storytelling as a foundation to literacy development for aboriginal children: Culturally and developmentally appropriate practices. *Canadian Psychology, 49*(2), 148–154.

McKinlay, L., & Ross, H. (2008). *You and others: Reflective practice for group effectiveness in human services*. Toronto, ON: Pearson Education Canada.

McNaughton, K., & Drenz, C. (2007). The Construction Site Project: Transforming early childhood teacher practice. *Theory into Practice, 46*(1), 65–73.

Meeting the needs of refugee families. (2007, March 15). *SWIS News & Notes, 18*. Retrieved from http://wiki.settlementatwork .org/wiki/SWIS_News_and_Notes_Newsletter

Miller, K. (2016). Learning about children's school preparation through photographs: The use of photo elicitation interviews with low-income families. *Journal of Early Childhood Research, 14*(3), 261–279.

Mills, H., & O'Keefe, T. (2010, Spring). Collaborative inquiry: From kidwatching to responsive teaching. *Association for Childhood Education International, 169,* 1–100.

Mistrett, S. G. (2017). *Universal design for learning: A checklist for early childhood environments.* Center on Technology and Disability. Retrieved from https://www.ctdinstitute.org/ sites/default/files/file_attachments/ UDL-Checklist-EC.pdf

Mistrett, S., & Ruffino, A. G. (2006). *Universal design for play guidelines.* Retrieved from http://letsplay.buffalo.edu/UD/ UDP%20Guidelines.pdf

Mitchell, L. M. (2007). Using technology in Reggio Emilia–inspired programs. *Theory into Practice, 46*(1), 32–39.

Moore, G. T., Sugiyama, T., & O'Donnell, L. (2003). *Children's Physical Environments Rating Scale.* Sydney, Australia: Environment, Behaviour and Society Research Group, University of Sydney. Retrieved from http://sydney.edu.au/ architecture/documents/staff/garymoore/112.pdf

Morgan, H. (2014). Enhancing instruction and communication with Twitter. *Childhood Education, 90*(1), 75–78.

Moss, P. (2011, February). *Early childhood policy, provisions and practice: Critical questions about care and education.* Symposium conducted at Ryerson University, Toronto, Ontario.

National Association for the Education of Young Children. (2005). *NAEYC accreditation criteria for physical environments: Standard 9.* Retrieved from http://www.naeyc.org/torch

National Association for the Education of Young Children. (2009). *Developmentally appropriate practice in early childhood programs serving children from birth through age 8* [Position Statement]. Retrieved from http://www .naeyc.org/files/naeyc/file/positions/PSDAP.pdf

National Child Care Accreditation Council. (2011, March). Nurturing children's spirituality. *Putting Children First, 37,* 11–13.

National Collaborating Centre for Aboriginal Health. (2010a). *A framework for Indigenous school health: Foundations in cultural principles.* Retrieved from https://www .ccnsanccah.ca/495/A_framework_for_Indigenous _school_health__Foundations_in_cultural_principles _.nccah?id=42

National Collaborating Centre for Aboriginal Health. (2010b). *Inunnguiniq: Caring for children the Inuit way.* Retrieved from http://www.ottawainuitchildrens.com/wp-content/ uploads/2015/01/Inuit-caring-EN-web.pdf

National Collaborating Centre for Aboriginal Health. (2010c). *Supporting Aboriginal parents: Teachings for the future.* Retrieved from https://www.ccnsa-nccah.ca/docs/health/ RPT-SupportingAboriginalParents-Irvine-EN.pdf

National Collaborating Centre For Aboriginal Health. (2013a). Caregiver-infant attachment for Aboriginal families. *Child and Youth Health.* Retrieved from https://www.ccnsa -nccah.ca/docs/health/FS-InfantAttachment-Hardy -Bellamy-EN.pdf

National Collaborating Centre for Aboriginal Health. (2013b). *Messages from the heart: Caring for our children.* Retrieved from https://www.ccnsa-nccah.ca/docs/health/ RPT-MessageHeartCaringChildren-EN.pdf

National Collaborating Centre for Aboriginal Health. (2013c). *Parents as First Teachers: A resource booklet about how children learn for First Nations and Métis parents in BC.* Retrieved from http://www.fnha.ca/Documents/parentteacher.pdf

National Collaborating Centre For Aboriginal Health. (2016). *Culture and language as social determinants of First Nations, Inuit, and Métis health.* Retrieved from https://www.ccnsa-nccah.ca/docs/determinants/ FS-CultureLanguage-SDOH-FNMI-EN.pdf

Native Women's Centre. (2008). *Traditional teachings handbook.* Hamilton, Ontario: Aboriginal Healing & Outreach Centre. Retrieved from http://www.nativewomenscentre .com/files/Traditional_Teachings_Booklet.pdf

Navarrete, A. (2015). *Assessment in the early years: ePerspectives and practices of early childhood educators.* (Master's dissertation, Dublin Institute of Technology). Retrieved from https://arrow.dit.ie/cgi/viewcontent.cgi?article=1091 &context=aaschssldis

Neeganagwedgin, E. (2011). A critical review of Aboriginal education in Canada: Eurocentric dominance impact and everyday denial. *Aboriginal Policy Research Consortium International* (APRCi). Paper 440. Retrieved from https://ir.lib.uwo.ca/aprci/440/?utm_ source=ir.lib.uwo.ca%2Faprci%2F440&utm_ medium=PDF&utm_campaign=PDFCoverPages

New Brunswick Department of Education and Early Childhood Development. (2016). *Early intervention service standards.* Retrieved from http://www2.gnb.ca/content/dam/gnb/ Departments/ed/pdf/ELCC/ECHDPE/EarlyIntervention.pdf

Newfoundland and Labrador Teachers' Association. (2011). *Code of ethics.* Retrieved from http://files.nlta.nl.ca/wp -Content/uploads/public/documents/memos_posters/ code_of_ethics.pdf

New Zealand Ministry of Education. (2017). *Te Whāriki: He whāriki mwhārikitauranga mwhāriki ngwhāriki mokopuna o Aotearoa early childhood curriculum.* Retrieved from https://www.education.govt.nz/assets/Documents/Early -Childhood/FINAL-ELS-Te-Whariki-ENG-A2-Poster.pdf

Niguidula, D. (2005). Documenting learning with digital portfolios. *Educational Leadership, 63*(3), 44–47.

Nilsen, B. (2014). *Week by week: Plans for documenting children's development* (6th ed.). Belmont, CA: Wadsworth Cengage Learning.

Nipissing District Developmental Screen Intellectual Property Association. (2018). *Looksee Checklist by ndds®.* North Bay, ON.

Nissen, H., & Hawkins, C. J. (2010). Promoting cultural competence in the preschool classroom. *Childhood Education, 86*(4), 255–259.

Northwest Territories Teachers' Association. (n.d.). *Code of ethics*. Retrieved from http://www.sahtudec.ca/documents/general/NWTTA%20Code%20of%20Ethics.pdf

Nova Scotia Child Care Association. (2014). *NSCCA code of ethics*. Retrieved from http://nschildcareassociation.org/wp-content/uploads/2014/01/NSCCA-Code-of-Ethics.pdf

O'Connor, A., & Diggins, C. (2002). *On reflection: Reflective practice for early childhood educators*. Lower Hutt, New Zealand: Open Mind.

Ontario College of Teachers. (2013). *Ethical standards for the teaching profession: Anishinaabe art*. Ontario College of Teachers. Retrieved from https://www.oct.ca/resources/categories/ethical-standards-anishnaabe-art

Ontario College of Teachers. (2015). *Professional advisory: Duty to report*. Retrieved from https://www.oct.ca/-/media/PDF/2015%20Professional%20Advisory%20Duty%20to%20ReportENWEB2.pdf

Ontario College of Teachers. (2017). *Professional advisory: Maintaining professionalism—use of electronic communication and social media*. Retrieved from https://www.oct.ca/-/media/PDF/Advisory%20Social%20Media/ProfAdvSocMediaENPRINT.pdf

Ontario College of Teachers. (2018). *Ethical standards*. Retrieved from https://www.oct.ca/public/professional-standards/ethical-standards

Ontario Ministry of Children and Youth Services. (2012). *Reporting child abuse and neglect: It's your duty*. Retrieved from http://www.children.gov.on.ca/htdocs/English/topics/childrensaid/reportingabuse/abuseandneglect/abuseandneglect.aspx

Ontario Ministry of Children and Youth Services, Best Start Expert Panel on Early Learning. (2007, January). *Early learning for every child today: A framework for Ontario early childhood settings*. Retrieved from http://www.cfcollaborative.ca/wp-content/uploads/2010/10/ELECT.pdf

Ontario Ministry of Education. (2002). *Ontario curriculum unit planner: Assessment strategies companion*. Toronto, ON: Queen's Printer for Ontario.

Ontario Ministry of Education. (2004). *The Individual Education Plan (IEP): A resource guide.* Retrieved from http://www.edu.gov.on.ca/eng/general/elemsec/speced/guide/resource/iepresguid.pdf

Ontario Ministry of Education. (2005). *Many roots, many voices: Supporting English language learners in every classroom. A practical guide for Ontario educators*. Toronto, ON: Queen's Printer for Ontario. Retrieved from http://www.edu.gov.on.ca/eng/document/manyroots/manyroots.pdf

Ontario Ministry of Education. (2008). *Growing success: Assessment, evaluation and reporting: Improving student learning*. Toronto, ON: Queen's Printer for Ontario. Retrieved from https://faculty.nipissingu.ca/douglasg/EDUC4315/Resources/GrowingSuccessAssessmentevaluationandreportingimprovingstudentlearning.pdf

Ontario Ministry of Education. (2010). *Growing success*. Retrieved from http://www.edu.gov.on.ca/eng/policyfunding/growingSuccessAddendum.html#gs2

Ontario Ministry of Education. (2012, October). *Pedagogical documentation: Leading learning in the early years and beyond*. Capacity Building Series K–2. Secretariat Special Edition, *30*, 1–8.

Ontario Ministry of Education. (2013). *Think, feel, act: Lessons from research about young children*. Retrieved from http://www.edu.gov.on.ca/childcare/document.html

Ontario Ministry of Education. (2014a, September). *Collaborative inquiry in Ontario: What we have learned and where we are now*. Ontario Ministry of Education, Capacity Building Series K–12, special edition #39. Retrieved from http://www.edu.gov.on.ca/eng/literacynumeracy/inspire/research/CBS_CollaborativeInquiry.pdf

Ontario Ministry of Education. (2014b). *Equity and inclusive education in Ontario schools: Guidelines for policy development and implementation*. Ontario Ministry of Education. Retrieved from http://www.edu.gov.on.ca/eng/policyfunding/inclusiveguide.pdf

Ontario Ministry of Education. (2014c). *How does learning happen? Ontario's pedagogy for the early years*. Retrieved from http://www.edu.gov.on.ca/childcare/HowLearningHappens.pdf

Ontario Ministry of Education. (2015a). *An introduction to special education in Ontario*. Retrieved from http://www.edu.gov.on.ca/eng/general/elemsec/speced/ontario.html

Ontario Ministry of Education. (2015b). *Pedagogical documentation revisited*. Capacity Building Series. Retrieved from http://www.edu.gov.on.ca/eng/literacynumeracy/inspire/research/CBS_PedagogicalDocument.pdf

Ontario Ministry of Education. (2016a). *Assessing learning in the four frames learning module*. Retrieved from http://www.edugains.ca/newsite/Kindergarten/prolearnfac/training_resources.html

Ontario Ministry of Education. (2016b). *Growing Success: The Kindergarten Addendum: Assessment, evaluation and reporting in Ontario schools*. Retrieved from http://www.edu.gov.on.ca/eng/policyfunding/growingSuccessAddendum.html

Ontario Ministry of Education. (2016c). *The kindergarten program*. Retrieved from https://files.ontario.ca/books/kindergarten-program-en.pdf

Ontario Ministry of Education. (2017a). *Child care licensing manual*. Retrieved from https://www.earlyyears.edu.gov.on.ca/EYPortal/en/ChildCareLicensing/ChildCareLicensingResources/index.htm#P12_337

Ontario Ministry of Education. (2017b). *Special education in Ontario: Kindergarten to grade 12*. Retrieved from http://www.edu.gov.on.ca/eng/document/policy/os/onschools_2017e.pdf

Paige-Smith, A., & Craft, A. (Eds.). (2007). *Developing reflective practice in the early years*. Berkshire, England: Open University Press, McGraw-Hill.

Parekh, G., & Underwood, K. (2015). *Inclusion: Creating school and classroom communities where everyone belongs. Research, tips, and tools for educators and administrators*. (Research Report No. 15/16-09). Toronto, Ontario: Toronto District School Board.

Parsons, S. (2015a). Digital technologies for supporting the informed consent of children and young people in research: The potential for transforming current research ethics practice. *Social Inclusion, 3*(6), 1–8.

Parsons, S. (2015b). The potential of digital technologies for transforming informed consent practices with children and young people in social research. *Social Inclusion, 3*(6) doi:http://dx.doi.org.ezproxy.humber.ca/10.17645/si.v3i6.400

Pascal, C. E. (n.d.). *Every child every opportunity: Curriculum and pedagogy for the early learning program*. A compendium report to "With our best future in mind: Implementing early learning in Ontario." Retrieved from http://www.pcfk.on.ca/PDFs/Research_Ken/Every%20Child%20Every%20Opportunity.pdf

Pascal, C. E. (2009). *With our best future in mind: Implementing early learning in Ontario*. Report to the premier by the special advisor on early learning, Canadian council on learning. Retrieved from http://www.opha.on.ca/our_voice/consultations/docs/PascalReport-recommendations-27Jan10.pdf

Pascucci, S. (2013). The WE ARE Project. Retrieved from: https://crayonswandsandbuildingblocks.wordpress.com/2013/06/30/the-we-are-project/

Pearson, R. (2006). Respecting culture in our schools and classrooms. *Child & Family, 9*(2), 37.

Pellerin, M. (2012). Digital documentation: Using digital technologies to promote language assessment for the 21st century. *OLBI Working Papers, 4*, 19–36. Retrieved from https://uottawa.scholarsportal.info/ojs/index.php/ILOB-OLBI/article/view/1105/955

Pelo, A. (2006, November/December). Growing a culture of inquiry: Observation as professional development. *Child Care Exchange, 172*, 50–53.

Pence, A. (2006). Seeking the other 99 languages of ECE: A keynote address by Alan Pence. *Interaction, 20*(3), 28–29.

Perry, B., Dockett, S., & Harley, E. (2007). Learning stories and children's powerful mathematics. *Early Childhood Research and Practice, 9*(7). Retrieved from http://ecrp.uiuc.edu/v9n2/perry.html

Pimento, B., & Kernested, D. (2010). *Healthy foundations in early childhood settings* (4th ed.). Toronto, ON: Nelson Education.

Preston, J. (2014). *Early childhood education and care for Aboriginal children in Canada*. Retrieved from https://movingchildcareforward.ca/images/policybriefs/MCCF_aboriginal_childcare_canada.pdf

Preston, J. P. (2011). Aboriginal early childhood education in Canada: Issues of context. *Journal of Early Childhood Research, 10*(1), 3–18.

Pyle, A., & Deluca, C. (2013). Assessment in the kindergarten classroom: An empirical study of teachers' assessment approaches. *Early Childhood Education Journal, 41*(5), 373–380.

Reading, C. (2014). *Policies, programs and strategies to address Aboriginal racism: A Canadian perspective*. National Collaborating Centre for Aboriginal Health. Retrieved from https://www.ccnsa-nccah.ca/docs/determinants/FS-AddressAboriginalRacism-EN.pdf

Rees, R. W. (2015). *Capturing, assessing and communicating student thinking in a digital world*. Retrieved from https://dspace.library.uvic.ca/handle/1828/6951

Reeves, S., Goldman, J., & Oandasan, I. (2007). Key factors in planning and implementing interprofessional education in health care settings. *Journal of Allied Health, 36*(4), 231–235.

Rintakorpi, K. (2016). Documenting with early childhood education teachers: Pedagogical documentation as a tool for developing early childhood pedagogy and practices. *Early Years: An International Research Journal, 36*(4), 1–14.

Rooney, T. (2010). Trusting children: How do surveillance technologies alter a child's experience of trust, risk and responsibility? *Surveillance & Society, 7*(3–4), 344–355.

Rourke, L., Rourke, J., & Leduc, D. (2009, August). *Rourke baby record: Evidence-based infant/child health maintenance*. Retrieved from http://www.rourkebabyrecord.ca

Rowan, C. (2011). *Exploring the possibilities of learning stories as a meaningful approach to early childhood education in Nunavik* (Master's thesis). University of Victoria, BC. Retrieved from https://dspace.library.uvic.ca/bitstream/handle/1828/3483/Rowan_Marycaroline_2011-1.pdf?sequence=1

Rowena J. R. (2015). *Capturing, assessing and communicating student thinking in a digital world*. University of Victoria. Retrieved from https://www.google.ca/url?sa=t&rct=j&q=&esrc=s&source=web&cd=22&ved=0ahUKEwi_zM-ikafaAhWY14MKHRIZCuo4FBAWCC0wAQ&url=https%3A%2F%2Fdspace.library.uvic.ca%2Fbitstream%2Fhandle%2F1828%2F6951%2FRees_Rowena_%2520Jane_MEd_2015.pdf%3Fsequence%3D4%26isAllowed%3Dy&usg=AOvVaw24L4ROmRcZahKoZppFgbB1

Ryan, K. (2006). Learning stories. *Jigsaw, 41*, 25–26.

Ryan, S., & Grieshaber, S. (2004). It's more than child development: Critical theories, research, and teaching young children. *Young Children, 59*(6), 44–52.

Sachdev, G. (2016, October). Spirituality in the early childhood education in New Zealand and around the globe: Relevance, research and beyond. *Practitioner Researcher*. Retrieved from http://www.hekupu.ac.nz/Journal%20files/Issue4%20October%202016/Sachdev.pdf

Salend, S. J. (2008). *Creating inclusive classrooms: Effective and reflective practices* (6th ed.). Columbus, OH: Merrill/Prentice Hall.

Salend, S. J. (2009). Technology-based classroom assessments: Alternatives to testing. *Teaching Exceptional Children, 41*(6), 49–58.

Sansosti, F. J. (2009). Teaching social behavior to children with autism spectrum disorders using social stories: Implications for school-based practice. Best of the *Journal of Speech-Language Pathology & Applied Behavior Analysis, 4*, 170–179.

Schein, D. (2014). Nature's role in children's spiritual development. *Children, Youth, and Environments, 24*(2), 78–101.

Schön, D. A. (1983). *The reflective practitioner: How professionals think in action*. New York: Basic Books.

Schuster, D., & Leland, C. (2008). Considering context: Encouraging students to consider the content of an observation can invite further inquiry. *Science and Children*, *45*(6), 22–24.

Seitz, H. (2008, March). The power of documentation in the early childhood classroom. *Young Children*, *63*(2), 88–93.

Seitz, H., & Bartholomew C. (2008). Powerful portfolios for young children. *Early Childhood Education Journal*, *36*, 63–68.

Services and Supports to Promote the Social Inclusion of Persons with Developmental Disabilities Act, 2008, S.O. 2008, c. 14.

Shackell, A., Butler, N., Doyle, P., & Ball, D. (2008). *Design for play: A guide to creating successful play spaces*. Retrieved from http://www.playengland.org.uk/resources/design-for-play

Shier, H. (2002). Pathways to participation: Openings, opportunities and obligations. *Children and Society*, *10*, 107–117.

Shriver, C. (2014, Winter). E-portfolios. *Independent School*, *73*(2), 70.

Skouge, J. R., Kelly, M., Roberts, K. D., Leade, D. W., & Stodden, R. A. (2007). Technologies for self-determination for youth with developmental disabilities. *Education and Training in Developmental Disabilities*, *42*, 475–482.

Smith, A. (2002). Interpreting and supporting participation rights: Contributions from sociocultural theory. *International Journal of Children's Rights*, *10*, 73–88.

Snow, K. (2002–2016). *The case against "special needs."* Retrieved from https://nebula.wsimg.com/d2da928bdcdec774f6254d1756185396?AccessKeyId=9D6F6082FE5EE52C3DC6&disposition=0&alloworigin=1

Snow, K. (2005). *Disability is natural: Revolutionary common sense for raising successful children with disabilities* (2nd ed.). Woodland Park, CO: Braveheart Press.

Snow, K. (2010). *People first language*. Retrieved from http://www.disabilityisnatural.com

Sosna, T., & Mastergeorge, A. (2005, December). *The infant, preschool, family mental health initiative: Compendium of screening tools for early childhood social-emotional development*. Retrieved from http://www.cibhs.org/sites/main/files/file-attachments/the_infant_preschool_family_mental_health_initiative_compendium_of_screening_tools_for_early_childhood_social-emotional_deve.pdf

Squires, J., & Bricker, D. (2009). *Ages & Stages Questionnaires®: A parent-completed child monitoring system* (3rd ed.) (ASQ-3TM). Baltimore, Maryland: Paul H. Brookes Publishing Co., Inc.

Squires, J., Bricker, D., & Twombly, E. (2015). *Ages & Stages Questionnaires®: Social emotional; A parent-completed child monitoring system for social emotional behaviors* (2nd ed.) (ASQ:SE-2TM). Baltimore, Maryland: Paul H. Brookes Publishing Co., Inc.

Steeves, V., & Jones, O. (2010). Surveillance, children and childhood. *Surveillance & Society*, *7*(3–4), 187–191.

Steinfeld, E., Maisel, J., & Levine, D. (2012). *Universal design: Creating inclusive environments*. Retrieved from https://ebookcentral-proquest-com.ezproxy.humber.ca

Stevenson, A. (2013). I Wonder… "I Wonder" boards serve as springboard for scientific investigations. *Science and Children*, *50*(6), 74–80.

Stoyles, G. J., Stanford, B., Caputi, P., Keating, A., & Hyde, B. (2012, August). A measure of spiritual sensitivity for children. *International Journal of Children's Spirituality*, *17*(3), 203–215.

Tarr, P. (2011). Reflections and shadows. *Canadian Children*, *36*(2), 11–16.

Teaford, P., Wheat, J., & Baker, T. (2010). *Checklist items from HELP®: 3–6*. Palo Alto, CA: VORT Corporation.

Tebyani, V. (2011, March). Nurturing children's spirituality. *Putting Children First*, *37*, 11–13.

Thompson, J. R., Meadan, H., Fansler, K. W., Alber, S. B., & Balogh, P. A. (2007). Family assessment portfolios: A new way to jumpstart family/school collaboration. *Teaching Exceptional Children*, *39*(6), 19–25.

Tingle Broderick, J., & Bock Hong, S. (2011). Introducing the cycle of inquiry system: A reflective inquiry practice for early childhood teacher development. *Early Childhood and Parenting Collaborative*. Retrieved from http://ecrp.uiuc.edu/v13n2/broderick.html

Tingstrom, D. H., Wilczynski, S. M., & Scattone, D. (2006). Increasing appropriate social interactions of children with autism spectrum disorders using social stories. *Focus on Autism & Other Developmental Disabilities*, *21*(4), 211–222.

Toronto Children's Services. (n.d). *Confidentiality and information sharing guidelines for early childhood programs*. Retrieved from https://www1.toronto.ca/city_of_toronto/childrens_services/files/pdf/conf_guide_forms.pdf

Toronto Children's Services. (2014). *Early learning and care assessment for quality improvement*. Retrieved from http://www1.toronto.ca/City%20Of%20Toronto/Children's%20Services/Files/pdf/O/Operating%20criteria/oc_introduction.pdf

Toronto District School Board. (2013). *District process guide: K–12 School effectiveness framework*. Retrieved from http://www.tdsb.on.ca/Portals/ward11/docs/District%20Review%20Guide_F2%20(2).pdf

Toronto Public Health. (n.d.). *Early abilities: Communication checklist for children from birth to age four*. Retrieved from https://www.toronto.ca/wp-content/uploads/2017/11/9694-tph-ea-communication-checklist-eng-2016.pdf

Toronto Public Health. (n.d.). *Early identification in Toronto: Toronto red flags guide. A reference guide for working with young children*. Toronto, ON: Author.

Tremblay, M., Gokiert, R., Georgis, R., Edwards, K., & Skrypnek, B. (2013). Aboriginal perspectives on social-emotional competence in early childhood. *The International Indigenous Policy Journal*, *4*(4). Retrieved from http://ir.lib.uwo.ca/iipj/vol4/iss4/2

Truth and Reconciliation Commission of Canada. (2015). *Truth and reconciliation commission of Canada: Calls to action*. Retrieved from http://www.trc.ca/websites/trcinstitution/File/2015/Findings/Calls_to_Action_English2.pdf

Turner, T., & Gray Wilson, D. (2010). Reflections on documentation: A discussion with thought leaders from Reggio Emilia. *Theory into Practice*, 49(1), 5–13.

Underwood, K. (2012). Mapping the early intervention system in Ontario, Canada. *International Journal of Special Education*, 27(2), 126–135. Retrieved from https://files.eric.ed.gov/fulltext/EJ982867.pdf

Underwood, K., & Frankel, E. B. (2012). The developmental systems approach to early intervention in Canada. *Infants &Young Children*, 25(4), 286–296. Retrieved from http://iecss.blog.ryerson.ca/files/2015/01/Underwood-Frankel-2012.pdf

Underwood, K., & Langford, R. (2011). *Children with special educational needs in early childhood*. Toronto, ON: Atkinson Centre for Society and Child Development, OISE/University of Toronto.

UNICEF. (2013). *United Nations declaration on the rights of Indigenous Peoples for Indigenous adolescents*. Retrieved from https://www.unicef.ca/sites/default/files/legacy/imce_uploads/TAKE%20ACTION/ADVOCATE/DOCS/Youth-Friendly%20Declaration%20on%20the%20Rights%20of%20Indigenous%20Peoples.pdf

UNICEF. (2017). *Oh Canada: Our kids deserve better*. Retrieved from https://www.unicef.ca/sites/default/files/2017-06/RC14%20Canadian%20Companion_0.pdf

UNICEF Canada. (2016). *UNICEF report card 13: Fairness for children*. Retrieved from https://www.unicef.ca/sites/default/files/legacy/imce_uploads/images/advocacy/rc/rc13_infographen_media.pdf

United Nations. (2008). *United Nations declaration on the rights of Indigenous peoples*. Retrieved from http://www.un.org/esa/socdev/unpfii/documents/DRIPS_en.pdf

United Nations General Assembly. (1989, November). *The United Nations Convention on the Rights of the Child*. Retrieved from http://www.unicef.org/crc/files/Rights_overview.pdf

Universal Design for Play Project, University at Buffalo. (2005). *Universal design for play tool*. Retrieved from http://letsplay.buffalo.edu/UD/FINAL%20final%20Tool%207.pdf

University of British Columbia. (2016). *Indigenous peoples: Language guidelines*. Retrieved from http://assets.brand.ubc.ca/downloads/ubc_indigenous_peoples_language_guide.pdf

Valentino, L. (2004). *Handle with care* (3rd ed.). Toronto, ON: Thomson Nelson.

Vaughan, M. (2011). *UDL 101 in the early childhood environment. Innovations and Perspectives*. Retrieved from http://www.ttacnews.vcu.edu/2011/01/udl-101-in-the-early-childhood-environment/

Velez Laski, E. (2013, July). Portfolio picks: An approach for developing children's metacognition. *Young Children*, 68(3), 38–43. Retrieved from http://www.bclearninglab.bc.edu/downloads/Laski_YC2013.pdf

Versteeg, B. (2018). *Team 2 Eagles Blog*. Retrieved from http://edublog.amdsb.ca/team2eagles/

Walters, K. (2006). Capture the moment: Using digital photography in early childhood settings. *Early Childhood Australia*. Retrieved from https://files.eric.ed.gov/fulltext/ED497542.pdf

Wang, F., Kinzie, M. B., McGuire, P., & Pan, E. (2010). Applying technology to inquiry-based learning in early childhood education. *Early Childhood Education Journal*, 37, 381–389.

Warash, B, Curtis, R., Hursh, D., & Tucci, V. (2008). Skinner meets Piaget on the Reggio playground: Practical synthesis of applied behaviour analysis and developmentally appropriate practice orientations. *Journal of Research in Childhood Education*, 22(4), 441–453.

Wein, C. A. (2013). *Making learning visible through pedagogical documentation*. Toronto, ON: Queen's Printer for Ontario. Retrieved from http://www.edu.gov.on.ca/childcare/Wien.pdf

Wells, A. (2009). *The Reggio Emilia approach: A social constructivist pedagogy of inclusion*. University of Manitoba. Retrieved from https://umanitoba.ca/faculties/education/media/Wells-09.pdf

Wesley, P. W., Buysse, V., & Skinner, D. (2001). Early interventionists' perspectives on professional comfort as consultants. *Journal of Early Intervention*, 24(2), 112–128.

West, E. A., Perner, D. E., Laz, L., & Gartin, B. C. (2015). People-first and competence-orientated language. *International Journal of Whole Schooling*, 11(2), 16–28.

Whitney, D., & Trosten-Bloom, A. (2010). *The power of appreciative inquiry: A practice guide to positive change*. San Francisco, CA.: Berrett-Koehler Publishers, Inc.

Wiggins, G. (2006). *Healthier testing made easy: The idea of authentic assessment: Tests don't just measure absorption of facts. They teach what we value*. Retrieved from http://www.edutopia.org/healthier-testing-made-easy

Wilde, D. (2010). Personalities into teams. *Mechanical Engineering*, 132(2), 22–25.

Williams, R. (1999). Cultural safety—what does it mean for our work practice? *Australian and New Zealand Journal of Public Health*, 23(2), 213–214.

Williams, S. T. (2008, October). *Mental health screening and assessment tools for children*. Retrieved from http://humanservices.ucdavis.edu/academy/pdf/final2mentalhealthlitreview.pdf

Wilson, K. (2006). To speak, participate and decide: The child's right to be heard. *Interaction*, 20(3), 30–33.

Wilson, L. (2014). *Partnerships: Families and communities in early childhood*. Toronto, ON: Nelson.

Wong, A. (2010). *Teacher learning made visible: Collaboration and the study of pedagogical documentation in two childcare centres*. Retrieved from https://tspace.library.utoronto.ca/handle/1807/26438

Wong, D., & Waniganayake, M. (2013). Mentoring as a leadership development strategy in early childhood education. In E. Hujala, M. Waniganayake, & J. Rodd (Eds.), *Researching leadership in early childhood education* (pp. 163–180). Tampere, Finland: Tampere University Press.

Wozniak, N. M. (2012). Enhancing inquiry, evidence-based reflection, and integrative learning with the lifelong eportfolio process: The implementation of integrative eportfolios at Stony Brook University. *Journal of Educational Technology Systems*, *41*(3), 209–230. doi:10.2190/ET.41.3.b

Wright, R. J. (2010). *Multifaceted assessment for early childhood education*. Thousand Oaks, CA: Sage.

Wurm, J. (2005). *Working in the Reggio way: A beginner's guide for American teachers*. St. Paul, MN: Redleaf Press.

Yates, T., Ostrosky, M. M., Cheatham, G. A., Fettig, A., LaShorage Shaffer, & Milagros Santos, R. (2008). *Research synthesis on screening and assessing social -emotional competence*. Retrieved from http://csefel.vanderbilt.edu/documents/rs_screening_assessment.pdf

Yost, H., & Fan, S. (2014, June). Social media technologies for collaboration and communication: Perceptions of childcare professionals and families. *Australasian Journal of Early Childhood*, *39*(2), 36–41.

Yu, G. S. (2008). Documentation: Ideas and applications from the Reggio Emilia approach. *Teaching Artist Journal*, *6*(2), 126–134.

Zachary, L. (2009). Make mentoring work for you: Ten strategies for success. *T+D Magazine*, *63*(12), 76–77.

Zhang, M., Lundeberg, M., & Eberhardt, J. (2010). Seeing what you normally don't see. *Phi Delta Kappan*, *91*(6), 60–66.

Zuniga, R., & Fischer, J. M. (2010). Emotional intelligence and attitudes toward people with disabilities: A comparison between two cultures. *Journal of Applied Rehabilitation Counseling*, *31*(1), 12–18.

Zygmunt-Fillwalk, E. M., & Huffman, R. (2012). A picture is worth a thousand words! Using documentation to increase family involvement. *NALS Journal*, *2*(2), 1–8.

Index

Note: **Bold** page numbers indicate glossary terms.

A

ABC analysis, 168, **187**–191
  adapting, 190–191
  behaviourists and, 187–188
  format, 188–190
  purpose, 187
  unique feature, 187
Abecedarian study, 326
Aboriginal Elders, 5, 20
Aboriginal peoples, 29, 90, 145. *See also* Indigenous peoples
abscissas, **185**
Accessibility for Ontarians with Disabilities Act (AODA), **221**
accessibility issues, 221, 248–250, 303–304, 316
accommodate, **109**
accommodations, **289**
action research, **21**, **275**, 322–323
adaptations
  of ABC analysis, 190–191
  of anecdotal records, 124–126
  of checklists, 178
  of communication in early childhood, 86–87
  of early intervention, 290–291
  environmental, 21
  of observation and assessment, 290–291
  observation in, 21
  of participation charts, 194–195
  of profiles, 197–200
  of rating scales, 181
  video recordings, 155
adjectives, 81, 87
adverbs, 81, 87
advocate role, **29**
AECEO (Association of Early Childhood Educators of Ontario), **320**
agentic, **8**
Ages & Stages maturational approach, 107
Ages & Stages Questionnaires, 176–177, 282, 283, 287
analogue, **187**
anecdotal records, 98, 108, 118, **119**–127. *See also* ABC analysis; running records
  adapting, 124–126
  evaluative function, 123–124
  example of, 120

expanded observation, 123
  format, 119–121
  interpretations, 121–124, 147
  perceptions and cultural inferences, 126–127
  purpose, 119
  unique feature, 119
antecedents, **187**, 188
anti-bias, 42–44
anti-oppressive approach, **21**
AODA (Accessibility for Ontarians with Disabilities Act), **221**
appreciative inquiry, 5, **6**–12, 211–212
  anecdotal records, 119
  behaviour tallying and charting, 182–183
  with children on their learning, 7
  consent and, 56
  early intervention/early identification, 257–261, 264
  environment and, 299
  observation and, 107–108, 257–261
  pedagogical framework, 211–212, 227–231
  pedagogical leadership, 317
  process, 211–212
  questioning and, 9–12, 66–73
  of responsive, inclusive educators, 4–5
  stages of, 6, 7–9
Arnett Caregiver Interaction Scale, 312
artifacts, **138**, 142, 234–237, 244, 247
assessment
  authentic, 234, 244–248, 277–278, 279, 286
  diagnostic, 263
  early intervention/early identification, 263, 277–278
  environmental, 311–317
  functional, 263, 288
  Indigenous perspective, 285–286
  non-standardized, 277–278, 286
  screening, 263, 282–286, 287–288
  socio-cultural approaches, 275
  standardized, 234, 277, 279, 282–286
  three stages, 263
assessment portfolios, **246**–247
Association of Early Childhood Educators of Ontario (AECEO), **320**
Atkinson, K., 123

audio/digital recordings, 78, 118, **150**–153
  format, 151–152
  portfolios of children, 152–153
  purpose, 151
  unique feature, 151
aural world, **150**
Aussie Childcare Network, 147
Australia, reflective practice from, 97
authentic assessment, **234**, 244–248, 277–278, 279, 286
Authorization for Exchange of Information, 55–56
Authorization for Release of Information, 55–56
autism, 181, **273**

B

Baird, L., 317–318
Ball, J., 285
Battelle Developmental Inventory, 287
Beach, Jane, 315
Beard, Bruce K., 38
behaviourists, 187–188
behaviours, **187**
  ABC analysis, 187, 188
  defining in pedagogical documentation, 98–99, 101
  designing an observational tool, 171–172
  domains of child development, 106–107
  duration, 170–171
  frequency, 170–171
  observing, 61–63
  specific learning experience or event. *See* closed methods (recording)
  subsets of, 171
  unanticipated. *See* open methods (recording)
  variables affecting, 103–104
behaviour tallying and charting, 168, **182**–187
  conventional graphs, 185–186
  format, 183–185
  interpreting information, 186–187
  purpose, 182–183
  textbook/internet examples, 186
  unique feature, 182–183
Belonging, Being, and Becoming (Australian Department of Education), 97
Belonging, Engagement, Expression, and Well-Being, 105

U

unanticipated behaviour, 117
UN Convention on the Rights of the
    Child, 44–46, 57, 134, 163
*Understanding the British Columbia
    Early Learning Framework*, 10
UNICEF Canada, 35, 46
United Nations Declaration on the Rights
    of Indigenous Peoples, 90
Universal Design for Learning (UDL), **300**
    cycle of observation, 300–311
    physical environment, 303–308
    socio-emotional/psychological tone of
        environment, 301–302
    temporal environment, 308–311
University of British Columbia, 90
unobtrusive observation, **82, 83**

V

validity, **181**
verbs, 81, 87
Versteeg, Rebecca, 159, 160–161
video recordings, 118, **153**–158
    adapting, 155
    children with special needs, 157
    effectiveness, 158
    format, 156–157
    purpose, 153–156
    relationship building, 154
    socio-emotional development and,
        157–158
    unique features, 153–156
Viscardis, L., 271
visible listening, 63
visual communication, 136. *See also*
    photographs/photography; video
    recordings
visual schedules, **309**–310
vocabulary development, in pedagogical
    documentation, 81
Voice Assistant, 250
voice recordings. *See* audio/digital
    recordings
Voice Texting Pro, 250
voice-to-text software, 152, 250, 251
Vygotsky, Lev, 27, 41, 217

W

Waniganayake, M., 319
Watson, John B., 187
We Are Project, 140–141
webbing, **146**, 168, **206**–209
    emergent documentation, 207–208
    overview, 206–207
    "thinking and wondering," 208–209
Weebly, 247
well-being of children, 21–22, 35,
    291–293
Whitney, D., 6, 8
Wiarton Kids Den, 207
Williams, R., 285
Wilson, D., 117
wonder board, **147**
Wong, D., 319
working/developmental portfolios,
    245–246
*Working with Young Children Who
    Are Learning English as a New
    Language*, 254
writing style, 91–92
Wylie, Sally, v, Foreword: xiii–xiv, 56, 68,
    70, 85, 202, 203, 209

Y

Yost, H., 50